THE CHANGING ENVIRONMENT OF INTERNATIONAL FINANCIAL MARKETS

Also by Dilip K. Ghosh

INTERCOUNTRY LOAN, FINANCIAL RISK AND FOREIGN
  EXCHANGE POLICIES OF THE LDCS

INTERNATIONAL TRADE AND THIRD-WORLD
  DEVELOPMENT (*with P. Ghosh*)

MICROECONOMIC ANALYSIS

THE GLOBAL POLICIES OF GOLD: Problems in International
  Finance and Prospects for American Policy
  (*with A. J. Klinghoffer*)

TRADE, DISTORTION AND GROWTH

Also by Edgar Ortiz

CURRENT ECONOMIC AND FINANCIAL ISSUES OF THE
  NORTH AMERICAN AND CARIBBEAN COUNTRIES

PUBLIC ADMINISTRATION, ECONOMICS AND FINANCE:
  Current Issues in the North American and Caribbean Countries

PUBLIC ENTERPRISE: Current Issues in the North American
  and Caribbean Countries

The Changing Environment of International Financial Markets

Issues and Analysis

Edited by

Dilip K. Ghosh
Professor of Finance
Suffolk University, Massachusetts

and

Edgar Ortiz
Professor of Finance
Universidad Nacional Autónoma de México

St. Martin's Press

332.042
C 456

© Dilip K. Ghosh and Edgar Ortiz 1994

All rights reserved. No reproduction, copy or transmission of
this publication may be made without written permission.

No paragraph of this publication may be reproduced, copied or
transmitted save with written permission or in accordance with
the provisions of the Copyright, Designs and Patents Act 1988,
or under the terms of any licence permitting limited copying
issued by the Copyright Licensing Agency, 90 Tottenham Court
Road, London W1P 9HE.

Any person who does any unauthorised act in relation to this
publication may be liable to criminal prosecution and civil
claims for damages.

First published in Great Britain 1994 by
THE MACMILLAN PRESS LTD
Houndmills, Basingstoke, Hampshire RG21 2XS
and London
Companies and representatives
throughout the world

A catalogue record for this book is available
from the British Library.

ISBN 0–333–59589–0

Printed in Great Britain by
Ipswich Book Co Ltd
Ipswich, Suffolk

First published in the United States of America 1994 by
Scholarly and Reference Division,
ST. MARTIN'S PRESS, INC.,
175 Fifth Avenue,
New York, N.Y. 10010

ISBN 0–312–10189–9

Library of Congress Cataloging-in-Publication Data
The Changing environment of international financial markets : issues
and analysis / edited by Dilip K. Ghosh and Edgar Ortiz.
p. cm.
Includes index.
ISBN 0–312–10189–9
1. International finance. 2. Foreign exchange. 3. Interest
rates. 4. Balance of payments. 5. Debts, External. I. Ghosh,
Dilip K. (Dilip Kumar), 1947– . II. Ortiz, Edgar.
HG3881.C5163 1994
332'.042—dc20   93–17783
                                                    CIP

To Dipasri and Debasri

University Libraries
Carnegie Mellon University
Pittsburgh PA 15213-3890

Contents

Preface

The international financial markets have been continuously undergoing structural and fundamental changes owing to nascent developments in international economic and political landscapes in countries engaged and involved in transnational trade and investment to exploit better opportunities for either profit or national welfare. New financial engineering has also been reshaping the colour of changing conditions in the world economy and in national economies. While we have been witnessing all these outcomes emerging sporadically, it has dawned on us that there could be a cosmos in all these occurrences – a unifying sequence leading the way to this phenomenal growth. To have a better handle on that curiosity, we have been looking through research, interactive ideas, and so on. We arranged a conference on 'International Trade and Finance in a Rapidly Changing Environment' under the auspices of the International Trade and Finance Association in Laredo, Texas, on 22–25 April 1992 to discuss various issues of topical interest and growing concern. We had 53 sessions with over 200 papers from scholars from all over the world, presenting new researches in areas of unexplored topics of utmost usefulness from theoretical and practical points of view. Out of these presentations, we chose 21 articles which we felt met the requirement for the book we have been interested in for quite a while. Two of us living in two different countries spent a lot of time on facsimile transmittal, telephone conversations, and a number of cross-country meetings to finalize the contents of this book.

We are very satisfied with the final outcome. Many friends and peers, and many factors have, of course, contributed to make it a success. It will be difficult to mention in this short space all the names whose help and intellectual stimuli have made us pursue this project with our hard labour to fruition. Yet, we must acknowledge the support and inspiring guidance of Professor Khosrow Fatemi – our dear friend and fellow editor – for his regular words of wisdom and suggestions on editorial balance. Our universities – Suffolk University and Universidad Nacional Autónoma de México – must be recognized in this connection for their support in our free pursuit to our research project. Finally, we must express our sincere appreciation and a debt of gratitude to all the fellow contributors without whom the project could not come out of its embryonic stage.

DILIP K. GHOSH
EDGAR ORTIZ

Notes on the Contributors

Alejandra Cabello, Lecturer, Department of Finance, Universidad Nacional Autonoma de Mexico, Mexico, D.F.

Benoit Carmichael, Associate Professor, School of Business, Universite Laval, Quebec, PQ G1K 7PA, Canada.

Jean-Claude Cosset, Associate Professor, School of Business, Universite Laval, Quebec, PQ G1K 7PA, Canada.

Krishnan Dandapani, Associate Professor, Department of Finance, Florida International University, Miami, FL 33199, USA.

Gilles Duteil, Associate Professor, Groupe Ecole Internationale des Affaires, Domaine de Luminy, Case 921, 13288 Marseille, Cedex 9, France.

Christopher A. Erickson, Associate Professor, Department of Finance, New Mexico State University, Las Cruces, NM 88003, USA.

Irene Finel-Honigman, Professor of International Affairs, School of International and Public Affairs, Columbia University, New York, NY 10027, USA.

Klaus P. Fischer, Associate Professor, School of Business, Universite Laval, Quebec, PQ G1K 7PA, Canada.

Dilip K. Ghosh, Professor, Department of Finance, Suffolk University, 8 Ashburton Place, Boston, MA 02108, USA.

Shyamasri Ghosh, Economist, World Academy of Development, P.O. Box 326, Marlton, NJ 08053, USA.

Larry Guin, Professor, Department of Economics and Finance, Murray State University, Murray KY 42071, USA.

M. Anaam Hashmi, Associate Professor, Department of Economics, Mankato State University, MSU Box 14, Mankato, MN 56002, USA.

Jannett K. Highfill, Associate Professor, Department of Economics, Bradley University, Peoria, IL 61625, USA.

Anisul M. Islam, Assistant Professor, FACIS Department, University of Houston – Downtown, Houston, TX 77002, USA.

Muhammad M. Islam, Assistant Professor, Graduate School of International Trade and Business Administration, Laredo State University, Laredo, TX 78040, USA.

Moosa Khan, Assistant Professor, College of Business, Prairie View A & M University, Prairie View, TX 77446, USA.

Shahriar Khaksari, Professor, Department of Finance, Suffolk University, 8 Ashburton Place, Boston, MA 02108, USA.

Ramakrishnan S. Koundinya, Associate Professor, College of Business and Industry, University of Massachusetts – Dartmouth, North Dartmouth, MA 02747, USA.

John P. Lajaunie, Professor, Department of Economics and Finance, Nicholls State University, P.O. Box 2015, Thibodaux, LA 70310, USA.

Eric Youngkoo Lee, Professor, Department of Economics, Fairleigh Dickinson University, Madison, NJ 07940, USA.

Charles Maxwell, Professor, Department of Economics and Finance, Murray State University, Murray KY 42071, USA.

Bruce L. McManis, Professor, Department of Economics and Finance, Nicholls State University, P.O. Box 2015, Thibodaux, LA 70310, USA.

Mathew J. Morey, Associate Professor, Department of Economics, Illinois State University, Normal, IL 61761, USA.

Abraham Mulugetta, Associate Professor, School of Business, Ithaca College, Ithaca, NY 14850, USA.

Atsuyuki Naka, Associate Professor, Department of Economics, University of New Orleans, New Orleans, LA 70148, USA.

Edgar Ortiz, Professor of Finance, Universidad Nacional Autónoma de México, Mexico, DF.

A. P. Palasvirta, Associate Professor, School of Business, Memorial University of Newfoundland, St Johns, Newfoundland, Canada.

Joanna Poznanska, Associate Professor, School of Business and Economics, Seattle Pacific University, Seattle, WA 98119, USA.

Arun J. Prakash, Professor, Department of Finance, Florida International University, Miami, FL 33199, USA.

Emmanuel N. Roussakis, Professor, Department of Finance, Florida International University, Miami, FL 33199, USA.

Neil Seitz, Professor, Department of Finance, St Louis University, St Louis, MO 63130, USA.

Michael Szenberg, Professor, Department of Economics, Lubin Graduate School of Business, Pace University, New York, NY 10038, USA.

William V. Weber, Professor, Department of Economics, Eastern Illinois University, Charleston, IL 61920, USA.

Elliott Willman, Associate Professor, Department of Finance, New Mexico State University, Las Cruces, NM 88003, USA.

M. Raquibuz Zaman, Professor, Department of Economics, Ithaca College, Ithaka, NY 14850, USA.

Part I
Introduction

1 The Changing Environment of International Financial Markets: Introduction

Dilip K. Ghosh and Edgar Ortiz

The post-World War II era covering almost half a century has been continuously witnessing dramatic changes in the landscape of international finance as it relates to market structures, financial institutions and instruments. Since the conclusion of the Bretton Woods Conference with the inception of the International Monetary Fund (IMF) and the International Bank for Reconstruction and Development (IBRD or popularly known as the World Bank), the world has seen various developments in trade structures, investment designs, and the integration process. We have observed the emergence of the General Agreement to Borrow (GAB), test-tube monetary units or scrip currencies such as Special Drawing Rights (SDR), European Unit of Account (EUA), which later has become what is known now as the European Currency Unit (ECU), stability (or lack thereof) in foreign exchange markets, different currency alignments under Eurosnakes and supersnakes, FECOM (the French initial for European Monetary Cooperation Fund), European Monetary System (EMS), and other regional monetary blocs. The world has become a global village; communication networks and the technological pace of progress have integrated international capital markets. Incredible growth of Eurocurrency and accessibility of financial operators in this market have made sovereign national monetary authorities less powerful in controlling and regulating the behaviours of economic agents in these days. The collapse of the Bretton Woods system, the liquidation of the Gold Pool, the introduction of free and dirty floats, the institution of International Banking Facilities (IBFs) by the United States, and so on have all contributed to the unavoidably developing trends in international financial markets, dictated hardly by any country, but certainly by hard calculations through financial engineering in

3

international markets by way of arbitrage, hedging and speculation in national markets interconnected with each other by trading via telecommunications and computer networks. New and changing political scenarios have also shaped the need and structures of international financial framework. The disappearance of the Iron Curtain through the demise of communist regimes in the Soviet Union and in its satellite states, the attempted marketization of those economies, the demolition of the Berlin Wall and the reunification of Germany, the passage of the Maastricht Treaty, industrialization of the Pacific Rim Basin, the 'Big Bang' (creating progress towards around-the-clock trading), the establishment of SEAQ, the formation of the North American Free Trade Agreement (NAFTA), and so on have coloured as well as complicated the international picture of market environments and analytic frameworks. This is a sketchy history and a backdrop of the changing international financial markets. Within this market framework we have chosen the important issues and analyses thereof for this book.

Financial markets create values that contribute to corporate growth and profitability, and through the infrastructure of macroeconomic links, to domestic and international economic growth and development. Their efficiency and performance depend largely on complex interactions of institutional and market factors. Each one of them is in continuous change, and their interrelationships are in the mode of change as well as a result. International financial markets reflect such vicissitudes more than any other markets. During the last decade the international market environment has changed dramatically by a set of factors leading to greater internationalization and integration of world economic activities which we may call economic and financial globalization.

Technological progress in production has led to greater output, and differentials in technological changes have created differences in productivity and competitiveness among nations. A rapid expansion of trade and foreign direct and indirect investments, enhanced by technological changes, has induced internationalization of production. Multinational corporations have implemented global strategies in production, marketing and financing. Financial intermediaries have followed the trend, establishing 'full services' across borders to support trade and investments.

However, the potential of financial markets has been unleashed with economic liberalization and deregulation. Deregulation and financial liberalization have put down barriers that restricted the flow of capital across national borders. Restrictions on exchange rates and capital markets controls have been eliminated in many countries. Greater reliance has been placed on market forces to allocate capital and price the value of firms. Along with these factors, rapid pace in information and communication networks has contributed to accelerate the processes of data analysis and information dissemination. Moreover, fast-moving communication technologies have facilitated the trade of currencies and securities across national borders around the clock, which has led to increased financial activities and enhanced arbitrage opportunities between markets.

The increasing globalization has been changing the fundamental characteristics of financial markets. As countries look to market forces to promote their developments, international barriers in trade, investments and capital flows fall, financial activities increase, and yet competition gets tougher in the global village. Similarly, markets become more sensitive to fundamental factors on a worldwide basis. This reflects in quick financial markets adjustments. Agents resort to more sophisticated techniques of analysis for decision-making in order to attain greater efficiency and manage systemic and exchange rate risks characteristic of transnational transactions. Simultaneously, financial intermediaries and governments improve market institutions, innovate securitization and portfolio management.

This new competitive globalized environment has led to greater interdependency among markets and nations. Accordingly, economic downturns and divergences on economic policies have frequently led to turbulence in the international financial markets, rapidly transmitting that from one market to another. Three major, often concurrent turbulences, can be identified in the age of financial globalization. First, the debt crisis of the 1980s. Imprudent borrowing and mismanagement of the domestic economy weakened the solvency of borrowing Less Developed Countries (LDCs). Private banks, which had pursued aggressive lending practices during the mid-1970s and early 1980s were severely affected, creating great instability and uncertainty in the financial markets. Second, securities markets plunged in October 1987. The event marked the influence of information flows on market performance. It did not result from changes in physical wealth, neither did it affect that. The ability to transmit market information around the world in seconds increased apprehensions about the market and the world economy. This led to unexpected chain reactions in plunging financial markets around the world. Understanding the nature of the 1987 stock markets crisis has helped prevent over-reaction. However, as global finance continues, it has become clear that financial markets are highly sensitive to information changes and flows. Their performance has continued to experience some recurrent commotions as responses to fundamental factors become more uniform and information about them spreads instantly. Finally, international financial markets have been characterized by periodic instabilities in the exchange markets, accompanied and fed by instabilities in interest and inflation rates. Currency fluctuations have reflected worldwide changes in competitiveness among nations, particularly in the industrialized ones. Competition among nations has increased to the point that many industrialized countries, particularly the United States, face huge deficits in trade balances which have contributed to deepen currency changes, as currency instabilities in the European Economic Community prove it. Institutional arrangements have been insufficient to promote exchange rate stability. Pressured by domestic problems, countries have resorted to independent monetary and exchange policies, which ultimately have led to regional and worldwide adjustments in exchange rates.

These negative trends have often reflected a lack of cooperation among nations and shortcomings of the international trade and monetary systems and institutions. Indeed, the failure of the GATT to solve differences of interests among the most developed nations has led to the emergence of an opposite trend in the international scenario: formation of strong economic blocs as an alternative to compete more advantageously in the globalized economy. Thus as the European Economic Community tightens its economic and financial ties among its members, in the Western Hemisphere Canada, United States and Mexico negotiate the North American Free Trade Agreement (NAFTA), while other Latin American countries are in the mode of instituting several integration schemes among themselves. Similarly, in Asia Japan leads integration among east Asian countries. Integration schemes concentrate on trade and investments, which influence international financial markets. Indeed, financial integration schemes are underway in the European Economic Community. By the end of the millennium the Community purports to have one common currency and unified monetary policy. Nevertheless, this pendular movement will tend to complement globalization and formation of economic blocs. Countries are associating themselves to increase their welfare by meeting the challenges of globalization from a more advantageous position. Thus, their environment will continue to be shaped by further globalization and economic integration schemes.

The dramatic changes in the environment of financial markets, as outlined, underlie the works presented in this book. Within this increasingly globalized financial market structure, international finance has increased its relevance as a theoretical and analytical discipline. It is growing and gaining ground every day. New researchers are pouring in with new issues, insights and analysis. Many of the old-age basic questions and analytical structures have already been extended to new horizons, and hence the depth and breadth of scope of critical examination of those concepts and issues have become inescapable necessities and realities. The chapters included in this book explore the basic building blocks of finance that must be promoted to push the potential of international financial markets.

Following this 'Introduction', Part II deals with markets of exchange rates. The works included in this part introduce new models and innovative research techniques to bring about insights concerning the dilemmas of long-run exchange rate equilibrium and market efficiency, and unrestrained market fluctuations *vis-à-vis* government intervention, left unsolved by conventional econometric models. These analyses have important implications for corporations and economic agents in general seeking to improve their exchange risk management to compete more effectively in the globalized economy.

Chapter 2 of this volume, 'Foreign Exchange Market Efficiency: A Look at London', by John P. Lajaunie, Bruce L. McManis and Atsuyoki Naka, attempts to determine long-run relationships existing between the price series of various currencies. Efficient market hypothesis in the semi-strong form is tested for the London foreign exchange market, using cointegration techniques. Recent studies in the area of foreign exchange market efficiency have employed econometric techniques which test for the presence of long-run equilibrium relationships between the major currencies. The existence of such a relationship is a direct violation of the *efficient market hypothesis* and the existence of efficient speculative markets. In their study, the authors attempt to resolve the conflict in results found in prior empirical studies. The study also attempts to provide a limited generalization of the empirical results by extending the examination of market efficiency to an additional major foreign exchange market, London. Based on their tests, the authors conclude that the null hypothesis of the absence of a cointegrating relationship cannot be rejected for any of the models specified, which confirms their results on speculative markets and the efficient market hypothesis.

The free floating exchange rate system has come under heavy government intervention since the Group of Five intervention of 1985. In his chapter, 'Freedom of Free Floating Exchange Rate: Empirical Analysis of Currency Fluctuation Patterns' (Chapter 3), M. Anaam Hashmi examines fluctuations in selected currencies and determines whether fluctuations are a result of only market conditions or government intervention. The hypothesis of government intervention is rejected for most of the currencies, using daily exchange rates. However, findings are mixed for weekly and monthly data series. Therefore, Hashmi concludes that the foreign exchange market cannot easily be influenced by government intervention as market forces play a dominant role. Market signals should therefore be paid greater attention in the management of exchange risk exposure. Similarly, models designed for exchange rate management must give greater weight to market forces to avoid providing misleading signals, which has often been the case with current methods. Indeed, failure to take market forces adequately into account to measure exchange risk exposure can lead to disastrous business strategies. Firms and economic agents in general can fail to identify the instruments to hedge with and ensure their ability to fulfil their cash flow commitments. Since exchange markets are now truly international in scope, hedging techniques and instruments have also tended to become more universal. However, differences might arise, due to specific geographic, legal and cultural environments, and all these need to be identified and understood. The importance of this issue stands out in Chapter 3.

Part III explores international interest rates and underscores the importance of these rates in international financial markets. Eurocurrency and Treasury security interest rates have played a leading role in global financial transactions and global financial trends. Charles Maxwell and Larry Guin in their chapter, 'Statistical Analyses of Eurocurrency and Treasury Interest Rates from 1975 to 1991' (Chapter 4), examine the characteristics of each of these types of yields over the past 17 years. Moments around the mean, correlations between the markets, and other relationships are examined. Data analysed correspond to various types of US government securities on the one hand, and Eurocurrency interest rates on the other. The findings generally support the existing financial theory regarding the distribution of these yields. Examining subperiods of their 17-year period under analysis, the authors find no major changes in the moments around the mean. Correlations between both markets are high, confirming that money flows between both markets. Chapter 5, 'A Cross-Country Comparison of Consumer Discount Rates', by William V. Weber, Jannett K. Highfill and Mathew J. Morey, sheds some more light on interest rates. This work develops a new theoretical foundation for estimating the consumer discount rate and applies the method by deriving some international comparisons of consumer discount rates. The chapter takes a micro-foundation of macro approach, starting off with an intertemporal optimum control problem. It is shown that the consumer discount rate can be derived from an economy's per capita growth rate, its real interest rate, and its marginal propensity to consume. In Chapter 6, 'The Interest Rate Parity, Covered Interest Arbitrage and Speculation Under Market Imperfection', Dilip K. Ghosh derives the expression of interest rate parity first in a perfect market, and then gives twelve additional expressions of interest rate parity under different scenarios of money market and foreign exchange market imperfections. The conditions for arbitrage profits and speculative opportunities are then spelled out.

Complementing the chapters on exchange rates and interest rates, and inflation, Part IV of the book deals with the balance of payments and international reserves, two fundamental factors that influence the changing environment of international finance. The common ground of the chapters in this section is the preoccupation of the authors for determining the impact of external deficits on future domestic and international activities. Aptly, the cases of developed and developing economies are analysed, examining the cases of United States, the post-communist economies from Eastern European countries and the former Soviet Union, and a sample of small Latin-American countries.

Chapter 7 takes the issue of international reserves in a very timely fashion. Anisul N. Islam, Moosa Khan, and Mohammad M. Islam redefine in 'An Empirical Test of the Demand for International Reserves' the determinants and demand for international reserves under current financial market and world economic conditions. The chapter presents four theoretical models and estimates the demand function for international reserves for a sample of three Central American countries: Costa Rica, El Salvador and Panama, using econometric models and Box-Jenkins models. The overall estimation results are consistent with their models. However, the estimates made with the econometric model outperform Box-Jenkins models in terms of their ability to forecast reserve demands in the sample countries. The econometric model is reasonably stable over the 1960–89 period analyzed. It is worth noting, that contrary to some beliefs, the new international monetary system, based on flexible interest rates, had no impact on the reserves demand of the three Central American nations. Since econometric models clearly identify intervening variables in the determination of financial reserves, the logical implications of these findings are that, for policy making, to shelter from possible instabilities of the balance of payments, econometric models are more useful.

Delving further in the fundamentals that influence the environment of international financial markets, Eric Youngkoo Lee and Michael Szenberg explore the US external sector. Its dramatic deficit increases during the last two decades and its change to a net debtor position has kept business activity under unparalleled strains, as the problem continues to grow and confrontation with its industrialized trading partners heats up. Many analytical proposals have attempted to shed some light into the problem emphasizing prospects and alternatives. Chapter 8, 'An Intertemporal Interpretation of the US Current Account Deficit', is a contribution along these lines. Opposing doomsday views, the authors present an optimistic diagnosis. They show, using a simplified intertemporal model of current account, that in so far as the government budget deficit represents the deliberate choice of policy-makers and therefore is taken as given, the alternatives the United States faces are higher levels of private investments and a trade deficit or low levels of private investment and balanced trade. Given the low US savings rate, the current account deficit should not be viewed as a problem, but rather as a solution to the problem of not having sufficient domestic savings to finance additional investment. Only part of the increased output and income generated by the additional investment spending accrues to foreign investors in the form of interests and dividend payments. The net inflow of capital from abroad will allow a faster growth in the US capital stock and a higher future standard of living than it would otherwise be. Their analysis is also positive because the authors identify market-oriented policies to eliminate the gap between savings and investment avoiding a 'hard landing' of the dollar and hence prevent undesirable turbulence in international financial markets. Chapter 9, 'Balance-of-Payments Implications of the Break-up of the USSR for its Former Republics and the East

European Countries', by M. Raquibuz Zaman takes a fresh look into a new problem. The rise of market environment in the former Eastern European and ex-Soviet countries finds them with feeble financial institutions in need of sharp transformations before they can become an integral part of international markets. Their incorporation into the international financial markets is, however, imminent. Their transition can be enhanced by accelerating the changes needed in the real sector. This requires a thorough analysis about the changes taking place in the area of international relations of the post-communist economies. Trade is the point of departure, which is dealt by Zaman in this chapter. He points out that the economies of the East European countries and the former Soviet Union were not only based on a command structure of a centrally planned system, but also on a system of mutual cooperation and collaboration that manifested in barter trade of each other's merchandise. With the collapse of the system, each nation now faces the dual task of systematically dismantling the old structure and erecting in its place a market-based system that can withstand competitive forces. Based on an analysis of past patterns of trade and the nature of underlying changes, the author contends that for some time to come the East European economies will face economic chaos and massive deficits in their balance of payments. However, it can be predicted that impacts of these deficits on the international financial markets will be negligible, although these initial impacts will tend to increase as integration of those nations with Western Europe and the rest of the world strengthens.

A somewhat similar situation but in a different dimension can be detected with respect to the developing countries. Although some developing countries are rapidly becoming integrated to world financial markets, many are experiencing difficulties in instituting reforms for their real and financial markets, and they remain cut-off from penetrating international markets. High debt payments and structural adjustments set back the economies of many developing countries during the 1980s to the point where the period has been identified as the 'lost decade'. Recent negotiations, carried out under the Brady Plan, have eased off payments somewhat, allowing benefited countries to return to their traditional growth patterns. However, the problem is far from being solved. Debt levels are still high and in addition developing countries have built in a secular dependency on foreign borrowing, directly from syndicated banking institutions, or else through international capital markets. In addition many debtor countries have not ended negotiations to restructure their debt and

their economies continue experiencing a negative economic downturn. International macroeconomic conditions are better now than in
the late 1970s and early 1980s. Nevertheless, it is imperative to
continue shedding more light on the origins and nature of the debt
crisis to avoid its repetition. Country risk analysis also needs to be
revisited to accede to new techniques that improve it and enhance
banking practices in international lending.

Part V fills some of those needs. It examines foreign debt and
country-risk analysis and sets forth new lessons from the debt crisis.
In Chapter 10, 'Foreign Exchange Dynamics, Debt and the "Peso
Problem"', Dilip K. Ghosh presents the picture of Mexico suffering
under gargantuan foreign debt, intractable rates of inflation and
persistently plummeting value of the peso that has triggered a real
and fundamental disequilibrium in which the policy makers and
people have appeared totally helpless. In the chapter, it is pointed
out that since relation between sovereign borrowers and sovereign
lenders is like that of the partners in a three-legged race in which both
can run, limp or fall together, but cannot part company, it is absolutely necessary and expedient for both Mexico and its lenders to
agree upon a new schedule for loan amortization to their mutual
benefit, if not for their immediate relief. Christopher A. Erickson
and Elliott Willman, in 'International Lending and Sovereign Debt in
the Presence of Agency Costs: The Case of Mexico' (Chapter 11),
offer a powerful and novel analysis of foreign debt by introducing agency costs in their model. It is shown that as long as some
entrepreneurs are incompletely collateralized, the optimum government policy is to borrow the maximum possible amount from international lenders and transfer the proceeds to the private sector. It is
further demonstrated that any reduction in government borrowing
capacity results in a decline in domestic economic activities, and that
decline does not end until the government rehabilitates its maximal
borrowing capacity. Within the straitjacket of this analysis, Erickson
and Willman examine the Mexican economy.

Identification of information asymmetries in international lending
and debt capacity borrowing limitations capture the importance of
improved country-risk analysis. Although sophisticated tools for
country-risk analysis have been developed during the last few years,
international lenders still find it difficult to assess both the viability of
a project in a developing country and, above all, the likelihood that
unexpected events within a country weaken the ability of firms or the
government to repay a loan. An aspect that needs further refinements

concerns the criteria to be used. In Chapter 12, Ramakrishnan S. Koundinya deals with this problem in 'A New Look at Country Risk Analysis: An Analytical Approach to Judgmental Risk Scoring'. The author proposes the application of the *analytic hierarchy process* methodology to structure the judgmental scoring of country risk and evaluation of country risk profiles over time. He suggests a framework of analysis that enables incorporation of quantitative assessment of economic/financial performance and expert judgment on other qualitative factors. The preliminary model focuses on selected economic/financial variables for the evaluation of risk profiles. Conceptual attributes considered relevant in forming expectations about country risk exposure are defined for three hierarchy levels. Relevance of the model is confirmed with an application for a sample of selected developed and developing countries. In the next paper (Chapter 13), 'Political Risk in Latin American Stock Markets: A Rational Expectations Approach', Benoit Carmichael, Jean-Claude Cosset and Klaus P. Fischer investigate the impact of political risk on common stock returns of selected Latin American stock exchanges by taking a rational expectation approach on the relationship between the government policy menu and prices of securities in these stock exchanges.

One of the most profound changes in the environment of financial markets has been the globalization of securities markets. During the last decade international capital markets underwent an explosive growth. Simplification and harmonization of major stock exchanges taking place concurrently led to higher competition and important innovations in securitization and intermediation. These changes promoted intense cross-border equity and bond financing. However, growth of the securities markets was heavily influenced by unfavourable international conditions making their environment unstable and risky. We have also witnessed the adoption of financial deregulation and liberalization which linked markets even further and forced corporations to globalize financing of their investments.

Looking at these problems, Part VI takes an analytical look at capital markets and makes important extensions of modern investments and portfolio theory as well as agency theory to take into account increased international competition and globalization of financial markets. Patterns of changes in the international capital markets are examined to determine their efficiency; conventional paradigms and research techniques are extended to test global efficiency and formulate new theories and tests for the case of emerging

capital markets. The issues have attracted the attention of practitioners and researchers, but disagreements remain on the nature of
global exchange markets. One point of concern refers to the degree
of integration among international stock exchanges and their ability
to process information. Shahriar Khaksari and Neil Seitz conduct
new tests to answer this question. In Chapter 14, 'A Real Return Test
of International Market Efficiency', the authors aim at determining
whether the mean-variance frontier available to an internationally
diversified investor is affected by the choice of the country in which
ultimate consumption is to occur. Limitations of previous studies are
overcome by including dividends as well as price changes in computing equity returns, by including long and short-term debt securities as
well as equity, and by adjusting returns for inflation so that both real
and nominal return efficient frontiers could be examined. Empirical
findings show that the location of the mean-variance efficient frontier
is affected by the country in which ultimate consumption takes place.
The chapter therefore provides evidence that international capital
markets are not fully integrated.

Financial globalization has mainly taken place among the leading
industrialized countries. Nevertheless, developing countries have
also been impacted by financial innovations around the world and are
rapidly assimilating to the new international financial markets structures. Moreover, in the aftermath of the debt crisis, developing
countries have been seeking alternative ways of financing. Consequently, to mobilize international savings to their markets, they have
adopted ambitious economic reform programmes, including deregulation and liberalization of their financial markets. Free from the
bonds of government, their financial markets seem to be bursting and
are 'emerging' as an important part of world financial activity.
However, they are still characterized by imperfections that pose a big
challenge to overcome them. Unfortunately, understanding of these
'emerging markets' remains limited, and theories to explain their
behaviour and relationships with the real markets are non-existent.
Moreover, finance theory has not been extended to take into account
market imperfections found in the developing countries. One important fact, which restrains the growth of financial markets, is the
existing forms of organization and governance of firms in the developing countries. Firms remain largely family-owned, with little or
no stocks sold in financial markets. Klaus P. Fischer, Edgar Ortiz,
and A. P. Palasvirta make an important contribution in this direction.
In their chapter, 'Risk Management and Corporate Governance in

Imperfect Capital Markets' (Chapter 15), Fischer, Ortiz and Palasvirta explicate the issues concerning corporate governance and risk
management under imperfect capital markets. Finance theory commonly explains these issues in terms of perfect capital markets. The
authors present an alternative paradigm to take into account the case
of entrepreneurs taking their decisions in the absence of arms' length
capital markets. Based on this conceptual framework and previous
empirical studies, these authors conclude that in the absence of
developed financial markets where risk can be bundled and price of
the corporation is fair, owner-managers have no incentives to relinquish control and diversify risk through financial markets. They
present and discuss three propositions about corporate control and
risk management by owner managers in the developing countries.
They also identify the reasons underlying the existence of 'industrial
groups' – a sort of family-owned conglomerates – and the set of
opportunities that under imperfect financial markets, entrepreneurs
have to invest and diversify risk, particularly high systematic risk
associated with 'political risk' derived from excessive state interven-
tionism in the economy. Four strategies used by owner-managers
to diversify risk are identified and discussed: export capital (international diversification); diversify in the real sector through atomized
projects – firms – which leads to the creation of groups; leverage up
through group-owned financial intermediaries; and generate rents
through permanent monopoly profits, often resulting from distorted
government practices. The propositions presented by the authors
have important implications for capital market development. They
identify some distortions from the real and financial markets that
must be dealt with to enhance their expansion and integration with
world financial markets so that their contributions to development
are optimized. Concretely, governments should induce changes in the
supply and demand side of the capital markets so that corporations
find it attractive to become public, and investors find adequate diversification opportunities due to the existence of an attractive frontier
of risk return alternatives. However, changes in the financial markets
must go along with changes in the real markets. Lesser intervention
of the state in the economy should be enforced to eliminate monopoly
profits which due to government intervention are not transient in
nature, like in common corporate entrepreneurship, but permanent
and do distort the potential growth of corporations and the economy.

These implications are finely exemplified by the South Korean case
– also an emerging financial market. Although liberalization of its

financial markets has been considered exemplary, some limitations are becoming apparent. Joanna Poznanska makes this point in Chapter 16, 'Structural Changes in the Korean Financial Market'. She shows that South Korea has reached the stage of industrial maturity without a developed financial system, and then she analyses reforms implemented in the banking system and the securities markets, and identifies the nature of Korean financial internationalization. These analyses lead her to assert that to sustain further growth Korea will have to adopt various types of liberalization policies. The essence of needed reforms lies in the activation of market competition through divestment of state assets and deregulation of financial markets. By freeing interest rates in the financial markets the government hopes that interest rate will reflect availability of funds. To promote corporate growth, the government has opened the local stock market to foreign investors. Korean government intervention aims to strengthen the market to enable it to become the regulating force of the economy. However, the government intends to pursue reforms slowly, in a gradual fashion, but market forces may overtake the process. The main targets of the reform, the *chaebol*, the Korean family firm, and the commercial banks are finding it difficult to adjust to proposed changes. In conclusion, Poznanska argues for furthering financial and real reforms in Korea as the means to ensure its continued economic growth.

An important feature of the new financial environment is the emergence of equity markets of quotation systems. In Chapter 17, 'An Analysis of Equity Markets of Quotation Systems', Gilles Duteil and Abraham Mulugetta provide a useful exposition and examination of equity markets, highlighting the operational efficiency, liquidity, and other 'qualities'. They bring out the French market microstructure of the Paris Bourse's continuous quotation system that has been inspired by the Toronto Stock Exchange CATS system and make a number of useful observations on liquidity and depth. It is concluded that actual market organization does not seem to be suitable for bloc trading (except OTC) and for future growth of harmonization of financial services in Europe. It is contended further that the active competition of the London SEAQ international market in which most of the French 'blue chips' are traded by market makers is likely to increase since it provides a firm price and immediacy to block traders.

One important reason why international financial markets find restraints to their integration is differences in tax systems among nations. The international financial environment is continuously influenced by changes in the treatment to corporate dividends and capital gains. Similarly, restrictive tax systems have tended to distort capital markets development at the domestic level. On the other hand, increased globalization is firmly leading the way towards greater harmonization of tax laws. Part VII of the book brings out tax issues and models of tax structure under closed and open economies, and examines various facets of this type of price distortion, discusses the implications of existing municipal taxation systems in Mexico on the North American Free Trade Agreement. In this part, focus is also put on international banking globalization. Historical patterns of globalization of the French banking system and the details of off-shore banking trends are examined. Alejandra Cabello's 'Economic Integration and Mexican Municipal Finances' (Chapter 18) attempts to study the implications of existing municipal taxation systems in Mexico on the North American Free Trade Agreement (NAFTA). She puts forth an important point: potential benefits to Mexico from its integration with Canada and the United States might be limited due to existing asymmetries among the three nations. Uneven regional development is a factor that could create severe bottlenecks in the North American integration processes, hindering Mexico's trade and investment opportunities that could be gained from the NAFTA. This conclusion is reached after a careful analysis of Mexican municipal finances. To this effect, she first reflects on the interrelationships between economic integration and municipal development and finances. She argues for more resources and greater autonomy in municipal taxation as a means to promote 'grass root' development. Her empirical analysis corroborates this assertion. In the long run, she finds, municipal revenues tend to decrease in real terms and Federal revenue shares become the most important source of local revenues, amounting to nearly 70 per cent of Mexican municipal funds. The problem can be identified with a weak federalism leading to a strong intervention by the central government in local economic activity. Poor training in municipal management and lack of adequate accounting systems also account for this problem. For this reason Cabello proposes an accounting system for municipalities, based on private accounting, and some policies to decentralize public municipal finances. The author also proposes a forward looking attitude in these policies so that harmonization with its Northern trade partners can be achieved at all levels of taxation. In the context of an international financial markets, the implications of this study are straightforward. In a nation, financial markets can only flourish if its economy is fully integrated. Similarly, outward financial integration cannot succeed, or at least will be limited in scope in the absence of arm's length well integrated financial markets in one of the participant countries.

Another angle of taxation is explored in Chapter 19. Alternative tax structures in closed and open economy frameworks are modelled and discussed by Dilip K. Ghosh and Shyamasri Ghosh in 'Optimum Distortions in Closed and Open Economies: Some Aspects of the Theory of Second Best'. Their point of departure is the search by policy makers for optimum economic policies in an imperfect market environment. The issue has been brilliantly dealt with in the literature of 'second best', but researchers have failed to present a coherent structure of optimum distortions. Ghosh and Ghosh tackle this problem. They determine the structure of optimum distortions in different postulated set-ups, and discuss the issues on possible tax structure in closed and open economic frameworks. Then, the authors attempt to ascertain when uniform rather than differentiated and when differentiated rather than uniform tax structure would be optimal for the taxing country. Many other results in the area of 'second best' are reviewed and extended, looking up at the problem of tariff manipulation. In this context, the authors provide conditions for successful trade liberalization and creation of trading blocs and customs unions. In the emerging environment of economic integration such as the European Monetary System (EMS), the North American Free Trade Agreement (NAFTA), and the like, if or when removal or reduction of tariffs is called for, and in the event that is warranted, what the structure of elimination or reduction ought to be has been enunciated in this work within the framework of welfare maximization. In Chapter 20, 'Socio-History of French Banks and Banking: Role Model for Global Banking', Irene Finel Honigman turns to historical evidence to assess patterns of internationalization and draws lessons to the present banking internationalization. The author finds that fear of speculation and risk since the financial fiascos of the eighteenth century coupled with a sense of historical presence and cultural identity have led France to adopt long term, well hedged protective policies while developing and maintaining vast inter-country and international banking networks. French banking has always depended on effective government intervention from Napoleon III 'Saint Simonien' capitalism (1860–71) to de Gaulle's nationalization of major banks (1946) to Mitterrand's complex manoeuvres from nationalization to privatization (1981–88).

A specific study of the Crédit Lyonnais's role from its inception in 1863, its foreign subsidiaries following the Franco-Prussian war, its presence as global bank, illustrates the paradoxical nature of government control and capitalist initiative. French banks dominated world markets through networks of branches, representative offices and foreign investment. She contends that at a time when we note a sense of crisis in the domestic American banking system and the emergence of unified monetary markets and economic hyperstructures in Europe, France's historical experience will help her to play a leading role in the European Monetary Union (EMU), and the promotion of a Euro Fed will continue to help shape the future of global banking policies.

Aggressive and innovative banking management has led to a higher degree of competition in international banking. To enhance their competitiveness, US banks have established offshore banking centres to strengthen their international operations. Offshore centres allow them to lower costs and overcome limitations due to tax laws or regulatory policies meant to ensure sound banking management and confidence on the financial system. As a result, US banks carry out a significant amount of foreign lending activities through offshore banking centres. In the last chapter of this book, 'Offshore Banking Centres: Prospects and Issues' (Chapter 21), Emmanuel Roussakis, Krishnan Dandapani and Arun Prakash focus on the main issues surrounding this international banking practice. They present the environment of offshore banking and explicate the problems thoroughly, and then shed some light on its prospects. They conclude with their significant empirical analysis that barriers all over the world are crumbling and the world is becoming a global market place. In this changing environment of international financial markets the offshore banking centres which can provide excellent quality of service and can maintain high regulatory and supervisory standards can be expected to survive in decades to come, and this requirement will in turn strengthen the banking system worldwide.

This book thus presents a wide spectrum of the analytical as well as empirical examination of several developments in our changing environment of international financial markets. As time moves forward, new developments will take shape, new problems will surface, and new challenges will be met. This work will be a guide for confronting some of those upcoming events, and we will also learn on the way to restructure and modify our analytical skill, theoretical frameworks and empirical designs to cope with the new situations and scenarios.

REFERENCES

AGLIETTA, M., BRENDER, A. and COUDERT, V., *Globalisation Financière: L'Aventure Obligée* (Paris: Centre d'Etudes Prospectives et d'Informations Internationales, 1990).

ANDERE, E. and KESSEL, G., (Comp.). *Mexico y el Tratado Trilateral de Libre Comercio. Impacto Sectorial* (México, D.F.: McGraw-Hill, 1992).

ARGY, V. and DE GRAUWE, P., *Choosing an Exchange Rate Regime: The Challenge for Smaller Industrial Countries* (Washington, DC: International Monetary Fund, 1990).

BARTH, J. R. and BARTHOLOMEW, P. F. (eds), *Emerging Challenges for the International Financial Industry. Research in International Business and Finance*, vol. 9 (Greenwich, CT: JAI Press, 1992).

BERGSTEN, C. F., *America in the World Economy. A Strategy for the 1990s* (Washington, DC: Institute for International Economics, 1988).

BRANSON, W. H., FRENKEL, J. A. and GOLDSTEIN, M. (eds), *International Policy Coordination and Exchange Rate Fluctuations* (Chicago: University of Chicago Press, 1990).

CANTO, V. A. and LAFFER, A. B. (eds), *Monetary Policy, Taxation, and International Investment Strategy* (New York: Quorum Books, 1990).

CANTO, V. A., LAFFER, A. B. and WEBB, R. I. (eds), *Investment Strategy and State and Local Economic Policy* (New York: Quorum Books, 1992).

CHUPPE, T. M., HAWORTH, H. R. and WATKINS, M. G., 'Global Finance: Causes, Consequences and Prospects for the Future', *The Global Finance Journal*, vol. 1, no. 1, (1989) pp. 1–20.

CLAASSEN, E. M., *International and European Monetary Systems* (New York: Praeger, 1990).

DAMANPOUR, F., *The Evolution of Foreign Banking Institutions in the United States* (New York: Quorum Books, 1990).

DERMINE, J. (ed.), *European Banking in the 1990s* (Cambridge, MA: Basil Blackwell, 1990).

DRACHE, D. and GERTLER, M. S. (eds), *The New Era of Global Competition. State Policy and Market Power* (Montreal and Kingston: McGill-Queen's University Press, 1991).

EDWARDS, F. R. and PATRICK, H. T. (eds), *Regulating International Financial Markets: Issues and Policies* (Boston: Kluwer Academic Publishers, 1992).

FELIX, D. (ed.), *Debt and Transfiguration? Prospects for Latin America's Economic Revival* (Armonk, NY: M.E. Sharpe, 1990).

FIELEKE, N. S., 'International Payments Imbalances in the 1980s', *New England Economic Review* (Federal Reserve Bank of Boston, Mar.–Apr. 1989) pp. 4–14.

FISCHER, K. and PAPAIOANNOU, G. J. (eds), *Business Finance in Less Developed Capital Markets* (Westport, CT.: Greenwood Press, 1992).

FRATIANNI, M. and HAGEN, J., *The European Monetary System and European Monetary Union* (Boulder: Westview, 1992).

GHOSH, D. K., *Trade, Distortion and Growth* (New Delhi: Concept Press, Jan. 1984).

GHOSH, D. K., *Intercountry Loan, Financial Risk and Foreign Exchange Policies of the LDCs* (World Academy Press, College Park, Maryland, Nov. 1984).

GHOSH, D. K. and KHAKSARI, S., 'International Equity Markets: Integrated or Segmented?', in *Handbook of International Market Integration*, ed. Stanley R. Stansell (Oxford: Basil Blackwell, UK, forthcoming).

GHOSH, D. K., 'Interest Rate Parity: Seven Expressions', *Financial Management* (FM Letter) (Winter, 1991).

GHOSH, P. K. and GHOSH, D. K., (eds), *International Trade and Third World Development* (Westport, CT: Greenwood Press, Oct. 1984).

GOLBERG, S., *Global Pursuit* (Toronto: McGraw-Hill Ryerson, 1991).

GUTTMANN, R., *Reforming Money and Finance. Institutions and Markets Flux* (Armonk, NY: M.E. Sharpe, 1989).

HAKKIO, C. S., 'Interest Rates and Exchange Rates – What is the Relationship?', *Economic Review* (Federal Reserve Bank of Kansas City, Nov. 1986) pp. 33–43.

HUBBARD, R. G., *Financial Markets and Financial Crisis* (Chicago: University of Chicago Press, 1990).

KHADEMIAN, A. M., *The SEC and Capital Market Regulation. The Politics of Expertise* (Pittsburgh: University of Pittsburgh Press, 1992).

KHOURY, S. J., *The Deregulation of the World Financial Markets. Myths, Realities and Impact* (New York: Quorum Books, 1990).

KHOURY, S. J., *Recent Developments in International Banking and Finance* (Amsterdam: North-Holland, 1992).

KLINGHOFFER, A. J., and GHOSH, D. K., *The Global Politics of Gold: Problems of International Finance and Prospects for American Policy* (World Academy Press, College Park, Maryland, Oct. 1984).

KOSTERS, M. H. and MELTZER, A. H., *International Competitiveness in Financial Services* (Boston: Kluwer Academic Publishers, 1991).

KRAINER, R. E., *Finance in a Theory of the Business Cycle. Production and Distribution in a Debt and Equity Economy* (Cambridge, MA: Blackwell, 1992).

LESSARD, D. R., 'Corporate Finance in the 1990s – Implications of a Changing Competitive and Financial Context', *Journal of International Financial Management and Accounting*, vol. 1, no. 3 (1989) pp. 209–31.

LESSARD, D. R., 'Global Competition and Corporate Finance in the 1990s', *Journal of Applied Corporate Finance* (Winter, 1991) pp. 59–72.

MADRID, R. L., *Overexposed. U.S. Banks Confront the Third World Debt Crisis* (Boulder: Westview Press, 1992).

MARRINAN, J., 'Exchange Rate Determination: Sorting Out Theory and Evidence', *New England Economic Review* (Nov.–Dec. 1989) pp. 39–51.

MEDEWITZ, J. N., ABDULLAH, F. A. and OLSON, K., 'Integration of World Equity Markets: The Recent Evidence', *The International Journal of Finance*, vol. 4, no. 1, (Autumn 1991) pp. 34–46.

MISTRY, P. S., 'Globalization of Financial Markets: Implications for Asian Developing Countries', *Journal of Development Banking*, vol. 5, no. 2 (July 1987) pp. 3–20.

OECD, *Integration des Pays en Developpement dans le Systeme Commercial International* (Paris: OECD, 1992).

OECD, *Noveaux Défix pour les Banques* (Paris: OECD, 1992).

ORTIZ, E. and CABELLO, A., 'La Globalizacion de los Mercados Financieros y sus Implicaciones en los Países en Desarrollo', mimeo (FCPyS/ Universidad Nacional Autonoma de Mexico, 1990).

OXELHWEIM, L., *International Financial Integration* (Berlin: Springer-Verlag, 1990).

PAULY, L. W., *Opening Financial Markets. Banking Politics in the Pacific Rim* (Ithaca: Cornell University Press, 1988).

QUIGLEY, J. M. (ed.), *Perspectives on Local Public Finance and Public Policy* (3 vols). (Greenwich, CT: JAI Press. 1983, 1985, 1987).

PISCHKE, J. D., *Finance at the Frontier. Debt Capacity and the Role of Credit in the Private Economy* (Washington, DC: The World Bank, 1991).

RANDALL, S. J., KONRAD, H. and SILVERMAN, S., *North America Without Borders? Integrating Canada, the United States and Mexico* (Calgary: University of Calgary Press, 1992).

RHEE, S. G. and CHANG, R. P., *Pacific-Basin Capital Markets Research*, vol. II (Amsterdam: North-Holland, 1991).

ROLL, R., 'The International Crash of October 1987', *The International Finance Reader*. R. W. Kolb (ed.) (Miami: Kolb Publishing Company, 1991).

Sachs, J. D. (ed.), *Developing Country Debt and Economic Performance. Volume 1. The International Financial System* (Chicago: University of Chicago Press, 1989).

SACHS, J. D. (ed.), *Developing Country Debt and Economic Performance. Volume 1. The International Financial System* (Chicago: University of Chicago Press, 1989).

SACHS, J. D. and COLLINS, S. M. (eds), *Developing Country Debt and Economic Performance. Volume 3. Country Studies – Indonesia, Korea, Philippines, Turkey* (Chicago: University of Chicago Press, 1989).

SAINI, K. G. and BATES, P. S., 'A Survey of Quantitative Approaches to Country Risk Analysis', *Journal of Banking and Finance* (June 1984) pp. 341–55.

SHOVEN, J. B. and WALEY, J., (eds), *Canada – U.S. Tax Comparisons* (Chicago: University of Chicago Press, 1992).

SURAJARAS, P. and SWEENEY, R. J., *Profit Making Speculation in Foreign Exchange Markets* (Boulder: Westview Press, 1992).

TONDKAR, R. H., ADHIKARI, A. and COFFMAN, E. N., 'The Internationalization of Equity Markets: Motivations for Foreign Corporate Listing and Filing and Listing Requirements of Five Major Stock Exchanges', *The International Journal of Accounting*, vol. 24, no. 1 (1989) pp. 144–63.

TUNG, R. L. and MILLER, E. L., 'Managing in the Twentieth-first Century: The Need for Global Orientation', *Management International Review*, vol. 30, no. 1, (1990), pp. 5–18.

VEGA CANOVAS, G. (Coord.), *Mexico Ante el Libre Comercio con America del Norte* (Mexico, D.F.: El Colegio de Mexico, 1991).

VOLCKER, P. A. and GYOHTEN, T., *Changing Fortunes. The World's Money and the Threat to American Leadership* (New York: Times Books, 1992).

VOSGERAU, H. J. (ed.), *New Institutional Arrangements for the World Economy* (Berlin: Springer-Verlag, 1989).

WATSON, W. G., *North American Free Trade Area* (Kingston, Ontario: John Deuth Institute, 1991).

WAVERMAN, L. (ed.), *Negotiating and Implementing a North American Free Trade Agreement* (Toronto: Fraser Institute/Centre for International Studies, University of Toronto, 1992).

WONNACOTT, R. J., *The Economics of Overlapping Free Trade Areas and the Mexican Challenge* (Toronto: C.D. Howe Institute, 1991).

Part II
Exchange Rate Markets

Part II deals with markets of exchange rates. The works included in this part introduce new models and innovative research techniques to bring insights concerning the dilemmas of long-run exchange rate equilibrium and market efficiency, and unrestrained market fluctuations *vis-à-vis* government intervention, left unsolved by conventional econometric models. These analyses have important implications for corporations and economic agents in general seeking to improve their exchange risk management to compete more effectively in the globalized economy.

2 Foreign Exchange Market Efficiency: A Look at London

John P. Lajaunie, Bruce L. McManis and Atsuyuki Naka

2.1 INTRODUCTION

The purpose of this study is to test the Efficient Market Hypothesis (EMH) in the London foreign exchange market. The study relates the EMH to the information set which includes past prices for four foreign currencies. The goal is to determine if a long-run equilibrium relationship exists between the price series for the different currencies. The existence of such a relationship will be considered a direct violation of the EMH.

For the EMH to hold, all current asset prices must reflect all past price information which is currently available (Fama, 1970). Furthermore, Granger (1986) indicates that if X and Y are price series for two different assets from a jointly efficient speculative market, they cannot be cointegrated (Granger, 1986).

This theoretical implication provides a plausible basis for formulating a test of the EMH. Given the price series for different foreign currency assets and the implication for integrated time series in an efficient market, a test for the presence of a cointegrating relationship between the price series for the different foreign exchange assets constitutes a test of the EMH (Hakkio and Rush, 1989; Baillie and Bollerslev, 1989a, b; Copeland, 1991). In the case of cointegrated time series, the rejection of the EMH is based on the existence of an information set which contains past and current prices that can be employed *vis-à-vis* an error correction model to forecast future price movements in the market.

2.2 LITERATURE REVIEW

Hakkio and Rush (1989) employed cointegration techniques to test the spot and one month forward rates for the Pound Sterling and the Deutsche Mark exchange rates in the United Kingdom and German foreign exchange markets for conformity to the EMH. The tests employed monthly data for the period July 1975 to October 1986. The methodology employed was a two-step test procedure for cointegration between the price series developed by Granger (1986). First, each price series in each of the markets was tested for stationarity, i.e. the price series was an integrated process of order zero, $I(0)$, with no unit roots in the series.[1] The test statistic employed was the Box–Pierce–Ljung Q statistic. Second, the null hypothesis of no cointegration and the validity of an error correction model was tested.[2]

The test results rejected the stationarity of the price series for both spot and forward rates specified in the levels. This implied each of the series contained a single unit root in its autoregressive (AR) representation. A stationary series integrated of order zero was obtained by taking the first differences of the series thereby yielding white noise disturbance terms in an AR representation of the series. The test for the absence of cointegration between the price series of the different currencies was unable to reject the null hypothesis for any pair of series at the 5 per cent level of significance. Overall, these results suggested that the markets for spot and forward foreign exchange in the United Kingdom and Germany were semi-strong form efficient.

Baillie and Bollerslev (1989a, b) examined the price series for seven spot and forward exchange rates from the New York Foreign Exchange Market for the period 1 March 1980 to 28 January 1985.[3] The data consisted of the daily opening bid prices for the Pound Sterling, Deutsche Mark, French Franc, Italian Lira, Swiss Franc, Japanese Yen and Canadian Dollar *vis-à-vis* the US dollar. Tests were conducted for the presence of a unit root in each of the series and the presence of cointegration between the different pairs of price series.

Baillie and Bollerslev (1989a, b) employed the Phillips–Perron tests which allowed for the presence of a unit root with or without a drift term in the exchange rate series.[4] The test results failed to reject the null hypothesis of a unit root in each of the price series.

Additionally, Baillie and Bollerslev extended their analysis by employing a full information maximum likelihood estimation procedure for the number of independent unit roots in a system of exchange rates as suggested by Johansen (1988). The test results indicated the existence of six independent unit roots for the seven pairs for the spot and forward exchange rates. This implied a single cointegrating relationship existed for the two sets of seven exchange rates which suggested the changes in the system were partly determined by a common long-run equilibrium error term. In the absence of a time-varying risk premium and utilizing the theoretical results for cointegrated variables these results implied a deviation from the EMH.

Copeland (1991) tested foreign exchange market efficiency through the use of cointegration analysis. After establishing the existence of a unit root in each of the series, Copeland employed the Johansen procedure to test the different pairs of spot exchange rates for the Deutsche Mark, Pound Sterling, French Franc, Swiss Franc and Japanese Yen, from 1976 to 1989, for the existence of a cointegrating relationship.[5]

The test results for the cross-market study rejected the existence of a cointegrating relationship between any of the pairs of currencies. This suggested the spot markets for the individual foreign currencies were efficient as an error correction model could not be employed to forecast future price movements.

2.3 METHODOLOGY

The methodology for this study is consistent with the theory of integrated time series (Granger, 1986) and the prior empirical studies (Hakkio and Rush, 1989; Baillie and Bollerslev, 1989a, b; Copeland, 1991). The purpose of employing a similar methodology is to examine the following hypothesis and make a valid comparison of the results with those from prior studies.

H_0: Price series of spot rates for different currencies in the London market are not cointegrated.
H_a: Price series of spot rates for different currencies in the London market are cointegrated.

Rejection of the null hypothesis of no cointegration is inconsistent with the theory of efficient speculative markets as set forth by Granger (1986) and the semi-strong form of the EMH of Fama (1970).

First, the individual spot price series are tested for the presence of a unit root. The Phillips–Perron tests, which allow for a greater generality in the error generating process in the AR representation of the price series, are employed (see Phillips, 1987; Perron, 1988; Phillips and Perron, 1988). The greater generality of the error process allows for weak forms of serial dependency through the use of a non-parametric Parzen's truncated lag window in the estimation process (Phillips, 1987).

The equations for the Phillips–Perron tests are shown as follows:

$$Y_t = \hat{\alpha} Y_{t-1} + \hat{u}_t \tag{1a}$$

$$Y_t = \mu^* + \alpha^* Y_{t-1} + u_t^* \tag{1b}$$

$$Y_t = \tilde{\mu} + \tilde{B}\,(t-n/2) + \tilde{\alpha} Y_{t-1} + \tilde{u}_t \tag{1c}$$

where μ^* and $\tilde{\mu}$ are drift terms, $(t-n/2)$ is a time trend variable, and $\hat{u}$, u^* and $\tilde{u}$ are error terms.

The critical values for the test are provided by Dickey and Fuller (1981).

Second, the different pairs of spot exchange rates are used to test the null hypothesis of an absence of cointegration. Both, the two variable and multiple variable specifications of the single equation model are employed for this testing (Granger, 1986; Engle and Granger, 1987; Engle and Yoo, 1987). The specifications of the two single equation cointegration models are shown below.

$$(two) \quad X_t = c + dY_t + u_t \tag{2a}$$

$$(multiple) \quad X_t = C + d_1 Y_{1,t} + d_2 Y_{2,t} + u_t \tag{2b}$$

First, the Durbin-Watson (DW) test statistic for each of the cointegrating regressions is examined (Durlauf and Phillips, 1988). Second, the test technique for the presence of a unit root in the residuals from the cointegrating regression is evaluated (Phillips and Ouliaris, 1990). The failure to reject the null hypothesis of a unit root in the residual series from a cointegrating regression implies the null hypothesis of no cointegration cannot be rejected either. If the coefficient on the lagged residuals is positive and significantly greater than zero, the null hypothesis of no cointegration is rejected. The evaluation of the other coefficient estimates in the model allows for definitive statements concerning a time trend or a drift term in the AR process.

The final test for the presence of a cointegrating relationship employed is a full information maximum likelihood method of estimation for a system of equations (Johansen, 1988; Johansen and Juselius, 1990). The systems approach allows for the presence of a common equilibrium error term between the different exchange rates in the system. The test employs the residuals from the ordinary least squares regression of the first difference and the lagged value of the asset price on the first difference of the $N-1$ remaining price series in the system. The computation of the cross-canonical correlation coefficients is based on the cross-product matrix of the error terms from the original least squares regressions. The test procedure involves the estimation of the matrix of cointegrating coefficients, beta. The test procedure employed also allows for the testing for the absence of a linear trend component in the impact matrix. The likelihood ratio test statistic is calculated as follows.

$$LRS = -T \sum_{i=r+1}^{N} \ln (1 - \hat{\lambda}_i) \tag{3}$$

where T is the number of observations and $\hat{\lambda}_i$ is the ith eigenvalue in the system.

The data employed in this study consist of the ask side of the daily closing prices for the Pound Sterling, Japanese Yen, Deutsche Mark and the Canadian Dollar from the London financial markets for the period 1 October 1986 to 1 April 1991. The exchange rates are stated in terms of the number of foreign currency units per US Dollar.[6]

2.4 RESULTS

The results of the tests for the stationarity of the price series in the levels from the London market point are presented in Table 2.1. For the price series presented in the levels, the Phillips–Perron procedure fails to reject the null hypothesis of a unit root. The parameter estimates for Rho in each case are very close to unity.

The test results for the presence of a unit root in the first differences of the price series for the London market are displayed in Table 2.2. The coefficient estimates for Rho in each case are substantially below unity. The test statistics rejected the presence of a unit root in each of the series. The data suggest the price series for foreign exchange assets are $I(1)$, non-stationary, in the levels and stationary, $I(0)$, in the first differences.

Table 2.1   Phillips-Perron unit root test results on the price levels

Currency	Rho	Tâ	t-ratio	Φ_1/Φ_2	Φ_3
Japanese Yen	0.99257	−7.456	−2.255	2.754	n.a.
Japanese Yen	0.99254	−7.493	−2.266	2.16	3.03
Canadian $	0.99618	−3.429	−2.149	4.669	n.a.
Canadian $	0.98720	−11.59	−2.542	4.009	4.003
British Pound	0.99243	−8.881	−2.451	3.169	n.a.
British Pound	0.99274	−8.814	−2.207	2.107	2.996
German Mark	0.99495	−6.889	−1.972	2.0165	n.a.
German Mark	0.99449	−8.112	−1.964	1.448	2.1005

1. Tâ: $A(1)=0$ (Table Ic, PO, 1990).
2. t-ratio: $A(1)=0$ (Table I, DF, 1981).
3. Φ_1: (ROW 1): $A(0)=A(1)=0$ (Table IV, DF, 1981).
4. Φ_2: (ROW 2): $A(0)=A(1)=A(2)=0$ (Table V, DF, 1981).
5. Φ_3: $A(1)=A(2)=0$ (Table VI, DF, 1981).

Table 2.2   Phillips-Perron unit root test resuls on the first differences

Currency	Rho	Tâ	t-ratio	Φ_1/Φ_2	Φ_3
Japanese Yen	−0.0194	−1177**	−32.46**	526.9**	n.a.
Japanese Yen	−0.0204	−1171**	−32.45**	351.2**	526.7**
Canadian $	−0.0276	−929**	−32.84**	539.0**	n.a.
Canadian $	−0.029	−915**	−32.97**	362.0**	543.1**
British Pound	−0.0061	−1127**	−31.97**	511.0**	n.a.
British Pound	0.00762	−1119**	−31.97**	340.8**	511.2**
German Mark	0.01956	−1139**	−31.39**	492.7**	n.a.
German Mark	0.01905	−1138**	−31.38**	328.4**	492.5**

The results for the pairwise analysis from the London market are reported in Table 2.3.

Using the different pairs of spot exchange rates, the Phillips–Ouliaris test for the presence of a unit root in the residuals of the cointegrating regression fails to reject the null hypothesis of no cointegrating relationship. Additionally, the DW statistic is close to zero for each equation. Thus, the London market shows no sign of a cointegrating relationship between the different spot exchange rate series.

The results of the test for the null hypothesis of no cointegration using a single equation multivariate model are reported in Table 2.4.

Table 2.3   Two variable cointegration test results

Currency	Equation*	DW	Tâ*	t-ratio	LAG/M
CD, DM	A	0.004 210	−3.774 4	−1.743 5	29/2
	B	0.035 79	−19.090	−3.193 3	0 /2
CD, BP	A	0.004 744	−3.016 8	−1.381 8	0 /2
	B	0.023 58	−12.171	−2.608 8	29/2
CD, JY	A	0.003 508	−3.350 6	−1.800 9	15/2
	B	0.028 02	−14.526	−2.685 1	15/2
BP, DM	A	0.011 50	−7.547 7	−2.237 8	15/2
	B	0.011 49	−7.564 9	−2.245 5	15/2
BP, JY	A	0.010 32	−5.856 7	−1.807 9	13/2
	B	0.015 21	−6.809 8	−1.718 6	13/2
DM, JY	A	0.006 359	−5.061 0	−1.652 1	30/2
	B	0.008 978	−6.079 5	−1.668 1	30/2

* Equation B incorporates a time trend.
1. The critical values for the Ta* and the *t*-ratio test statistic are found in Phillips and Ouliaris (1990, pp. 189–92).

Table 2.4   Multiple variable model for all currencies

DW	LAG/M	Tâ*	t-ratio
0.0446	15/4	−21.334	−3.2677
0.04871	14/4	−23.654	−3.4391

The test statistics fail to reject the null hypothesis for the multivariate model. The DW for each equation is close to zero for each of the regression equations.

The likelihood ratio statistics based on Johansen's full information maximum likelihood procedure are reported in Table 2.5

The test results fail to reject the null hypothesis of zero cointegrating vectors for the four–dimensional system. This confirms the results reported for the single equation model of no long-run relationship between the price series in the London foreign exchange market. Also, the likelihood ratio test for the null hypothesis of the absence of a linear trend is highly significant.[7]

Table 2.5   Results for the Johansen cointegration test for London
Variables: (CD, DM, BP, JY)
Lambda: (0.01364203, 0.01144550, 0.004127735, 0.00005604016)
LC = 14.66896**

Beta (*normalized*)

β_1	β_2	β_3	β_4
−1.0	−1.0	−1.0	−1.0
0.100 328 2	0.448 174 4	14.408 142	−0.256 452 2
1.146 394	−0.440 172 1	−9.460 464 6	0.239 883 8
0.151 009 3	−0.006 903 6	−2.576 31	0.106 902 7

Test statistics

LRS	λ-MAX	TRACE	M	R
32.089 33	27.341	48.419	4	0
17.064 99	21.279	31.256	3	$R \leqslant 1$
4.569 63	14.595	17.844	2	$R \leqslant 2$
0.061 09	8.083	8.803	1	$R \leqslant 3$

1. The critical values for λ-MAX and TRACE are in Johansen and Juselius
   (1990, Table d-2, Appendix D). LC is the likelihood ratio test for the
   absence of a linear trend which is distributed Chi-square with 4 degrees of
   freedom.

2.5   CONCLUSION

Given the results from the empirical tests, the null hypothesis of the
absence of a cointegrating relationship cannot be rejected for any of
the models specified. These results are consistent with the theory for
integrated time series in speculative efficient markets (Granger, 1986)
and the EMH (Fama, 1970). The results confirm the findings of the
prior studies by Hakkio and Rush (1986) and Copeland (1991).
Therefore, the hypothesis of an efficient market for the London
foreign exchange market cannot be rejected.

The results presented above contradict the findings of Baillie and
Bollerslev (1989b). There are two possible reasons for this difference.
First, the test technique employed by Baillie and Bollerslev (1989b)
did not account for the presence of a linear trend component in the
impact matrix. Second, the use of approximated critical values for the
seven-dimensional system may also have contributed to this difference.

Notes

1. The presence of unit roots in the price series for foreign exchange is well documented. For the original work see Meese and Singleton (1982).
2. The specification of an error correction model is provided in Engle and Granger (1987).
3. Baillie and Bollerslev note the rapid appreciation of the US dollar over this period may have influenced some of the results of the study.
4. The Phillips–Perron unit root test is robust with respect to heteroskedastic behaviour in the error terms. Baillie and Bollerslev refer to their prior work on conditional heteroskedastic processes in the *Journal of Business and Economic Statistics*, 1989 (also see Phillips, 1987; Perron, 1988; Phillips and Perron, 1988).
5. Copeland cited two reasons for using the spot exchange rate series. First, the spot market was viewed as having greater ease of access to new information. Second, the spot market was not obscured by the existence of a time varying risk premium.
6. The data is transformed to natural logarithms to avoid the well documented problems associated with Jensen's inequality and exchange rate data.
7. The test statistic is distributed chi-square with one degree of freedom. For reference, see Johansen and Juselius (1990, p. 21).

REFERENCES

BAILLIE, R. T. and BOLLERSLEV, T. (1989a) 'Common Stochastic Trends in a System of Exchange Rates', *Journal of Finance*, vol. 44, no. 1, (Mar.) pp. 167–81.

BAILLIE, R. T. and BOLLERSLEV, T. (1989b) 'The Message in Daily Exchange Rates: a Conditional Variance Tale', *Journal of Business and Economic Statistics*, vol. 7, no. 3 (July) pp. 297–305.

COPELAND, L. S. (1991) 'Cointegration Tests with Daily Exchange Rate Data', *Oxford Bulletin of Economics and Statistics*, vol. 53, no. 2, pp. 185–99.

DICKEY, D. A. and FULLER W. A. (1981) 'Likelihood Ratio Statistics for Autoregressive Time Series with a Unit Root', *Econometrica*, vol. 49, no. 4 (July) pp. 1057–72.

DURLAUF, S. and PHILLIPS, P. C. B. (1988) 'Trends Versus Random Walks in Time Series Analysis', *Econometrica*, vol. 56, no. 6 (Nov.) pp. 1333–54.

ENGLE, R. and GRANGER, C. W. J. (1987) 'Cointegration and Error Correction: Representation, Estimation, and Testing', *Econometrica*, vol. 55, no. 2 (Mar.) pp. 251–76.

ENGLE, R. and YOO, S. B. (1987) 'Forecasting and Testing Cointegrated Systems', *Journal of Econometrics*, vol. 35 (July/Aug.) pp. 143–59.

FAMA, E. (1970) 'Efficient Capital Markets: A Review of Theory and Empirical Work', *Journal of Finance*, vol. 25, no. 2 (May) pp. 383–417.

GRANGER, C. W. J. (1986) 'Developments in the Study of Cointegrated Variables', *Oxford Bulletin of Economics and Statistics*, vol. 48, no. 3 (Aug.) pp. 213–28.

HAKKIO, C. S. and RUSH, M. (1989) 'Market Efficiency and Cointegration: An Application to the Sterling and Deutschemark Exchange Market', *Journal of International Money and Finance*, vol. 8, no. 1, pp. 75–88.

JOHANSEN, S. (1988) 'Statistical Analysis of Cointegration Vectors', *Journal of Economic Dynamics and Control*, vol. 12, pp. 231–54.

JOHANSEN, S. and JUSELIUS, K. (1990) 'The Full Information Maximum Likelihood Procedure for Inference on Cointegration with Applications', *Oxford Bulletin of Economics and Statistics*, vol. 52, no. 2 (May) pp. 169–210.

MEESE, R. and SINGLETON K. (1982) 'On Unit Roots and the Empirical Modeling of Exchange Rates', *Journal of Finance*, vol. 37, no. 4, (Sept.) pp. 1029–35.

PERRON, P. (1988) 'Trends and Random Walks in Macroeconomic Time Series', *Journal of Economic Dynamics and Control*, vol. 12, pp. 297–332.

PHILLIPS, P. C. B. (1987) 'Time Series Regression with a Unit Root', *Econometrica*, vol. 55, no. 2 (March) pp. 277–301.

PHILLIPS, P. C. B. and PERRON, P. (1988) 'Testing for a Unit root in Time Series Regression', *Biometrika*, vol. 75, no. 2 (June) pp. 335–44.

PHILLIPS, P. C. B. and OULIARIS, S. (1990) 'Asymptotic Properties of Residual Based Tests for Cointegration', *Econometrica*, vol. 58, no. 1 (Jan.) pp. 165–93.

3 Freedom of Free Floating Exchange Rate: Empirical Analysis of Currency Fluctuation Patterns

M. Anaam Hashmi

3.1 INTRODUCTION AND LITERATURE REVIEW

For more than twenty years, a free floating exchange rate had been advocated by central banks and academicians alike. It was believed that market forces should play a major role in exchange rate determination. Between 1970 and 1973, leading currencies were allowed to fluctuate and an exchange rate which might be described as 'flexible', was established. This study has attempted to look back on sixteen years (1973–89) over which flexible rates have been the norm.

How has the system of free floating exchange rates worked so far? Upon close examination, we realize that exchange rates were not really free to fluctuate in response to supply and demand and other market forces. Typically, a given currency would be maintained by the intervention of its central bank at a value determined by that country to be appropriate to its balance-of-payments position, conducive to maintaining a satisfactory level of reserves, and in some cases, in fixed relation to some key currency of the world such as the US dollar. Countries have different foreign exchange rate systems. The two systems, namely the independent floating system and the European Monetary System (EMS) are close to free market systems. Countries using these two systems have constantly intervened in the foreign exchange markets to influence the currency exchange rate.

At any given time a currency might be stable, depreciating, or appreciating, in relation to a chosen key currency. In general, one may say that it is common practice for countries to seek a stable exchange rate in the short run but to allow long-run forces, as they become cumulatively strong, to manifest themselves. Thus, for most leading currencies, periods of exchange-rate fluctuation would be punctuated by periods of stability.

It has long been recognized that many financial time series such as foreign exchange rates are non-stationary (Singleton and Meese, 1982). The issue of non-stationary data is not merely just a statistical curiosity but has several important implications for the modelling of exchange rates. It minimizes the controversy over the appropriate transformations to use when conducting tests of whether the forward rate is an unbiased and efficient predictor of the future spot exchange rate, making it easier to explain the sharing of long-run movements by many exchange rates, and also to identify exactly which or how many stochastic trends are responsible for driving the exchange rate system. To put it simply, the autoregressive conditional heteroscedasticity (ARCH) model framework of Engle (1982), and similar analysis using the Engle model by other researchers, are performed by Westerfield (1977), Vinso (1978), Hsieh (1988), and Baillie and Bollerslev (1989). All of these studies find that the fundamental system of exchange rates is tied to one long-run equilibrium path. The random errors around this equilibrium path can be contributed to the various innovations in successive changes and shocks in the exchange rate market.

Baillie and Bollerslev's (1989) study (which constitutes a total of 1245 observations) encompasses the daily spot and thirty-day forward exchange rate data from the New York Foreign Exchange Market between 1 March 1980 to 28 January 1985. The data are provided by the Data Resource Incorporated (DRI) and are of the opening bid prices for the UK, West Germany, France, Italy, Switzerland, Japan, and Canada *vis-à-vis* the US dollar. The six different test statistics are calculated from all seven countries. It is concluded that after taking account of any ARCH effects, the assumption of conditional normality is a reasonable approximation on monthly and fortnightly data, whereas for weekly data, it varies among currencies. With daily data, one can not predict its outcome, because there are no reasons to expect normality under any of the conditions for any of the selected currency.

Baillie and Bollerslev (1989) research on foreign exchange rates clearly shows that the speculative selling (or buying) pressure is far too large for official offsetting by any nation on any given day in the foreign exchange market. It furthers the notion that the foreign exchange market existing today is a world market, thanks in most part, to the advent of electronics and telecommunications media. The result of improved banking functions, the instantaneous flow of private sector funds across national frontiers, and high volume transactions have made foreign exchange markets undoubtedly world markets. The total capital transactions effecting the balance of payments often become so large that they shadow both the visible and invisible transactions of the current account and their rapidly diminishing influence upon exchange rates. (Presently, foreign exchange market transactions regularly dwarf public-sector operations, making them insignificant when compared with exchange market transaction at all time.) Therefore, one can argue that the intermittent but heavy intervention by central banks and the widespread swap arrangements to which governmental institutions resort may cause foreign exchange markets unpredictable, and encourage unfounded practices of precautionary (by the business sector) and speculative (by the financial investment sector) movements in the market. This creates irrational events day-in and day-out to the amazement of all interested parties and participants in the foreign exchange market.

To explain Baillie's finding in another way, the movements of capital funds are now potentially so great that their effect on the exchange rate cannot be offset by exchange fund operations by governmental institutions. Consequently, it is obvious that the reserve holdings of any central bank, perhaps even a group of central banks, may be insufficient to regulate and to manipulate the short-run exchange rate that in any way directly contradicts the direction of the market movement.

The notion that capital moves are far more easily made than anticipated, and that barriers such as exchange controls and limitations do not work can be easily seen by looking at several examples. One such example is as follows:

In November 1985, because of a computer failure, the Bank of New York was able to receive incoming or buy orders but was unable to execute outgoing or sell orders. The bank soon began to develop a massive negative balance and was obligated to overdraw its Federal Reserve account by $22.6 billion U.S. dollars (Spero, 1988–9).

This is just the volume of one bank's capital flow for one day, the cumulative sum of the world's banking system put the figure close to the trillion dollar range. Foreign exchange transactions per day (worldwide) are included in Table 3.1. It is believed that no central banks

Table 3.1   Exchange transactions/day worldwide

Year	Transactions/day (billion US$)
1979	75
1984	150
1986	300
1987	425*
1989	720[†]

* P. Sherrid, 'The Games Behind The Dollar's Fall', *U.S. News and World Report*, 16 Feb. 1987, pp. 43–44.
† April 1989, Exchange Market Survey, (Federal Reserve Bank of New York, 1989).

Sources: A. Murray and P. Truell, *The Wall Street Journal*, 22 Sept. 1989, A12. Morgan Stanley Bank estimate, 1979–1987.

can influence these active foreign exchange markets. It is suggested that in today's markets, central bank intervention may be futile. This concept is the key to this study and the independence of foreign exchange markets is analysed using a time-series model.

3.2   RESEARCH METHODOLOGY

For this study six leading international currencies are selected from January 1987 to July 1989 noon rates in the London Foreign Exchange Market. The exchange rate data series are tabulated for daily (669 days), weekly (134 weeks), and monthly (31 months) intervals. For empirical testing a first-order auto-regressive model, specifically the ARIMA (1, 0, 0) Cx model, is applied using daily, weekly, and monthly data series for all six currencies.

It is understood that individual currency will fluctuate as a result of domestic variables as well as international variables. The variables can also be influenced by central bank intervention in the foreign exchange market. We assume that the free floating exchange rate system is in place and foreign exchange markets are unbiased (free of white noise), the sample auto-correlation coefficients have normal distribution, with mean 0 and standard deviation $1/T$. It means that data series consist of independently distributed random variables. By using the ARIMA (1, 0, 0) model, if no white noise is detected, it can be concluded that exchange rates are influenced by market forces and no central bank intervention is observed. On the other hand, existence of white noise means the foreign exchange rate system is not free of central bank intervention. The following hypothesis is tested for this study.

HYPOTHESIS: Foreign exchange rate for floating currencies is influenced by government's (central bank) intervention.

3.3 DATA ANALYSIS AND DISCUSSION

The monthly, weekly, and daily data for all six currencies are analysed using the ARIMA (1, 0, 0) Cx model. Further Chi-square statistics are compiled for 90 per cent and 95 per cent level of significance. The results are tabulated in Table 3.2 (monthly data), Table 3.3 (weekly data), and Table 3.4 (daily data).

For monthly data, at 23 DF (degree of freedom) and 90 per cent and 95 per cent confidence, DM, Y and SF data series are free of white noise. It implies that during the January 1987–July 1989 period, monthly data series do not detect any statistically significant government intervention. For three other data series (FF, A$ and Peseta) government intervention is noticed (Table 3.2).

Table 3.2   Determination of white noise for monthly foreign exchange rates

Degree of freedom accept/reject	11	23	11 90%	23 90%	11 95%	23 95%
C16 Australian $	13.50	23.50	A	R	A	A
C17 Deutsche Mark	13.70	24.00	A	R	A	R
C18 French Franc	11.30	21.00	A	A	A	A
C19 Japanese Yen	13.60	24.30	A	R	A	R
C20 Spanish Peseta	0.30	4.20	A	A	A	A
C21 Swiss Franc	11.80	29.00	A	R	A	R

Chi-square at 90%	17.2750	21.0642
Chi-square at 95%	19.6751	23.6848

Source: ARIMA (1,0,0) Cx run on minitab version 7.1 of 134 monthly data points for each.
Currency. A, Accept monthly Chi-square value at 11/23 DF within 90% and 95% confidence levels. R, Reject monthly Chi-square value at 11/23 DF within 90% and 95% confidence levels.

Table 3.3   Determination of white noise for weekly exchange rates

D.O.F.	11	23	35	47	11	23	35	47	11	23	35	47
Accept/reject the model as white noise									90%		95%	
Australian Dollar												
C9	18.5	37.1	48.4	59.4	R	R	R	A	A	R	A	A
Deutschemark												
C10	19.5	26.7	34.8	46.5	R	R	A	A	A	R	A	A
French Franc												
C11	15.6	19.9	24.0	36.0	A	A	A	A	A	A	A	A
Japanese Yen												
C12	18.5	25.1	36.0	51.3	R	R	A	R	A	R	A	A
Spanish Peseta												
C13	16.9	27.9	32.3	38.9	A	R	A	A	A	R	A	A
Swiss Franc												
C14	5.4	16.1	47.6	53.4	A	A	R	R	A	A	A	A

Chi-square at 90%	17.2750	21.0642	46.0305[†]	49.7657*
Chi-square at 95%	19.6751	23.6848	63.1671[†]	67.5048*

[†] Average between DF30 and DF40.

A, Accept weekly chi-square value at 11/23/35/47 DF within 90% and 95% confidence level. R, reject weekly chi-square value at 11/23/35/47 DF within 90% and 95% confidence level.

Source: Arima (1,0,0) Cx run on minitab version 7.1 of 134 weekly data points for each currency.

For weekly data, only SF and Y data series are free of white noise at 47 degree of freedom and 90 per cent confidence level. It is concluded that no government intervention is noticed for SF and Y weekly data. Government intervention is found for four other currencies (90 per cent confidence level), and all the six currencies (95 per cent confidence level). (Table 3.3).

For daily data, no white noise is observed at 47 degree of freedom (90 per cent confidence level) for all five currencies except of Japanese Yen. Similarly at 47 degrees of freedom (95 per cent confidence level) no white noise is noticed with the exception of Japanese Yen and Spanish Peseta (Table 3.4). Japanese Yen has consistently exhibited government intervention and Spanish Peseta market intervention is noticed only at 95 per cent confidence level. It explains

Table 3.4   Determination of white noise for daily exchange rates

D.O.F. 11	23	35	47	11	23	35	47	11	23	35	47
Accept/reject the model as white noise								_____90%		_____95%	_____
Australian dollar											
C2 69.0	73.1	84.7	105.4	R	R	R	R	R	R	R	R
Deutsche Mark											
C3 122.6	160.0	216.9	295.9	R	R	R	R	R	R	R	R
French Franc											
C4 52.8	59.6	68.8	73.3	R	R	R	R	R	R	R	R
Japanese Yen											
C5 11.5	18.7	35.4	40.2	A	A	A	A	A	A	A	A
Spanish Peseta											
C6 16.9	33.9	45.9	51.7	A	R	A	R	A	R	A	A
Swiss Franc											
C7 52.9	58.1	59.8	69.8	R	R	A	R	R	R	A	R

Chi-square at 90%	17.2750	21.0642	46.0305*	49.7657†
Chi-square at 95%	19.6751	23.6848	63.1671*	67.5048†

* Average between DF30 and DF40.
† Use DF50 values.
A, Accept weekly chi-square value at 11/23/3/47 DF within 90% and 95% confidence level of significance. R, reject weekly chi-square value at 11/23/35/47 DF within 90% and 95% confidence level of significance.

Source: Arima (1,0,0) Cx run on minitab version 7.1 daily data points for each currency.

that Japanese Yen and Spanish Peseta markets have witnessed government intervention from January 1987–July 1989 period. Other four currencies do not reveal statistically significant government intervention for that period.

The hypothesis of government intervention is rejected for most of the currencies using daily exchange rates (90 per cent confidence). The findings are mixed for monthly and weekly data series. Thus, it is concluded that the foreign exchange market cannot easily be influenced by government intervention and market forces play a dominant role. Further, correlation coefficients are tabulated among all six currencies using monthly, weekly and daily data series. The findings are tabulated in Table 3.5. It is revealed that the Japanese Yen (independently floating currency) bear high correlation only

Table 3.5   Correlation of daily, weekly, and monthly foreign currency exchange rates

Daily data	Columns	C2	C3	C4	C5	C6
Australian $	C2					
Deutsche Mark	C3	-0.104				
French Franc	C4	-0.288	0.863			
Japanese Yen	C5	0.694	0.498	0.355		
Spanish Peseta	C6	0.405	0.667	0.561	0.863	
Swiss Franc	C7	-0.225	0.880	0.944	0.403	0.566
Weekly data	**Columns**	**C2**	**C3**	**C4**	**C5**	**C6**
Australian $	C9					
Deutsche Mark	C10	-0.104				
French Franc	C11	-0.309				
Japanese Yen	C12	0.694	0.520	0.378		
Spanish Peseta	C13	0.401	0.703	0.593	0.867	
Swiss Franc	C14	-0.283	0.957	0.969	0.379	0.554
Monthly data	**Columns**	**C2**	**C3**	**C4**	**C5**	**C6**
Australian $	C16					
Deutsche Mark	C17	-0.104				
French Franc	C18	-0.332	0.979			
Japanese Yen	C19	0.712	0.507	0.351		
Spanish Peseta	C20	0.377	0.313	0.234	0.494	
Swiss Franc	C21	-0.281	0.973	0.982	0.385	0.245

Source: Correlation run of C2–C7, C9–C14, C16–21, daily, weekly and monthly data points on minitab version 7.1.

with the Australian Dollar and Spanish Peseta, other independently floating currencies. The correlation of the Swiss Franc with the Deutsche Mark and French Franc is significantly strong. Similarly, correlation between the Deutsche Mark and French Franc is substantially higher for monthly, weekly and daily data. The Spanish Peseta does not reveal any strong correlation with other currencies with the exception of the Japanese Yen.

This analysis confirms that independently floating currencies (A$, Y Peseta) fluctuate in a similar pattern for the chosen time period. Also, strong correlation is found among co-operative system currencies, DM, FF, and SF. For details, refer to Table 3.5.

In conclusion, there is enough evidence that foreign exchange markets are influenced by the type of floating rate system (independently float or co-operative arrangement). Also, there is strong evidence (with few exceptions) that the selected six currency markets are not influenced by government intervention and market forces played a dominant role during the January 1987–July 1989 time period. Perhaps the foreign exchange markets have become too complicated to be controlled by one or two central banks.

REFERENCES

BAILLIE, R. T. and BOLLERSLEV, T. (1989) 'The Message in Daily Exchange Rates: A Conditional-Variance Tale', *Journal of Business and Economic Statistics*, vol. 7, no. 3 (July) pp. 297–305.

ENGLE, R. R. (1982) 'Autoregressive Conditional Heteroscedasticity with Estimates of the Variance of U.K. Inflation', *Econometrica*, vol. 50, pp. 987–1008.

EXCHANGE MARKET SURVEY (1989) Federal Reserve Bank of New York, April.

HSIEH, D. A. (1988) 'The Statistical Properties of Daily Foreign Exchange Rates: 1974–1983', *Journal of International Economics*, vol. 24, pp. 129–45.

INTERNATIONAL FINANCIAL STATISTICS, International Monetary Fund, Washington, DC., 1987, 1988, 1989, and 1990 Yearbooks.

ISARD, P. (1978) 'Exchange Rate Determination: A Survey of Popular Views and Recent Models', *International Finance Section*, vol. 42 (May).

MUSSA, M. 'Empirical Regularities in the Behavior of the Foreign Exchange Market', *Policies for Employment, Prices, and Exchange Rate*, Carnegie–Rochester Conference Series on Public Policy, vol. 11 (North-Holland) pp. 9-57.

SINGLETON, K. J. and MEESE, R. A. (1982) 'On Unit Roots and the Empirical Modeling of Exchange Rates', *Journal of Finance* (Sept.) pp. 1029–35.

SPERO, J. E. (1988–9) 'Guiding Global Finance', *Foreign Policy*, Winter, pp. 127.

VINSO, J. D. and ROGALSKI, R. J. (1978) 'Empirical Properties of Foreign Exchange Rates', *Journal of International Business Studies*, vol. 9, pp. 69–79.

WESTERFIELD, J. M. (1977) 'An Examination of Foreign Exchange Risk Under Fixed and Floating Rate Regimes', *Journal of International Economics*, vol. 7, no. 2 (May) pp. 1981–2000.

Part III

International Interest Rates

Part III explores international interest rates and underscores the importance of these rates in international financial markets. Eurocurrency *vis-à-vis* Treasury security interest rates, consumer discount rate, and the Interest Rate Parity, Covered Interest Arbitrage and Speculation under Market Imperfection are the focus of this section.

4 Statistical Analyses of Eurocurrency and Treasury Interest Rates from 1975 to 1991

Charles Maxwell and Larry Guin

4.1 INTRODUCTION

Eurocurrency and Treasury security interest rates are primary movers in global financial transactions. From these two interest rate groups come most developed and developing nation interest rate movements, and, coincidentally, changes in currency exchange values which may lead to alterations in global trade patterns and volumes. During the past fifteen years, the world has been witness to significant changes in trade patterns, currency values, political systems, and leadership in global finance. But a question that still remains to be answered in a satisfactory manner is how Eurocurrency and Treasury interest rates have acted, or responded, in relation to these changes. In a statistical sense, what form have these interest rates taken? What are their statistical characteristics around the mean? How do they correlate with similar securities? How do changes in interest rates correlate with changes in currency rates or with changes in other global securities?

4.2 A REVIEW

Published reports relating to results of statistical analyses of economic and financial data are legion, with foreign exchange rates receiving the most attention. Examples include that by Calderon-Rossell and Ben-Horim (1982) that (a) supported the random nature of exchange rates and (b) determined that government policies largely determined foreign exchange behaviour. Some of the technical aspects of the study were subsequently disputed (So *et al.*, 1986) but the general results were not denied. Results relating to unit roots of spot and forward exchange rates (Meese and Singleton, 1982) also lent support to the random walk hypothesis.

Studies seeking to determine the statistical characteristics of economic data also exist, with perhaps the best known being that of Nelson and Plosser (1982). In this particular study, the authors sought to determine native characteristics of a wide range of economic data. A few similar studies were reported (McFarland *et al.*, 1982; Hoffman and Schlagenhauf, 1985; Ito, 1990; Peterson and Tucker, 1988) on various aspects of exchange rate determination with no universally concrete result yet established.

Studies seeking to determine the statistical characteristics of interest rates also have been reported. One (Karfakis and Moschos, 1990) finds no systematic interest rate relationships in the long run between Germany and the other EMS countries,[1] while a second (Beenstock and Longbottom, 1981) investigates the interrelationship between interest rates of different nations. Their primary goal is to determine whether the interest rates of one nation are indeed independent, as postulated by existing interest rate theories, or interdependent, as suggested by the interest rate parity theory.

4.3   GOAL OF THE CHAPTER AND METHODS OF ANALYSIS

4.3.1   Goal

The goal of this study is to further the research in the statistical characteristics of interest rates. To achieve this goal, we seek to determine some of the statistical moments around the mean of Eurocurrency and Treasury security interest rates, and to measure the relationship between the two types of securities. Specifically, data to be analysed are divided into two groups: Group I consists of US fed funds, 90- and 180-day Treasury bills, 1 year- and 5-year Treasury notes, long-term Treasury bonds. Group II consists of Eurocurrency interest rates, including overnight funds, 7-day, 30-day, 90-day, and 180-day rates as well as 1-year Eurocurrency rates. An *a priori* assumption of the chapter is that the series studied represent a random walk similar to that determined by Giddy and Dufey (1975), Nelson and Plosser (1982), or Liu and He (1991).[2]

4.3.2 Analytical methods

To accomplish our goal, two distinctive methods of analyses are employed: first the data are analysed in their nominal form, and second they are again analysed after taking a first difference, which typically implies non-stationarity of data (random walk). The period analysed is from January 1975 to December 1991. Data are analysed over the total period as well as by specific subperiods to determine the four moments about the mean, that is, the mean, the standard deviation, kurtosis, and skewness. Traditional ancillary standard error estimates also are made. Accompanying these analyses are correlation analyses of the US yields with the Eurocurrency yields.

4.4 DATABASE

The database used in this analysis is a proprietary database that consists of 119 economic variables taken on a weekly basis beginning in 1975 and ending in 1991, for a total of almost 890 observations for each variable. Specifically, Eurocurrency interest rates were taken from *Selected Interest and Exchange Rates*, published by the Board of Governors of the Federal Reserve System, and Treasury interest rates were taken from *U.S. Financial Data*, published by the Federal Reserve Bank of St Louis. In all cases the data were coordinated by reporting date.

4.5 FINDINGS

4.5.1 Moments about the mean

Upon examination, the Eurocurrency market exhibits several definite trends based on the maturity structure of the securities. The first four moments about the mean for each security were calculated for the period 1975–91. Table 4.1 summarizes the findings for the period.

The following patterns are apparent from Table 4.1.

- As the maturity of the Eurocurrency increases, the mean return increases as well. This is consistent with existing financial theory, particularly the liquidity premium theory, which maintains that the

Table 4.1   Characteristics of Eurocurrency yields

Security	Mean (%)	Std deviation (%)	Skewness	Kurtosis
Overnight	9.2	3.7	1.085	0.635
7-day	9.3	3.7	1.052	0.529
30-day	9.4	3.7	1.051	0.466
90-day	9.7	3.7	0.952	0.102
6-month	9.9	3.5	0.861	−0.152
1 year	10.0	3.2	0.717	−0.415

higher return on the longer-term securities is necessary to offset the additional risk caused by the longer maturity.

• The standard deviation of the returns decreases slightly as well. This is also no surprise, as short-term rates are more volatile than long-term rates in most financial markets.

• The third moment about the mean, the skewness, decreases noticeably as the maturity increases. If the distribution of returns was exactly normal, the values for the skewness would be zero. The short-term maturities exhibit a much greater positive skewness (tail toward the larger yields) than do the longer-term maturities, although all of the distributions are positively skewed.

• The fourth moment about the mean, the kurtosis, would also have a value of zero if the distribution were normal. The longer maturities of the Eurocurrencies have much heavier tails (i.e. are more 'platykurtic') than the shorter-term securities. During the period, the shorter-term Eurocurrencies appeared to have a preferred habitat in the range of 5–10 per cent while the longer Eurocurrencies were more evenly distributed over a wider range.

These relationships may be seen more clearly by comparing two graphs of the frequency distribution for the Eurocurrencies. First, consider the frequency distribution of weekly yields for the overnight Eurodollar transaction. The distribution is skewed noticeably to the right and exhibits a relatively high degree of kurtosis, as seen in Figure 4.1.

As seen in Figure 4.2, however, the pattern for the one-year Eurodollar exhibits more 'normality' in its shape with less skewness and less of a 'peaked' distribution.

US Treasury securities feature these same patterns, although with greater variety in their mean returns. As the maturities increase, the US securities demonstrate (1) a lower variation in absolute returns,

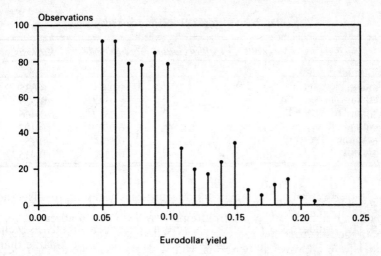

Figure 4.1   Frequency distribution of overnight Eurodollar-returns

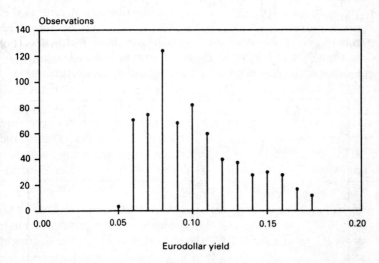

Figure 4.2   Frequency distribution of one-year Eurodollar returns

(2) a noticeably lower degree of skewness, and (3) a rapidly falling degree of kurtosis. These trends are indicated in Table 4.2.

Upon examination of several subperiods of the seventeen-year period to see if the financial characteristics had changed materially over time, no such changes were found. The trends are unchanged over time.

Table 4.2   Characteristics of US yields

Security	Mean (%)	Std deviation (%)	Skewness	Kurtosis
US federal funds	8.8	3.3	1.327	1.572
90-day Treasury bill	7.9	2.7	1.169	0.885
180-day Treasury bill	8.6	2.6	0.930	0.211
1-year Treasury bill	8.1	2.4	0.929	0.184
5-year Treasury note	9.4	2.3	0.911	−0.105
Long-term Treasury bonds	9.6	2.0	0.722	−0.548

First-difference tests. A first-difference test was then applied to the data to determine if the distributions were normal. In all cases, for both the Eurocurrency rates and the US domestic yields, the distributions were approximately normal with a skewness approaching zero. Although space does not permit a full listing of the distributions, a graph of the overnight Eurodollar yield changes is shown in Figure 4.3 as an example. (Skewness for the overnight Eurodollar is 0.06.)

Correlation. How do the Eurocurrencies correlate with their US counterparts? Very highly, as Table 4.3 demonstrates. The correlation coefficients indicated on the diagonal (northwest to southeast) of

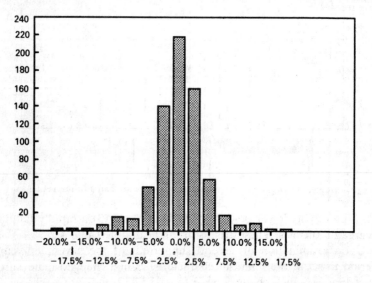

Figure 4.3   Distribution of overnight Eurodollar yield changes

Table 4.3   Correlation of Eurocurrency yields to US yields

Treasury Eurodollar	US federal funds rate	Treasury bills (3 months)	Treasury bills (6 months)	Treasury bills (1 year)
Overnight rate	0.9799	0.9652	0.9539	0.9342
3-month rate	0.9760	0.9808	0.9813	0.9710
6-month rate	0.9617	0.9764	0.9855	0.9823
1-year rate	0.9409	0.9655	0.9834	0.9911

Table 4.3 show the correlation among the most comparable securities. The lowest of these correlation coefficients is approximately 0.98, indicating an extremely high degree of correlation among the movement of interest rates in the two markets. As we examine the other coefficients, we notice a decline in the relationships, as would be expected as we move across the maturity spectrum.

A closer examination of two of these comparable securities, the overnight Eurodollar rate and the US federal funds rate, illustrates this relationship with more detail. If we subtract the federal funds rate on any given day from the overnight Eurodollar rate and examine the excess (or shortage), we can see the relationship shown in Figure 4.4.

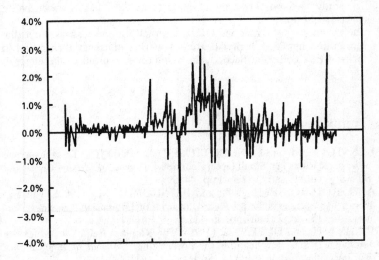

Figure 4.4   Overnight Eurodollar rate minus federal funds rate

We can see that, with a few notable exceptions where one market got ahead of the other, the markets move very closely together. On those occasions where one market led the other, market opportunities quickly forced the markets to converge.

The seventeen-year period of the study was broken down into several subperiods to examine whether the correlation between the two markets had changed over time. No such changes were discovered upon this examination.

4.6 SUMMARY

The findings of the chapter support the generally accepted financial beliefs regarding interest rate movements. In examining subperiods of the seventeen-year examination period, no major changes in the moments about the mean were found. Correlations between the two types of markets is very high, indicative of the money flows between the two markets. Again, when examining subperiods of the entire period, no major changes over time were discovered.

Notes

1. The study used monthly nominal interest rate data, hardly conducive to conclusive results.
2. The assumption of a random walk is accepted for two reasons. First, the assumption implies a higher degree of market efficiency than found in series with a unit root. Second, the assumption neutralizes the effect of trading rules.

REFERENCES

BEENSTOCK, M. and LONGBOTTOM, J. A. (1981) 'The Term Structure of Interest Rates in a Small Open Economy', *Journal of Money, Credit and Banking*, vol. 13, no. 1 (Feb.) pp. 44–59.
CALDERON-ROSSELL, J. R. and BEN-HORIM, M., (1982) 'The Behavior of Foreign Exchange Rates', *Journal of International Business Studies*, vol. 13, no. 2 (Fall) pp. 99–111.
GIDDY, I. H. and DUFEY, G. (1975) 'The Random Behavior of Flexible Exchange Rates: Implications for Forecasting', *Journal of International Business Studies*, vol. 6, no. 1 (Spring) pp. 1–31.
HOFFMAN, D. L. and SCHLAGENHAUF, D. E. (1985) 'The Impact of

News and Alternative Theories of Exchange Rate Determination', *Journal of Money, Credit and Banking*, vol. 17, no. 3 (Aug.) pp. 328–46.

ITO, T. (1990) 'Foreign Exchange Rate Expectations: Micro Survey Data', *American Economic Review*, vol. 80, no. 3 (June) pp. 434–49.

KARFAKIS, C. J. and MOSCHOS, D. M. (1990) 'Interest Rate Linkages Within the European Monetary System: A Time Series Analysis', *Journal of Money, Credit and Banking*, vol. 22, no. 3 (Aug.) pp. 388–94.

LIU, C. Y. and HE, J. (1991) 'A Variance-ratio Test of Random Walks in Foreign Exchange Rates', *Journal of Finance*, vol. 46, no. 2 (June) pp. 773–85.

MCFARLAND, J. W., PETTIT, R. R. and SUNG, S. K. (1982) 'The Distribution of Foreign Exchange Price Changes: Trading Day Effects and Risk Management', *Journal of Finance*, vol. 37, no. 3 (June) pp. 693–715.

MEESE, R. A. and SINGLETON, K. J. (1982) 'On Unit Roots and the Empirical Modeling of Exchange Rates', *Journal of Finance*, vol. 37, no. 4 (Sept.) pp. 1029–35.

NELSON, C. I. and PLOSSER, C. R. (1982) 'Trends and Random Walks in Macroeconomic Time Series', *Journal of Monetary Economics*, vol. 10, no. 1, pp. 9–162.

PETERSON, D. R. and TUCKER, A. L. (1988) 'Implied Spot Rates as Predictors of Currency Returns: A Note', *Journal of Finance*, vol. 43, no. 1 (Mar.) pp. 247–58.

SO, J. C., CALDERON-ROSSELL, J. R., and BEN-HORIM, M. (1986) 'The Behavior of Foreign Exchange Rates – Comment/Reply', *Journal of International Business Studies*, vol. 17, no. 3 (Fall) pp. 165–80.

5 A Cross-Country Comparison of Consumer Discount Rates

William V. Weber, Jannett K. Highfill and Mathew J. Morey

5.1 INTRODUCTION

The consumer discount rate is a fundamental concept underlying virtually all intertemporal consumer-choice and capital-growth models. The discount rate is defined to be the rate at which a consumer, whose consumption path is assumed to be constant over time, must be paid to substitute future consumption for present consumption and still remain indifferent. In other words, the discount rate is the intertemporal marginal rate of substitution, evaluated at a stationary consumption path, minus 1. This chapter develops a new theoretical foundation for estimating the consumer discount rate and applies the method by deriving some international comparisons of discount rates.

Previous attempts to estimate the consumer discount rate have provided disappointing results at best. The traditional approach to estimating the consumer discount rate, what may be called the Friedman approach, is derived from the theory of the aggregate consumption function. (The description here is adapted from Dougherty (1980, p. 40).) Briefly, assuming an adaptive expectations mechanisms, and letting Y_t^p and Y_t denote permanent and actual income at time t, respectively, Friedman assumes $\Delta Y_t^p = \beta(Y_t - Y_{t-1}^p)$. This equation then implies $Y_t^p = \beta Y_t + \beta(1-\beta)Y_{t-1} + \beta(1-\beta)^2 Y_{t-2} + \ldots$. The reaction factor β is then interpreted as the consumer's subjective discount rate. As Dougherty (1980, p. 40) says, 'the main problem with this procedure is that it is not at all obvious why the way in which an individual discounts past income for prediction purposes should have any connection with the way in which he discounts future consumption in his intertemporal preference ordering'. The assumption that these two kinds of discounting are identical is probably

56

erroneous, and thus the estimates obtained using this method have been much too high. Friedman (1960, 1963), Laumas (1969), and Landsberger (1971) obtain estimates of about 0.35 per year. Higher estimates of 0.7–0.8 and 1.3–3.3 have been obtained by Wright (1969) and Holbrook (1967), respectively.

Loewenstein and Thaler (1989), in the context of the psychology of decision making and experimental economics, report the results from a number of experiments on the consumer discount rate. They find a large amount of variability in the results. Among the studies they survey, one reports discount rates in the 0.15–0.30 range, while another measures discount rates as high as 3.00. Although Loewenstein and Thaler do not report any estimates that were less than 0.10, they do mention the common observation that it seems possible that people may have negative discount rates (e.g., people arrange their withholdings to guarantee income tax refunds in April), and they also mention that life-cycle studies indicate that rising consumption patterns might, under certain assumptions, indicate a negative discount rate.

This chapter takes a microfoundations-of-macro approach to derive an equation which can be used to estimate the consumer discount rate. Section 5.2 introduces a basic intertemporal consumer-choice model and shows how a version of the permanent income hypothesis can be derived. Section 5.3 shows that Fisher separation preserves this result when capital investment is possible. In Section 5.4, a Keynesian consumption function is derived from an aggregated version of the permanent income hypothesis equation from Section 5.2. Finally, OECD data is used to provide some numerical illustrations and international comparisons in Section 5.5. It will be shown that the consumer discount rate can be estimated from an economy's growth rate, its real interest rate, and its marginal propensity to consume.

5.2 A MICROFOUNDATION FOR THE PERMANENT INCOME HYPOTHESIS

Consider a consumer with perfect foresight who is maximizing intertemporal utility over the course of his lifetime of T years. His intertemporal utility is given by an instantaneous utility function u and an instantaneous discount rate ρ. The consumer has an initial stock of wealth w_0 and faces a dynamic wealth constraint. The rate of change in the consumer's wealth $w(\cdot)$ is denoted by $\dot{w}$ and is determined by his income flow $I(\cdot)$, the interest earned on his stock of wealth, and the cost of his consumption flow. The consumer's stock of wealth may become negative if he goes into debt, in which case interest is paid rather than earned. However, the consumer must be out of debt (i.e., his stock of wealth must be non-negative) at the end of his lifetime.

The consumer's utility maximization problem is thus given by

(Problem C) $\max\limits_{x,\,w} \int_0^T u(x(t))\, e^{-\rho t}\, dt$

subject to $\dot{w} = I + rw - \sum\limits_i p_i x_i$

$x(\cdot) \geq 0$

$w(0) = w_0 \; w(T) \geq 0,$

where $x(\cdot)$ is an n-coordinate vector representing the consumer's consumption stream, $p(\cdot)$ is the corresponding vector of prices, and r is the instantaneous interest rate.[1] All variables are assumed to be measured in real terms.

Standard optimal control procedures can be used to solve problem C. Let $u_i(t) = \partial u/(\partial x_i(x(t)))$. There exist non-negative constants λ_0 and γ and a function $\lambda_1(\cdot)$, not all equal to zero, such that

$$\lambda_0 u_i\, e^{-\rho t} - \lambda_1 p_i \leq 0, \quad \text{with equality if } x_i > 0 \tag{C1}$$

$$\lambda_1 = -r\lambda_1,\; \lambda_1(T) = \gamma \tag{C2}$$

$$\gamma w(T) = 0 \tag{C3}$$

when evaluated at the optimum. As in El-Hodiri (1985), if for each t there exists an i with $x_i(t)$, $u_i(t)$, $p_i(t)$ all strictly positive, then we may take $\lambda_0 = 1$.[2]

El-Hodiri (1985) also provides a method for solving the first-order conditions. Solving equation (C2) yields $\lambda_1(t) = \gamma e^{r(T-t)}$, so equation (C1) may be rewritten as

$$u_i\, e^{-\rho t} \leq \gamma p_i\, e^{r(T-t)}. \tag{C4}$$

If $\gamma = 0$, then $u_i \leq 0$ for all i and all t, which would contradict the standard assumptions on marginal utility. Thus $\gamma > 0$, and by equation (C3), $w(T) = 0$.

Equation (C4) can be put in terms of expenditure by multiplying both sides by x_i and summing over i:

$$\sum u_i x_i \, e^{-\rho t} = \gamma \sum p_i x_i \, e^{r(T-t)}. \tag{C5}$$

The consumer's wealth constraint can be rewritten as $\sum p_i x_i = I + rw - \dot{w}$. Substituting this expression into equation (C5) and solving for $\dot{w}$ yields

$$\dot{w} = rw + I - \frac{1}{\gamma} \sum u_i x_i \, e^{-\rho t - r(T-t)}. \tag{C6}$$

Using the initial condition $w(0) = w_0$, equation (C6) may be solved for the consumer's stream of wealth $w(\cdot)$:

$$w(t) = e^{rt} \left[w_0 + \int_0^t I(s) \, e^{-rs} \, ds - \frac{1}{\gamma e^{rT}} \int_0^t \sum u_i x_i \, e^{-\rho s} \, ds \right]. \tag{C7}$$

It has been proven than $w(T) = 0$, so equation (C7) may be used to solve for γ:

$$\gamma = \frac{\displaystyle\int_0^T \sum u_i x_i \, e^{-\rho s} \, ds}{e^{rT} \left(w_0 + \displaystyle\int_0^T I(s) \, e^{-rs} \, ds \right)}. \tag{C8}$$

Applying equation (C8) to equation (C5) and rearranging terms gives the equation

$$\sum p_i x_i \, e^{-rt} = \frac{\sum u_i x_i \, e^{-\rho t}}{\displaystyle\int_0^T \sum u_i x_i \, e^{-\rho s} \, ds} \left(w_0 + \int_0^T I(s) \, e^{-rs} \, ds \right). \tag{C9}$$

El-Hodiri (1985) shows that cumulative, rather than instantaneous, demand analysis is appropriate for the continuous-time framework. Assume that time is measured in years, so that the period from $t = 0$ to $t = 1$ represents the current year. Accordingly, current annual expenditure and lifetime income are then defined by $C_0 = \int_0^1 \sum p_i x_i \, e^{-rt} \, dt$ and $M = w_0 + \int_0^T I(t) \, e^{-rt} \, dt$. Integrating equation (C9) from

$t = 0$ to $t = 1$ gives the equation

$$C_0 = \frac{\int_0^1 \sum u_i x_i \, e^{-\rho t} \, dt}{\int_0^T \sum u_i x_i \, e^{-\rho t} \, dt} \cdot M. \tag{C10}$$

Equation (C10) is a weak form of the permanent income hypothesis (PIH). (In general, the term $\sum u_i x_i$ is not totally independent of M; it depends on present-value prices normalized by lifetime income. The standard version of the PIH requires that the proportionality constant be independent of M.) However, if instantaneous utility is log-linear, then equation (C10) reduces to a simple version of the PIH:

$$C_0 = \frac{\int_0^1 e^{-\rho t} \, dt}{\int_0^T e^{-\rho t} \, dt} \cdot M = \frac{1 - e^{-\rho}}{1 - e^{-\rho T}} \cdot M. \tag{C11}$$

Because of the simplified structure of the proportionality constant in equation (C11), this version of the PIH provides an appropriate basis for estimating the consumer discount rate ρ.

5.3   FISHER SEPARATION

We wish to apply equation (C11) to a macroeconomic framework. Because the PIH was derived in the context of a simple utility-maximization problem, the question arises as to whether or not the solution remains valid in more general situations. Using a simple capital-theory model, it will be shown that Fisher separation allows the consumer's utility maximization problem (problem C) to be 'split off' from the problem of maximizing the value of productive assets.

Suppose that a capital stock K is available. Capital is assumed to grow naturally over time at the rate c. Let y denote the vector of capital flows to industries, and let $f(y) = (f_1(y_1), \ldots, f_n(y_n))$ be the production function, which is assumed to be neoclassical in each coordinate. The income flow created by the economy's production is given by $I = \sum_i p_i f_i(y_i)$, where p is the vector of prices of the consumption goods.

For convenience, assume all consumers have identical time horizons, discount rates, and instantaneous utility functions. Under these assumptions, the basic macroeconomic problem is given by

(Problem E) $\displaystyle\max_{x, y, w, K} \int_0^T u(x(t))\, e^{-\rho t}\, dt$

       subject to $\dot{w} = rw - \sum p_i(f_i(y_i) - x_i)$
                              $\dot{K} = cK - \sum y_i$
                              $x(\cdot) \geqslant 0;\; y(\cdot) \geqslant 0$
                              $w(0) = w_0,\; w(T) \geqslant 0$
                              $K(0) = K_0,\; K(\cdot) \geqslant 0.$

Let $\lambda_1(\cdot)$ and $\lambda_2(\cdot)$ be the multipliers associated with the dynamic wealth and capital constraints, respectively. Also let γ be the non-negative multiplier associated with the inequality constraint on $w(T)$, and let $v(\cdot)$ be the multiplier for the non-negativity constraint on the capital stock K. Then the first-order conditions are

$$\lambda_0 u_i\, e^{-\rho t} - \lambda_1 p_i \leqslant 0, \qquad \text{with equality if } x_i > 0 \qquad \text{(E1a)}$$

$$\lambda_1 p_i f_i'(y_i) - (\lambda_2 + v) \leqslant 0, \qquad \text{with equality if } y_i > 0 \qquad \text{(E1b)}$$

$$\dot{\lambda_1} = -r\lambda_1,\; \lambda_1(T) = \gamma \qquad \text{(E2a)}$$

$$\dot{\lambda_2} = -c(\lambda_2 + v) \qquad \text{(E2b)}$$

$$\gamma w(T) = 0 \qquad \text{(E3a)}$$

$$v \geqslant 0,\; \dot{v} \leqslant 0,\; \dot{v}K = 0. \qquad \text{(E3b)}$$

Equations (E1a), (E2a), and (E3a) are identical to equations (C1), (C2) and (C3). As shown in the previous section, these equations can be solved to obtain a weak version of the PIH.

Moreover, a Fisher separation theorem can be proven in this framework. Define the producer's problem to be

(Problem P) $\displaystyle\max_{y, K} \int_0^T \sum p_i f_i(y_i)\, e^{-rt}\, dt$

       subject to $\dot{K} = cK - \sum y_i$
                              $y(\cdot) \geqslant 0$
                              $K(0) = K_0,\; K(\cdot) \geqslant 0.$

The Fisher separation theorem states that $(y^*(\cdot), K^*(\cdot))$ solves Prob-

lem P and $(x^*(\cdot), w^*(\cdot))$ solves Problem C if and only if $(x^*(\cdot), y^*(\cdot),$
$w^*(\cdot), K^*(\cdot))$ solves Problem E. (See the Appendix for the proof.) In
other words, the basic consumer's problem can be 'split off' from the
productive considerations in the macroeconomic problem and be
solved independently. Therefore, the PIH equations (C10) and (C11)
remain valid in more general situations.

5.4 DERIVATION OF A KEYNESIAN CONSUMPTION FUNCTION

In this section, the microeconomic PIH equation derived in Section
5.2 is used to develop a macroeconomic consumption function.
Assume that all consumers have the same time horizon and the same
discount rate, as was done in the previous section. Also assume that
all consumers have log-linear instantaneous utility. Then equation
(C11) implies

$$\mathbf{C} = \frac{1 - e^{-\rho}}{1 - e^{-\rho T}} \cdot \left(\mathbf{W}_0 + \int_0^T Y(t)\, e^{-rt}\, dt \right), \tag{M1}$$

where $\mathbf{C}$ is aggregate annual real consumption expenditures, $\mathbf{W}_0$ is
the initial aggregate stock of wealth, and $\mathbf{Y}(\cdot)$ is the aggregate real
income flow.[3]

Suppose the macroeconomy is in a steady state, with aggregate
income growing at the instantaneous rate g. Then $\mathbf{Y}(t) = \mathbf{y}_0\, e^{gt}$ for
some initial income level $\mathbf{y}_0$, which allows equation (M1) to be rewritten as

$$\mathbf{C} = \frac{1 - e^{-\rho}}{1 - e^{-\rho T}} \cdot \left(\mathbf{W}_0 + \mathbf{y}_0 \int_0^T e^{-(r-g)t}\, dt \right). \tag{M2}$$

Recall from Section 5.2 that annual figures, like $\mathbf{C}$, are obtained by
integrating from $t = 0$ to $t = 1$. Thus in this framework, aggregate
income for the current year is defined by

$$\mathbf{Y} = \int_0^1 Y(t) e^{-rt}\, dt = \mathbf{y}_0 \int_0^1 e^{-(r-g)t}\, dt.$$

Substituting this expression into equation (M2) yields

$$\mathbf{C} = \frac{1 - e^{-\rho}}{1 - e^{-\rho T}} \cdot \left(\mathbf{W}_0 + \frac{\displaystyle\int_0^T e^{-(r-g)t}\, dt}{\displaystyle\int_0^1 e^{-(r-g)t}\, dt} \cdot \mathbf{Y} \right) \tag{M3}$$

$$= \left(\frac{1 - e^{-\rho}}{1 - e^{-\rho T}} \cdot \mathbf{W}_0 \right) + \left(\frac{1 - e^{-\rho}}{1 - e^{-\rho T}} \cdot \frac{1 - e^{-(r-g)T}}{1 - e^{-(r-g)}} \right) \cdot \mathbf{Y}.$$

The last expression in equation (M3) is in the form of a Keynesian consumption function. Autonomous consumption is a fraction of the initial aggregate stock of wealth, and the marginal propensity to consume (MPC) depends on the consumer discount rate, the time horizon, the real interest rate, and the economy's real rate of growth.

5.5 NUMERICAL ESTIMATES OF CONSUMER DISCOUNT RATES

The theoretical framework developed in the previous sections has provided an equation which is an appropriate basis for estimating consumer discount rates:

$$MPC = \frac{1 - e^{-\rho}}{1 - e^{-\rho T}} \times \frac{e^{-(r-g)T}}{1 - e^{-(r-g)}}. \tag{M4}$$

In this section, some numerical illustrations showing the implications of this equation are developed. OECD data for real interest rates, real per capita growth rates, real disposable income, and real consumption expenditures are used to derive some international comparisons.

OECD data for seven countries – the US, Japan, Germany, France, the UK, Italy, and Canada – are used to illustrate the range of consumer discount rates implied by equation (M4). The results are summarized in Table 5.1. The average real long-term interest rate for the years 1980–89 (obtained from OECD (1990, p. 106)) is used for the value of r in equation (M4). The average real per capita growth rate (obtained from OECD (1990, p. 48)), again for the years 1980–89, is used for the value of g.[4] The MPC listed in Table 5.1 is the result of using OLS to regress real disposable income per capita

Table 5.1   Consumer discount rates from equation (M4)

	OECD data			Discount rate ρ		
	MPC	*r*	*g*	*T* = 30	*T* = 100	*T* → ∞
US	0.948 7	0.055	0.018	0.031 8	0.034 2	0.034 4
Canada	0.888 3	0.057	0.021	0.025 3	0.030 6	0.031 2
France	0.885 9	0.047	0.016	0.020 7	0.026 2	0.026 9
Germany	0.931 8	0.045	0.017	0.021 8	0.025 1	0.025 6
UK	0.910 6	0.034	0.021	0.005 89	0.010 4	0.011 6
Japan	0.836 7	0.048	0.035	−0.000 216	0.008 17	0.010 5
Italy	0.885 7	0.027	0.023	−0.004 45	0.001 34	0.003 46

against real private final consumption expenditure per capita for the years 1971–89.[5] In the data for these regressions, disposable income was calculated as the sum of private final consumption expenditure and private net saving, which are found in OECD, *National Accounts*, vol. II, Detailed Tables, 'Accounts for Households and Private Unincorporated Enterprises' (Table 8). These values were converted to real terms (1980 base year) using the GDP implicit price deflators in national currencies found in United Nations (1991, pp. 223–56). Population figures found in OECD (1991a, pp. 18–19), were used to convert figures to per capita terms.

When the variables *r*, *g*, and *MPC* are known, equation (M4) then implicitly defines the discount rate ρ as a function of the time horizon *T*. Several different values for *T* are used to obtain a range for the value of ρ. Table 5.1 reports the value for ρ obtained from the time horizons *T* = 30 years and *T* = 100 years. Table 5.1 also shows the value of $\lim_{T \to \infty} \rho(T)$ to illustrate the values obtained from extremely long time horizons.[6]

The ranges for ρ obtained from equation (M4) are reasonable. For example, the estimated consumer discount rate ranges from 3.2 per cent to 3.4 per cent for the US and from 2.5 per cent to 3.1 per cent for Canada. For the shortest time horizon, *T* = 30 years, the negative discount rates for Japan and Italy indicate a small amount of patience, while the values for all other countries indicate varying degrees of impatience. As the time horizon becomes infinitely large, the data indicate mild impatience in all countries, with ρ ranging from 0.34 per cent in Italy to 3.4 per cent in the US.

The international comparisons in Table 5.1 also support intuitive preconceptions about consumer discount rates. High MPCs, like those in the US and Germany, are associated with relatively high discount rates, while low MPCs, like Japan's, tend to correspond to relatively low discount rates. Real interest rates that are high relative to the economy's real per capita growth are also associated with impatience. For example, France, Italy, and Canada have nearly identical MPCs, but the real interest rate is about 3 times higher than the real growth rate in France and Canada, while the real interest rate is only slightly higher than the real growth rate in Italy. Consequently, the discount rates estimated for France and Canada indicate substantially more impatience than the value estimated for Italy.

As the time horizon is extended, the effect of the MPC on the estimated discount rate diminishes, and the effect of the difference between the real interest rate and the real growth rate is enhanced. For instance, Japan has a substantially lower MPC than does the UK, but the interest rate is 1.3 percentage points higher than the growth rate in both countries. The difference in their MPCs suggests that Japan's discount rate should be significantly lower than the UK's, and this is certainly true for $T = 30$ years, but the difference between their estimated discount rates becomes substantially smaller as the time horizon is lengthened. A similar pattern holds for Germany and France. Germany has the higher MPC, while France has a slightly higher interest rate and slightly lower growth rate. For $T = 30$ years, the difference in their MPCs dominates and Germany has the higher discount rate. For the longer time horizons, however, the situation is reversed and the larger difference between the interest and growth rates causes France to have the higher estimate for ρ.

5.4 SUMMARY AND CONCLUSIONS

The concept of discounting is fundamental in economics, but acceptable measurements of the consumer discount rate have been elusive. Neither Friedman's adaptive expectations approach nor experimental economics have provided consistent, satisfactory estimates. This chapter offers a new theoretical foundation for estimating consumer discount rates from basic macroeconomic data. The method is based on an aggregated version of a simple PIH equation, which shows that the discount rate depends on the marginal propensity to consume and the difference between the real interest rate and the economy's real growth rate. Although the assumptions underlying the theoretical development are severe, the results are both reasonable and intuitive. As shown by the numerical examples calculated from OECD data, countries with high MPCs and countries in which the real interest rate greatly exceeds the real growth rate tend to have the highest consumer discount rates.

The results of this chapter also offer an attractive alternative to selecting the proper social rate of discount for use in evaluating public projects. The standard approach in public finance is to adjust the market rate of interest for tax distortions, but as Loewenstein and Thaler (1989, p. 192) note, the problems involved are 'far from trivial'. They also observe that experimental economics offers another approach – estimating the social discount rate from time preferences measured at the individual level – but there is no obvious way to choose from the wide range of esimates obtained from different experimental situations. The microfoundations-of-macro approach suggested in this chapter has a dual advantage: it is based on standard intertemporal consumer-choice theory, and it provides a relatively easy way to calculate the discount rate from basic macroeconomic data.

APPENDIX: PROOF OF THE FISHER SEPARATION THEOREM

To prove the Fisher separation theorem stated in Section 5.3, first consider the solution to Problem P. Let $\lambda_2(\cdot)$ be the multiplier associated with the dynamic capital constraint, and let $v(\cdot)$ be the multiplier associated with the non-negativity constraint on the capital stock. The first-order conditions are

$$\lambda_0 p_i f_i'(y_i) - (\lambda_2 + v) \leq 0, \qquad \text{with equality if } y_i > 0 \tag{P1}$$

$$\dot{\lambda}_2 = -c(\lambda_2 + v) \tag{P2}$$

$$v \geq 0, \dot{v} \leq 0, \dot{v}K = 0. \tag{P3}$$

The multiplier λ_0 may be taken as a positive constant, if normality can be demonstrated. Assume that for each t, there exists an i with $p_i > 0$ and $y_i > 0$. If $\lambda_0 = 0$, then equation (P1) implies that $\lambda_2 + v = 0$. Both multipliers are non-negative, thus $\lambda_2 \equiv 0$ and $v \equiv 0$. However, not all multipliers can equal zero, and so we have a contradiction. Thus, $\lambda_0 > 0$. (In fact, if $p_i > 0$ and $\lim_{y_i \to 0} f_i'(y_i) = \infty$, then the first-order conditions imply $p_i f_i'(y_i) e^{-rt} = A e^{-ct}$ for some constant A. This equation says that the present value of the marginal revenue product of capital decays at rate c.)

To prove the Fisher separation theorem, set $\lambda_0 = \gamma e^{rT}$ in the first-order conditions for Problem P, where γ is the multiplier solved for in Problem C. Then equation (P1) becomes $(\gamma e^{r(T-t)}) p_i f_i'(y_i) - (\lambda_2 + v) \leq 0$. However, in the solution to Problem C, it was shown that equation (C2) implies $\lambda_1(t) = \gamma e^{r(T-t)}$, and thus equation (P1) can be rewritten as

$$\lambda_1 p_i f_i'(y_i) - (\lambda_2 + v) \leq 0, \text{ with equality if } y_i > 0. \tag{P1*}$$

The Fisher separation theorem stated in Section 5.3 is now obvious. The first-order conditions to Problem C (equations (C1), (C2) and (C3) and Problem P (equations (P1*), (P2) and (P3) are identical to the first-order conditions of Problem E (equations (E1a), (E1b), (E2a), (E2b), (E3a) and (E3b).

Notes

1. The interest rate r and the discount rate ρ are, for convenience, assumed to be constant over time. The model can be easily generalized to the case where r and ρ are functions of time.
2. If $\lambda_0 = 0$, then equation (C1) implies $\lambda_1 (\cdot) \equiv 0$. Equation (C2) then implies that $\gamma = 0$, which contradicts the fact that not all multipliers can be zero.
3. Bold letters are used to denote macroeconomic aggregates.
4. The interest and growth rates in the OECD data are *annual* rates, while equation (M4) uses *instantaneous* rates. An annual rate a and an instantaneous rate α are related by the equations $a = e^{\alpha} - 1$ and $\alpha = \ln(a + 1)$. The interest and growth rates were converted to instantaneous terms before they were substituted into equation (M4). The discount rate obtained from equation (M4) was converted to annual terms before being reported in Table 5.1. Thus all rates reported in Table 5.1 are annual rates.
5. See Bunting (1989) for a discussion of the validity of this method to estimate the MPC. All estimated MPCs were significant at the 1 per cent level. To check for bias, the MPCs were also estimated using two-stage least squares, adding a basis GDP equation introducing investment and net exports. No significant differences in the coefficients were found.
6. The solution to the consumer-choice problem (Problem C) is ony valid when the time horizon is finite, and so the value of $\lim_{T \to \infty} \rho(T)$ cannot be interpreted as the solution to the infinite-horizon consumer-choice problem. This value is calculated and provided only for illustrative purposes.

REFERENCES

BUNTING, D. (1989) 'The Consumption Function "Paradox"', *Journal of Post Keynesian Economics*, vol. 11, no. 3 (Spring) pp. 347–59.
DOUGHERTY, C. (1980) *Interest and Profit* (New York: Columbia University Press).
EL-HODIRI, M. A. (1985) 'Properties of Consumers over Time Demand Functions', in G. FEICHTINGER (ed.), *Optimal Control Theory and Economic Analysis 2* (Amsterdam: North-Holland).

FRIEDMAN, M. (1960) 'Comments', in I. FRIEND and R. JONES (eds), *Consumption and Saving*, vol. II (Philadelphia: University of Philadelphia).

FRIEDMAN, M. (1963) 'Windfalls, the "Horizon," and Related Concepts in the Permanent-Income Hypothesis", in C. F. CHRIST *et al.*, *Measurement in Economics* (Stanford: Stanford University Press).

HOLBROOK, R. S. (1967) 'The Three-Year Horizon: An Analysis of the Evidence', *Journal of Political Economy*, vol. 75, pp. 750–54.

LANDSBERGER, M. (1971) 'Consumer Discount Rate and the Horizon: New Evidence', *Journal of Political Economy*, vol. 79, pp. 1346–59.

LAUMAS, P. S. (1969) 'A Test of the Permanent Income Hypothesis', *Journal of Political Economy*, vol. 77, pp. 857–61.

LOEWENSTEIN, G. and THALER, R. H. (1989) 'Intertemporal Choice', *Journal of Economic Perspectives*, vol. 3, no. 4 (Fall) pp. 181–93.

OECD (1985) *National Accounts, 1971–1983*, vol. II, Detailed Tables (Paris).

OECD (1990) *Historical Statistics, 1960–1989* (Paris).

OECD (1991a) *Labour Force Statistics, 1969–1989* (Paris).

OECD (1991b) *National Accounts, 1977–1989*, vol. II, Detailed Tables (Paris).

United Nations (1991) *National Accounts Statistics: Analysis of the Main Aggregates, 1988–1989* (New York).

WRIGHT, C. (1969) 'Estimating Permanent Income: A Note', *Journal of Political Economy*, vol. 77, pp. 845–50.

6 The Interest Rate Parity, Covered Interest Arbitrage and Speculation under Market Imperfection

Dilip K. Ghosh

6.1 INTRODUCTION

The interest rate parity is important in international finance for at least two reasons. It explains covered interest arbitrage, and it specifies conditions for speculation in currency markets (see Ghosh, 1991; 1992; Niehans, 1984). It was Keynes (1923) who had initiated via interest rate parity the discussion on short-term capital flows, and later, Spraos (1953), Tsiang (1959), Branson (1969), Aliber (1973), and others have extended it and/or reinterpreted it. The idea of interest rate parity is simple in perfect market conditions. Consider an investor who has the opportunity to borrow and invest at home and abroad. Under this situation, he will invest abroad if the amount earned there exceeds the dollar amount earned at home; in an opposite situation, he will invest at home, and in the event the two alternative choices yield exactly the same rate of return – which is the case of interest rate parity – he will be indifferent. Let S be the current spot rate of exchange (in direct quote), F the one-year forward rate, r and r^* the domestic and the foreign rates of interest, respectively. Then, if he invests his investible funds, say $\$S$, in the domestic market, his rate of return is r; but if he converts his $\$S$ for 1 British Pound (£1), and then invests £1 at r^*, he turns it into £1($1 + r^*$) at the end of one year. Since the exchange rate one year from now may change, he can hedge now by selling £1($1 + r^*$) at forward exchange rate F and without risk make $\$(1 + r^*)F$. His rate of return from the foreign investment is then equal to:

$[(1 + r^*)F - S]/S.$

If he finds that

$$r \lesseqgtr [(1 + r^*)F - S]/S, \tag{1}$$

he should invest abroad, remain indifferent or invest at home, respectively.[1] When the equality holds, it is the *celebrated* interest rate parity. The situations with inequalities define departures from parity and create conditions for profitable arbitrage. An algebraic simplification of (1) yields:

$$F/S \lesseqgtr (1 + r)/(1 + r^*) \tag{1*}$$

or

$$[(F - S)/S] (1 + r^*) \lesseqgtr (r - r^*). \tag{1.1}$$

One can now understand that if $F > S (1 + r)/(1 + r^*)$ in (1*), the investor should borrow dollars at r, buy British Pound with dollars at S, lend (invest) British Pound at r^* and sell British Pound forward at F. If the inequality is reversed, it is profitable for the investor to borrow British Pound at r^*, sell British Pound for dollars at the spot rate of exchange, lend (invest) dollars at r and buy British Pound forward. So, it appears clear that the comparison of two rates of return, given in equation (1), defines the interest rate parity or its absence, in which case arbitrage profit can be exploited. It can also be shown that if:[2]

$$F < (S^+)^2/[S (1 + r)/(1 + r^*)]$$

and

$$F < S (1 + r)/(1 + r^*),$$

then the investor should speculate and buy foreign currency forward. Here S^+ is the expected future (1 year from now) rate of exchange. Similarly, other conditions for speculative 'sell forward', 'buy spot', and 'sell spot' can be ascertained with, among other things, by parity rate $S(1 + r)/(1 + r^*)$. The interest rate parity is thus extremely powerful. However, it should be noted that the results discussed above are grounded on a perfectly competitive market in which transaction costs or any distortion are non-existent.

6.2 MARKET IMPERFECTIONS AND CURRENCY ARBITRAGE

So it is appropriate then to extend the interest rate parity against the backdrop of market imperfections which subsumes transaction costs and affects the investor's decision-making calculations. It should be noted that in the same country, an investor's rate of borrowing is not *necessarily* equal to his rate of lending (investing). The spread between these rates is one form of transaction cost for the investor. So, when he has to consider two countries, he faces usually four rates – two in each country, and they are domestic rate of borrowing (r_B), domestic rate of lending (investing) (r_L), foreign rate of borrowing (r_B^*), and foreign rate of lending (r_L^*). There is another transaction cost in his financial operations, and that is embedded in his purchase and sale prices of the currencies concerned. The bank's *ask* price is the investor's purchase price, and the investor's sale price is the bank's *bid* price. The spread between the bank's ask and bid prices is the transaction cost of the investor. Because of market imperfections, a typical investor accepts all these transaction costs and adjusts his market positions with respect to his investment funds. It is instructive now to see how the interest parity is modified under market imperfections conditioned by all these transaction costs. Following Frenkel and Levich (1975), and Deardorff (1979), several modellings have factored in transaction costs with respect to purchase and sale of foreign exchange by way of introducing a middle rate between the ask and bid prices and then adding plus or minus transaction cost (see, for example, Blenman, 1991, 1992; Callier, 1981a; 1981b; Niehans, 1984). This method of introducing the transaction cost is correct, but to capture the full measure of transaction costs it is being implicitly assumed that the volume of purchase of a currency from the bank equals the volume of sale of the currency to the bank. Secondly, since some of these treatments allow only two interest rates, r and r^*, the practical usefulness of the covered interest parity is still limited when the investor in reality faces possibly two different interest rates in each country – that is, the rate of borrowing at home (r_B), the rate of lending (investing) at home (r_L), the rate of borrowing abroad (r_B^*), and the rate of lending abroad (r_L^*). Under the circumstances, one can ask the question: what is the interest rate parity, or alternatively, what constitute(s) the conditions for covered interest arbitrage? It is obvious that if $r_B \neq r_L$ and $r_B^* \neq r_L^*$,[3] and the *bid* and *ask* prices are the same, investor faces four choices: (i) he can borrow, say $\$S$, at home at r_B, convert $\$S$ into £1, invest (lend) £1 at r_L^*, then sell £1$(1 + r_L^*)$ forward and get $\$(1 + r_L^*)F$, and realize the net rate of return:

$$[(1 + r_L^*)F - S(1 + r_B)]/S; \tag{2}$$

(ii) he can borrow, say £1, at r_B^* and exchange £1 for $\$S$ at the spot rate, and then lend (invest) $\$S$ at r_L. Since at the end of one year he has to pay back $\$ (1 + r_B^*)F$, his net rate of return is:

$$[S(1 + r_L) - (1 + r_B^*)F]/S; \tag{3}$$

(iii) he can borrow at home at r_B and lend at r_L to realize the net rate of return of $(r_L - r_B)$, or (iv) he can borrow abroad at r_B^* and lend at the rate r_L^* and earn the net rate of return equal to $(r_L^* + r_B^*)$. Since there are four net rates of return, and two rates can be compared at a time, the possible combinations are *six* $(= 4C2)$, and hence there are six manifestations of interest rate parity. Thus, if the rates of return from choice (i) and choice (ii) are compared, that is, if:

$$[(1 + r_L^*)F - S(1 + r_B)]/S \lessgtr [S(1 + r_L) - (1 + r_B^*)F]/S \tag{4}$$

one obtains the following:

$$[(F - S)/S][(1 + r_L^*) + (1 + r_B^*)] \lessgtr (r_L + r_B) - (r_L^* + r_B^*) \tag{4.1}$$

Look at the similarity between (4.1) and (1.1). If $r_L = r_B$ and $r_L^* = r_B^*$, (4.1) collapses into (1.1). Next, consider the comparison of rates of return given by choices (i) and (iii), and that means:

$$[(1 + r_L^*)F - (1 + r_B)S]/S \lessgtr (r_L - r_B), \tag{5}$$

whence:

$$[(F - S)/S](1 + r_L^*) \lessgtr (r_L - r_L^*). \tag{5.1}$$

If the investor compares the rates of return that he can earn by his choice (ii) with that of choice (iv) he derives the following:

$$[(F - S/S](1 + r_B^*) \lesseqqgtr (r_L - r_L^*).$$ (6.1)

Three other possible comparisons of net rates are as follows:

$$[S(1 + r_L) - (1 + r_B^*)F]/S \lesseqqgtr (r_L - r_B),$$ (7)

$$[(1 + r_L^*)F - S(1 + r_B)]/S \lesseqqgtr (r_L^* - r_B^*),$$ (8)

and $(r_L - r_B) \lesseqqgtr (r_L^* - r_B^*)$, which is equivalent to:

$$S(r_L - r_B) \lesseqqgtr (r_L^* - r^{*B})F.$$ (9)

From (7) one can derive the following:

$$[(F - S)/S](1 + r_B^*) \lesseqqgtr (r_B - r_B^*).$$ (7.1)

The expression (8) yields the following:

$$[(F - S)/S](1 + r^*) \lesseqqgtr (r_B - r_B^*),$$ (8.1)

and from (9) we get:

$$[(F - S)/S]\{(1 + r^*) - (1 + r_B^*)\} \lesseqqgtr (r_L - r_B) - (r_L^* - r^{*B}).$$ (9.1)

These are the seven expressions of covered interest parity (in the case of equality), given by Ghosh (1991). Blenman (1992) observes that some of these expressions will be dominated by others. But as long as that proof is yet to come, it is probably instructive to keep all the expressions in one place. His second point, that if the investor borrows and invests both in the foreign market, then there is no need to cover his position, appears untenable as long as the investor decides to redeem his foreign earnings in domestic currency terms and wants to compare them with the domestic net rate of returns.

Thus far we have factored in only the market imperfections embedded through interest rate differentials, but the spreads in the foreign exchange rates in spot and forward transactions we have mentioned earlier have been ignored up to this point. It is therefore time to recompute the covered interest rate parity or its absence under the new realities. So, let S^a, F^a, S^b, and F^b be the bank's spot and forward *ask* and *bid* (and hence the investor's *buy* and *sell*) rates of foreign exchange, respectively. At this stage, one has to change the notations S and F in the expressions (4.1) to (9.1) by appropriately assigning the superscripts a and b to those notations. Note here once again that (4.1) has been derived by comparing the rates of return generated by choice (i) and choice (ii), and so if we go back to the steps involved in choice (i) and choice (ii), we can modify (4.1) and come up with the correct expression under the new situation. Going back to choice (i), the investor now borrows \$$S^a$ (= £1) at r_B, converts the dollar amount into pound sterling and then investing the sterling amount at r_L^* makes the net rate of return: $\{(1 + r_L^*)S^b - (1 + r_B^*)\}/S^a$. His choice (ii) yields the rate of return: $\{(1 + r_L)S^b - (1 + r_B^*)F^b\}/S^b$. The comparison of the rates of return from choice (i) and choice (ii) then results in the following expression:

$$[(F^b - S^a/S^a][(1 + r_{.L}) + ((1 + r_B^*)/(1 + \tau)] \lesseqgtr \{(r_L + r_B) -$$
$$(r_L^* + (1 + r_B^*)/(1 + \tau))\}, \tag{4.1*}$$

where $\tau \equiv (S^a - S^b)/S^b$.

The similar comparison of the rates of return from choices (i) and (iii) yields:

$$[(F^b - S^a)/S^a](1 + r_L^*) \lesseqgtr (r_L - r_L^*). \tag{5.1*}$$

By the very same procedure one can now modify (6.1), (7.1), (8.1), and (9.1) respectively as follows:

$$[(F^b - S^b)/S^b](1 + r_B^*) \lesseqgtr (r_L - r_L^*), \tag{6.1*}$$

$$[(F^b - S^b)/S^b](1 + r_B^*) \lesseqgtr (r_B - r_B^*), \tag{7.1*}$$

$$[(F^b - S^a)/S^a](1 + r_L^*) \lesseqgtr (r_B - r_B^*), \tag{8.1*}$$

and

$$[(F^b - S^b)/S^b]\{(1 + r_L^*) - (1 + r_B^*)\} \lesseqgtr \{(r_L - r_B)$$
$$- (r_L^* - r_B^*)\}. \tag{9.1*}$$

We have all the six expressions of interest rate parity, and they are in situations of equality in (4.1), (5.1), (6.1), (7.1), (8.1), and (9.1) when transaction costs are incurred through interest rate differential on borrowing and lending; but when these transaction costs are reflected through the bank's *ask* and *bid* rate on foreign exchange quotes as well, then they are given by (4.1*), (5.1*), (6.1*), (7.1*), (8.1*), and (9.1*). When inequalities hold in these expressions, we have deviations from parity, which mean conditions for riskless profit opportunities. If equality holds in all these six expressions, interest rate parity prevails in every scenario, and then it is a matter of indifference for the investor as to where he should borrow from and where to lend out or invest in. However, if he has the inequalities before him, he must ascertain where the difference between F and $(1 + Z/G)S$ is the largest, and it is where covered interest arbitraging must be undertaken. Note here Z is all the terms in the right-hand side of these expressions and G is the multiplier of $(F - S)/S$ on the left-hand side of these inequalities.

6.3 DESIGNS OF SPECULATIVE STRATEGIES

Speculation is an assumption of risk by choice for the investor. He bears the risk for an expectation of profit. In the previous section, no unknown has been factored in, and as a result no risk appears in the picture. In this section, we consider an investor taking a position on the future spot market (which is unknown at this point). The question then is: what should be his speculative strategies under different possible scenarios?

6.3.1 Perfect market structure

First we bring out the speculative rules under conditions of perfect market in which transaction costs of any sort are conspicuous by their absence. Let S^+ be the (expected) spot rate of exchange one year from today. Let $S\{(1 + r)/(1 + r^*)\}$ be called, in the absence of any better term, the *parity rate of exchange* (P_E). It is obvious that if the investor expects S^+ to be the spot rate of exchange a year from today, he can enter into forward speculation or into spot speculation. If $S^+ > F$, he should take a position to buy pound sterling forward, because by doing so, he can make profit. For instance, if $F = 2.15$ and $S^+ = 2.65$, he can buy pound forward by paying \$2.15 for £1, and then he can sell £1 for \$2.65, and make a net profit of \$0.50. Again, if $S^+ > S\{(1 + r)/(1 + r^*)\}$, he can profit by spot speculation (that is, by borrowing dollars at r, buying pound at spot rate, investing pound at r^*, and finally selling the pound sterling at S^+. When the investor is confronted with two such choices, both yielding profit, he must calculate which option offers him the better rate of profit. One can see that if:

$$(S/S^+).(1 + r)/(1 + r^*) > S^+/F \qquad (10)$$

selling spot is preferable to buying forward. One can see immediately that the exact same condition specifies that forward sales of pound to be superior to spot purchases. We can easily see that if:

$(F/S^+) > (S/S^+).(1 + r)/(1 + r^*)$ holds, (that is, $F > P_E$), it means selling pound forward is more profitable than selling spot and spot purchases are better than forward purchases. All these can be summarized as follows:

When

$F > P_E$ and $F > (S^+)^2/P_E$: sell pound forward,

$F > P_E$ and $F < (S^+)^2/P_E$: buy pound forward,

$F < P_E$ and $F > (S^+)^2/P_E$: sell pound spot, and

$F < P_E$ and $F < (S^+)^2/P_E$: buy pound forward.

6.3.2 Imperfect market structure

In this section, we assume that $r_L \neq r_B$, $r_L^* \neq r_B^*$, and spread between *ask* and *bid* exists in current spot, forward and future spot markets. Let future spot ask and bid rates be denoted by $S^{+(a)}$ and $S^{+(b)}$, respectively. From (4.1*) to (9.1*) one can derive the following:

$$F^b \lesseqqgtr S^a \{(1 + r_L) + (1 + r_B)\}/\{(1 + r_L^*)$$
$$+ [(1 + r_B^*)/(1 + r)]\} \qquad (4.1^{**})$$

$$F^b \lesseqqgtr S^a \{(1 + r_L)/(1 + r_L^*)\}, \qquad (5.1^{**})$$

$$F^b \lesseqqgtr S^a \{(1 + r_L) + (1 + r_B^*) - (1 + r_L^*)\}/(1 + r_B^*), \qquad (6.1^{**})$$

$$F^b \lesseqqgtr S^b \{(1 + r_B)/(1 + r_B^*)\}, \qquad (7.1^{**})$$

$$F^b \lesseqqgtr S^a \{(1 + r_B) + (1 + r_L^*) - (1 + r_B^*)\}/(1 + r_L^*), \qquad (8.1^{**})$$

$$F^b \lesseqqgtr S^b \{(r_L - r_B)/(r_L^* - r_B^*)\} \qquad (9.1^{**})$$

A careful scrutiny of these new parity expressions should yield strategies for a speculative investor in the currency markets. If we consider (4.1**), it should come out that when:
$S^{+(b)} > S^a \{(1 + r_L) + (1 + r_B)\}/\{(1 + r_L^*) + [(1 + r_B^*)/(1 + \tau)]\}$, he should buy pound spot, and $S^{+(a)} < S^a \{(1 + r_L) + (1 + r_B)\{/\}(1 + r_L^*) + [(1 + r_B^*)/(1 + \tau)]\}$, he should sell pound spot. If $S^{+(b)} > F^a$, he should buy pound forward, and when $S^{+(a)} < F^b$, he should sell pound forward. If other parity rates such as (5.1**) to (9.1**) are considered, then other conditions will be derived in the same way. There are choices to be made between spot market speculation and forward market speculation, and it appears that cases exist when speculation is out of money. The detailed analysis on this issue is dealt with by Ghosh (1992) in a separate work.

Notes

1. Alternatively, one can derive the result as follows: suppose the investor borrows $\$S$ in the domestic market, and exchanges the amount for pound sterling at the current spot rate (S) and gets 1 BP, which he invests at r^* and turns the amount into $1(1 + r^*)$ BP at the end of the year. Since the exchange rate one year from now may change, he may cover his position by selling $1(1 + r^*)$ BP at forward exchange rate (F) and without risk make $\$(1 + r^*)F$. Note, since he borrowed $\$S$ at the rate r, his year-end liability is $\$S(1 + r)$. His calculation is then as follows:

$$\text{if } [(1 + r^*)F - S(1 + r)]/S \lesseqgtr 0, \quad \begin{array}{l} \text{he should invest abroad;} \\ \text{he should be indifferent;} \\ \text{he should invest at home.} \end{array}$$

2. For details on this, see Ghosh 1989 and Niehans (1984).
3. More specifically, we should only consider cases where $r_L > r_B$ and $r_L^* > r_B^*$.

REFERENCES

ALIBER, R. G. (1973) 'The Interest Rate Parity Theorem: A Reinterpretation', *Journal of Political Economy*, vol. 81 (Nov./Dec.) pp. 1451–9.
BAHMANI-OSKOOEE, M. and DAS, S. P. (1985) 'Transaction Costs and Interest Parity Theorem', *Journal of Political Economy*, vol. 93, no. 4 (June) pp. 793–9.

78   *Interest Rate Parity, Covered Arbitrage and Speculation*

BLENMAN, L. P. (1991) 'A Model of Covered Interest Arbitrage under Market Segmentation', *Journal of Money, Credit and Banking*, vol. 23, no. 4 (Nov.) pp. 706–717.

BLENMAN, L. P. (1992) 'The Interest Rate Parity: Seven Expressions: A Reply', *Financial Management*, (FM Letter), Autumn.

BRANSON, W. H. (1969) 'The Minimum Covered Interest Differential Needed for International Arbitrage Activity', *Journal of Political Economy*, vol. 77 (Nov./Dec.) pp. 1028–35.

CALLIER, P. (1981a) 'Covered Arbitrage Margin and Transaction Costs', *Weltwirtschaftliches Archiv*, vol. 117 (Dec.) pp. 262–75.

CALLIER, P. (1981b) 'One-way Arbitrage, Foreign Exchange and Securities Markets: A Note', *Journal of Finance*, vol. 36 (Dec.) pp. 1177–86.

CLINTON, K. (1988) 'Transactions Costs and Covered Interest Arbitrage: Theory and Evidence', *Journal of Political Economy*, vol. 96 (Apr.) pp. 358–70.

DEARDORFF, A. V. (1979) 'One-Way Arbitrage and its Implications for the Foreign Exchange Markets', *Journal of Political Economy*, Apr.

DOOLEY, M. P. (1974) 'A Model of Arbitrage and Short-Term Capital Flows', International Finance Discussion Paper No. 40 (Washington, DC: Federal Reserve Board).

FRENKEL, J. A. and LEVICH, R. M. (1975) 'Covered Interest Arbitrage: Unexploited Profits?', *Journal of Political Economy*, vol. 83 (Apr.) pp. 325–38.

GHOSH, D. K. (1989) 'Speculation, Currency Substitution and Capital Flight: Japanese Experience', *Proceedings of the Inaugural International Conference on Asian-Pacific Financial Markets*, National University of Singapore, Nov.

GHOSH, D. K. (1991) 'The Interest Rate Parity: Seven Expressions', *Financial Management* (FM Letter), Winter.

GHOSH, D. K. (1992) 'Speculative Strategies in Currency Markets', Jan. (mimeo).

KEYNES, J. M. (1923) *A Tract on Monetary Reform* (London: Macmillan)

LESSARD, D. R. (ed.) (1979) *International Financial Management* (John Wiley & Sons) 2nd ed.

McCORMICK, F. (1979) 'Covered Interest Arbitrage: Unexploited Profits? – Comment', *Journal of Political Economy*, vol. 87 (Apr.) pp. 411–17.

NIEHANS J. (1984) *International Monetary Economics* (Johns Hopkins University Press).

OFFICER, L. H. and WILLET, T. D. (1970) 'The Covered – Arbitrage Schedule: A Critical Survey of Recent Developments', *Journal of Money, Credit and Banking*, vol. 2 (May) pp. 247–57.

OTANI, I. and TIWARI, S. (1981) 'Capital Controls and Interest Rate Parity: The Japanese Experience, 1978–81', *International Monetary Fund Staff Papers*, vol. 28, pp. 793–815.

PRACHOWNY, M. F. J. (1970) 'A Note on Interest Parity and the Supply of Arbitrage Funds', *Journal of Political Economy*, vol. 78 (May/June) pp. 340–45.

ROLL, R. W. and SOLNIK, B. (1979) 'On Some Parity Conditions Frequently Encountered in International Finance', *Journal of Macroeconomics*, vol. 1 (Summer) pp. 267–83.

SPRAOS, J. (1953) 'The Theory of Forward Exchange and Recent Practice', *Manchester School Economics and Social Studies*, vol. 21 (May) pp. 87–117.

TSIANG, SHO-CHIEH (1959) 'The Theory of Forward Exchange and Effects of Government Intervention on the Forward Exchange Market', *International Monetary Fund Staff Papers*, vol. 7 (Apr.) pp. 75–106.

Part IV

Balance of Payments and International Reserves

Part IV of the book deals with balance of payments and international reserves, two fundamental factors that influence the changing environment of international finance. The common ground of the chapters in this section is the preoccupation of the authors with determining the impact of external deficits on future domestic and international activities. Aptly, the cases of developed and developing economies are analysed, examining the cases of United States, the post-communist economies from Eastern European countries and the former Soviet Union, and a sample of small Latin American countries.

7 An Empirical Test of the Demand for International Reserves

Anisul M. Islam, Moosa Khan and
Muhammad M. Islam

7.1 INTRODUCTION

The demand for international reserves (henceforth called reserves)
has been extensively studied by various researchers (see, for example,
Bahmani-Oskooee, 1985; Edwards, 1984; 1985; Heller and Khan,
1978; Iyoha, 1976; Lizondo and Mathieson, 1987; Williamson, 1973)
in the past and in recent years. A country desires to hold reserves for
a variety of reasons. One primary reason is to keep reserves as a
buffer stock against a possible instability in its balance of payments
(BOP). This can be considered as a precautionary motive for holding
reserves. Other reasons for holding reserves arise mainly from a
country's desire to carry out international transactions effectively
(transaction motive), to enhance its ability to borrow in the global
financial markets, and to improve a country's confidence in its ability
to meet external obligations.

Theoretically, reserves demand would be high under a pegged
exchange rate system. Under this system, persistent BOP deficits
would exert enormous pressure on the external value of a country's
currency. This outcome can be avoided if a country has an adequate
amount of reserves to pay for those deficits at the same time maintaining its current pegged rate. On the other hand, under a floating
exchange rate system, any imbalance in the BOP would be automatically adjusted by a required movement in the exchange rate. Thus the
need for holding foreign reserves would be reduced or eliminated
(Heberler, 1977). However, under a managed float system, a country
has to intervene in the market in order to maintain exchange rate
fluctuations within an acceptable limit. Therefore, the demand for
reserves would be reduced rather than eliminated. The situation is a
little complex for those developing countries which are following a

pegged exchange rate system within an international environment of managed float because of the added uncertainty caused by fluctuations in the value of major currencies against which their own currencies are pegged (Frenkel, 1978; Heller and Khan, 1978). This is clearly an important issue which needs to be resolved by more empirical studies based on those countries which are still under a pegged exchange rate regime. This chapter therefore estimates the demand for international reserves for three Central American countries: Costa Rica, El Salvador and Panama. These three countries are selected for several reasons: first, they are under a pegged exchange rate regime; secondly, they have been undergoing severe BOP deficits over the past several years, causing serious strains on their foreign reserves and finally, no empirical studies exist for these countries in this respect.

The remainder of this chapter is organized as follows. The second section briefly reviews the demand for international reserves theories. The third section discusses model specifications. Research methodology and data sources are presented in Section 7.4 which is followed by empirical test results. The final section concludes the chapter.

7.2 REVIEW OF CURRENT THEORIES

A critical analysis of existing theories (see, for example, Bahmani-Oskooee, 1985; Edwards, 1984; Frenkel, 1978; Heller and Khan, 1978; Iyoha, 1976; Kenen and Yudin, 1965; Lizondo and Mathieson, 1987) reveals the following major problems. First, most of these studies are conducted at a highly aggregative level involving broad country groups. The results obtained from such studies are subject to serious aggregation bias. Different countries with different political, legal, institutional and socio-economic factors are lumped together into a single group as if they were drawn from a homogeneous population (Heller and Khan, 1978). A few studies (Landell-Mills, 1989) attempted to reduce the aggregation bias probably by introducing dummy variables or by estimating country-specific factors from the error structures in their regressions (Edwards, 1984; Lizondo and Mathieson, 1987). Their approaches, however, did not eliminate the aggregation bias problem. However, some recent studies (see Burkett, Ramirez and Javier, 1987; Elbadawi, 1990) are conducted at individual country levels which overcome this problem. Secondly, most of these researches used cross-section (or pooled cross-section and time series) data to estimate the reserves demand function. This was done presumably because of the lack of data for a sufficient length of time to the time-series studies. Such studies implicitly assume long-run equilibrium behaviour and, therefore, do not allow for intertemporal adjustments of reserves with respect to changes to various internal and external factors. Finally, most of these studies fail to incorporate any measure of opportunity cost in their models. From a theoretical point of view this is a serious flaw possibly causing specification bias in estimation. In order to avoid aggregation bias, our study will develop three separate models for the three individual countries (Costa Rica, El Salvador and Panama) using time series data. The present study uses a reasonable proxy variable in order to avoid the specification bias. In addition, our study covers a longer period (1960 to 1989) than any other previous study. Moreover, as is stated above this is a first attempt to analyse the demand for international reserves for these three Central American countries in this respect.

7.3   MODEL SPECIFICATION

A survey of the literature indicates that four major explanatory variables determine the demand for international reserves. First, a scale variable representing the level of transactions is proxied by the level of imports (M). Second, a variable representing the propensity to import or the degree of openness of the economy. This is usually proxied by the ratio of import to GDP (MY). Third, a measure of the opportunity cost (OC) of holding reserves. Fourth, a variable measuring the disturbance or variability (VAR) of BOP. Using these variables and taking a log linear function, the reserve demand function can be specified as follows:

$$\ln R_t = \alpha + \beta_1 \ln M_t + \beta_2 \ln MY_t + \beta_3 \ln OC_t$$
$$+ \beta_4 \ln VAR_t + U_t \tag{1}$$

ln stands for natural logarithms, R stands for the amount of international reserves held by a country, β_i coefficients are elasticities of respective variables, U stands for a stochastic (disturbance) term, and t is the time subscript. Logarithmic transformation also reduces the problem of heteroscedasticity in the data set (if any).

The justification for the theoretical signs of the above four explanatory variables are given below. The expected effect of the scale variable M on the dependent variable R is positive because an increase in the level of imports will generate a higher demand for foreign reserves (other things remaining the same). Moreover, the elasticity of this variable being less than unity would imply the presence of economies of scale. The expected relationship between MY and R is ambiguous. In the Keynesian 'priceless' model, it acts as a proxy for the marginal propensity to import, and therefore, its inverse association is an indication of the amount of domestic adjustment required to produce a particular level of reserves. On the other hand, this variable also measures the degree of openness of the economy, thus measuring the extent to which the economy is vulnerable to external disruption justifying the direct association with R.

Frenkel (1978) has shown that in a model that emphasizes the role of relative prices, the price level, and the demand for money, the relationship between MY and R can not be unambiguously determined, but under certain reasonable conditions, the effect would be positive. The available empirical results are mixed and therefore, provide support for both.[1] The OC variable is expected to have a negative effect on R, because foreign reserve is a scarce resource which has alternative use. The VAR variable is expected to have a positive effect on R, because the monetary authorities would try to protect against greater payments uncertainties by holding a larger amount of foreign reserves.

7.4 METHODOLOGY AND DATA DESCRIPTIONS

The dependent variable R is the amount of non-gold international reserves consisting of convertible foreign currency reserves, reserve position in the IMF, and the holdings of SDR.[2] The scale variable M is measured by the level of imports, and the MY variable is measured as the ratio of imports to GDP. It is difficult to find an appropriate proxy for the OC variable. This is why most researchers[3] have ignored this variable in their model. Since the US dollar is a major currency for international trade and reserve holdings, and since these three countries currencies are pegged against the US dollar, we use the short-term US money market rate as a reasonable proxy for the OC variable. Foreign money market rate is used because reserves are typically held in foreign currencies. A short-term rate is more appropriate because reserves are usually invested (if at all) in short-term financial instruments in order to maintain a high degree of liquidity (Hipple, 1979). Finally, the measurement of the *VAR* variable can be measured in several alternative ways; however, we have followed the Heller and Khan two-step procedure involving the Box-Jenkins ARIMA model.[4] In the first stage, an ARIMA model is fitted to the dependent variable R. After ensuring stationarity to the R variable, the process involved fitting an appropriate ARIMA (p, d, q) model of the form:

$$\phi(L)R_t^1 = \theta(L)V_t \qquad (2)$$

where $\phi(L)$ and $\theta(L)$ are polynomial functions of the lag operator L, R_t^1 is an appropriately transformed stationary series based on R_t, and V_t represents a whie noise term. The estimated residuals from equation (2) are squared to obtain an estimate of the variability (V_t^2) of the payment deficits.

Since both past and present values of V_t^2 affect the values of the reserves, in the second stage, we estimate the behavioural model (equation (1)) with a polynomial lag structure imposed on the estimated V_t^2 as follows:

$$\ln R_t = \alpha + \beta_1 \ln M_t + \beta_2 \ln MY_t + \beta_3 \ln OC_t$$
$$+ \beta_4 \sum b_i \ln V_{t-i}^2 + U_t \qquad (3)$$

where $k = 10$ lags were found to be satisfactory, V_t^2 is defined above, and b_i are the weights attached to the current and the lagged values of V_t^2, and the weights are estimated as a second degree polynomial with a constraint of zero at lag 10th.

Finally, our desired variable *VAR* was constructed as a weighted moving average of the V_t^2 values using the estimated weights (b_is) obtained from equation (3), beginning at the period when the weight became significantly positive at the 5 per cent level of significance until the last significant weight. *VAR* was thus calculated using the following lag structures with the corresponding b_i coefficients:

Costa Rica: $\qquad VAR = b_i \sum_{i=1}^{7} V_{t-i}^2 \qquad$ (4)

El Salvador: $\qquad VAR = b_i \sum_{i=0}^{5} V_{t-i}^2 \qquad$ (5)

Panama: $$VAR = b_i \sum_{i=0}^{0} V^2_{t-i} \qquad (6)$$

Since the stochastic term U_t in equation (1) may have autoregressive and/or moving average components, we have identified the appropriate ARIMA (p, d, q) structure, and then corrections are made to make the disturbance term U_t a white noise. The identification process shows the following error structures for the three countries:

Costa Rica: $$U_t = p_1 u_{t-1} + p_2 u_{t-2} + w_t \qquad (7)$$

El Salvador: $$U_t = q_1 e_{t-3} + w_t \qquad (8)$$

Panama: $$U_t = r_1 e_{t-3} + w_t \qquad (9)$$

where w_ts are the white noise terms.

The data used in this study are annual time series data for three Central American countries covering the time period 1960 to 1989. The data are collected from the *International Financial Statistics Yearbook 1990*, published by the IMF. Because of non-availability of quarterly data for GDP series annual data were used. All variables are converted into US dollars (in millions) using country-specific appropriate exchange rates.

7.5   EMPIRICAL RESULTS

The empirical results are reported in Table 7.1 and in Table 7.2. Estimation results of ARIMA model (equation (2)) and the behavioural model (equation (1)) are reported in Table 7.1 and Table 7.2 respectively. The former is required to estimate the variable VAR which is then used as an argument in the behavioural model. These models are estimated separately for each country.

The ARIMA model (equation (2)) is identified as ARIMA (1, 0, 0) for Costa Rica, ARIMA (1, 0, 3) for El Salvador, and ARIMA (2, 0, 4) for Panama. The results are reported in Table 7.1. The Box–Pierce Q statistics indicate that the residuals are free from serial correlation. These residuals are then extracted, squared, and then applied to the second stage regressions to construct the variable VAR as discussed in the previous section.[5] The behavioural model (equation (1)) estimates are reported in Table 7.2. Based on the adjusted R-squared values, the models explain 93 per cent, 88 per cent, and 93

Table 7.1   Arima model (equation (2)).
Estimates for three Central American countries

Costa Rica
  $(1 - 1.1171\ L)\ R'_t = -64.48 + v_t$
      (23.72)   (-0.49)
  Box–Pierce $Q = 13.15$; $R^2 = 0.95$; $F = 562.6$; $DF = 19$; $N = 29$.

El Salvador
  $(1 - 0.9907\ L)\ R'_t = 1085.64 + (1 + 0.6108\ L^3)\ v_t$
      (9.56)   (0.09)   (-2.52)
  Box–Pierce $Q = 10.71$; $R^2 = 0.77$; $F = 44.4$; $DF = 16$; $N = 29$.

Panama
  $(1 - 0.5158\ L - 0.4092\ L^2)\ R'_t = 171.21 + (1 + 0.5020\ L^4)\ v_t$
      (2.92)   (2.32)   (0.90)   (-2.29)
  Box–Pierce $Q = 4.06$; $R^2 = 0.70$; $F = 18.96$; $DF = 13$; $N = 28$.

The values in the parentheses below the coefficients are the *t*-values. The theoretical values of the χ^2 (Chi-square) at the 5 per cent level of significance and with the appropriate degrees of freedom are 30.14, 26.3 and 22.4 respectively for Costa Rica, El Salvador and Panama.

per cent of the variation in reserves for Costa Rica, El Salvador, and Panama respectively. The *F*-statistics is highly significant (at 1 per cent level) for each country implies that all explanatory variables taken together explains quite well to the variation of the dependent variable *R*. Durbin–Watson test statistics indicate that the error terms are serially uncorrelated. Thus the behavioural model estimates appear to be quite satisfactory.

The coefficient of the scale variable *M* is positive as is expected and is significant at the 1 per cent level. However, the elasticity is found to be greater than unity indicating the presence of some diseconomies of scale. This result is different from that obtained by Officer (1976), Edwards (1984), Lizondo and Mathieson (1987) using aggregate data for groups of countries. On the other hand, Heller and Khan (1978) found elasticity to be close to unity.

The elasticity of the *MY* variable is negative and is found statistically significant only for Panama supporting the Keynesian hypothesis and also consistent with Heller and Khan (1978) result. The sign of the coefficient of the *OC* variable is consistent with the theoretical sign for Costa Rica and El Salvador and is also found statistically significant at the 1 per cent level for the latter country. The elasticity is also less than unity. In case of Panama the coefficient came up with

Table 7.2   Regression results of behavioural model (equation (1)) for three Central American countries

---

Costa Rica

$\ln R_t = -0.55 + 1.25^a \ln M_t - 1.02 \ln MY_t - 0.61^b \ln OP_t + 1.36^a \ln VAR_t;$
$\qquad (-0.29) \quad (5.12) \qquad (-1.48) \qquad\qquad (-1.46) \qquad\qquad (3.60)$

$p_1 = 0.59^b; \qquad p_2 = -0.49^c$
$\quad (2.58) \qquad\qquad (-1.98)$

Adj $R^2 = 0.93$; $SEE = 0.33$; $F = 46.7^a$; $DW = 1.93$; $N = 22$.

El Salvador

$\ln R_t = -0.43 + 1.22^a \ln M_t - 0.30 \ln MY_t - 0.74 \ln OP_t + 0.19 \ln VAR_t$
$\qquad (-0.48) \quad (7.20) \qquad (-1.23) \qquad\qquad (-3.73) \qquad\quad (-0.60)$

$q_3 = -0.57^c;$
$\quad (-2.05)$

Adj $R^2 = 0.88$; $SEE = 0.21$; $F = 31.3^a$; $DW = 1.86$; $N = 21$.

Panama

$\ln R_t = -4.54^a + 1.91^a \ln M_t - 1.24^b \ln MY_t + 0.07 \ln OP_t + 1.04^b \ln VAR_t;$
$\qquad (-3.37) \quad (8.96) \qquad (-2.26) \qquad\qquad (-0.22) \qquad\quad (1.72)$

$+ 0.53^a D_1 - 0.72^b D_2; r_3 = -0.58^c;$
$\quad (2.55) \qquad (-1.87) \qquad (-1.83)$

Adj $R^2 = 0.93$; $SEE = 0.31$; $F = 49.2^a$; $DW = 2.22$; $N = 25$.

A two-tailed test was applied for the variable *MY* while a one-tailed test was applied for the other variables. The values in the parentheses below the regression coefficients are the *t*-values. 'a' indicates significance at 1 per cent, 'b' at 5 per cent and 'c' at 10 per cent level of significance.

a wrong sign (positive). However, according to *t*-test, the coefficient was found insignificant. The elasticity of VAR variable appears with a correct sign for both in Costa Rica and Panama. According to *t*-test it is found also significant at the 1 per cent level for Costa Rica and at the 5 per cent level for Panama. In the case of El Salvador the sign of the coefficient is wrong but is not statistically significant.

The variability of the payments elasticity is found to be slightly above unity for Costa Rica and approximately unity for Panama. These results indicate that an increase in variability of payments would require an upward adjustment of reserves by 1 per cent or more.

Two dummy variables are introduced in the regressions in order to capture for a possible shift in the reserve demand functions. The dummy variable D1 assumed a value one for 1971, 1972 and 1973, and zero otherwise. This was intended to capture two shocks occurring at that time: one is the OPEC shock and the other is the shock due to change in the international monetary system in 1973. This dummy variable was found to be positive (as expected) and also highly significant for Panama. It was not significant for the other two countries and therefore was dropped. The second dummy variable D2 was assumed to have a value one for the period since 1982 and zero otherwise. It was intended to capture any shift in the function due to international debt crisis which seriously affected some Latin American countries (Bahmani-Oskooee, 1985). This variable is found statistically significant (but negative) for Panama and insignificant for the other two countries. The above findings indicate that the reserve demand functions are quite stable for Costa Rica and El Salvador but somewhat unstable for Panama.

7.6 SUMMARY AND CONCLUSIONS

This chapter estimated the demand function for international reserves for three Central American countries: Costa Rica, El Salvador and Panama using the econometric (behavioural) model and the Box–Jenkins (ARIMA) model. The behavioural model outperformed the ARIMA model in terms of its ability to forecasting reserve demands in these countries. It was also found that the behavioural model has been reasonably stable over the sample period except for Panama. For Panama, the function appears to have shifted in the early 1970s (due to the OPEC oil crisis) as well as the early 1980s (due to the Latin American debt crisis). However, the new international monetary system did not have any significant effect on the reserve for these countries. This is not surprising given the fact that these countries continued to maintain the pegged exchange rate system.

The scale variable is found to be highly significant with a correct sign (positive) for all these countries. However, it does not provide any support to the 'economies of scale' in using reserves. The variable representing payments uncertainty was found to be positive and significant for Costa Rica and Panama, while the opportunity cost variable was found significant only for El Salvador. The import–GDP ratio was generally not significant with the exception of Panama. The results obtained in our study can be considered more accurate because the models were estimated using country-specific longer (1960 to 1989) time series data, thus trying to avoid some serious limitations to previous studies.

Notes

1. Negative effect was found by Bahmini-Oskooee (1985a, b) and Heller and Khan (1978), among others, while positive effect was reported by Frenkel (1978), Heller and Khan (1978), Hipple (1972) and Iyoha (1976), among others.

2. Gold is excluded because it is usually measured using official rather market prices and thus its inclusion can create serious measurement bias. Moreover, the opportunity cost variable in our model does not capture the opportunity cost of holding gold as reserves. This exclusion is not expected to seriously bias our results because gold constitutes only a small portion of total reserves in these countries.

3. For example, Williamson (1973) used various proxies without any success. Kenen and Yudin (1965) used income per capita as a proxy for it and came up with an incorrect sign. Similarly, lack of success with this variable was reported by Frenkel and Jovanovic (1981). Others such as Frenkel (1978), Heller and Khan (1978) have simply ignored this variable. Edwards (1985) has criticized previous studies for incorrectly measuring this variable. Using the spread between the interest rate at which a country can borrow from abroad and LIBOR as a reasonable proxy for the 'net' opportunity cost of holding reserves, Edwards found a significant negative effect of this variable on the reserve demand for a group of developing countries.

4. For alternative ways of measuring VAR, see Frenkel (1978), among others. Following Heller and Khan (1978) and others, it is assumed here that the variability of reserves reflect the variability of the BOP of a country.

5. For alternative ways of measuring VAR, see Clark (1970), Frenkel (1978), among others. Following Heller and Khan (1978) variability of reserves reflect the variability of the BOP of a country.

REFERENCES

BAHMANI-OSKOOEE, M. (1985a) 'Demand for and Supply of International Reserves: a Simultaneous Approach', *Journal of Post Keynesian Economics*, vol. 7, no. 4, (Summer) pp. 493–503.

BAHMANI-OSKOOEE, M. (1985b) 'Demand for International Reserves: Survey of Recent Empirical Studies', *Applied Economics*, vol. 17, no. 2 (April) pp. 359–75.

BURKETT, P., RAMIREZ, J. and JAVIER, M. (1984) 'The Demand for International Reserves and Monetary Equilibrium: Some Evidence from Developing Countries', *Review of Economics and Statistics*, vol. 66, no. 3, pp. 494–500.

BURKETT, P., RAMIREZ, J. and JAVIER, M. (1985) 'On the Interest Rate Elasticity of the Demand for International Reserves: Some Evidence from Developing Countries', *Journal of International Money and Finance*, vol. 4, no. 2 (June) pp. 287–95.

BURKETT, P., RAMIREZ, J. and JAVIER, M. (1987) 'The Determinants of International Reserves in the Small Open Economy: The Case of Honduras', *Journal of Macroeconomics*, vol. 9, no. 3, (Summer) pp. 439–50.

CLARK, P. B. (1970) 'Demand for International Reserves: A Cross-Country Analysis', *Canadian Journal of Economics*, vol. 3, November 1970, pp. 577–94.

EDWARDS, S. (1984) 'The Demand for International Reserves and Monetary Equilibrium: Some Evidence from Developing Countries,' *Review of Economics and Statistics*, vol. 66, no. 3, 1984, pp. 595–600.

EDWARDS, S. (1985) 'On the Interest Rate Elasticity of the Demand for International Reserves: Some Evidence from Developing Countries, *Journal of International Money and Finance*, vol. 4, no. 2, June 1985, pp. 287–95.

ELBADAWI, I. A. (1990) 'The Sudan Demand for International Reserves: A Case of a Labor Exporting Country', *Economica*, vol. 57, no. 225 (Feb.) pp. 73–79.

FRENKEL, J. A. (1978) 'International Reserves: Pegged Exchange Rates and Managed Float', in K. Brunner and A. H. Meltzer (eds), *Public Policies in Open Economies*, Carnegie–Rochester Conference Series on Public Policy, vol. 9 (Amsterdam) pp. 111–40.

FRENKEL, J. A. and JOVANOVIC, B. (1981) 'Optimal International Reserves: A Stochastic Framework', *Economic Journal*, vol. 91, no. 362, (June) pp. 507–14.

HEBERLER, G. (1977) 'How Important is Control over International Reserves?', in R. A. Mundell and J. J. Polak (eds), *The New International Monetary System* (Columbia University Press) pp. 111–32.

HELLER, H. R. and KHAN, M. S. (1978) 'The Demand for International Reserves Under Fixed and Floating Exchange Rates', *IMF Staff Papers*, vol. 25, no. 4 (Dec.) pp. 623–49.

HIPPLE, F. S. (1974) 'The Disturbances Approach to the Demand for International Reserves', *Princeton Studies in International Finance*, vol. 35, pp. 1–46.

HIPPLE, F. S. (1979) 'A Note on the Measurement of the Holding Cost of International Reserves', *Review of Economics and Statistics*, vol. 61, no. 4, (Nov.) pp. 612–14.

IYOHA, M. A. (1976) 'Demand for International Reserves in Less Developed Countries: A Distributed Lag Specification', *Review of Economics and Statistics*, vol. 58 (Aug.) pp. 351–55.

KENEN, P. B. and YUDIN, E. B. (1965) 'The Demand for International Reserves', *Review of Economics and Statistics*, vol. 47 (Aug.) pp. 242–50.

LANDELL-MILLS, J. M. (1989) 'The Demand for International Reserves and their Opportunity Cost', *IMF Staff Papers*, vol. 36, no. 3 (Sept.) pp. 708–32.

LIZONDO, J. S. and MATHIESON, D. J. (1987) 'The Stability of the Demand for International Reserves' *Journal of International Money and Finance*, vol. 6, no. 3 (Sept.) pp. 251–82.

OFFICER, L. H. (1976) 'The Demand for International Liquidity: A Test of the Square Root Law', *Journal of Money, Credit and Banking*, Aug., pp. 325–37.

SUSS, E. C. (1976) 'A Note on Reserve Use Under Alternative Exchange Rate Regimes', *IMF Staff Papers*, vol. 23, pp. 387–94.

WILLIAMSON, J. (1973) 'Surveys in Applied Economics: International Liquidity', *Economic Journal*, vol. 83 (Sept.) pp. 685–746.

8 An Intertemporal Interpretation of the US Current Account Deficit

Eric Youngkoo Lee and Michael Szenberg

8.1 INTRODUCTION

During the last decade the huge current account deficits, averaging over $100 billion, and the corresponding net capital inflows have reduced the US foreign investment position steadily, turning the United States into a net foreign debtor in 1985.

One major concern that the growing status as a net debtor has rasied is that future generations of Americans may face reduced living standards because they will be forced to transfer much of their income to foreigners to service the accumulated foreign debt.

To assess the validity of the concern that foreign capital inflows could produce a burden on future generations in the form of a lowered standard of living, we need to understand the economic factors that generated large net capital inflows into the United States during the ten years 1982–91.

Fundamentally, current account deficits and corresponding capital inflows reflect macroeconomic imbalances. The persistent US current account deficits have merely reflected the excess of the nation's expenditures or absorption over its output or, equivalently, the short-fall of national saving from investment, for the rising government budget deficit was not matched by an increase in private saving.

Table 8.1 shows that although national saving declined from about 16.6 per cent of GNP in 1980–81 to about 13.4 per cent in 1984–88, investment remained virtually unchanged as a share of GNP except for the recession years of 1982–83; investment averaged about 16.4 per cent of GNP during the earlier period and about the same during the latter years despite the precipitous fall in national saving. The implication is that the inflow of capital from abroad allowed continuing growth in the US capital stock. In the absence of foreign

Table 8.1 US saving, investment and the current account
(per cent of GNP)

Year	Business saving (1)	Personal saving (2)	Government saving (3)	National saving (4)=(1)+(2)+(3)	Investment spending (5)	Saving less investment (6)=(4)−(5)	Current account balance* (7)
1980	12.5	5.0	-1.3	16.2	16.0	0.2	0.0
1981	12.8	5.2	-1.0	17.0	16.9	0.2	0.2
1982	12.7	4.9	-3.5	14.1	14.1	0.0	0.2
1983	13.6	3.8	-3.8	13.6	14.8	-1.2	-1.2
1984	13.5	4.4	-2.8	13.5	17.6	-4.1	-2.6
1985	13.4	3.1	-3.3	13.3	16.0	-2.7	-3.1
1986	12.9	3.0	-3.4	12.4	15.6	-3.2	-3.4
1987	12.4	2.3	-2.4	12.2	15.5	-3.3	-3.6
1988	12.2	3.0	-2.0	13.2	15.4	-2.2	-2.7

*The discrepancy between the saving less investment balance (6) and the current account balance (7) is due to some minor data adjustments.

Source: International Financial Statistics Yearbook 1991 (Washington, DC: International Monetary Fund) and *Economic Report of the President* (Washington, DC: US Government Printing Office, January 1989).

capital inflows, a drop in national saving would have to be accompanied by a drop in investment.

The purpose of this chapter is to show that insofar as the government budget deficit represents the deliberate choice of policy-makers and, as a result, the low domestic savings rate is taken as given, the alternatives the US faces are either higher levels of investment and a current account deficit or low levels of investment and balanced trade. We will show that given the low US domestic savings rate for whatever the cause we shall not pursue here the question of whether the government budget deficit is desirable or not for the country – the current account deficit with its corresponding net capital inflow should not be viewed as a problem but rather as a solution to the problem of not having sufficient domestic savings to exploit profitable domestic investment opportunities. Additional spending on new plant and equipment generates higher output and income in the future, but only part of the increased output accrue to foreign investors in the form of interest and dividend payments.

The chapter is organized in the following manner. In Section 8.2, the determination of the general equilibrium levels of investment, consumption, savings and the various accounts of the balance of payments is rigorously examined, using a two-period model of a small, open economy, facing a given world rate of interest. In Section 8.3, an intertemporal interpretation of the deterioration in the US current account, beginning 1982, is presented in the light of our model. Policy implications and concluding remarks are offered in Section 8.4.

8.2   AN INTERTEMPORAL MODEL OF THE CURRENT ACCOUNT

Current account movements are best analysed in a multiperiod macroeconomic model, for they represent international borrowing and lending, thus reflecting intertemporal savings and investment decisions of households, firms and governments (see Abel and Blanchard, 1983).

In this section, we present a simplified two-period version of the intertemporal model that provides a theoretical framework for analysing the current account.

The model assumes perfect foresight, optimal behaviour by individual agents, and perfect international capital mobility. Output is supply-determined as full employment is assumed. These assumptions make the model the most appropriate for a longer-run analysis in which aggregate demand effects on output may be ignored.

We begin with certain accounting identities that must be satisfied by the measurement of aggregate income and expenditure flows (see Sachs, 1981). The current account surplus can be expressed as the export of goods and services minus their import plus income transfers, as national income minus national absorption, or as national saving minus domestic investment.

More formally,

$$Y = Q + F \tag{1}$$

where Y is gross national product (GNP), Q is gross domestic product (GDP), and F is net factor payments from abroad such as remittances or interest on foreign bonds. Also GNP plus net unilateral transfers from abroad, R, may be used for consumption, C, gross private saving, Sp and taxes, T:

$$Y + R = C + Sp + T. \tag{2}$$

Government saving, Sg is given by $T–G$, where G is government consumption of goods and services. Output market equilibrium requires.

$$Q = C + I + G + X - M. \tag{3}$$

Since the current account surplus, CA, is defined as the net export of goods and services plus unilateral transfers and net factor payments from abroad, three equivalent definitions of CA are derived from the above three equations.

$$CA = X - M + F + R \tag{4a}$$

$$CA = Y - (C + I + G) + R \tag{4b}$$

$$CA = (Sp + Sg) - I. \tag{4c}$$

Equation (4a) represents the standard definition of CA. Equation (4b) reflects the insight that the surplus must also equal income minus absorption $(C + I + G)$. Equation (4c) shows CA as the excess of saving over investment. Although any of the three forms of the

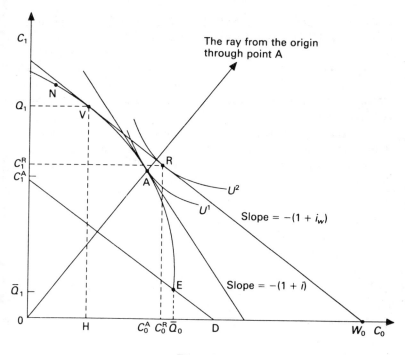

Figure 8.1

current account identity is ultimately as good as any other, the saving minus investment view shifts the emphasis to the role of intertemporal choices in determining saving, investment and the current account.

We begin by considering a small country in an intertemporal framework (see Layard and Walters, 1978; Hirshleifer, 1965). Let there be only two periods, present and future, indexed $t = 0$ and 1 respectively. The country is represented by a single consumer whose utility function is $U(C_0, C_1)$, where C_0 and C_1 denote period 0 and period 1 consumption levels. We start by specifying the supply side of the model.

Figure 8.1 shows an economy that is endowed with an initial sequence of income flows, $\bar{Q}_0$ and $\bar{Q}_1$, where the subscripts zero and one specify the present and future periods. The endowed income in period zero may be consumed, or alternatively, it may be invested in the intertemporal production process. Such an investment process alters the intertemporal pattern of available output flows (GDP). During the second (and last) period, total income is fully consumed.

Formally, output in the future period Q_1 is linked to the initial endowment $\bar{Q}_0$, through the production function.

$$Q_1 = \bar{Q}_0 + f(I_0) \tag{5}$$

where I_0 represents investment which is equal to the level of output not consumed in period zero, that is, $I_0 = \bar{Q}_0 - C_0$.

We assumed that the production function exhibits positive and diminishing marginal product, that is, $f'(I_0) > 0$ and $f''(I_0) < 0$. The investment opportunities consist of a set of projects, each of which involves a sacrifice of current consumption C_0 and an increase in future consumption C_1. The rate of return, r, on a project is given by

$$\frac{\Delta C_1}{-\Delta C_0} = \frac{\text{return}}{\text{cost}} = \frac{\text{return} - \text{cost}}{\text{cost}} + 1 = r + 1. \tag{6}$$

Adding projects in order of their rates of return traces out a concave production frontier reaching northwest from point E in Figure 8.1, whose slope at any point is $(1 + r)$, r being the rate of return on the marginal project.

In autarky, the representative consumer's production frontier is also his consumption frontier. His problem is thus:

Maximize $U(C_0, C_1)$ $\tag{7}$

subject to the production constraint.

$$F(C_0 - \bar{Q}_0, C_1 - \bar{Q}_1) = 0.$$

His optimum is at a tangency between his production frontier and the indifference curve U^1, where their slopes are equal,

$$\frac{F_0}{F_1} = \frac{U_0}{U_1}, \tag{8}$$

using the usual notation for derivatives. The absolute slope of the indifference curve is,

$$\frac{-dC_1}{dC_0} = \frac{U_0}{U_1} = \frac{U_0 - U_1}{U_1} + 1 = p + 1, \tag{9a}$$

where p denotes the 'rate of time preference', which measures the proportion by which the value of consumption today exceeds that of consumption tomorrow. The absolute slope of the production frontier is:

$$\frac{-dC_1}{dC_0} = \frac{F_0}{F_1} = \frac{F_0 - F_1}{F_1} + 1 = r + 1. \tag{9b}$$

In equilibrium, therefore $p = r$, implying that at less investment than the optimum, p is less than r but as additional investment is undertaken p rises and r falls until they are equalized.

At the optimal production and consumption point A, the representative consumer has determined not only his rate of saving and investment (both of which equal $\bar{Q}_0 - C_0^A$), but also his equilibrium rate of time preference $\bar{p}$, which serves as the (*ex post*) discount rate as well as the autarky interest rate i. Therefore, in autarky, saving (i.e., refraining from current consumption to release resources for investment) must necessarily equal investment.[1]

However, once there is a possibility of borrowing and lending in the world capital market, the saving investment equality need no longer apply for any single country.

Now assume that the country is opened up to the world capital market, where it can borrow at the going world interest rate i_w which is lower than the autarky interest rate i.

We now show that the home country will borrow in the world capital market, thereby incurring a current account deficit (and a capital account surplus) and this is the outcome of profit maximization by firms and utility maximization by households.[2]

Firms are assumed to maximize the present value of profits, PV,

$$PV = a_w f(I_0) - I_0, \tag{10}$$

where $a_w = 1/(1 + i_w)$ denotes the present value factor.

As the interest rate falls from i to i_w, the representative firm will increase the level of investment, I_0, until the rate of return on the marginal project, r, equals the world rate of interest. The value-maximizing level of investment, $\tilde{I}_0$, now occurs at point V in terms of Figure 8.1, where the (absolute value of the) slope of the intertemporal transformation function equals that of the iso-value locus VW_0.

$\tilde{I}_0$ is measured in a leftward direction from $\bar{Q}_0$ to H and the maximized present value of profits, $\widetilde{PV}$, can be measured by the distance DW_0, for the line ED is a zero-value locus. The iso-value line VW_0 then is associated with the maximum attainable level of the country's wealth W_0, which is defined as the present value of the stream of income (net of investment outlays) discounted at the world interest rate,

$$H + a_w Q_1 = \bar{Q}_0 + a_w \bar{Q}_1 + \widetilde{PV} \equiv W_0. \tag{11}$$

Choosing the scale of investment that maximizes wealth guarantees for the economy that the consumption frontier or the budget constraint is pushed as far to the right as possible. The representative consumer can then choose a preferred intertemporal balance of consumption between present and future.

Then the intertemporal budget constraint for the representative consumer is,

$$C_0 + a_w C_1 = \bar{Q}_0 + a_w \bar{Q}_1 + \widetilde{PV} \equiv W_0. \tag{12}$$

This present-value budget constraint highlights the fact that the key decisions that the representative consumer makes concern the choices of C_0 and C_1 as well as the magnitude of external borrowing, which appears explicitly in the two temporal budget constraints below.

The first-period budget constraint is

$$C_0 = \bar{Q}_0 + B_0 - \tilde{I}_0 \tag{13}$$

and the second-period budget constraint is

$$C_1 = \bar{Q}_1 + f(\tilde{I}_0) - (1 + i_w)B_0, \tag{14}$$

where B_0 denotes first-period external borrowing and $-(1 + i_w)B_0$ denotes the repayment of the loan plus interest in the second period. $\tilde{I}_0$ corresponds to the losses of firms (negative dividends) while $f(\tilde{I}_0)$ corresponds to the profits of firms, which are paid out as dividends.

It can be seen that the specification in the two temporal budget constraint equations above conform with national income accounting, where $C + I + CA = GNP$. In terms of equation (13), $\bar{Q}_0$ represents GNP as well as GDP as factor income payment, F, is zero, and the current account deficit (equal to the capital account surplus) is equal to B_0. The current account deficit also equals the trade account deficit. Alternatively, the current account deficit also equals savings $(\bar{Q}_0 - C_0)$ minus investment $(\tilde{I}_0)$. In terms of equation (14), $Q_1 - i_w B_0$ represents GNP, $(1 + i_w)B_0$ represents the trade account surplus and B_0 represents the current account surplus. Alternatively, the current account surplus also equals saving $(Q_1 - i_w B_0 - C_1)$.

Here intertemporal solvency implies that the discounted sum of the first period trade account deficit and second period surplus equal zero.

$$(TA)_0 + a_w(TA)_1 = 0 \tag{15}$$

However, a similar property does not apply to the intertemporal pattern of the current account.

$$(CA)_0 + a_w(CA)_1 + a_w(F)_1 = 0 \tag{16}$$

Formally, the individual's maximization problem is

$$\tilde{U} = \max_{\{C_0,\, C_1\}} U\,(C_0,\, C_1)$$

subject to $C_0 + a_w C_1 = W_0$.

In Figure 8.1, the solution to this maximization problem is represented by point R, where the indifference curve U^2 is tangent to the budget line associated with point W_0. This 'consumption basket' (C_0^R, C_1^R) represents the preferred intertemporal consumption pattern, where the marginal rate of time preference is equal to the world rate of interest.

To facilitate the exposition, we assume that the utility function $U(C_0, C_1)$ is homothetic, which implies that for a given rate of interest the ratio of consumption in the two periods is independent of the level of wealth. Thus the wealth-consumption path is the ray from the origin going through the initial equilibrium point A.

Figure 8.1 shows that the representative consumer borrows $(C_0^R - H)$ in period zero and repays $(Q_1 - C_1^R) = (1 + i_w) \times (C_0^R - H)$ in period 1 but we cannot say how much of the loan is a consumption loan, or an investment loan for that matter. At any rate, the economy runs a current account deficit in the amount of the borrowing $(C_0^R - H)$, which represents the excess of investment $(\bar{Q}_0 - H)$ over saving $(\bar{Q}_0 - C_0^R)$.

Because of the homotheticity assumption, we can show that the present level of consumption C_0^R is greater than C_0^A, the present level of consumption in autarky, since both the wealth and substitution effects reinforce each other. The future level of consumption is also shown to be higher than the autarky level C_1^A if we assume that the positive wealth effect more than offsets the negative substitution effect that is due to the increase in the relative price of future consumption, namely, $1/(1 + i)$.

Now international borrowing and lending can be interpreted as a kind of international trade of goods today for goods in the future, otherwise known as intertemporal trade. In our model, the home country with its higher autarky interest rate then has a comparative advantage in the production of future goods, whereas the rest of the world with its lower interest rate has a comparative advantage in the production of present goods. So if we open up the possibility of intertemporal trade, we would expect the home country to export future goods in return for imports of present goods. Since a low relative price of future goods in terms of present goods implied by the high interest rate corresponds to a high return on investment, the home country borrows in the world capital market because it has highly productive investment opportunities available relative to current productive capacity.

Figure 8.1 shows how the home country's production and consumption patterns of present and future consumption goods are determined for a given world intertemporal terms of trade, that is, the world rate of interest. Point R, where the home country's budget constraint touches the highest attainable indifference curve, shows the present and future consumption levels chosen by the economy, which is far superior to what could have been achieved by isolated production.

The home country's demand for present consumption, C_0^R, is larger than its production of present consumption, H; so it imports (that is, borrows) $C_0^R - H$ units of present consumption from the rest of the world, which equals its trade deficit.

Correspondingly, the home country exports $Q_1 - C_1^R$ units of future consumption to the rest of the world when it repays its first-period loans with interest, which equals its trade surplus in the second period. The intertemporal budget constraint implies that $(Q_1 - C_1^R) = (1 + i_w) \times (C_0^R - H)$, so that trade is intertemporarily balanced.

Here again we cannot say how much of the first-period borrowing is a consumption loan in the sense that it finances consumption directly.

8.3 AN INTERTEMPORAL INTERPRETATION OF THE DETERIORATION IN THE US CURRENT ACCOUNT

Our intertemporal analysis offers an appropriate framework to analyse the deterioration in the US current account since 1982.

We will make the simplifying assumption that the US interest rate was equal to the world rate in 1980–81, during which period the US current account was approximately balanced. So in terms of Figure 8.1, the initial equilibrium representing both productive and consumptive optimum for the US economy would be at point V, where the highest indifference curve attainable (undrawn in order to avoid clutter) is tangent to the production frontier.

Now the fall in national saving caused by the huge federal budget deficit that developed in the 1980s can be interpreted as a shift in national demand from future consumption to present consumption, that is, an increase in the national rate of time preference.

In terms of Figure 8.1, the US consumptive and productive optimum would move from point V to, say, point A in the absence of international capital movements as the US indifference curves shift so as to increase relative preferences for present versus future consumption. The drop in domestic saving associated with the increase in the government budget deficit would then have to be accompanied by a corresponding drop in domestic investment and a rise in the domestic interest rate; the budget deficit 'crowds out' domestic investment by raising the interest rate.

However in a world of international capital mobility, this would transform a balanced US current account into a large deficit instead, as new general equilibrium levels of investment, consumption, savings and the various accounts of the balance of payments emerge at point R in Figure 8.1. It can be seen easily that the exogenous fall in national saving caused by the budget deficit 'crowds out' net exports (that is, enlarges the trade account deficit) but not domestic investment.

A low propensity to save in the United States relative to other countries generates current account deficits. Protectionist trade policies would influence the structure of international trade, not the overall trade balance. Currency devaluations would lead to domestic inflation and an increase in the money supply without affecting the trade balance either (see Alexander, 1952; Sachs, 1988; McKinnon and Ohno, 1988; Lee, 1989).

8.4   CONCLUDING REMARKS

Throughout this chapter, we elaborated the view that the current account imbalances represent national savings or borrowing *vis-à-vis* the rest of the world and therefore are the outcome of intertemporal choices of households, firms and governments.

A major theme developed in the chapter is that in a world of capital mobility, shifts in national saving propensities relative to investment opportunities lead to corresponding shifts in the current account.

The model presented in the chapter assumes that output is supply-determined as a function of the capital stock and not affected by aggregate demand; real interest rates are tied to the marginal productivity of capital and not influenced by monetary policies. These assumptions make the model the most appropriate for explaining the current account in the intermediate or longer-run, over which full employment is assumed.

Steps taken to reduce the current account deficit can only be effective if they also narrow the gap between national saving and investment. Exogenous changes in the currency exchange rate would merely generate changes in the domestic price level and money supply without affecting the current account balance. Protectionist trade policies would simply alter the structure of international trade, not the overall current account balance.

One instrument the United States could use in achieving current account adjustments is a regulatory restriction on international borrowing and lending.[3]

If binding capital restrictions are imposed to eliminate net foreign capital inflow, the US interest rate rises until the current account is balanced. With no net capital inflows allowed by capital controls, higher interest rates will stimulate more savings; higher interest rates will cause domestic investment to decline. The outcome will be a balance between savings and investment and elimination of the excess absorption that caused the current account deficit in the first place.

Another possibility of the US current account being eliminated is the extreme scenario of a 'hard landing' of the dollar, where the perceptions of the riskiness of holding dollar-denominated assets worsen to the point where foreign capital inflow is drastically curtailed so as to eliminate the US current account deficit (see Marris, 1985).

Neither of the above two possibilities of having the US current account balanced would be desirable because of the resulting drop in investment and slower growth in the US capital stock.

In this chapter we did not pursue the question of whether the budget deficit is desirable or not for the country. However, if we assume that the budget deficit represents the deliberate choice of policymakers, it follows that the associated current account deficit must be preferred to the alternative.

Insofar as the low national saving is taken as given, the alternatives the US faces are either higher levels of private investment made possible by a trade account deficit or low levels of private investment and balanced trade.

Therefore, the current account deficit should not be viewed as a problem but rather as a solution to the problem of lacking sufficient domestic savings to exploit productive investment opportunities. In the absence of net foreign capital inflows, a drop in national saving for whatever the cause would have to be accompanied by a drop in investment.

Additional spending on new investment in plant and equipment generates higher output and incomes. Only part of the increased income accrue to foreign investors in the form of interest and dividend payments. The inflow of capital from abroad allows a faster growth in the capital stock and a higher US standard of living in the future than it would otherwise be. Nevertheless, the rate of US income growth would be even higher, had more of the investment been financed by domestic saving rather than foreign saving, for then less of the returns to that new capital would accrue to foreigners. But that is another story.

Notes

1. At the (*ex-post*) discount rate i, the representative household or the representative firm that it owns undertakes all investment projects for which $r > \bar{p}$ or, equivalently, all projects which have positive present values when future flows are discounted at i.
2. The development of a small, open economy model in this section draws heavily on Frenkel and Razin (1989).
3. Capital controls can appear in myriad ways, such as explicit prohibitions on various types of investments, as taxes on the purchases of assets, and intricate rules on reporting and approval of investment activities that serve to discourage their undertaking.

REFERENCES

ABEL, A. B. and BLANCHARD, O. J. (1983) 'An Intertemporal Model of Saving and Investment', *Econometrica*, 51 (May) pp. 675–92.

ALEXANDER, S. S. (1952) 'Effects of a Devaluation on a Trade Balance', *International Monetary Funds Staff Papers*, 2, 263–78. Reprinted in R. E. Caves and H. G. Johnson (eds), *Readings in International Economics* (Homewood: Irwin, 1968).

Economic Report of the President, (Washington DC: Government Printing Office, January).

FRENKEL J. A. and RAZIN, A. (1989) *Fiscal Policies and the World Economy: An Intertemporal Approach* (Cambridge, Mass.: MIT Press) pp. 139–51.

HIRSHLEIFER, J. (1965) 'On the Theory of Optimal Investment', *Journal of Political Economy*, vol. 66 (Aug.) pp. 329–51.

International Financial Statistics Yearbook (1991) (Washington DC: International Monetary Fund).

LAYARD, P. R. G. and WALTERS, A. A. (1978) *Microeconomic Theory* (New York: McGraw-Hill) pp. 326–32.

LEE, E. Y. (1989) 'The Persistent U. S. External Imbalance: Its Causes and Policy Message', *The American Economist*, vol. XXXIII, (Spring) pp. 28–35.

MARRIS, S. (1985) 'Deficits and the Dollar: The World Economy at Risk' *International Economics, Policy Studies in the International Economy*, No. 14 (Washington, DC).

MCKINNON, R. I. and OHNO, K. (1988) 'Getting the Exchange Rate Right: Insular vs. Open Economies', *Seoul Journal of Economics*, vol. 1 (Mar.) pp. 19–40.

SACHS, J. D. (1981) 'The Current Account and Macroeconomic Adjustment in the 1970s', *Brookings Papers on Economic Activity*, no. 1, pp. 201–68.

SACHS, J. D. (1988) 'Prospects for Global Trade Imbalances: A Simulation Approach', *Seoul Journal of Economics*, vol. 1 (Mar.) pp. 41–74.

9 Balance-of-Payments Implications of the Break-Up of the USSR for Its Former Republics and the East European Countries

M. Raquibuz Zaman

9.1 INTRODUCTION

The collapse of the Soviet Union following the unsuccessful coup of August 1991 not only brought an end to the 'Cold War', but also the demise of the Marxist system of economic management and the economic alliance between the East European countries. The former Soviet Union seemed to have used its CMEA alliance countries (Council for Mutual Economic Assistance) principally to absorb its exports of raw materials and fuels in exchange for their manufactured products, and at times, agricultural and food items (*World Economic Outlook*, October 1991, p. 26). Within its own borders, the Soviet Union promoted industrial production in gigantic state-owned monopolies which produced a final product for distribution across the boundaries of its republics (Stanglin *et al.*, 1991, p. 38). As a consequence, the economies of the republics are heavily interdependent on one another, at a time when each aspires to be an independent and sovereign nation. With the break-up of the former Soviet Union and the Marxist regimes in the other CMEA countries (Bulgaria, Czechoslovakia, former East Germany, Hungary, Poland and Romania), the republics and the states not only have to restructure their domestic economic operations in line with the market economies, but also have to learn how to trade competitively in convertible currencies. The hard fall from the decades of economic mismanagement was cushioned by the abilities of the CMEA members to barter each other's inefficient and, at times, inferior goods and services. Now that the alliance is gone, it will be difficult for them to find new markets in a competitive world. The short- and long-term prospects of these economies in international trade are the focus of this chapter. Before the future outlook is discussed, it is important to re-examine the recent past trading relations among the former Soviet Union's republics and the East European countries.

9.2 TRADE RELATIONS AMONG THE CMEA COUNTRIES

Table 9.1 presents data on intra-regional exports of the CMEA countries for 1989, the last year before the complete collapse of the alliance. It is clear that most of the exports of Bulgaria, former East Germany, Czechoslovakia, Hungary, and the Soviet Union went to the region. West Germany has also been included in the table to show how important it was for the trade of some of the CMEA countries. Roughly 22 per cent of East German exports went to West Germany, followed by Poland's 14 per cent, Hungary's 12 per cent, Czechoslovakia's 8 per cent, and Romania's 7.5 per cent. Even before the German reunification, East Germany exported almost as much to

Table 9.1   Regional trade of the East European countries in 1989 (percentage of exports)

	From						
	Bulgaria	Czechos-lovakia	East Germany	Hungary	Poland	Romania	USSR*
Bulgaria	—	2.3	2.0	0.7	1.6	1.7	9.1
Czechoslovakia	4.4	—	5.5	5.1	5.5	2.6	9.5
East Germany	5.6	6.6	—	5.4	4.2	4.2	10.7
West Germany†	1.1	8.3	21.4	11.9	14.2	7.5	3.6
Hungary	1.4	4.0	4.0	—	1.6	2.4	6.7
Poland	3.9	8.5	4.5	3.2	—	3.5	9.4
Romania	2.1	1.8	2.0	1.5	1.1	—	3.5
USSR	65.8	30.5	23.8	25.1	20.8	21.4	—
Total	84.3	62.0	63.2	52.9	49.0	43.3	52.5

* Data are for 1988.
† West Germany is included here because of its importance to East European trade.

Source: *The Europa World Yearbook, 1991*, vols I and II (London: Europa Publications).

Table 9.2   Regional trade of the East European countries in 1989
(percentage of imports)

	Bulgaria	Czechos-lovakia	East Germany	Hungary	Poland	Romania	USSR*
				To			
Bulgaria	—	2.2	1.8	0.1	1.3	3.0	10.6
Czechoslovakia	5.0	—	4.6	5.2	5.7	3.3	10.5
East Germany	5.8	7.8	—	6.2	4.4	5.8	10.8
West Germany†	4.9	9.3	19.8	16.0	15.7	3.4	5.0
Hungary	1.4	4.8	3.4	—	1.6	2.8	7.6
Poland	4.8	8.6	4.4	3.3	—	5.5	10.9
Romania	1.9	1.7	1.8	1.6	1.0	—	3.7
USSR	53.6	29.7	22.0	22.1	18.1	22.4	—
Total	77.4	64.1	57.8	54.5	47.8	46.2	59.1

* Data are for 1988.
† West Germany is included here because of its importance to East European trade.

Source: *The Europa World Yearbook, 1991*, vols I and II (London: Europa Publications).

West Germany as it did to its largest partner, the Soviet Union. Dependence on the Soviet export market was highest for Bulgaria, followed by Czechoslovakia, Hungary, East Germany, Romania and Poland.

Table 9.2 data show the percentage distribution of imports for the CMEA. Import data again reconfirm the extent of dependency of the countries in question to the former Soviet Union. The latter's trade seems to have been evenly divided among the CMEA countries, except with Romania and, to some extent, Hungary (see Tables 9.1 and 9.2). Although roughly over half of Soviet exports and imports were with the CMEA alliance, it was not overly dependent on any one of its satellite countries. This has not been so for the other nations in CMEA. Collapse of the old order would have been most disastrous for Bulgaria and least for the Soviet Union, if the latter would not have disintegrated into independent republics and nation states.

Perhaps, for a better understanding of the trading relations between the CMEA countries, one needs to examine the nature and composition of their exports and imports. Table 9.3 presents data on the distribution of exports by principal commodities for the CMEA nations. The major components of exports of each country, except

Table 9.3 Per cent distribution of exports by principal commodities in
1989

Commodity	Country						
	Bulgaria	Czechos-lovakia	East Germany	Hungary	Poland	Romania[†]	USSR*
CmdtyA	4.0	4.6	4.9	18.5	9.6	6.9[‡]	N.A.
CmdtyB	11.7	—	1.8	1.3	4.1[§]	‡	N.A.
CmdtyC	7.0[¶]	3.7	2.9	4.1	§	27.1[¶]	N.A.
CmdtyD	¶	5.2	8.3	2.9	9.6	¶	29.4[‖]
CmdtyE	—	—	0.1	—	§	—	N.A.
CmdtyF	3.4	7.6	12.1	12.4	10.5	8.6	N.A.
CmdtyG	1.9	22.4	18.7	17.0	10.5	—	N.A.
CmdtyH	60.5	44.4	36.5	30.2	38.4	37.6	16.2
CmdtyI	11.5	12.1	14.7	13.6	17.3	19.8	N.A.

CmdtyA: Food and live animals.
CmdtyB: Beverages and tobacco.
CmdtyC: Crude materials (inedible) except fuels.
CmdtyD: Mineral fuels, lubricants, etc.
CmdtyE: Animal and vegetable oils, fats and waxes.
CmdtyF: Chemicals and related products.
CmdtyG: Basic manufactures.
CmdtyH: Machinery and transport equipment.
CmdtyI: Misc. manufactured articles and other.

— Indicates data not available in this category, but have been included elsewhere.

* Data are for 1988.
† Data for 1987.
‡ 6.9 per cent for both categories.
§ 4.1 per cent includes all three categories.
¶ 7.0 per cent for both categories.
‖ Petroleum and petroleum products only.

Source: *The Europa World Yearbook, 1991*, vol. II (London: Europa Publications).

the Soviet Union, were 'machinery and transport equipment'. For the
Soviet Union, these were 'mineral fuels, lubricants, etc.' The bulk of
the exports as well as imports (see Table 9.4) seem to have consisted
of manufactured products (see the last four rows of Tables 9.3 and
9.4). However, these included very little of consumption goods as is
evident from the size of percentages in the last row of the two tables.
Hungary seems to have produced enough food products to export
sizeable amounts to the CMEA alliance countries, especially to the
former Soviet Union. Poland followed Hungary in generating export
surpluses in food and agricultural products (see Table 9.3).

Table 9.4   Per cent distribution of imports by principal commodities in 1989

Commodity	Country						
	Bulgaria*	Czechos-lovakia	East Germany	Hungary	Poland	Romania†	USSR*
CmdtyA	‡	6.9	8.8	6.2	13.6§	1.3¶	N.A.
CmdtyB	—	—	1.9	—	§	¶	N.A.
CmdtyC	36.7‖	8.8	6.3	6.3	8.7	53.5‖	N.A.
CmdtyD	‖	17.3	14.5	11.8	12.7	‖	N.A.
CmdtyE	5.4‡	—	0.3	—	§	—	N.A.
CmdtyF	5.4	2.5	9.0	16.3	15.0	5.0	2.5
CmdtyG	—	10.4	18.6	17.5	9.5	—	N.A.
CmdtyH	41.6	36.9	31.6	33.4	37.0	28.4	40.9
CmdtyI	7.8	6.2	9.0	6.9	3.5	11.8	N.A.

CmdtyA, food and live animals; CmdtyB, beverages and tobacco; CmdtyC, crude materials (inedible) except fuels; CmdtyD, mineral fuels, lubricants, etc.; CmdtyE, animal and vegetable oils, fats and waxes; CmdtyF, chemicals and related products; CmdtyG, basic manufactures; CmdtyH, machinery and transport equipment; CmdtyI, Misc. manufactured articles and other.

— Indicates data not available in this category, but have been included elsewhere.

* Data are for 1988.
† Data for 1987.
‡ 5.4 per cent for both categories.
§ 13.6 per cent includes all three categories.
¶ 1.3 per cent for both categories.
‖ 53.5 per cent for both categories.

Source: *The Europa World Yearbook, 1991*, vol. II (London: Europa Publications).

From the International Monetary Fund sources, it appears that Czechoslovakia had small current account surpluses during the 1986–1989 period, while it generated a deficit of $817 million in 1990 (IMF, 1991b, p. 325). Hungary experienced current account deficits during the 1986–1989 period in amounts ranging from $800 million to $1.5 billion (IMF, 1991b, p. 423). Poland had small current account deficits in 1987 and 1988. However, in 1989 the deficit jumped to $1.586 billion (IMF, 1991b, p. 613). Romania, which pursued a policy of repaying foreign debts by choking the domestic economy, generated substantial current account surpluses between 1982 and 1989 (IMF, 1991b, p. 623; 1991c, p. 334). With the fall of the Marxist regime and the increased trade with non-CMEA countries, it accumulated a deficit of over $3 billion in 1990. According to the *Direction of Trade*

Statistics Yearbook, 1991, exports and imports of Bulgaria, East Germany, and the USSR were essentially in balance through 1990 (IMF, 1991c, p. 36). Not much data are available on the inter-republic trade of the former USSR. Turkmenistan was the most and Russia the least dependent on inter-republic trade (*The Economist*, 1991). In 1988 such trade (7.9 billion roubles of exports plus imports) was equivalent to around 76 per cent of Turkmenistan's total output. The next most dependent republic was Armenia with about 58 per cent (7.7 billion roubles of exports and imports), followed by Molda-via with 52 per cent (9.8 billion roubles); Estonia 52 per cent (5.7 billion roubles); Latvia with 50 per cent (9.1 billion roubles); Byelo-russia with 48 per cent (32.4 billion roubles); Lithuania with 48 per cent (11.7 billion roubles); Tadzhikistan with 46 per cent (5.0 billion roubles); Georgia with 45 per cent (10.7 billion roubles); Kirghizia with 44 per cent (5.5. billion roubles); Azerbaijan with 42 per cent (11.7 billion roubles); Uzbekistan with 40 per cent (20.6 billion roubles); Ukraine with 30 per cent (83.1 billion roubles); Kazakhstan with 30 per cent (22 billion roubles); and the least dependent Russia with around 13 per cent (138.3 billion roubles). With the collapse of the USSR and the rising aspiration for economic independence among the former republics, it may not be far-fetched to assert that their economic as well as balance-of-payments problems may roughly approximate the proportion of their inter-republic export–import trade to their individual domestic outputs.

Internal trade deficit as percentage of output for 1988 (Passell, 1991, p. A13) was 32 per cent for Moldavia, the highest among the republics, if one excludes the now-independent states of Lithuania (38 per cent), Estonia (29 per cent), and Latvia (16 per cent). The second highest deficit was for Kazakhstan (24 per cent); followed by Armenia and Tadzhikistan (each with 20 per cent); Georgia and Kirghizia (each with 18 per cent deficit); Uzbekistan (10 per cent), Byelorussia (8 per cent), Azerbaijan (4 per cent), and Ukraine (3 per cent). Turkmenistan's trade was in balance, while Russia had a trade surplus of 8 per cent. Since Russia's domestic output was roughly 50 per cent of the former Soviet Union, the trade surplus in absolute size was substantial (*The Economist*, 1991, p. 22).

Table 9.5   Composition of net material product[1] in 1989
(Percentages)

Sector	Country						
	Bulgaria*	Czechos-lovakia	East Germany	Hungary[†]	Poland	Romania[‡]	USSR[§]
Sctr.A	12.6	9.1	10.0[¶]	14.1[¶]	13.1	—	20.4[¶]
Sctr.B	0.4	0.01	[¶]	[¶]	1.2	—	[¶]
Sctr.C	58.1	58.2	64.9	29.8	50.2	60.0	44.8
Sctr.D	9.4	10.6	7.2	6.3	9.6	—	12.5
Sctr.E	8.4	16.2	8.9	9.4	18.6	—	[‖]
Sctr.F	7.0	3.5	5.3**	7.3**	4.3	—	6.1**
Sctr.G	1.8	0.01	**	**	0.06	—	**
Sctr.H	2.3	0.01	3.7	33.1[††]	2.3	—	16.2[‖]

Sctr.A, agriculture and fishery; Sctr.B, forestry; Sctr.C, industry; Sctr.D, construction; Sctr.E, trade, restaurants, etc.; Sctr.F, transportation and storage; Sctr.G, communications; Sctr.H, others.

[1] Net Material Product or NMP is defined as 'the total net value of goods and "productive" services, including turnover taxes, produced by the economy. This excludes economic activities not contributing directly to material production, such as public administration, defence and personal and professional services.' (See source below.)

* Data for 1988.
† Data are for GDP.
‡ Data are not available for Romania. In 1985 industry contributed more than 60 per cent to NMP.
§ Data are for 1987, latest available.
¶ Sectors A and B combined.
‖ 'Others' include trade, distribution, etc.
** Sectors F and G combined.
†† This data cannot be compared with those of other countries in the table because of GDP figures used.

Source: *The Europa World Yearbook, 1991*, vol. II (London: Europa Publications).

9.3   COMPOSITION OF THE ECONOMIES AND FUTURE SHAPE OF THEIR BALANCE OF PAYMENTS

Table 9.5 presents data on the Net Material Product, NMP (see note in Table 9.5 for definition) of the CMEA countries for 1989. Consistent data are not available for these countries and, as such, inter-country comparisons are at best approximations. One thing is clear from the data and that is, the CMEA countries paid little attention to the development of the services sector (services are included under

'Others' in Table 9.5). Hungary is the only country in this group which had a semblance of a service sector, and even that is inadequate by Western standards, where it represents well over 50 per cent of GDPs (see *World Development Report 1991*, p. 209). Non-material services constituted around 20 per cent of Hungary's GDP in 1989 (Boote and Somogyi, 1991, Table 3, p. 32).

There are quite a few similarities between the CMEA countries as far as the percentage share of 'industry' to NMP is concerned. 'Industry', which includes principally manufacturing, mining, electricity, gas and water supply, constitute the bulk of the material output of all the countries except Hungary (see Table 9.5). Agriculture, fishery, and forestry contributed anywhere from 9.2 per cent for Czechoslovakia to 20.4 per cent for the USSR. Contribution of 'construction' ranges from 6.3 per cent for Hungary to 12.5 per cent for USSR. Percentage share of 'construction,' 'Trade, restaurants, etc.,' also vary among the former CMEA members in a similar fashion. Because of lack of adequate and reliable data, not much can be said about the contribution of the other sectors in the CMEA economies.

One characteristic that was common among the East European countries was the predominance of the state-owned sectors in the value-added in national incomes. In the mid-1980s the share of the state-owned sector was 97 per cent for Czechoslovakia and East Germany, 96 per cent for the Soviet Union, 86 per cent for Hungary, and 82 per cent for Poland (*The Economist*: A Survey of Business in Eastern Europe, 21 September 1991, Survey, p. 10). Not only the state sector accounted for most of the value-added, in the case of the Soviet Union, state industrial enterprises were concentrated in single giant plants, often located in a single republic. According to a report (Stanglin *et al.*, 1991, p. 38), more than 2000 products, including 80 per cent of industrial machines, were produced in one giant plant. Thus, Azerbaijan supplied 100 per cent of all oil-well pumps used in the former Soviet Union. Similarly, 99 per cent of die-casting machines came from Moldavia; Ukraine supplied 86 per cent of the USSR's fork-lifts, and 100 per cent of corn harvesters; Uzbekistan supplied 100 per cent of cotton harvesters; Russia produced 100 per cent of tramway rails and sewing machines; and Armenia contributed 100 per cent of cigarette filters (Stanglin *et al.*, 1991). Such an overwhelming dependence for major industrial products on a single republic complicates future trade relationships among the members of the former Soviet Union. The task of converting these economies into a market system, as if it were not difficult enough for the republics of former Soviet Union, they had to endure the August 1991 failed coup attempt by the Soviet hardliners. Its GNP declined by 6.4 per cent in 1990 from that of 1989, and possibly another 17 per cent or so in 1991 (Forman, 1991, p. A1) because of the complete breakdown of the Union.

The fall of the communist regimes and the struggle to establish market economies brought with it economic declines throughout Eastern Europe. Poland's GNP declined by 12 per cent in 1990 and possibly another 4 per cent in 1991 (*The Economist*, ibid., p. 5); Czechoslovakia experienced declines of 3.1 and 9.8 per cent, respectively, for 1990 and 1991; comparable figures for Romania were around 10 per cent each year; for Hungary 3.5 per cent and 6 per cent; and for Bulgaria 11.8 and 19.8 per cent. According to the IMF sources, real GDP in these countries (excluding the USSR) was expected to fall by 12 per cent in 1991 or a drop of 19 per cent for 1990–91 period (*World Economic Outlook*, October 1991, p. 20). The decline in the real GDP of the former USSR was expected to be far larger.

The declines in trade among the former CMEA partners were expected to be far more severe than what they saw in their GDPs. For example, the IMF estimates indicate that CMEA exports in 1991 to Hungary and the USSR probably declined by 35 to 45 per cent; by 50 to 65 per cent to Bulgaria, Czechoslovakia, and Romania, and by 75 per cent to Poland (ibid., p. 26). Greater the dependence on the CMEA trade, more severe is likely to be the decline in the GDP. For example, *Bulgaria* with 83 per cent of exports going to and 73 per cent of imports coming from the CMEA countries experienced a dramatic reduction in liquidity, in industries geared for exports, and in the process brought down the real wages by two-thirds in the first half of 1991 (ibid., p. 27). Unemployment rose sharply to 5–6 per cent in an economy where it used to be less than 2 per cent in December 1990.

Czechoslovakia, whose industries were geared for exports to the Soviet markets (see Table 9.1) and the other CMEA nations, will find it difficult to redirect its exports to other regions. In 1990, its sales of machinery and transport equipment to the Soviet Union dropped by 30 per cent and possibly by a larger percentage in 1991. Sales of chemicals and other products also declined by 25 to 30 per cent in 1990.

Hungary faced more than a 50 per cent drop in its trade of most products in 1990 with the CMEA members. The only bright picture for Hungary is the increase in trade in machinery with non-CMEA countries. Since this trade with the CMEA countries consisted of products that were labour intensive, Hungary's unemployment rate was expected to shoot up to 6–8 per cent by the end of 1991 from a low of 2 per cent of the labour force early in the year (ibid., p. 28).

Romania experienced a 17 per cent decline in its production of industrial goods in the first half of 1991 from the same period in 1990 because of contraction of exports to CMEA countries. It also witnessed a jump in unemployment in its labour force – from 2 per cent to around 8 per cent in 1991 (ibid., p. 28).

The collapse of the alliance, particularly the disintegration of the former Soviet Union, not only deprived the East European countries of each other's assured markets, but also left in each country large amounts of wasted capital stocks in the form of useless plants, equipment, and facilities that cannot be salvaged to produce for the market economy (Junz, 1991, p. 176). To compete successfully in the world arena, these countries will have to invest heavily in modern infrastructure, technologically advanced plants and facilities, and in developing a viable service sector. Among the former CMEA nations, Hungary got a head start. Since 1968, it has been experimenting with market-oriented reforms, while Poland has pursued some reform since 1981–82 (Wolf, 1991, p. 45). Because of the lack of political will, not much headway was made by either country until recent years. It is estimated that roughly 25–30 per cent of Hungary's and up to 40 per cent of Poland's economies are now under private sector (*The Economist*, Survey, ibid., p. 14; see also Hare, 1991, pp. 195–201).

A beginning towards a market economy was made in Bulgaria on 1 February 1990, when most prices except basic foodstuffs were liberalized. However, economic reorganization will be a long and hard one for Bulgaria, especially since its economy was geared towards the needs of the CMEA's interests (in subsidized industries) rather than based on its comparative advantage in agriculture (Jackson, 1991, pp. 203–9).

Czechoslovakia has been pursuing the policy of privatization for its economy since 1990 with issuance of vouchers to citizens which will allow them to bid for shares of firms to be privatized (Brada, 1991, pp. 171–77). The process has been slow because of the continuation of some of the old rules and regulations. Romania has not yet been able to shed all its connection with the communist past. The present government does not command much confidence of its people and, as such, is not conducive to the growth of a market economy (Ben-Ner and Montias, 1991, pp. 163–70). Romania's economy as well as its trade is likely to continue to shrink in the near future.

The picture within the former Soviet Union is at best muddled. Before the break-up of the Union, Byelorussia had the highest per capita income ($5960) among the republics, followed by Russia ($5810), Armenia ($4710), Ukraine ($4700), Georgia ($4410), Moldavia ($3830), Azerbaijan ($3750), Kazakhstan ($3720), Turkmenistan ($3370), Kirghizia ($3030), Uzbekistan ($2750), and Tadzhikistan ($2340). These 1989 figures (*The New York Times*, 1991, p. F6) are probably over-estimates of the republics' GNPs since they all experienced significant declines in their economies in 1990 and 1991. At the time of writing, their economies are in shambles. Of all the republics, Ukraine has the best potential for economic growth, followed closely by Russia (Passeil, 1991, p. A13), with Tadzhikistan the least. However, it all depends on political stability and the zeal with which the peoples and their governments accept privatization and the market economy. Each republic faces internal discord from diverse ethnic groups, and each has to reorient its economy in line with its resource base and away from the needs of the central planners from Moscow. The giant plants and factories erected by the Soviet Union to fuel its armament-based economy are now white elephants. Investment in new technologies to produce marketable goods and services will require not only economic co-operation among the republics, but also massive support from abroad (Dentzer, 1991, p. 43), which may not be forthcoming soon, given the economic downturn in the West.

As of November 1991, aid pledged to East Europe amounted to around $45 billion (Montgomery, 1991, p. D20), of which only 20 per cent was actually disbursed. The need is far greater than what the developed West can afford to advance to the former CMEA nations. Given the disparate needs for aid by the poorer countries of Africa, Asia and Latin America, it will be morally difficult to justify pouring in aid to the middle income countries of Eastern Europe (Collins, 1991, pp. 219–27). Unless there are massive uprisings and chaos within the region, aid money will flow in at a pace the individual economies can absorb meaningfully. In the meantime, each of the countries will amass significant amounts of deficits in their balance of payments for the foreseeable future. Even the mineral resource rich Republic of Russia faces huge deficits as it struggles to modernize its extractive industries.

9.4 CONCLUSION

The former Soviet Union and its CMEA alliance countries face the dual task of dismantling the outmoded factories and plants along with the economic system that brought them, and rebuilding their economies to meet the needs of their people and the world market. It seems that the first task of dismantling of the old systems is yet to start in earnest (*The Economist*, 1992, p. 43) and only time will tell how soon the newly privatized ventures begin to bear fruit. One thing is certain though, these countries, trade balances will be in deficit for some time to come.

REFERENCES

BEN-NER, A. and MONTIAS, J. M. (1991) 'The Introduction of Markets in a Hypercentralized Economy: The Case of Romania', *Journal of Economic Perspectives*, vol. 5. no. 4 (Fall) pp. 163–70.

BOOTE, A. R. and SOMOGYI, J. (1991) *Economic Reform in Hungary Since 1968*, Occasional Paper No. 83 (Washington DC: International Monetary Fund, July)

BRADA, J. C. (1991) 'The Economic Transition of Czechoslovakia from Plan to Market', *Journal of Economic Perspectives*, vol. 5, no. 4 (Fall) pp. 171–77.

COLLINS, S. M. (1991) 'Policy Watch: U.S. Economic Policy Toward the Soviet Union and Eastern Europe', *Journal of Economic Perspectives*, vol. 5, no. 4 (Fall) pp. 219–27.

DENTZER, S. (1991) 'The Moment of Truth: The Economic Choice is Now between Strong Medicine and Disaster', *U.S. News & World Report*, 23 December p. 43.

The Economist (1991) 'Russia's Future: Whither the Flying Troika?', *The Economist*, 7 December 1991, pp. 21–4.

The Economist (1992) 'Russia: A Taste of Spring', and 'The Moscow Circus', *The Economist*, 8 February 1992, p. 43.

Europa Publications, *The Europa World Yearbook 1991*, vols. I and II (London: Europa Publications).

FORMAN, C. (1991) 'Freedom's Perils: Soviet Economy Holds Potential for Disaster as the Union Weakens', *The Wall Street Journal*, 4 September pp. A1 and A8.

HARE, P. G. (1991) 'Hungary: In Transition to a Market Economy', *Journal of Economic Perspectives*, vol. 5, no. 4 (Fall) pp. 195–201.

IMF (1991a) *World Economic Outlook, October 1991* (Washington DC: International Monetary Fund, 1991) p. 26.

IMF (1991b) *International Financial Statistics Yearbook 1991* (Washington DC: International Monetary Fund)

IMF (1991c) *Direction of Trade Statistics Yearbook 1991* (Washington DC: International Monetary Fund).

JACKSON, M. (1991) 'The Rise and Decay of the Socialist Economy in Bulgaria', *Journal of Economic Perspectives*, vol. 5, no. 4 (Fall) pp. 203–9.

JUNZ, H. B. (1991) 'Integration of Eastern Europe into the World Trading System', *The American Economic Review*, vol. 81, no. 2 (May) pp. 176–80.

MONTGOMERY, P. L. (1991) Aid to East Europe Put at $45 billion', *The New York Times*, 12 Nov. p. D20.

The New York Times (1991) Figure entitled, 'All Across the U.S.S.R: The Soviet Republics by Region', *The New York Times*, 1 September 1991, p. F6.

PASSELL, P. (1991) 'A Centerless Soviet Economy May Not be So Bad, Western Experts Say', *The New York Times*, 5 Sept. p. A13.

STANGLIN, D. *et al.* (1991) 'Now the Birth of a Nation', *U.S. News & World Report*, 23 December 1991, pp. 34–41.

WOLF, T. A. (1991) "The Lessons of Limited Market-Oriented Reform', *Journal of Economic Prospects*, vol. 5, no. 4 (Fall) pp. 45–58.

The World Bank (1991) *World Development Report 1991* (Washington DC: The World Bank).

Part V

Foreign Debt and Country Risk Analysis

Part V examines foreign debt and country risk analysis, and sets forth new lessons from the debt crisis. In Chapter 10, 'Foreign Exchange Dynamics, Debt and the "Peso Problem"', Dilip K. Ghosh presents the picture of Mexico suffering under gargantuan foreign debt, intractable rates of inflation and persistently plummeting value of the peso that has triggered a real and fundamental disequilibrium in which the policy makers and people have appeared totally helpless. In the chapter, it has been pointed out that since relation between sovereign borrowers and sovereign lenders is like that of the partners in a three-legged race in which both can run, limp or fall together, but cannot part company, it is absolutely necessary and expedient for both Mexico and its lenders to agree upon a new schedule for loan amortization to their mutual benefit, if not for their immediate relief. Christopher A. Erickson and Elliott Willman, in 'International Lending and Sovereign Debt in the Presence of Agency Costs: the Case of Mexico' (Chapter 11), offer a powerful and novel analysis of foreign debt by introducing agency costs in their model. It is shown that as long as some entrepreneurs are incompletely collateralized, the optimum government policy is to borrow the maximum possible amount from international lenders and transfer the proceeds to the private sector. It is further demonstrated that any reduction in government borrowing capacity results in a decline in domestic economic activities, and that decline does not end until the government rehabilitates its maximal borrowing capacity. Within the straitjacket of this analysis, Erickson and Willman examine the Mexican economy. Chapter 12 explains how country risk analysis can be profitably made by analytic hierarchy process. Chapter 13 provides an exposition of political risk by taking a rational expectation approach on Latin American stock markets.

10 Foreign Exchange Dynamics, Debt and the 'Peso Problem'

Dilip K. Ghosh

10.1 INTRODUCTION

Located next to the largest economy of the world, Mexico – the second largest Latin American nation – has been experiencing a process of painful adjustments for over a decade and half. Its financial woe owing to its gargantuan foreign debt, intractable rates of inflation and plummeting value of the peso has brought about real and fundamental economic disequilibrium, and the economy hardly seems to be pulled back toward an order by any centripetal forces or by any governmental policy menu. The Government has been trying seriously to correct or, at least to contain, the continuous downslide of the economy, but nothing appears to be working well. It is quite ironic that when the peso is greatly depreciating in the market, it is often getting overvalued in reality by the combined effects of the *Fisher Open Principle* and the *Purchasing Power Parity*.[1] This sort of turn or twist causing the paradox of appreciation in the midst of depreciation probably further sustains the plunging condition of the Mexican currency. Some analysts argue that since the foreign exchange market is not always efficient, even a low probability of an event may cause a large change in the exchange rates, and this is what is happening with the peso. This is the so-called 'peso problem'. It is, unlike 'speculating bubbles', as amplified by Blanchard (1979), Tirole (1982) and Blanchard and Watson (1982), an exchange rate dynamics of disequilibrium in which expectation of expansionary policy menu induces an actual erosion in current exchange rate and thus forces current inflationary pressures ahead of any expansion. Lizondo (1983) and Krasker (1982) highlight this problem, and Salant and Henderson (1978) contend that it is a generic problem of asset markets with speculators actively over-reacting, or to put it in the words of Dornbusch (1982) (it is a problem where) 'asset market-oriented adjustment of exchange rate works with an overkill'. In this study, we re-examine the peso problem and attempt to ascertain the reasons behind this problem. To do so effectively, it is incumbent as well as instructive that we review some of the vital statistics of Mexico that may provide an insight and a useful backdrop against which our analysis may be duly appreciated.

10.2   THE ECONOMIC BACKDROP

Since the exchange rate of a currency is essentially determined at the balance-of-payments equilibrium – by traders', speculators' and arbitrageurs' activities – it is instructive that we look into the balance-of-payments conditions of Mexico, and since the term 'peso problem' was coined because of the anticipated trouble with this currency just around its devaluation in 1976, it is important that we exhibit the data on current account balance (CUB), capital account balance (CAB), unilateral transfers (UT), official reserve account (ORA), net errors and omissions (NRO), different price indices and foreign debts from that year on. Tables 10.1, 10.2 and 10.3 show a summary picture of the Mexican economy.

Table 10.1   Balance of payments (millions of US dollars)

Year	Current account	Capital account	Unilateral transfers	Official reserve	Net errors and omissions
1976	−3 408	5 545	157	1 188	−2 618
1977	−1 854	2 473	169	1 649	−56
1978	−3 171	3 701	192	1 842	−87
1979	−5 459	5 144	225	2 072	314
1980	−8 162	12 890	275	2 960	−3 933
1981	−13 899	23 208	289	4 074	−8 840
1982	−6 307	1 463	303	834	−6 157
1983	5 403	−8 786	302	3 913	−925
1984	4 194	−3 890	410	7 272	−973
1985	1 130	−3 071	1 000	4 906	−1 765
1986	−1 673	764	464	5 670	458
1987	3 968	−2 453	648	12 464	2 605
1988	−2 905	−6 691	615	5 279	−467
1989		−3 595			

Source: *IMF International Financial Statistics*, Feb. 1984 and Dec. 1989.

Table 10.2   Percentage change in prices

Year	GDP deflator	Consumer prices	Wholesale prices
1976	0.42	15.8	22.0
1977	0.55	29.0	41.2
1978	0.65	17.5	15.8
1979	0.78	18.2	18.3
1980	1.00	26.4	24.5
1981	1.27	27.9	24.4
1982	2.01	58.9	56.1
1983	0.40	101.6	107.6
1984	0.65	65.5	70.4
1985	1.00	57.7	53.6
1986	1.81	86.2	88.4
1987		131.8	135.6
1988		114.2	107.8
1989		24.7	17.9

Source: *IMF International Financial Statistics*, Feb. 1984 and Dec. 1989.

Table 10.3   Foreign debt

Year	Foreign debt	Year	Foreign debt
1976	27.33	1984	95.8
1977	30.63	1985	96.86
1978	33.80	1986	100.87
1979	40.40	1987	109.45
1980	48.60	1988	100.75
1981	75.30	1989	95.64
1982	87.60	1990	–
1983	93.80		

Source: IMF International Financial Statistics.

Table 10.1 clearly portrays the continuing disequilibrium in the balance-of-payments accounts and it certainly spells out that the foreign exchange market for Mexico is in turbulence and disarray. The official reserve account as an accommodating balance has been seriously ineffective because of the negative reserve positions in most of the years under examinations. The external shock, triggered by contractions in exports, increase in imports and hikes in interest rates on foreign borrowing, has produced an overall adverse terms of trade for the country, and as a result current account balance has been consistently in the red until 1982 – the year when the peso became devalued again – (initially 40 per cent – on the night of 17 February) and the two-tier exchange rate was instituted (on 6 August). The current account improved in 1983 and has stayed in the black more often since then, but the magnitude has been on the decrease. One should note that capital account balance dropped dramatically in 1983 and it maintained its negative value in the subsequent years with the exception only of 1986 when it turned positive. Since the announcement of the dual exchange structure, speculation against the peso started and soon escalated to the extent that dollar-denominated deposits in the Mexican banks could not be withdrawn in dollars and the banks were ordered to suspend temporarily foreign exchange transactions. President Lopez Portillo's announcement of bank nationalization and foreign exchange controls on 1 September 1982, created a good deal of panic for everyone involved with Mexico. This created a lot of confusion, and all markets were out of balance.

10.3   THEORETICAL ANALYSIS

It is well known that when:[2]

$$BOP = ep^m x(p^m, e) - p^u m(p^m, e, y^m) + UT + K(r^m - r^u) + ORA + NRO = 0,$$

the external market is cleared and the equilibrium exchange rate is determined. Theoretically, when traders', speculators' and arbitrageurs' reaction functions are taken in tandem, we obtain the following schedules of optimum excess demand and supply of the currency under consideration, and their intersection determines the equilibrium value of the exchange rate in the spot and the forward markets (see Figure 10.1(a), (b), (c)).

Here along the vertical axis we measure current forward exchange rate ($e_{f(o)}$) in Figure 10.1(a), current spot exchange rate ($e_{s(o)}$) in Figure 10.1(b), and current forward spot exchange rate ratio ($e_{f(o)}/e_{s(o)}$) in Figure 10.1(c), and along the horizontal axis demand and supply of the peso are measured. In Figure 10.1(a), the demand schedule *DD*, that reflects the speculative behaviour, is the lateral (horizontal) summation of the excess demand for the peso of all speculators in the forward market. Figure 10.1(b), with a little sim-

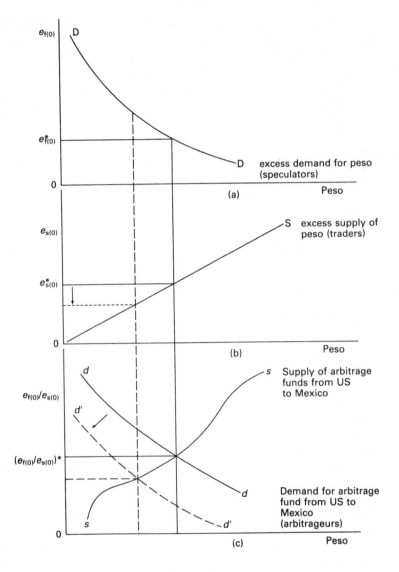

Figure 10.1

plification, illustrates that excess supply of the peso in the spot market, derived from the exports and imports of goods and services. Finally, in Figure 10.1(c), the demand for arbitrage funds is represented by the *dd* schedule, and the supply of it is given by the *ss* schedule. The

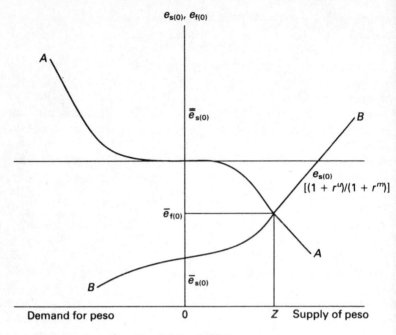

Figure 10.2

intersection of the *dd* curve and *ss* curve determines the equilibrium, and, in this illustrative diagram $e^*_{s(o)}$ and $e^*_{f(o)}$ are the equilibrium values of the current spot and forward rates of exchange. The continuous variations in trade flows, capital movements, currency speculations and so on keep impacting on the momentary values of the exchange rate. A speculation against the peso, as we have noted already since August 1982, causes a shift of the *dd* curve to the *d'd'* curve and triggers the downward revision of the peso's external value. Drawn slightly differently, following the classic work of Grubel (1966), the equilibrating forces are as shown in Figure 10.2.

Here *AA* and *BB* represent, respectively, the arbitrageurs' and speculators–traders' schedule of reactions at different rates of exchange. If the current spot rate is $\bar{e}_{s(o)}$, and if it is less than the forward parity, i.e., $e_{s(o)} [(1 + r^u)/(1 + r^m)]$, as in Figure 10.2, market clearing conditions dictate speculators and traders to hold a forward commitment of $0Z$ amount of the peso for delivery and arbitrageurs to take the delivery at the equilibrium forward rate $\bar{e}_{f(o)}$. In such a situation, speculative sentiment would expect a stable spot rate. But if the spot rate happens to be $\bar{e}_{s(o)}$ ($> e_{s(o)} [(1 + r^u)/(1 + r^m)]$), speculators would anticipate the devaluation of the peso, and as a result of this anticipation, there will be a capital flight from Mexico to the United States. This is a case where speculation induces the spot market funds to move from high-interest economy Mexico to low-interest economy United States. This analysis fits well with the ongoing Mexican conditions in the foreign exchange market, and the result is that there is a constant pounding on the peso and a continuing dollarization of Mexican assets. Against the backdrop of this theoretical analysis, it is appropriate to point out that the peso does not have a forward market, and the equilibrium, as envisaged in the theoretical explanation of exchange rate movements, does not exist. This criticism, although quite meaningful, is not a serious problem, since upon reflection, one can recognize that in a highly interdependent world, international market participants create through currency substitutions as good a forward market as a visible one that exists for a hard currency such as US dollars. People with the pesos are constantly converting this currency into other currencies in the spot market and taking spot/forward positions in anticipation of future spot rates and speculative gains. What is happening with the peso is a continuing triangular intertemporal currency substitution by traders, hedgers, speculators and arbitrageurs with their unending anticipation of fluctuations in the value of the currency. 'The peso problem', which is virtually the replay of pre-Poincaré French episode of the franc's continuous tumbling (1925–26), reminds us of Ragnar Nurkse's (1944) famous observations:

anticipations are apt to bring about their own realization. Anticipatory purchases of foreign exchange tend to produce or at any rate to hasten the anticipated fall in the exchange value of the national currency, and the actual fall may be set up or strengthen expectations of a further fall . . . Exchange rates in such circumstances are bound to become highly unstable, and the influence of psychological factors may at times be overwhelming.

Baumol (1957), Stein (1961) and Kemp (1963) stress very pointedly this destabilizing character of speculative binge, although Friedman (1956) has a strong case against it. Following Blanchard (1979), Dornbusch (1982) shows that a 'rational' speculative bubble consists of three factors as follows:

Table 10.4   Main interest rates

	Mexico			United States		
Year	T-Bill	Time deposits	Commercial bank lending	T-Bill	Time deposits	Commercial bank lending
1976				4.99	6.77	6.84
1977		11.0		5.27	6.69	6.82
1978	12.75	12.0	18.2	7.22	8.29	9.06
1979	17.89	16.75	19.9	10.04	9.71	12.67
1980	27.73	26.15	28.1	11.62	11.55	15.27
1981	33.23	31.82	36.6	14.08	14.44	18.87
1982	57.44	52.54	46.02	10.72	12.92	14.86
1983	53.78	54.70	63.03	8.62	10.45	10.79
1984	49.18	47.78	54.73	9.57	11.89	12.04
1985	63.36	59.48	55.23	7.49	8.05	9.93
1986	88.57	84.68	75.91	5.97	6.52	8.35
1987	103.07	97.24	92.44	5.83	6.86	8.21
1988	61.95	52.93	52.70	6.67	7.73	9.32
1989	54.43	31.75	31.05	7.85	8.73	10.66

Source: *IMF International Financial Statistics*, Feb. 1984 and Dec. 1989.

$$e_{s(t+1)} - e_{s(t)} = (1-a)^{-1}(r^m - r^u) + a(1-a)^{-1}[e_{s(t)} - \bar{e}_{s(t)}]$$

where a is the probability of a crash to the fundamental spot rate at time t, $e_{s(t)}$. These factors are the international interest rate differential, $(r^m - r^u)$, a and undervaluation of the exchange rate, $(e_{s(t)} - \bar{e}_{s(t)}$. The more undervalued the exchange rate, the higher the interest rate differential and higher the probability of crash, the greater the rate of depreciation. Table 10.4 exhibits the interest rates of two countries only for a simple illustrative purpose. It is evident that the positive interest rate differential between Mexico and the United States is regularly blowing the bubble up and triggering the nose-dive of the peso in the external market. It can, however, be contended, as Salant and Henderson (1978) show, that if the people's fear and frenzy get magnified because the contingencies contemplated by the public are not in fact the intentions of the policy makers, the external value of any currency will stay off course. The peso problem is a corroboration of this thesis.

10.4 THE FOREIGN DEBT

One might still wonder if all these adequately explain the downswing of the peso. It is imperative, therefore, at this juncture that we focus our attention on the foreign debt Mexico has incurred over the years (see Table 10.3). Although the balance-of-payments accounts do not explicitly show an item such as foreign debt, there is a relationship as pointed out by Dornbusch in Smith and Cuddington (1985), and it is as follows:

increase in gross foreign debt = current account deficit − direct and long-term portfolio capital inflows + official and reserve increases + other private capital outflows.

It is now not too difficult to see how growth of external debt has a negative impact on the exchange value of a currency. One can note that until 1980 the external debt was, by the current standard, moderate probably because borrowing was relatively cheap, the interest rate hovering around 10 per cent in nominal terms and minus 5 per cent in real terms.[3] But in 1981 foreign debt jumped to $75.3 billion and thereafter it has been steadily increasing. At the end of 1985 the foreign debt stood at $96 billion and the servicing charge is approximately $11 billion. This debt crisis escalated owing to, among other things, a significant drop in oil prices, SEPAFIN's policy of bumping buyers unwilling to pay, the Mexican prices from PEMEX's customers' list, virtual depletion of foreign exchange reserves in 1982 and foreign banks' reluctance to extend medium-term loans to Mexico. The IMF managing director also took a decision of not recommending the approval of the IMF Agreement (with the Mexican Administration calling for a net flow of funds from private foreign banks to the Mexican public sector in 1983) to the Executive Board of the IMF without assurances from both official sources and commercial banks that adequate external financing would be in place for the success of the Mexican Adjustment Program and the IMF Agreement, and that the principles of a realistic restructuring scheme of the Mexican debt would be favourably considered by the community. But because of the active role of the IMF and the US Federal Reserve, 526 foreign banks finally extended credit at the rate of 2.5 per cent over LIBOR and thus the IMF managing director's position and Mexican problems were, at least temporarily, overcome. The Government of Mexico adopted the corrective measures by way of devaluation and import

Table 10.5   Average exchange rates

Year	Nominal	Real*
1976	15.43	26.93
1977	22.57	31.80
1978	22.77	29.15
1979	22.81	26.29
1980	22.95	22.56
1981	24.52	20.75
1982	54.99	31.24
1983	120.09	276.81
1984	167.83	247.81
1985	256.90	254.07
1986	611.80	344.10
1987	1 378.20	
1988	2 273.10	
1989	2 568.00	

*Real = (Nominal • US GDP Deflator)/Mexico's GDP Deflator.

Source: *IMF International Financial Statistics*, Feb. 1984 and Dec. 1989.

restrictions, imposition of exchange control, institution of a two-tier exchange system and restructuring the external debt payments. From September 1983 to December 1984, the rates were allowed, under the central bank supervision, to depreciate by 13 centavos against the dollar on a daily basis. In December 1984 the rate of depreciation rose to 17 centavos a day to the dollar, and in March 1985 to 21 centavos a day. On 8 May 1985 the controlled rate of exchange was 216.67 pesos per US dollar, the free market rate was 234.08 pesos to the dollar, and the black market rate was much worse. On 11 October 1985 the free market rate dipped to 399 pesos and the controlled rate to 310 pesos per US dollar. On the yearly basis, the mean value of the exchange rate from 1976 through 1989 has been as shown in Table 10.5.

10.5   THE PROSPECT

Since relations between sovereign borrowers and lenders is like that of partners in a three-legged race that they can run, limp or fall together, but they cannot part company, it is absolutely necessary and economically expedient for both Mexico and its lenders to agree

Table 10.6   Debt amortization schedule (in millions of US dollars)

Year	Before	After
1985	9 371	3 221
1986	8 498	1 565
1987	13 469	3 685
1988	11 778	2 443
1989	10 097	3 771
1990	8 032	4 409

Source: PP.23, *Quarterly Economic Reviews of Mexico*, 1985 Annual Supplement, the Economist Intelligence Unit, London, UK.

upon a new schedule for loan amortization to their mutual benefit, it not to their immediate relief. The IMF has already extended a $3.9 billion loan over a three-year adjustment period and the US Treasury has recently drafted a $29 billion aid package from which Mexico is expected to be the first recipient of $4 billion. The Baker Plan in October 1985 and the Brady Plan in March 1989 and the call for swap of debt for new long-term bonds at 35 per cent discount, and other schemes of lessening the burden of debt have certainly created much better conditions for Mexico. The amortization schedule of public external debt before and after restructuring (inclusive of bank debts) appears as shown in Table 10.6.

Peter Kenen (1990) still insists that an *International Debt Discount Corporation (IDDC)* should be established, and he argues that the risks assumed by the sponsoring countries and their taxpayers will not be large in so far as debtors lie on the downward sloping side of the *debt relief Laffer curve*. It is hoped that this would take a good deal of pressure off Mexico and the country would feel less constrained to pursue a policy of recovery and development. At this point, Mexico is still confronted with a set of situations conditioned by the existing restrictions and policy distortions, and whether these regulations are choking the economic ebullience and stifling the financial freedom it needs so deeply and desperately to put itself on a rejuvenated path of prosperity and warranted growth should be a subject for further scrutiny. As already noted, Mexico is maintaining a neomercantilist policy of protectionism by way of tariffs, other impediments and dual exchange policy in a time when the dollar is on the rise on a trend basis. Adams and Greenwood (1985) have shown that the dual exchange system is tantamount to protectionism and it is essentially another commercial policy distortion such as a tariff. Kumcu (1985) establishes, under the 'small' country assumption, that tariff and export subsidy have an effect on the exchange rate, which is a function of the factor shares. It appears, therefore, that the imposition of tariff and exchange control would simply overdo correcting the economic imbalances. President Miguel de la Madrid's decision that his nation would join the GATT was an important development. It is true that so many trade-inhibiting restraints on the openness of the Mexican economy may be seriously non-optimal in the world of second best; but it is not clear that elimination of some of the trade barriers would necessarily increase the economic well-being. Gale (1971, 1974) and Ghosh (1977) have shown that trade imbalance may persist and the economy can be in steady-state with such an imbalance. In the Mexican case, therefore, imbalance should not be construed as the necessary evil; the real culprit should, however, be detected as early and as correctly as possible. Following Bhagwati, one should closely examine the economic as well as non-economic objectives of this immiserized economy and then suitably bring in the correct amount of corrective policy menu. For debt management, the Mexican authority should strive for an indexing of debt amortization with its net foreign exchange earnings, and this needs the co-operative spirits of both the creditors and the debtors. Since this spirit is noticeable, the magic of Mexican charm can turn the peso problem around within a reasonable time frame.

Notes

1. It refers to the equality of buying power of two sovereign currencies in real terms obtained upon adjustments of inflation and interest rates in those two countries.
2. BOP = balance of payments, of Mexico in US dollars; e = foreign exchange rate: amount of dollars per peso; x = Mexico's export volume in physical terms; m = Mexico's import volume in physical terms; p^m, r^m and p^u and r^u stand, respectively for Mexican price and interest rate and US price. (Here the United States is a proxy for the rest of the world for Mexico. Since Mexico's trade with the United States is nearly 60 per cent of its total volume, and the US dollar is the vehicle currency of the world, this assumption is reasonable.)
3. This is taken from Smith and Cuddington (1985), p. 261.

REFERENCES

ADAMS, C. and GREENWOOD, J. (1985) 'Dual Exchange Rate Systems and Capital Controls: An Investigation', *Journal of International Economics*, vol. 18, no. 1/2 (Feb.) pp. 43–63.
BAUMOL, W. J. (1957) 'Speculation, Profitability, and Stability', *Review of Economics and Statistics*, vol. XXXIX, (Aug.) pp. 263–71.
BHAGWATI, J. N. (1971) 'The Generalized Theory of Distortions and Welfare'. In J. N. Bhagwati *et al.* (eds), *Trade, Balance of Payments and Growth*.
BLANCHARD, O. J. (1979) 'Speculative Bubbles, Crashes and Rational Expectations', *Economic Letters*, 1979, pp. 387–89.
BLANCHARD, O. J. and WATSON, M. W. (1982) 'Bubbles, Rational Expectations, and Financial Markets'. Mimeo.
BULOW, J. and ROGOFF, K. (1988) 'The Buyback Boondoggle', *Brookings Papers on Economic Activity*.
CORDEN, W. M. (1988) 'Debt Relief and Adjustment Incentives', *International Monetary Fund Staff Papers*, Dec.
DORNBUSCH, R. (1982) 'Equilibrium and Disequilibrium Exchange Rates', *Zeitschrift fur Wirtschafts und Sozialwissenschaften*, vol. 102, no. 6, pp. 573–99.
FRIEDMAN, M. (1956) 'The Case for Flexible Exchange Rates', *Essays in Positive Economics* (University of Chicago Press).
GALE, D. (1971) 'General Equilibrium with Imbalances of Trade', *Journal of International Economics*, pp. 159–88.
GALE, D. (1974) 'The Trade Imbalance Story', *Journal of International Economics*, pp. 118–37.
GHOSH, D. K. (1977) 'Trade Imbalance Persists: A Simple Proof.' Presented at the Annual *Econometric Society Meetings*, Atlantic City, September 1976 and documented by the State Department, the US Government.
GRUBEL, H. G. (1966) *Forward Exchange, Speculation, and the International Flow of Capital* (Stanford, California: Stanford University Press).
KEMP, M. C. (1963) 'Speculation, Profitability, and Price Stability', *Review of Economics and Statistics*, vol. XIV (May) pp. 1985–9.
KENEN, P. B. (1990) 'Organizing Debt Relief: The Need for a New Institution', *Journal of Economic Perspectives*, Winter.
KRASKER, W. (1982) 'The Peso-Problem in Testing the Efficiency of Forward Exchange Markets', *Journal of Monetary Economics*, vol. 6, pp. 269–76.
KUMCU, M. E. (1985) 'The Theory of Commercial Policy in a Monetary Economy with Sticky Wages', *Journal of International Economics*, vol. 18, no. 1/2 (Feb.) pp. 159–76.
LIZONDO, J. S. (1983) 'Foreign Exchange Futures Prices Under Fixed Exchange Rates', *Journal of International Economics*, vol. 4, pp. 69–84.
NURKSE, R. (1944) *International Currency Experience: Lessons of the Inter-War Period* (Princeton, New Jersey: League of Nations).
SACHS, J. D. (1990) 'A Strategy for Efficient Debt Reduction', *Journal of Economic Perspectives*, Winter.

SALANT, S. and HENDERSON, D. (1978) 'Market Anticipations of Government Policies and the Price of Gold', *Journal of Political Economy*, vol. 86.

SMITH, G. W. and CUDDINGTON, J. T. (eds) (1985) *International Debt and the Developing Countries*, A World Bank Symposium. (Washington, DC: World Bank) March.

STEIN, J. L. (1961) 'Destabilizing Speculative Activity Can be Profitable', *Review of Economics and Statistics*, vol. XLIII, (Aug.) pp. 301–2.

TIROLE, J. (1982) 'On the Possibility of Speculation Under Rational Expectations', *Econometrica*, Sept.

11 International Lending and Sovereign Debt in the Presence of Agency Costs: The Case of Mexico

Christopher A. Erickson and
Elliott Willman

11.1 INTRODUCTION

For Mexico, the 1970s were a period of rapid economic progress. Between 1970 and 1980, real GDP per capita increased by an annual average of 3.4 per cent, real consumption per capita increased by 5.2 per cent, and fixed investment increased by 3.8 per cent.[1] Moreover, given its large proven reserves, the increase in the world price of oil substantially increased Mexico's ability to generate current account surpluses.

Rapid growth coupled with expected current account surpluses led international lenders to substantially revise upward Mexico's creditworthiness during the 1970s. Mexico used its increased borrowing capacity and increased its external sovereign debt. By June 1982 Mexico owed $64 billion to developed country banks (Rukstad, 1992).

The decline in world oil prices following the collapse of OPEC reduced Mexico's ability to repay its foreign debt. By June 1982, it had become evident that Mexico could not service its external debt and only with difficulty be able to roll-over its existing debt. Subsequent to this debt crisis, the growth rate of consumption and domestic capital formation fell off substantially.

In fact, the 1980s can at best be characterized as a period of stagnation and limited development. Between 1981 and 1986, GDP per capita declined on average by 2.3 per cent per annum, consumption per capita fell by 1.9 per cent, and aggregate fixed investment fell by 4.3 per cent. Capital formation was actually negative in 1982, 1986 and 1987.

Many analysts have argued that the poor economic performance of Mexico during the 1980s can be traced directly to the debt crisis. Certainly the timing of the two events argues for this conclusion. Yet a convincing economic model is needed if this conclusion is to be accepted unhesitatingly. This chapter presents a first pass at such a model. In particular, we develop a model which can explain the main stylized facts of the Mexican economy: (1) maximum sovereign borrowing, (2) a magnified effect on domestic production and consumption from sovereign borrowing, and (3) a positive relationship between sovereign borrowing and domestic fixed investment.

11.2 THE MODEL

In this section, we develop a model of an economy with international borrowing and lending, which rationalizes the stylized facts about the Mexican economy outlined in the previous section. The economy consists of two sectors – an export sector controlled by the government and a competitive sector producing the domestic consumption good. In the context of Mexico, the export sector represents the petroleum industry while the competitive sector represents domestic manufacturing.[2] The model is a variation on Bernanke and Gertler (1989). Asymmetric information plays a central role by introducing agency costs.

The important modification that we make is that the home country government controls an asset which is illiquid in the sense that the government can not transfer control of the asset to another. The government can, however, borrow in international markets against the future cash flow generated by the asset. The home government can then channel borrowed funds to private sector businesses.[3] Because the transfer payments increase private sector net worth, agency costs are mitigated and economic efficiency increased. An adverse shock to the expected cash flow of the government controlled asset reduces its value as collateral. The home country government must reduce the transfers to the private sector and economic efficiency is reduced.

More formally, we assume that there are three types of agents – entrepreneurs, the home country government and the international lender. Entrepreneurs and the lender are assumed to be risk neutral wealth maximizers and the government is assumed to only care about the welfare of entrepreneurs. There are two time periods. In period 0, contracts are entered into and investments undertaken. In period 1, outcomes from investment projects are determined, output allocated subject to period 0 contracts, and consumption occurs.

There are three goods – a capital good, a domestic consumption good and an export good. The government has control of the asset which produces B units of the export good. The export good is then sold in world markets in exchange for the consumption good. The export asset is illiquid in the sense that the government cannot transfer control of the asset. The government can, however, borrow capital from the international lender against expected cash flow from the asset. The government's credit limit, or borrowing capacity is assumed to be B/r, where r is the required return to the international lender.[4] At the beginning of period 1, the government uses revenue from exports to repay its international debt and distributes the remainder, if any, to entrepreneurs lump sum.

In period 0, each entrepreneur is endowed with S units of the capital good. There are two technologies available for transforming capital into period 1 consumption. The first technology, called storage, is riskless and pays a certain return, r. The other technology is an investment technology, which involves risk. The investment technology comes in discrete units referred to as projects. Each entrepreneur is endowed with one of these projects. Each entrepreneur is indexed by ω, with low ω having a lower cost of investment. ω is assumed to be uniformly distributed on $(0, 1)$. An entrepreneur with efficiency of ω requires exactly $x(\omega)$ units of capital to complete her project. That is, if less than $x(\omega)$ is invested, output from the project is zero. On the other hand, if more than $x(\omega)$ is invested, the marginal product is zero. For simplicity, output from investment projects is assumed to take only two possible values, denoted θ_i with $\theta_1 > \theta_2$. It is assumed that with probability π_i, the outcome is θ_i.

We introduce asymmetric information by assuming that the outcome of a particular project can be observed costlessly only by the entrepreneur who operates it. An entrepreneur, however, has an incentive to misrepresent the outcome from her project. Specifically, if she under-reports output, she can retain the excess output for her own consumption. Other agents can only infer the output from a project by incurring an auditing cost γ. Once audited, the output from a project can be observed by all agents costlessly without error. It is assumed that random auditing is possible. We also assume that the outcome to investment projects are independently distributed and that there is accountable infinity of agents. These two assumptions together mean that there is no aggregate uncertainty.

11.3   THE INVESTMENT DECISION

The optimal policy for the government is to borrow from international lenders and then redistribute the proceeds to entrepreneurs. To show this, it is necessary to derive the optimal investment rule for an individual entrepreneur. In deriving the optimal investment rule, we use a two-step approach. In the first step, the optimal financial contract is derived, assuming that investment will occur. Then, in the second step, the entrepreneur's investment rule is derived taking the optimal contract as given.

The optimal financial contract involves the choice of four variables – the probability of an audit (p), the entrepreneur's consumption when an audit occurs (c^a), and the level of consumption in the absence of an audit in state 1 (c_1) and in state 2 (c_2). The optimal contract is found by solving:

$$\max \pi_1 \left(pc^a + (1 - p) c_1 \right) + \pi_2 c_2$$

subject to adequate return to lenders:

$$\pi_i[\theta_1 - p (c^a + \gamma) - (1 - p) c_1] + \pi_2 [\theta_2 - c_2] \geq r [x(\omega) - (S + \tau)]$$

incentive compatibility:

$$c_2 \geq (1 - p) [(\theta_2 - \theta_1) + c_1]$$

limited liability:

$$c_1, c^a \geq 0$$

and to $0 \leq p \leq 1$. τ is the transfer received by the entrepreneur from the government. This transfer is assumed to be treated as given by an individual entrepreneur, although it is determined optimally by the government.

Since audits are costly, an audit will only occur if there is a default.

Sufficiently efficient entrepreneurs, however, will not default even in the bad state. Define S^* by

$$S^*(\omega) = \frac{\theta_1}{r} - x(\omega).$$

An investor with $S^* \leqslant S$ is fully collateralized since she will always have sufficient resources to repay any borrowings. It is never necessary to audit a fully collateralized entrepreneur ($p = 0$) and no agency costs are incurred. If $\omega > \omega^*$, audits may occur in the bad state ($p > 0$). In this case, it can be shown that $c_1 = c^a = 0$. Thus the optimal auditing probability function is given by

$$p = \max\left\{\frac{r[x(\omega) - (S + \tau)] - \theta_1}{\pi_2(\theta_2 - \theta_1) - \pi_1\gamma}, 0\right\}.$$

Notice that p is decreasing in τ, hence expected agency costs are also decreasing in τ.

Given the optimal financial contract, the decision to invest depends on the efficiency of the individual entrepreneur. Define $\underline{\omega}$ by $\theta - rx(\omega) - \pi_1\gamma = 0$ and define $\bar{\omega}$ by $\theta - rx(\bar{\omega}) = 0$. A high efficiency entrepreneur ($\omega \leqslant \underline{\omega}$) will always invest because, even if an audit is certain in the bad state, her project always has a positive expected return. A low efficiency entrepreneur ($\omega > \bar{\omega}$) will never invest because, even in the absence of auditing, her project has a negative expected return. An intermediate efficiency entrepreneur ($\bar{\omega} \geqslant \omega > \underline{\omega}$) will invest only if expected agency costs are sufficiently low.

Return to entrepreneurs who do not invest in their projects is $r(S + \tau)$. Since no agency cost is incurred, the expected return to a fully collateralized entrepreneur is expected output less required return to lenders:

$$R_{fc} = \theta - r[x(\omega) - (S + \tau)].$$

For incompletely collateralized entrepreneurs, expected return is:

$$R_{ic} = \alpha[\theta - r[x(\omega) - (S + \tau) - \pi_1\gamma]$$

where $\alpha = [\pi_2(\theta_2 - \theta_2)]/[\pi_1(\theta_2 - \theta_1) - \pi_1\gamma] > 1$. Notice $\partial R_{ic}/\partial \tau = \alpha r > r$. That is, the increase in return to incompletely collateralized entrepreneurs from transfers is positive and greater than the cost of funds in international loan markets. It is this result which provides scope for Pareto improving government borrowing. By committing export earnings as collateral and borrowing to finance transfers, the government can reduced expected agency costs, allowing increased consumption by incompletely collateralized entrepreneurs.

11.4 THE OPTIMAL GOVERNMENT POLICY

The government is assumed to maximize consumption by its choice of $\tau(\omega)$. We restrict discussion to the subset of Pareto improving policies which involve positive transfers.[5] The government's optimal policy is the solution to:

$$\max C = \int_{\bar{\omega}}^{1} r(S + \tau)\, d\omega + \int_{\underline{\omega}}^{\omega^*} i(\omega) R_{ic} + [1 - i(\omega)]\, r(S + \tau)\, d\omega$$
$$+ \int_{0}^{\omega^*} R_{fc}\, d\omega + \left[B - r \int_{0}^{1} \tau\, d\omega \right]$$

subject to the government borrowing constraint:

$$r \int_{0}^{1} \tau(\omega)\, d\omega \leq B$$

and to the positive transfer constraint:

$$\tau(\omega) \geq 0$$

where $i(\omega)$ is an indicator variable which takes the value one if investment is undertaken. The Kuhn–Tucker conditions to the government's problem are:

$$\alpha - 1 + \mu(\omega) - \lambda \leq 0$$

for incompletely collateralized investors, and

$$\mu(\omega) - \lambda r \leq 0$$

otherwise, with strict equality if either constraint is binding. μ is the Lagrangian multiplier from the positive transfer constraint, and λ is the Lagrangian multiplier from the borrowing constraint.

It is now possible to evaluate the model in the context of the

stylized facts of the Mexican debt crisis. First notice that government's borrowing constraint is binding as long as there exists incomplete collateralization. This result arises because, as long as there is
incomplete collateralization, agency costs can be reduced by increasing the equity available to incompletely collateralized entrepreneurs.
As long as there are incompletely collateralized entrepreneurs, the
government will borrow up to its borrowing capacity. *Thus the model
is consistent with the stylized fact that Mexico exhausted its borrowing
capacity.*

By the envelope theorem, $dC/dB = 1 + \lambda = \alpha > 1$. Thus an increase
or decrease in the borrowing capacity of the government results in a
multiple expansion or contraction in domestic consumption. Moreover, the change will persist until the government borrowing capacity
is restored. The reason for this is that transfers financed through
borrowing affects consumption directly and also indirectly through its
effect on agency costs. *Thus the model is consistent with rapid growth
in consumption per capita during the 1970s and the decline during the
1980s.*

The relationship between the government's borrowing capacity
and domestic investment is complicated. This is because agency costs
arc linear in B. More formally, domestic investment is:

$$I = \int_0^{\omega^*} rx(\omega)\ d\omega + \int_{\omega^*}^{\bar{\omega}} i(\omega)\ rx(\omega)\ d\omega.$$

From the entrepreneur's maximization problem, it is possible to solve
for the investment indicator variable as a weakly increasing function
of transfers (i.e. $i(\omega) = i(\omega, \tau)\ \omega$). Thus the government can design
policy to affect investment. One policy rule consistent with the government's maximization problem would be $\tau \geqslant 0$ only if $i(\omega, 0) = 1$.
In this case, investment would be unrelated to borrowing capacity.
Another policy rule would be to choose τ to max $\int i(\omega)\ d\omega$, in which
case investment would be an increasing function of B. In fact, it is
possible to construct pathological policy rules for which investment is
a decreasing function of B. *Thus there is no set relationship between
investment and borrowing capacity.*[6]

11.5 CONCLUSION

We have developed a simple model which explicitly incorporates
agency costs. We have shown that, as long as some entrepreneurs are
incompletely collateralized, the optimal government policy is to borrow the maximum amount possible from international lenders and

transfer the proceeds to the private sector. Any reduction in the government's borrowing capacity results in a decline in domestic production and a multiple decline in domestic production and hence consumption. Moreover, the effects on production and consumption are permanent. Recovery does not occur until the government rehabilitates its borrowing capacity. The model is also consistent with reduced domestic investment. The model is generally consistent with the stylized facts of economic performance during the period leading up and following the Mexican debt crisis.

Notes

1. Source for all data used in this section is the *International Financial Statistics Year Book*, 1989.
2. Historically, Mexico has adopted rather protectionist measures. This is consistent with the model since we do not allow for international trade in the consumption good. We abstract from measures which restrict domestic competition.
3. Note these transfers could take extralegal forms (i.e. via corruption and graft).
4. More generally, *B* would be determined endogenously. See Bulow and Rogoff (1989).
5. Allowing negative transfer i.e. allowing taxation) in period 0 is only Pareto improving when the taxpayer receives a compensating repayment in period 1. The repayment must be sufficient to allow the taxpayer to maintain at least the same level of consumption as would be possible without taxation. Such repayments could be financed from agency cost savings generated from redistributing equity. The discussion of such schemes, however, would require considerable additional notation without altering our main conclusions, so we do not pursue the issue here.
6. This result is an artefact of the discrete nature of investment in the model. If investment were continuous, a decrease in borrowing capacity would unambiguously reduce investment.

REFERENCES

BERNANKE, B. and GERTLER, M. (1989) 'Agency Costs, Net Worth, and Business Fluctuations', *American Economic Review*, vol. 79, no. 1, pp. 14–31.
BULOW, J. and ROGOFF, K. (1989) 'A Constant Recontracting Model of Sovereign Debt', *Journal of Political Economy*, vol. 97, no. 1, pp. 155–78.
RUKSTAD, M. G. (1992) *Macroeconomic Decision Making in the Real World* (New York: Dryden Press).

12 A New Look at Country Risk Analysis: An Analytical Approach to Judgmental Risk Scoring

Ramakrishnan S. Koundinya

12.1 INTRODUCTION

Country risk analysis is generally accepted as the process of assessing a country's economic, political, and social situation as determinants of its ability and willingness to service its foreign financial obligations. It is a well researched area during the past two decades. Significant involvement of commercial banks in lending to developing nations forced the need for such analysis and evaluation systems. These have become essential components of the country credit granting process.

The variety of approaches adopted cover a whole spectrum of methodologies: with purely qualitative assessment at one extreme to the other extreme of quantitative assessment using multivariate statistical techniques. The 1976 Eximbank survey of country risk analysis systems in US banks classified these into fully qualitative; structural qualitative; checklist (quantitative); and other quantitative (Burton and Inoue, 1983). A number of such approaches are discussed in the literature (see Ensor (1981) for a collection of country risk assessment methods). A number of quantitative studies are reviewed in Saini and Bates (1984). While the various approaches differ in analytical content and in the scope of information used, they all work with incomplete, imprecise economic and financial data, vague notions of sociopolitical factors, and inadequate surrogates for representation of risk (default) events. Inevitably the final synthesis has to be formulated based on the subjective judgments of credit management professionals. These judgments relate both to the usefulness of information contained in the set of variables deemed pertinent, and to the importance (weight) to be assigned to such information in determining the overall creditworthiness of a country. The role of

147

judgment thus dominates country risk analysis. Such reliance on judgment in its very nature neither reveals the process through which judgments were made, nor the means to ensure consistency in the application of the process to different countries. This means that such evaluation processes cannot be replicated if it proved to be effective in predicting future risk, nor can it be improved if it proved to be inadequate. Alternative methodological frameworks that formalize the judgmental process followed in the formation of *ex-ante* country risk expectations should enable documentation of the country risk evaluation system, and ensure consistency in its application to different countries.

This chapter proposes the application of the analytic hierarchy process methodology (Saaty, 1977, 1987) to structure the judgmental scoring of country risk and evaluation of country risk profiles over time. The purpose of this research is to suggest a framework that enables incorporation of quantitative assessments of economic/financial performance and expert judgment on other qualitative factors. The preliminary model focuses on selected economic/financial variables for the evaluation of risk profiles.

12.2 COUNTRY RISK ASSESSMENT: A BRIEF OVERVIEW

The early impetus for the need to assess a country's ability to service foreign debt came from the role the World Bank (IBRD) took as financiers of economic growth in developing nations. The first major study in this area by Avromovic (1958) formalized the linkage between the performance on debt service and debt bearing capacity. An important early empirical study by Frank and Cline (1971) focused on short-run debt repayment difficulties and assessed selected economic factors as indicators of debt renegotiation exercises. The increasing involvement of commercial banks beginning in the early 1970s forced the need for in-house methods for country risk exposure assessment. The variety of approaches reflected the differences in the perspectives of the user bank, their expertise, and most of all their desire to participate in the growing area of international lending. By and large these approaches are more of a process than an application of a standard technique. Typically the bank gathers data on economic/financial variables on domestic economic performance, trade and balance of payments, and sociopolitical climate. Country reports assessing the data are prepared by economic staff groups, and reviewed by credit/lending committees and judgments on risk exposure are made.

A major difficulty with these approaches is the lack of a mechanism to formalize the judgmental process so as to ensure consistency in application. Often the process was driven by commercial considerations (Baird, 1983). The need is for an evaluation process that would provide full scope for judgment and a mechanism to document these judgments.

12.3 THE ANALYTIC HIERARCHY PROCESS METHODOLOGY

The analytic hierarchy process methodology is a procedure well suited to solve complex decision problems involving multi criteria and activities. The methodology offers a structured approach to incorporate judgmental and quantitative assessment of criteria and activities. The decision problem is set up as a hierarchy of structural and/or functional relationships linking objectives to activities/decisions. A pairwise comparison of activities in a given hierarchy in relation to an objective at a higher level are obtained using responses based on a scale of 1 to 9. This matrix of responses is a reciprocal matrix of ratios of weights assigned to activities taken in pairs. The weights are recovered from these ratios by computing the normalized eigenvectors corresponding to the maximum eigenvalue. The weights corresponding to the activities in each hierarchy level are synthesized to arrive at the composite weight for the activities at the lowest level of the hierarchy. This methodology has been extensively applied to diverse problem areas involving prioritization, planning, resource allocation, and prediction.

12.4 COUNTRY RISK SCORING MODEL

The analytic hierarchy process method offers a systematic approach to incorporate judgmental and quantitative assessment of multiple criteria/factors that are deemed useful in the country risk analysis process. The method enables incorporation of the lack of precision in the economic/financial information used, and offers an analytical procedure to assess and synthesize the relative importance of the variables/factors in the analysis. The risk-scoring procedure is structured

Level 0	Max risk class efficiency			
Level 1 factors	LP	PC	TC	FC
Level 2 variables	RETOIM RETOIV	XGR YGR	EXTOY RETOY	EXTOIM EXTOIV

Figure 12.1

as a hierarchy linking the objective of maximal risk assessment efficiency to the country's economic/financial performance measured by the selected variables. A preliminary specification of the hierarchy model is in Figure 12.1.

Conceptual attributes considered relevant in forming expectations about country risk exposure that form the hierarchy level 1 factors are liquidity position (LP), productive capacity (PC), transfer capacity (TC), and funding capacity (FC). Selected economic/financial variables used to measure these attributes form hierarchy level 2. The variables selected are from the Koundinya (1983) study. These are: reserves to imports and reserves to investment income ratios for liquidity position; exports, and income growth rates for productive capacity; exports to income, and reserves to income ratios for transfer capacity; and exports to imports, and exports to investment income ratios for funding capacity. Hierarchy level 3 is the quality of credit risk rated as high, medium, and low relative to a selected risk class of countries. For this preliminary analysis selected industrial countries are used as a reference risk class. Relative importance of attributes/factors in level 1, the variables in level 2, and quality of performance on variables in level 3 are computed from a series of responses to pairwise comparisons of elements in each level in the hierarchy. For each pair these responses measure the importance of one item over the other on a scale of 1 (equal importance) to 9 (extremely most important). Sets of priority weights for each level are computed using an eigenvalue procedure. These weights are synthesized to arrive at country scores for risk quality categories for each attribute – variable combination.

12.4 COUNTRY RISK SCORES

The overall risk scores are computed using a series of response matrices for each hierarchy level. The response matrix for hierarchy

level 1 in Table 12.1 represents judgments about the relative importance of liquidity position, productive capacity, transfer capacity, and
funding capacity taken in pairs.

Table 12.1

Factors	LP	PC	TC	FC	Weights
LP	1	0.5	0.25	1	0.13
PC	2	1	0.5	2	0.27
TC	4	2	1	2	0.45
FC	1	0.33	0.5	1	0.15

The responses in Table 12.1 indicate that in the author's judgment
transfer capacity is significantly more important (4 times) than liquidity position, slightly more important (2 times) than productive capacity, and funding capacity in determining a country's credit quality.
The productive capacity is slightly more important (2 times) than
liquidity position, and funding capacity. The funding capacity is
about of equal importance (1 time) as liquidity position.

The priority weights of the factors in Level 1 of the hierarchy are
the normalized eigenvector computed from the matrix using the
geometric approximation method (see Saaty and Kerns, 1985, p. 32).
These weights are in the last column of Table 12.1. As can be noted
transfer capacity and productive capacity account for over 70 per cent
of the contribution to credit quality according to this author.

From a set of four response matrices corresponding to hierarchy
level 2 the priority weights for the economic/financial variables are
computed. For example, using the response matrix for productive
capacity shown in Table 12.2 the priority weights for export growth
(XGR) and income growth (YGR) are computed.

Table 12.2

PCVARS	XGR	YGR	WTPCV
XGR	1	3	0.75
YGR	0.33	1	0.25

This table indicates that in the judgment of the author export
growth (XGR) is relatively more important (3 times) than income
growth (YGR) in determining productive capacity impacting quality

Table 12.3

	LP		PC		TC		FC
RETOIM	0.8	XGR	0.75	EXTOY	0.83	EXTOIM	0.67
RETOIV	0.2	YGR	0.25	RETOY	0.17	EXTOIV	0.33

of credit. This implies a 75 per cent contribution from export growth. Table 12.3 lists the weights assigned to Level 2 variables computed from the respective response matrices.

Hierarchy level 3 rates the country's risk position relative to the group of selected industrial countries. For this preliminary analysis the group consist of US, Japan, Germany, UK, Canada, France and Italy. The priority weights for this level are assessed using the response matrix in Table 12.4.

Table 12.4

RCLASS	High	Medium	Low	Weights
High	1	3	6	1
Medium	0.33	1	2	0.33
Low	0.17	0.5	1	0.16

The risk classes high, medium, and low indicate a high, medium, and low performance on the selected economic/financial variables relative to the group of selected industrial countries. The responses in Table 12.4 indicate for example an assessment of high (performance) rating is highly significant (6 times) in comparison to low (performance) rating while moderately significant (3 times) in comparison to medium (performance) rating. The priority weights for the risk classes are in the last column of the Table 12.4. Normalized priority weights are adjusted to reflect the categorical nature of the risk class intervals by assigning proportionate values.

The total score for credit quality for factor/variable/performance class were computed by multiplying the respective weights. These total scores are in Table 12.5.

The total score of 6.72 for productive capacity/export growth/ medium performance is obtained by multiplying productive capacity weight (0.27), export growth weight (0.75), and medium performance class weight (0.33 per cent).

Table 12.5   Total country scores

Variable	Quality rating class		
	High	Medium	Low
RETOIM	10.76	3.59	1.79
RETOIV	2.69	0.9	0.45
XGR	20.17	6.72	3.36
YGR	6.72	2.24	1.12
EXTOY	37.68	12.56	6.28
RETOY	7.54	2.51	1.26
EXTOIM	9.63	3.21	1.61
EXTOIV	4.82	1.61	0.8

12.5   COUNTRY RISK PROFILES

For this preliminary study of risk profiles the countries selected are: Venezuela, Korea, Brazil, Thailand, India, Nigeria, Jordan, Egypt, Tanzania, Zambia and Turkey.

The first step in the scoring process is the computation of the Means and Standard deviations of the selected performance variables for the reference group of industrial countries. Time series data for the period 76–85 was used for this purpose. For the periods 76–85 for each country the standardized deviations (Z scores) of the performance variables relative to the reference group are computed. Performance was rated high for z-scores greater than or equal to 0.25, medium for z scores 0.25 to -0.5, and low for Z scores less than -0.5. Scores from the Table 12.5 corresponding to the performance variables were assigned to the country for each time period, for each of the 24 factor/risk class and summed to arrive at the total scores. A high score reflects a low exposure to credit risk while a low score reflects a high exposure. In other words these scores are measures of credit quality of the borrower nation.

12.6   ANALYSIS OF RISK PROFILES

The preliminary hierarchy based model proposed here is to show that the framework used offers a unique approach to develop quantitative credit quality scores using expert judgments rather than relying on purely statistical assessment of past data. The model presented here is limited by choice to the use of financial/economic variables reflecting transfer capacity. However, the risk scores generated by this preliminary model are analysed for information content as measures of country credit quality in the following discussion.

For purposes of comparative analysis data on country credit ratings published in the September 1979–1985 issues of *Institutional Investor* (II) is used as benchmark. These country credit ratings are 'based on ratings provided by leading international banks.' These ratings are on a scale of zero to 100. The higher the rating the better the credit quality of the country. *Institutional Investor* arrives at a composite rating by weighting the responses from the sample group of 25–100 bankers.

The country risk scores and corresponding II credit ratings for the sample group of developing nations are in Table 12.6 to 12.9.

The country risk score profiles for a selected sample of developing countries and the model scores are in Figures 12.2–12.5, and Tables 12.6–12.9 respectively. Table 12.6 has the model scores for Venezuela (VENRS), Brazil (BRZRS), AND Korea (KORRS). These countries are rated by the *Institutional Investor* credit rating system as group 6 and 7 countries. *Institutional Investor* scores for Venezuela (VENIS), Brazil (BRZIS) and Korea (KORIS) are also presented in Table 12.6. The profiles of the model scores and *Institutional Investor* scores for group 6 and 7 countries are graphed in Figure 12.2. Model scores, and II scores for group 5 countries Thailand, Nigeria, and India and corresponding profiles are in Table 12.7, and Figure 12.3. Jordan, Egypt (group 3 and 4) scores, and Turkey, Zambia, and Tanzania (group 1 and 2) scores are in Tables 12.8 and 12.9. Profiles for these countries are in Figures 12.4 and 12.5.

The data in the tables and the profiles in the figures indicate the relative volatility of the model scores. The model scores reflect more closely the balance-of-payment difficulties experienced by the developing nations during the 1980s. These are more pronounced for oil exporting countries. Except for Turkey the II credit-rating profiles show a secular decline in credit quality. In most cases, the II rating lag the model scores with about a year's lag. This is suggestive of a relatively longer-term view and an averaging process. The model scores when smoothed as one year moving averages the profiles parallel more closely with the II ratings. Except for Turkey the II ratings profiles by and large fall below that of the model score profiles, the dispersion being most pronounced for oil exporting

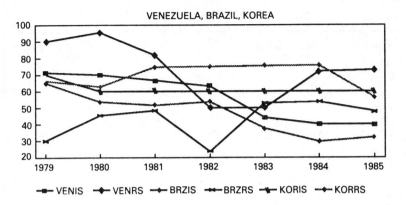

Figure 12.2 Group 6 and 7 countries

Table 12.6

Year	VENIS	VENRS	BRZIS	BRZRS	KORIS	KORRS
1979	72.4	90.52	64.9	30.24	71.2	64.56
1980	69.4	95	52.9	44.81	56.9	58.96
1981	66	81.55	48.9	46.41	57.1	72.98
1982	60.3	48.59	52.2	22.44	57.2	72.98
1983	43.4	48.59	37.6	51.71	56.4	74.59
1984	37.4	72.59	29.7	52.83	56.9	74.59
1985	37.3	72.59	30.9	47.47	57.3	55.54

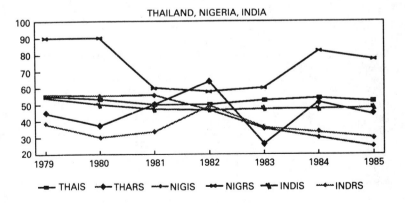

Figure 12.3 Group 5 countries

Table 12.7

Year	THAIS	THARS	NIGIS	NIGRS	INDIS	INDRS
1979	54.7	43.92	54.1	89.4	54.2	37.64
1980	52.6	36.21	53.9	89.4	49.8	29.26
1981	51.7	50.2	55.4	58.51	48.3	32.62
1982	51.3	61.85	48.1	55.6	46.6	50.54
1983	52.2	26.57	36.3	56.72	46.2	35.84
1984	53.4	50.2	29.9	83.35	46.9	32.62
1985	52	39.44	25.4	74.38	46.3	29.26

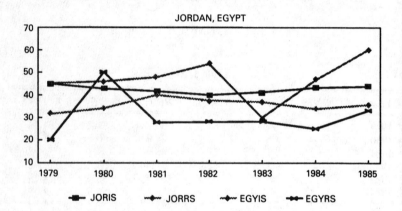

Figure 12.4   Group 3 and 4 countries

Table 12.8

Year	JORIS	JORRS	EGYIS	EGYRS
1979	44.7	44.81	33.9	19.71
1980	42.2	44.81	34.9	49.29
1981	39.7	44.81	38.8	26.88
1982	37.5	49.29	35.7	26.88
1983	37	28	33.5	26.88
1984	37.3	43.69	32.7	23.52
1985	38.1	60.75	35	34.72

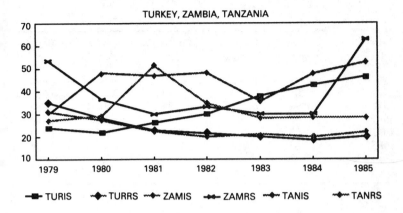

Figure 12.5   Group 1 and 2 countries

Table 12.9

Year	TURIS	TURRS	ZAMIS	ZAMRS	TANIS	TANRS
1979	14.8	20.83	20.7	43.87	25	17.92
1980	12.7	36.52	17.7	27.06	18.2	19.04
1981	16	35.84	13.9	19.04	13.5	40.32
1982	20.2	36.52	11.7	22.4	10.6	23.52
1983	26	24.33	9.1	19.52	9.8	17.92
1984	30.6	37.1	9.8	19.52	8.22	17.92
1985	34.8	40.32	10.5	51.71	9.5	17.92

countries. In general the II ratings declined at a faster pace after 1982, reflecting the serious concerns of debt servicing problems of developing nations as a group, particularly in the Latin American region.

A clear inference that surfaces from the comparative profiles is the role of qualitative factors in the assessment of risk by bankers. II ratings include such factors while the preliminary model does not. To determine the information content of the model scores, and the role of non-quantifiable qualitative factors in the risk assessment process a set of regression models are estimated using cross-section data on the sample of countries studied for the years 1979–85. While a number of qualitative factors may play a role, one qualitative factor that distinguish the perception of credit quality of the reference group of industrial countries and the other developing nations clearly is their

Table 12.10   Regressions

Year	Dstat coefficient value	Dstat Tstat	CSCORE coefficient value	CSCORE Tsat	RSQUARE
1979	1.05	5.6	0.46	2.5	0.72
1980	0.99	5.19	0.37	1.97	0.71
1981	0.98	5.35	0.48	2.24	0.74
1982	1.03	5.47	0.34	1.7	0.72
1983	1.06	6.23	0.37	1.89	0.78
1984	1.12	6.09	0.25	1.36	0.75
1985	1.11	5.64	0.06	0.27	0.71

development status. A dummy variable Dstat is defined to distinguish this qualitative assessment. A value of 1 is assigned for reference group of industrial countries and 0.5 for the developing countries. The model estimated for each year is of the form:

II Rating = Dstat + Model score + Error term

Results of the estimated regression models using cross-section data for years 1979–85 are presented in Table 12.10.

As can be noted the two dependent variables, the development status and the model scores explain between 70 and 80 per cent of the variations in the II ratings. The development status is extremely significant. The *t* stat for this variable is over five in every regression suggestive of the crucial role played by qualitative judgment of perceived development status. Developing nations as a class are rated as more risky. Equally important to note is that the model scores are also statistically significant with *t* stats relatively close to 2.0 in most years except 1985. The coefficient values are also relatively stable except for 1985. These results clearly validate a judgmental approach to the country risk assessment process.

12.7   CONCLUSIONS

The hierarchy process model provides not only a structured approach to integrate judgments on multiple factors that include qualitative and quantitative aspects, but also lead to quantitative scores that can be validated.

The preliminary model presented in the chapter as limited as it is in its scope clearly shows the validity of the judgmental approach. In this instance, the analysis strongly suggests the scope for further research in identifying the set of unique qualitative variables that are implicit in the Dstat variable used as a surrogate for development status. The model can be readily extended to include additional variables as well as additional levels of hierarchies. More importantly this approach offers a unique methodology to construct bank specific risk scoring models that can document the judgmental process followed in the scoring of credit quality of countries.

REFERENCES

AVROMOVIC, D. (1958) *Economic Growth and External Debt* (Baltimore, MD: Johns Hopkins Press).

BAIRD, J. (1983) 'Where did Country Risk Analysts go Wrong', *Institutional Investor*, May, pp. 227–9.

BURTON, F. N. and INOUE, H. (1983) 'Country Risk Evaluation Methods: a Survey of Systems in Use', *The Banker*, Jan. pp. 41–43.

ENSOR, R. (1981) *Assessing Country Risk* (London: Euromoney).

FRANK, C. R. and CLINE, W. R. (1971) 'Measurement of Debt Servicing Capacity: an Application of Discriminant Analysis', *Journal of International Economics*, vol. 1, pp. 327–44.

KOUNDINYA, R. S. (1983) 'Country Risk Exposure and Credit Policy Formulation: Application of Cluster Analysis Techniques', *Academy of International Business Conference San Francisco*.

SAATY, T. L. (1977) 'A Scaling Method for Priorities in Hierarchical Structures', *Journal of Mathematical Psychology*, vol. 15, no. 773, pp. 223–81.

SAATY, T. L. (1987) 'Concepts, Theory and Techniques: Rank Generation, Preservation and Reversal in Analytic Hierarchy Decision Process', *Decision Sciences*, vol. 18, pp. 157–77.

SAATY, T. L. and KERNS, K. P. (1985) *Analytical Planning: The Organizational Systems*, (New York: Pergamon Press).

SAINI, K. G. and BATES, P. S. (1984) 'A Survey of the Quantitative Approaches to Country Risk Analysis', *Journal of Banking and Finance*, vol. 8, no. 2, pp. 341–56.

13 Political Risk in Latin American Stock Markets: A Rational Expectations Approach

Benoit Carmichael, Jean-Claude Cosset and Klaus P. Fischer

13.1 INTRODUCTION

Emerging equities markets (EEM) are becoming the focus of much attention. There are two reasons for this. First, governments and international development agencies assign an increasing importance to the securitized markets to finance development and promote capital transfers. Second, they are an interesting target to internationally-minded portfolio managers seeking new opportunities to enhance the performance of their portfolios.

As a result, LDC governments in every continent are re-regulating their securities markets and investing in their infrastructure. They are being encouraged in their efforts by the international financial community and supported by agencies such as the International Finance Corporation and the United States Securities and Exchange Commission. Although attention has been paid to securitized debt instruments also, the emphasis seems to be placed on equities.

This chapter addresses the concern of these two constituencies: governments and international investors. First, since we focus on the impact of monetary and fiscal policy variables on the stock market performance it informs governments about the role of their own actions on the behaviour of the markets they are trying to develop. Second, from the point of view of international investors, it helps them to better understand the link between government policy and stock market behaviour. The importance of a better knowledge of this link has been emphasized by Solnik (1991, p. 23).

The trend toward more reliance on equity markets to allocate resources in the economy, requires a better understanding of these

160

markets. In economies such as the United States, Japan and the United Kingdom the functioning of the market is relatively well known. However, securitized markets in emerging markets are quite a different matter. Efforts undertaken recently in various parts of the world suggest that it is unfeasible to rapidly boost their development to the level of the bigger counterparts.

Age of the market does not seem to be a factor in explaining the differences in development. Take for example some of Latin American (LA) stock exchanges. They were created by the middle of last century (e.g. Buenos Aires, 1854; Montevideo, 1864, Brazil, 1876). Contemporaneous or even later exchanges have done much better (e.g. Toronto, 1858; Tokyo, 1878). Neither does it seem to be related, as suggested by some of the classical literature on financial markets developments, to the size of the economy or per capita income. To emphasize this point, in Table 13.1 we present market capitalization and turnover statistics adjusted for size of the economy (GNP) and per capital income (GNP per capita). Market capitalization, when adjusted for size of the economy and income, suggest a difference between the group of LA and industrialized country markets. However, statistically we cannot reject the hypothesis of equal means. This should not be surprising since market capitalization data are misleading in the sense that they actually overstate considerably the level of activity in these 'emerging markets'. The reason for this is that in most industrialized countries a very high proportion of the outstanding shares are traded in the market (liquid shares). In contrast, in most emerging markets this proportion is quite small (10–15 per cent) as shareholder entrepreneurs hold on to a large proportion of shares to guarantee control. Turnover statistics should be free of this bias. Indeed, these statistics emphasize the different dynamic operating in the LA and industrialized country markets. In fact, using a simple t-test we can reject the hypothesis that they come from the same sample with a 95 per cent confidence.

If equities markets are to play a role in financing development, it is critical to focus on their current functioning, and what is needed to boost their development. In particular, it is important to recognize the various sources of price volatility, which in itself is an important measure of market efficiency. Perhaps the best undertaken study in the academic literature is one supported by the IFC (Errunza and Losq, 1985). The paper investigates the behaviour of stock prices for a group of well established and newly emerging markets. Their focus was on the distributional properties of returns. The results would

Table 13.1 Comparative market statistics

	Market capitalization* (MC)	MC/GNP†	MC/GNPC‡	Turnover§ (TV)	TV/GNP	TV/GNPC
Argentina	8.7	1.26	0.40	2.4	0.35	0.11
Brazil	34.5	0.92	1.36	11.9	0.32	0.47
Chile	17.1	7.43	0.97	1.2	0.52	0.07
Columbia	2.2	0.57	0.18	0.1	0.03	0.01
Mexico	51.15	3.01	2.54	16.7	0.98	0.83
Venezuela	7	1.49	0.29	1.9	0.40	0.08
Mean		2.45	0.96		0.43	0.26
SD		2.58	0.32		0.32	0.90
Canada	266.7	5.35	1.40	79.9	1.60	0.42
France	360.2	3.60	2.02	118.2	1.18	0.66
Germany	379.3	2.99	1.86	816.9	6.45	4.00
Japan	3480.4	11.87	14.62	1799.7	6.14	7.56
United Kingdom	899.1	10.76	6.15	306.3	3.67	2.10
United States	3591.9	6.90	17.18	2028.7	3.90	9.70
Mean		6.91	7.20		3.82	4.07
SD		3.69	7.00		2.20	3.81
t-statistic		2.215	1.980		3.410	2.227
SD-pooled		3.186	4.987		1.571	2.706

* Market capitalization in billion dollars.
† Market capitalization over GNP times 100 000.
‡ Market capitalization over per-capita GNP times 100.
§ Turnover (traded value) in billion dollars.

suggest that emerging markets, even though not as efficient as major industrialized-country markets, are quite comparable to the smaller European markets. This is particularly true for the 'heavily traded segments' of the markets. On the other hand, a panoply of studies replicated quite closely the approaches used to test the efficiency of the US market. In most cases the authors were able to reject the random-walk hypothesis. This should not be surprising since this same result holds generally for the New York Stock Exchange. Tests of weak-form efficiency would have to be based on a rejection of the *fair-game* hypothesis in which trading strategies that exploit markets inefficiencies are used to obtain abnormal returns. These have not been done, thus ruling on this issue is still open. Lack of data has prevented many semi-strong and strong-form efficiency tests, but the ones available would suggest no efficiency. Again, an unsurprising outcome in the face of results of similar tests for developed country markets.

Of course, it would be a mistake to assign responsibility for the differences in functioning of these markets to any single factor. Much research will be needed before we have a reasonable understanding of the difference between an emerging and a developed market and what makes a market grow. In this chapter we propose to focus on a more general link between government activity and equities markets. The central proposition is that the government intervention in the economy affects the risk exposure of firms. We call this particular type of risk, *political risk* (PR).[1] Thus, we suggest that returns on domestic securities should thus respond to variations in government fiscal and policy variables. More specifically, the objective of this research project is twofold:

- First, like Agmon (1985) and Brewer (1985a) we stress that among the most important elements in the political environment of enterprises are the monetary, fiscal and expenditure policies of governments. Thus, these policies are a key determinant of firms' PR exposure.
- Second, based on this premise we attempt to establish the relationship between government *policy* variables (i.e. variables that are fully under the control of the government) and the performance of securities prices. We do this using a rational expectations approach on a sample of Latin American stock markets, namely Argentina, Brazil, Colombia and Venezuela. To allow for additional insights we present and compare results with those of a test made on the United States equities market.

The organization of the chapter is as follows: after this introduction we discuss the evolution of the concept of PR in the finance literature. This is important to narrow the scope of the definition of PR we propose. In the third section we present an elementary model of rational expectations that allows us to test the nature of the impact of changes in government policy variables on securities returns. In the fourth section we present briefly the data we use in the study and details of the statistical methodology. The fifth and sixth sections present a discussion of results and conclusions respectively.

13.2 EVOLUTION OF THE CONCEPT OF 'POLITICAL RISK' IN FINANCIAL RESEARCH

In this chapter we highlight the role of political risk in portfolio management, either domestic or for the purpose of international diversification. Thus we are concerned about the impact of government action on the return structure of financial assets. This is a rather unusual focus since it largely diverges from what has been studied in the traditional finance literature, both on the management of multinational corporations (MNCs) and the domestic or international capital asset pricing. To place our research in the context of the PR literature we need to review two bodies of research associated with the impact of government actions: first, the research on the impact of government actions on firms' cash flows, and second on the impact of those actions on financial asset pricing. Although there is an obvious relationship between the two, this relationship has not been formalized in the literature. We start the review by adopting a definition of PR by Robock (1971) that has been accepted as a point of departure in most of the literature on the subject. According to this author, *political risk can be defined as the risk associated with an unexpected change in government policy that affects the cash flows – and thus the rate of return – of an enterprise.* We will use Table 13.2 to help us to understand the various strains of the PR research literature.

In the last fifteen years or so, financial economics has come a long way in refining this concept by uncovering many nuances to the phenomenon. Initially, PR was seen as an issue associated with the impact on cash flows of changes in the legal environment of MNCs with operations in Third World countries. That is the focus was on direct (foreign) investment.[2] We include under this heading all the literature listed in the second column of Table 13.2. Consistent with

Table 13.2 Political risk in the finance literature

| | Direct foreign investment | | Portfolio investment | | |
	Legal aspects (restrictions, taxes, etc.)	Monetary and fiscal policies	Legal aspects (restrictions, taxes, etc.)	Monetary and fiscal policies	
Existing/ expected			Standard ICAPM with certain barriers Errunza & Losq (1985a, b, 1989) Stulz (1981)		Not political risk
Unexpected	Traditional PR literature Mahajan (1990) Kennedy & Baglioni (1988) Chase, Kuhle & Walther (1988) Burton & Inoue (1987) Brewer (1983) Nigh (1985) Levis (1979) Kobrin (1976, 1978, 1979) Shapiro (1978)	'New' PR literature Oxelheim & Wihlborg (1987) Agmon (1985) Brewer (1985a, 1985b)	CAPM with expected/ unexpected barriers Sellin (1991) Cosset & de la Rianderie (1985) Errunza & Losq (1987)	Policy variables and stock returns Darrat (1988) Alexakis & Petrakis (1991)	Political risk
Frequency	Discrete/rare events	Continuous/common events	Discrete/rare events	Continuous/common events	

Robock's definition most studies focused on unexpected events that affected this legal environment. Whether PR was relevant in a different context was not a point of discussion. Furthermore, it was seen predominantly as the result of acts of government that directly affected the cash flows of the MNCs subsidiaries with a certain emphasis on the dramatic, such as blockage of funds or expropriations. Models were developed that explicitly included consideration of PR in the financing and investment decisions of MNCs (e.g. Shapiro, 1978). Innovations in the evolution of the concept have taken three major directions.

First, with time researchers have come to recognize that PR is not an issue for MNCs operating in developing countries only. In fact, it was a type of risk exposure of assets that could occur theoretically in any economy, although, from a practical point of view PR was viewed as negligible in some economies. It was further argued that perhaps PR is just as relevant for domestic as for foreign assets. In this sense, for example, Phillips-Patrick (1989) compares the PR exposure of foreign and domestic firms in France, and recognizes that under certain conditions some domestic firms may even have a higher PR exposure than certain foreign firms.[3]

Second, throughout the years, research on PR has focused on *discrete events*, from expropriation and blockage of funds to social unrest and elections. In today's international environment the continued emphasis in this type of events seems disproportionate to the level of realization. Although few would insinuate that the era of expropriations and blockages of funds is gone forever, it is a fact that in the last ten years actual cases were rare if not absent altogether, while research continued focusing on these types of events.[4] Clearly, this almost exclusive focus on discrete political events is inappropriate. Focusing on discrete events is not only in conflict with reality, but it also ignores the fact that it is the day-to-day action of governments that is continuously affecting the economic environment in which firms operate. These actions range from obvious sources of PR that affect the legal environment of companies (such as changes in capital flow barriers and exchange controls) to some less-than-obvious such as monetary policy, fiscal policy and industrial policy. This latter group of actions in most cases have no impact on the legal environment of firms but affect their cash flows none the less. Further, even if we focus in discrete political events only, and in the process uncover that asset prices respond to these events (e.g. Cosset and de la Rianderie, 1985; Langohr and Viallet, 1984), the use of this acquired knowledge is limited. At best we can assert: (a) whether prices respond favourably to 'good news' and unfavourably to 'bad news', and (b) how efficiently markets respond, i.e. how fast is the news impounded in the price. It still remains unclear what is the structure of the price formation model to which assets are responding. In a further refinement that shifted the focus away from discrete events, it was recognized that PR is associated directly to the governments' macroeconomic policies (e.g. Brewer, 1985a, b; Oxelheim and Wihlborg, 1987). We include this literature under the heading of the third column in Table 13.2. This implies, among other things, the possibility that domestic as well as foreign firms may be indiscriminately and continuously affected.

Third, there is a-priori no reason why the impact of government actions, both of legal and policy nature, should affect firms' cash flows but not securities prices. We include the literature covering this particular form of PR risk under the heading of the fourth column of Table 13.2. As a rare case of explicit treatment of PR in portfolio management, we refer to the theoretical – albeit informal – speculations of Errunza and Losq (1987) in which relationships are drawn between PR and some existing model of international diversification and the international capital asset pricing model (ICAPM). For international portfolio diversification the case is clear: since it is precisely the stock of these domestic corporations that is of interest to portfolio managers engaged in international diversification, there is a need to focus on this very domestic aspect of PR. Both the focus on discrete events and the neglect of the impact of PR on domestic firms of extant research are not without some consequences to our understanding of international capital flows. For example, only recently are some models appearing that can incorporate PR variable in models useful for international portfolio management. For example, Peter Sellin (1991) introduces a ICAPM model in which cash flows may be expropriated at random times. However, note again the focus on 'confiscation' which, although it can take many forms from plain taxation to outright asset confiscation, still consists of an 'unexpected event' that is rare and thus should have little effect on actual asset prices.

We could not consider the review complete without some explicit consideration of important contributions to the literature of ICAPM with barriers, including Black (1974), Stulz (1981), Errunza and Losq (1985a, 1989) and others. This literature, although concerned with the existence of legal barriers to flows, does not address the issue of political risk. It is largely concerned with the impact of existing legal barriers on asset pricing. This is clearly a limiting case of political risk as defined by Robock (1971) with a probability of the event occurring equal to one. We have included this literature under the fourth column of Table 13.2.

Although not under the heading of PR, the efficient markets and rational expectations literature has focused on the impact of policy variables on the price of financial assets, including stocks. For example, Bonomo and Tanner (1983), in the context of the debate of 'natural rate' versus 'counter cyclical' monetary policy propositions, tests the proposition that *only* unexpected monetary changes have non-neutral effect on the USA stock market. Although all definitions of the model reject the hypothesis that 'rationally anticipated' monetary changes have systematic effect on stock prices, forecast revisions have some effect on relative prices. Two further studies by McMillin and Laumas (1988) for the USA and Darrat (1988) for Canada, test a theory by Blanchard (1981) suggesting a link between government policy variables, production and stock market prices. McMillin and Laumas find that in the USA anticipated as well as unanticipated fiscal policy actions affect real stock prices. Anticipated increases in money growth have similar effect, but the evidence is weaker in the case of unanticipated money growth. Darrat finds that in Canada, changes in the stance of fiscal policy play an important role in determining stock returns while monetary actions do not.[5]

In a related study, Alexakis and Petrakis (1991) use principal component analysis to identify the sources of variations in Greek stock returns. They find that the political variables chosen (left-wing participation in parliament and the hours of work lost due to strikes) rank fifth in explaining variation. Overall, the study finds that the behaviour of the share price index is more sensitive to alternative investment opportunities and sociopolitical factors than companies' or economic fundamentals.

13.3   A RE MODEL OF POLITICAL RISK

There are two aspects to the problem that need to be addressed. First, do government policies affect security returns? That is, does the market price uncertainties associated with policy variables? In this case we are focusing on the ability of the market to aggregate information about uncertainties that result from the government's policy making function. Second, assuming that PR *is* priced, how does the market process the information related to PR? This second question focuses on the efficiency of the market with respect to the set of information about government policy variables. The nature of the transmission mechanisms may indeed be complex. However, one of the great advantages of rational expectations (RE) analysis is that it allows the researcher to study the impact of information on market variables without having to specify the mechanism by which this impact operates. This does not imply that an in depth study of the transmission mechanisms is not feasible or even advisable. However, in the absence of a model capable of explaining how specific information impact prices, rational expectations provides parsimony to the effort of modelling unknown transmission mechanisms, as well as a econometric framework to do the modelling. Throughout the analysis we adopt a methodology that is close to that proposed by Mishkin (1983) for testing models of macroeconomic rational expectations.

The scenario we propose is that of investors facing an opportunity set of assets representing claims on domestic firms' cash flows. Investors operating in the market will not be systematically biased about the actions of governments and their impact on asset returns. This applies to both holders of financial as well as physical assets. The following example, albeit somewhat obvious, will make this clear. Assume that a public firm (that is, a firm for which publicly traded stocks exist) is a supplier of government inputs, in the extreme case this could be a military contractor. The cash flows associated to these assets are sensitive to the fiscal (spending) policy set by the government. Thus, a rational asset owner/manager will be an alert observer of the government's fiscal policies, π_f, and the independent observable variables, X_t, that influence these polices, $\pi_j = P(X_t)$. Further, he/she will form expectations of the government actions regarding government spending (maintaining, increasing or decreasing) and the probabilities associated with these shifts. For the moment we shall ignore *how* these expectations are formed – i.e. we will ignore the specific mechanism of expectation formation – but assume that unbiased expectations are formed. It is likely that the asset owner/manager will operate as to neutralize any negative effect, or exploit any opportunity, resulting from the government's action.

Similarly, investors holding claims on the assets (e.g. shares) will form unbiased expectations about both: the impact of the government's actions on the firm, and the competence of management to undertake these actions. Further, they will adjust the composition of their portfolios to reflect these expectations modifying the demand/ supply relationships of different financial assets. Thus, the price of the securities representing contingent claims on the firms' cash flows should reflect both market-wide expectations about the government's actions and the firms' competence to respond to these actions. Note that the impact of government actions may operate through a variety of channels in addition to firm's cash flows: e.g., affect the risk-free rate at which future cash flows of financial claims are discounted; affect the market-wide risk premium charged on risky claims; etc. Also, an observation common to this type of model will be repeated here. It is not necessary that all investors are well informed and rational, and act to eliminate abnormal return opportunities. The only condition required is that there are *some* informed market participants standing ready to eliminate the unexploited profit opportunities that may result from innovations in the information set.

Furthermore, events, such as fluctuations in fiscal and monetary policy, tend to affect the economy as a whole. Thus hedging opportunities through domestic portfolio diversification are limited. This characteristic of PR implies that the level of domestic systematic risk to which investors are exposed – non-diversifiable by the means available to an investor within the national economy – is pervasive and therefore will be priced.

RE theory starts from the premise that market participants' psychological, subjective expectations equal the true mathematical expectations of future values of the variables, conditional on all available past information. When applying this basic premise to the problem at hand, this implies that the market should form rational expectations about any government's policies, assess their impact on the market, and respond to this expectations by acting accordingly. They do this by shifting their investment behaviour. Consequently, the market's expectations about government action should be reflected in the price of assets that represent claims on the cash flows of the firm subject to PR.

In equilibrium any abnormal return $r_t - r_t^e$ to be obtained over the period $t - 1$ to t should be the result of *only*: (a) the arrival of new information into the market, mostly corrections to the information set $\varphi_{p,t-1}$ and realizations of relevant state variables, and (b) a random disturbance. These abnormal returns should be uncorrelated with the information set φ_{t-1}. The contrary would imply absence of market efficiency. This situation can be represented by the following equation

$$r_t - r_t^e = \beta(\mathbf{Y}_t - \mathbf{Y}_t^e) + \varepsilon_t, \tag{1}$$

where ε_t is a scalar error term such that $E(\varepsilon_t \mid \varphi_{t-1}) = 0$, implying that ε_t is serially uncorrelated and uncorrelated to forecast errors $(\mathbf{Y}_t - \mathbf{Y}_t^e)$; $\mathbf{Y}_t$ is a $k \times 1$ vector containing variables relevant to the pricing of the security at time t; this includes fiscal and monetary policy variables. $\mathbf{Y}_t^e$ is a $k \times 1$ vector of one period ahead rational forecasts of $\mathbf{Y}_t$, where

$$\mathbf{Y}_t^e = E_m(\mathbf{Y}_t \mid \varphi_{t-1}) = E(\mathbf{Y}_t \mid \varphi_{t-1});$$

β is a $1 \times k$ vector of coefficients; r_t is the stock return at time t; φ_{t-1} is the set of information available at time $t - 1$, $E_m(\dots \varphi_{t-1})$ is the subjective expectation assessed by the market, and $E(\dots \varphi_{t-1})$ is the objective expectation conditional on φ_{t-1}.

In the absence of an economic forecasting model, or a 'market forecast' generated by, for example, pooling of information (such as the Goldsmith–Nagan survey of interest rates forecasts from actual market participants in Friedman (1980)), or 'announcements' on future states of policy variables (as suggested by Blanchard (1981)), we specify an econometric forecasting model. We use a linear specification such as:

$$\mathbf{Y}_t = \mathbf{X}_{t-1} \gamma + \upsilon_t, \tag{2}$$

where $\mathbf{Y}_t$ is the $k \times 1$ vector of forecasted variable as defined above; $\mathbf{X}_{t-1}$ is a $m \times 1$ vector of variables used to forecast $\mathbf{Y}_t$ which are available at time $t - j, j = 1, 2, 3, \dots$ $\mathbf{X}_{t-1}$ may contain lagged values of $\mathbf{Y}_t$; γ is a $k \times m$ matrix of coefficients, and υ is a $k \times 1$ vector of error term assumed to be uncorrelated with any information available at time $t - 1$, including $\mathbf{X}_t$ and serially uncorrelated.

A forecast $\mathbf{Y}_t^e$ is obtained by taking expectations of (2),

$$\mathbf{Y}_t^e = E[\mathbf{Y}_t] = \mathbf{X}_{t-1}\gamma \tag{3}$$

that, when substituted in (1) yields

$$r_t - r_t^e = \beta(\mathbf{Y}_t - \mathbf{X}_t\gamma) + \varepsilon_r \tag{4}$$

We further assume that expectations about returns, r_t^e, are formed consistent with the following process

$$r_t^e = r_{t-1}^f + \bar{\phi}_t(\varphi_{t-1}).\tag{5}$$

That is, at any point in time the expected return over the period $t - 1$ to t is equal to the *ex ante* risk-free rate, r_{t-1}^f, plus a risk premium, a random variable, $\tilde{\phi}_t$, that is a function of the information set φ_{t-1}. Now, $\varphi_{t-1} = \varphi_{p,\,t-1} \cup \varphi'_{p,\,t-1}$, where $\varphi'_{p,\,t-1}$ is the complement of $\varphi_{p,\,t-1}$ in φ'_{t-1}, representing all 'other' information uncorrelated to $\varphi_{p,\,t-1}$. Thus we can partition the risk premium, $\tilde{\phi}_t$, into two orthogonal components associated to the respective information subsets or 'factors', $\psi_t(\varphi_{p,\,t-1})$, a *political risk premium*, and $\phi_t(\varphi_{p,\,t-1})$. That is, $\tilde{\phi} = \phi_t(\varphi_{p,\,t-1}) + \psi_t(\varphi_{p,\,t-1})$. We represent the first risk premium, $\psi_t(\varphi_{p,\,t-1})$, as a linear function of fiscal and monetary policy variables:

$$\psi_t(\varphi_{p,\,t-1}) = \delta Y_t^e + \xi_t\tag{6}$$

and

$$r_t^e = r_{t-1}^f + \phi_t + \delta Y_t^e + \xi_t,\tag{7}$$

where ξ_t is a white noise. That is, at any point in time the expected return over the period $t - 1$ to t, r_t^e, is equal to the risk-free rate, r_{t-1}^f, plus a risk premium ϕ_t that is either time variant or invariant,[6] plus a premium that is specific to the type of risk under study. Again, the parameter ϕ_t plays the role of capturing all sources of risk that may be priced but are not associated to the information set contained in Y_t^e.

Rearranging yields

$$r_t - r_{t-1}^f = \phi_t + \beta(Y_t - X_{t-1}\gamma^*) + \delta(X_{t-1}\gamma^*) + \varepsilon_t\tag{8}$$

In equation (8) the *ex-post* excess returns $r_t - r_{t-1}^f$ are function of innovations in the information set $\psi'(\varphi_{p,t})$ occurring at two points in time: First, at time $t - 1$, the expectations market participants form about the future state of the policy variables $E[Y_t]$. This effect, if it exists, will reflect in coefficient γ statistically different from zero. For example, a negative assessment of the impact of an upward shift of $E[Y_t]$ on the firms' value will increase the premium charged on stock, depressing the price P_{t-1} and increasing the expected (required) return on holding the stock. Thus $\delta > 0$. Second, at time t, as market participants observe the actual value of the state variables Y_t, they assess the impact of the 'surprise' and price the stock, P_t, accordingly. Pursuing the earlier example, if expectations of Y_t, $E[Y_t]$, fell short of the actual realization of Y_t, and this is considered to be 'bad news,' a correction will take place depressing the price, P_t, and depressing excess returns, $r_t - r_{t-1}^f$. In this case $\beta < 0$. Note that a similar assessment of the impact of the state variables on the value of the firm leads to opposite sign for the two coefficients in (8).

This model of the return structure has some important implications on the interpretation of results. In particular we cannot interpret a δ significantly different from zero as evidence of market efficiency. That interpretation would be correct only if the dependent variable is *abnormal returns*, $r_t - r_t^e$, which it is not. If one uses *excess returns*, $r_t - r_{t-1}^f$ – as in our study – or *total returns*, r_t – as in Darrat's (1988) study – then the implication is simply that there is a predictable component to returns that can be associated with policy variables. This may violate the random-walk hypothesis of the stock market but does not violate a fair-game hypothesis of that market. For other evidences of a predictable component of stock returns see Carmichael and Samson (1992), Bekaert and Hodrick (1990), Campbell and Hamao (1990), Cutler, Poterba and Summers (1990), Campbell and Shiller (1988), Fama and French (1988) and Campbell (1987), etc. These authors were able to predict *excess returns* with variables such as dividend yields, the term structure spread, the default risk spread in bonds, changes in short term interest rates and the January effect.

The rational expectations model estimation procedure consists of estimating equations (2) and (8) which we now present together as a system.

$$Y_t^e = E[Y_t] = X_{t-1}\gamma + \upsilon_t \tag{9–1}$$

$$r_t - r_{f,t} = \phi + \beta(Y_t - X_{t-1}\gamma^*) + \delta(X_{t-1}\gamma^*) + \varepsilon_t, \tag{9–2}$$

where υ_t and ε_t are assumed to have mean zero and be serially uncorrelated. Note that we have dropped the time subscript for the coefficient ϕ which, in the statistical implementation of the model, will be assumed to be time invariant.

13.4 DATA AND STATISTICAL METHODOLOGY

Monthly data for a sample of four LA countries for periods of various length between the years 1980 and 1991 is available. These countries are: Argentina, Brazil, Colombia and Venezuela. Variables used, their source, and transformations made to the data before entering into the statistical models (e.g. deseasonalization, differencing, etc.) are described in detail in the Appendix. It is important to note that the variables proxy for fiscal and monetary policy were carefully selected. Of all possible candidates of monetary and fiscal policy variables we chose those that were most under the control of the government and were least subject to external shocks. The proxies used were: for *fiscal policy*, the central government's expenditure and fiscal deficit, and for *monetary policy*, reserve money (money base minus currency in hand of the public).

The statistical methodology employed in this chapter is the so-called two-step procedure for rational expectations models.[7] This two-step procedure consists of: first, identifying and estimating the forecasting equation (9–1) and, second, estimating the rational expectations equation (9–2) using forecasts and forecast errors generated through equation (9–1). We now describe briefly the statistical methodology used to complete the two-step procedure. Statistical tests used throughout the analysis follow the specifications presented in Judge *et al.* (1985).

The first step, i.e. the selection and estimation of the forecasting model is actually the more involved portion of the statistical analysis. The statistical methodology used in the present study is vector autoregression (VAR) forecasting. This statistical model can be represented as follows:

$$\mathbf{Y}_t^e = \mathbf{v} + \sum_{p=1}^{L} \Theta \mathbf{Y}_{t-p} + \sum_{p'=1}^{L'} H \mathbf{X}_{t'_p} + \mathbf{v}_t. \qquad (10)$$

In this system of m equations (one equation per variable to be forecasted), $\mathbf{v}$ is an m-dimensional vector, the Θ and H are $m \times m$ coefficient matrices, Θ corresponding to the endogenous variables $\mathbf{Y}_{t-p}$, and H corresponding to the exogenous variables $\mathbf{X}_{t-p}$, and $\mathbf{v}_t$ is a vector white noise. Three aspects of this model needed to be identified:

(a) The length of the lag, L, of the endogenous variables in the VAR system. This was accomplished using the Schwartz criteria (SC). Although the Akaike Information Criteria (AIC) is better known and more widely used, Monte Carlo studies have shown that the SC chooses the correct lag order most often and the resulting estimated autoregressive process provides a better forecast (Judge *et al.*, 1985). The use of SC tends to result in models with shorter lags.

(b) The exogenous or instrumental variables that serve to improve the forecasting power of the model. This was done using a block exogeneity test. This test is a multivariate generalization of the Granger–Sims causality test and, in essence, consists of a likelihood ratio (LR) test. One by one, candidate exogenous variables were included into the system and their contribution to the forecasting power of the model tested with the block exogeneity test. The combination of exogenous variables selected for each country is presented in Table 12.3.

(c) The length of the lag, L', for the exogenous variables selected. This was done using again the SC. A uniform length was used for all exogenous variables. Lag length for both endogenous and exogenous variables are reported at the bottom of Table 13.3.

Estimation of equation (9–2) was done using a standard OLS regression procedure. As the measure of forecasting errors we use the residuals of system (10). Predictions were obtained by subtracting the residuals of system (10) from the series of actual observations. It is well known that returns may be abnormal around January. Thus we included a dummy variable for this month in the regression. Another dummy variable was added to the regressions for Argentina and the United States. In the case of Argentina it accounts for the short period of serious hyperinflation that occurred in May, 1989. It was around this time that the then president, Raul Alfonsin, was forced to hand over power early to the incoming president Carlos Menem. For the United States the dummy represents the crash of October 1987. The relatively mild drops that occurred in the Latin American economies around this date did not warrant the inclusion of a crash related dummy in the regressions.

13.5 ANALYSIS OF RESULTS

VAR systems can generate many coefficients and other statistics depending upon the lag lengths L and L'. The value, sign and significance of these statistics are of little help beyond a general appreciation of the power of the forecasting equation. The value and significance of the parameters corresponding to the rational expectations equation are reported in Table 13.4, for all four countries. The strength of the results is quite surprising. The F-statistic of all models suggests a good fit, and in two cases (Argentina and United States) the explanatory power of the regression is rather remarkable. We

Table 13.3   Selection of forecasting variables and lag length for forecasting equation

This table lists the dependent variables, candidate independent variables, selected independent variables and lag length used in the forecasting equation by country. The independent variables were selected using a χ^2 distributed block-exogeneity (multivariate Granger causality) test for each country. The lag length was chosen for each country using a Schwartz information criteria (SIC) test. Since we computed the optimal lag length for the endogenous and exogenous variables independently in the VAR system, we report both.

Dependent variables

Fiscal policy:
Government spending
Fiscal deficit.

Monetary policy:
Monetary base*

Candidate independent variables
Industrial production
Fiscal revenues
Balance of trade
Exchange rate
Discount rate
Inflation
FX reserves
Government LT-bond yield/Deposit rates†

Independent variables selected

Argentina
Industrial production
Fiscal revenues
Balance of trade
Exchange rate
Inflation
FX reserves
Commercial lending rates

Lags: 1/1

Brazil
Fiscal revenues
Inflation
FX reserves
Commercial lending rates

Lags: 1/1

Colombia
Fiscal revenues
Balance of trade
Exchange rate
Discount rate

Lags: 1/1

Venezuela
Fiscal deficit‡
Fiscal revenues
Balance of trade
Exchange rate
Discount rate
Inflation
FX reserves

Lags: 1/1

United States
Fiscal revenues
Discount rate
Inflation
FX reserves

Lags: 1/1

* In the case of Colombia Claims on Government (COG) was used, due to better availability of data.
† One or the other, depending upon availability. See also note § in the appendix.
‡ This variable was included in the model as an exogenous variable rather than as a policy variable. See footnotes to Table 12.4 for an explanation of this decision.

Table 13.4 Estimation of rational expectations equation

This table reports the values of the parameters and the corresponding computed t-test values (below the coefficients, in brackets) of the rational expectations equation. This corresponds to the second step of the two-step estimation procedure. The estimated equation is:

$$r_t - r_t^* = \phi + \beta(Y_t - X_t\gamma^*) + \delta(X_t\gamma^*) + \varepsilon_t$$

Country	φ Const.	Dummy*	January	β₁ Experr	β₂ Deferr	β₃ Monerr	δ₁ Expfor	δ₂ Deffor	δ₃ Monfor	F	DW	Adj. R²	Q (lags)	Period (NDF available)†
Argentina	0.241 (0.027)	424.109 (4.368)	7.7570 (0.260)	-2.7413 (-0.075)	-0.7310 (-0.086)	-2.3399 (-0.036)	-40.4545 (-3.214)	-611.1903 (-6.242)	-54.0848 (-4.213)	6.552	1.57	0.35	21.20 (27)	1983: 1–1991:12 (82)
Brazil	-1.365 (-1.238)	NA‡	0.0725 (1.460)	-0.1235 (-2.259)	-0.6093 (-0.940)	0.3205 (1.430)	-0.1195 (-1.031)	-3.9419 (-1.630)	3.7390 (4.327)	4.52	1.55	0.20	37.26 (25)	1977:06–1985:12 (102)
Colombia	-0.009 (-0.294)	NA	-0.0302 (-0.694)	-0.1222 (-1.359)	-0.1203 (-0.854)	-0.0151 (-0.083)	0.1345 (0.636)	2.7621 (2.983)	0.6040 (1.258)	1.968	1.96	0.18	9.91 (10)	1986:04–1990:08 (31)
Venezuela	0.0308 (1.817)	NA	0.0284 (0.603)	0.1347 (2.182)	NA	-0.0409 (-0.193)	0.3364 (1.990)	NA	-0.3342 (-0.851)	1.83	1.39	0.07	21.47 (17)	1985:12–1991:10 (57)
United States	-0.0001 (-0.044)	-0.244 (-5.675)	0.0091 (0.623)	NA	-0.0105 (-0.189)	-0.1033 (-0.317)	NA	-0.4227 (-3.181)	0.4604 (0.628)	8.16	2.15	0.25	24.45 (32)	1981: 3–1991:12 (130)

* These dummy variables mean different things for different countries. In the case of *Argentina* it accounts for the short period of serious hyperinflation that occurred in May, 1989. For the *United States* the dummy represents the crash of October 1987.

† This number represents the total degrees of freedom available after accounting for missing data within the period.

‡ We report an NA whenever we restricted the regression coefficient corresponding to the variable at the top of the column to be zero.

observe coefficients that are different from zero at the 5 per cent or the 10 per cent confidence level in every country, including the US. This is true even when using a very small sample such as in the case of Colombia. Most significant coefficients are associated with the forecasted variables rather than the forecasting errors. In the case of Argentina, all three coefficients associated to the forecast are significantly different from zero. The value and significance of the coefficients associated to the forecasted variables imply that investors develop expectations about the future state of the world in terms of the governments' fiscal and monetary policy, and price stocks accordingly.

On the other hand, only two coefficients associated to the forecasting errors are statistically different from zero. For those coefficients that are statistically different from zero, in one case the signs of the coefficients associated to the forecast and the forecast errors are opposite, consistent with theory, but in the other case not.

The rather weak result obtained for Colombia is none the less of interest. This result could be ascribed to more than one reason. First, the small sample available and the fact that the proxy of monetary policy is the variable claims on government rather than the monetary base. Second, and perhaps more importantly, the drug-based unofficial economy with a vast international market, could also explain this result. Perhaps the market is more responsive to fluctuations in this underground economy than to government policy. The absence of significance of even the constant may suggest that, without excluding the latter possibility, the first explanation may be at least partly responsible.

The theoretical part of the chapter suggest that the sign of the coefficients corresponding to the prediction and the prediction error should be opposite. However, there is no suggestion about what these signs should be specifically. This is so because macroeconomic theory's predictions of the impact of government policies on real variables are very sensitive to the assumptions made in the formulation of the model. The simple relaxation of an assumption such as price constancy in the real sector (in e.g., Blanchard, 1981) can lead to completely opposite results. Thus we have abstained, much to our discomfort, from making specific predictions about these signs. In fact, the signs of the coefficients vary considerably over the five countries used in the study. It is, none the less interesting to note that the sign of coefficients tend to be equal for the two economies whose governments' fiscal and monetary policy resemble most each other, Argentina and Brazil, and contrary to that which might be considered different, Venezuela and Colombia.

13.6 CONCLUSION

In this chapter we investigate in a rational expectations framework the impact of political risk on common stock returns and test the resulting model on a sample of Latin American stock exchanges. More specifically, we stress that the monetary and fiscal policies of governments are among the most important elements in the political environment of firms. Thus, these policies are a key determinant of firms' political risk exposure. Based on this premise, we attempt to establish the relationship between government policy variables (i.e. variables that are fully under the control of the government), and the performance of securities prices in four Latin American countries: Argentina, Brazil, Colombia and Venezuela.

The strength of the results is quite surprising. The results imply that investors develop expectations about the future state of the world in terms of the governments' fiscal and monetary policy, and price stocks accordingly. In other words, this implies, consistent with an efficient market hypothesis, that prices of stocks fully incorporate expectations about policy changes introduced by government. Also, quite rationally, they seem to respond to discrepancies between the expected and actual states of the world by adjusting prices consistently.

APPENDIX: DATA DESCRIPTION

Stock return data, r_t. Return on the stock market index including dividend yield. *Source*: International Finance Corporation's (IFC), Emerging Markets Database (EMDB).

Riskless interest rates, r_t^f. Source: International Financial Statistics (IFS). For Argentina, Colombia and Venezuela, in the absence of treasury bill rates we used end-of-month 90-days certificates of deposits (CD) rates reported in the *IFS*. Brazil: the discount rate calculated on the basis of sales quotations among financial institutions of 13-week treasury bills reported by the *IFS*; it is an arithmetic average of the daily rates.

Monetary and fiscal policy data, Y_t and X_t. Source: International Financial Statistics (IFS). Countries were selected in part by the availability of monthly observations for these data in the *IFS*. The table below lists the variables used, their code in the *IFS* database, and the transformation performed on the series before entering them into statistical model.

Table A–1 List of variables and data source
(all data monthly observations)

Variable	IFS code	Transformation
Policy/Endogenous (Y_t)		
Fiscal: (a) Government expenditure	82	Log of level, adjusted for inflation, deseasonalized*
(b) Fiscal deficit	80	Level, adjusted for inflation, deseasonalized, and adjusted for real activity[†]
Monetary: (a) Reserve money/Claims on govt.	14	Log of change, deseasonalized
Forecasting/Exogenous (X_t)		
Manufacturing productions	66ey	Log of change[‡]
Balance of trade	70, 71	Level, adjusted for inflation
Central bank discount rate	60	%, adjusted for inflation
Consumer price index (inflation)	64	Log of change
Real exchange rate	ae	Adjusted for inflation
Foreign exchange reserves	1.d.d.	Log of level
Government Bond Yield/Deposit rates	61a/JPM	%, adjusted for inflation[§]
Fiscal revenues	81	Log of level, adjusted for inflation

* Deseasonalized variables were computed using the following equation:

$$y_t^a = y_t - \beta_0 - \sum_{l=1}^{11} \beta_{1_l} S_l$$

where y_t^a represents the deseasonalized variable, y_t the original series, S_l a dummy variable for each month, and β_j are the coefficients obtained from regressing y_t against the monthly dummy variables.

† We adjusted the fiscal deficit variable for the level of business activity. The adjusted value of fiscal deficit y_t^a was obtained with the following equation:

$$y_t^a = y_t - \beta_0 - \sum_{l=1}^{11} \beta_{1_l} S_l - \beta_2 x_t$$

where y_t represents the original series, S_l a dummy variable for each month, x the level of industrial production, and β_j are coefficients obtained from the regression of y against S_l and x.

‡ When available. For Argentina and Brazil we used exports (*IFS–70d*). For Colombia we used coffee exports (*IFS–70d*) and Venezuela petroleum production (*IFS–66aa*)

§ The purpose of this variable is to provide a measure of interest rates in the economy. Government bond yields were available for Venezuela and the United States. For Argentina and Brazil we used commercial bank deposit rates that were obtained from *World Financial Markets* (Morgan Guaranty Trust Company, New York). It should be clear that these two variables are extremely imperfect substitutes of a measure of interest rates in the economy. For Colombia we obtained an estimate of interest rates in the economy assuming Fisher-open. We used dollar interest rates and black market spot exchange rates, obtained from the *World Currency Yearbook*, to compute the equilibrium domestic interest rate.

Notes

1. Brewer (1985) and more so Agmon (1985) also employ a similar definition of political risk. However, their focus remains on multinational corporations or country debt.
2. We could include here a quite extensive list of items which we chose to summarize under the concept of legal status, such as expropriations, confiscations, restrictions on repatriation of dividends, royalties, etc. In practice that included some events that disrupted the legal environment resulting from social or political upheavals that introduced uncertainty on the legal environment of the MNCs.
3. Another nuance identified in the concept is that political instability is not necessarily associated with PR (Robock, 1971; Kobrin, 1978; 1979; Errunza and Losq, 1987). Whether political instability translates into PR depends upon two factors. One is the level of involvement of government in the economy. *Ceteris paribus*, the lower this involvement the lower is the probability that political instability will translate in actions that directly affect a firm's cash flows. The other is the degree of continuity of economic policy that accompanies political instability.
4. It should then be no surprise that some of the recent studies have to search for their sample information quite far back in history (e.g., see, Burton and Inoue, 1987; Kennedy and Baglioni, 1988).
5. For further references on the response of financial market variables to monetary policy variables, see for example, Kaul (1987), Urich and Wachtel (1981); for influence of inflation (controllable by the government via monetary and fiscal policy), see e.g., Gultekin (1983); and a good summary by Ely and Robinson (1989).
6. Recent developments in the literature, e.g. Harvey (1991), strongly suggest that this risk premium is, most likely, time variant.
7. We are perfectly aware that this procedure will produce unbiased coefficients. However, as in most two-step procedures the t-statistics will be slightly overstated. This should be taken into consideration when interpreting the results.

REFERENCES

AGMON, T. (1985) *Political Economy and Risk in World Financial Markets* (Lexington, Mass.: Lexington Books, D.C. Heath).
ALEXAKIS, P. and PETRAKIS, P. (1991) 'Analyzing Stock Market Behavior in a Small Capital Market', *Journal of Banking and Finance*, 15, 471–83.
BEKAERT, G. and HODRICK, J. (1990) 'Characterizing Predictable Components in Excess Returns on Equity and Foreign Exchange Markets', Working Paper, Northwestern University. Aug.
BLACK, F. (1974) 'International Capital Market Equilibrium With Investment Barriers', *Journal of Financial Economics*, 40, 337–52.

BLANCHARD, O. J. (1981) 'Output, the Stock Market and Interest Rates', *American Economic Review*, 71, 132–43.

BONOMO, V. and TANNER, J. E. (1983) 'Expected Monetary Changes and Relative Prices: A Look at Evidence from the Stock Market', *Southern Economic Journal*, 50, 334–45.

BREWER, T. L. (1983) 'The Instability of Controls on MNE's Funds Transfers and the Instability of Governments', *Journal of International Business*, 14 (Winter), 147–57.

BREWER, T. L. (1985a) 'A Comparative Analysis of the Fiscal Policies of Industrial and Developing Countries: Policy Instability and Governmental Regime Instability', *Journal of Comparative Economics*, 9 (June), 191–6.

BREWER, T. L. (1985b) 'Times Series Forecasting: Illustrations and Issues', in T. L. Brewer (ed.) *Political Risk in International Business* (New York: Praeger).

BREWER, T. L. and RIVOLI, P. (1990) 'Politics and Perceived Country Creditworthiness in International Banking', *Journal of Money, Credit, and Banking*, 22, 357–69.

BURTON, F. N. and INOUE, H. (1987) 'A Country Risk Appraisal Model of Foreign Asset Expropriation in Developing Countries', *Applied Economics*, 19, 1009–48.

CAMPBELL, J. Y. (1987) 'Stock Returns and the Term Structure', *Journal of Financial Economics*, 18, 373–99.

CAMPBELL, J. Y. and HAMAO, Y. (1990) 'Predictable Stock Returns in the United States and Japan: a Study of Long-term Capital Market Integration', *National Bureau of Economic Research*, Working Paper No. 3191.

CAMPBELL, J. Y. and SHILLER, R. J. (1988) 'Stock Prices, Earnings and Expected Dividends', *Journal of Finance*. 43, 661–76.

CARMICHAEL, B. and SAMSON, L. (1992) 'La détermination des primes de risque: une approche dynamique avec attentes rationelles', *Working Paper* 9203 (Québec: Université Laval).

CHASE, C. D., KUHLE, J. L. and WALTHER, C. H. (1988) 'The Relevance of Political Risk in Direct Foreign Investment', *Management International Review*, 28, 31–8.

COSSET, J.-C. and DE LA RIANDERIE, B. D. (1985) 'Political Risk and Foreign Exchange Rates: An Efficient Market Approach', *Journal of International Business Studies* (Fall) 21–55.

CUTLER, D. M., POTERBA, J. and SUMMERS, L. H. (1990) 'Speculative Dynamics', *National Bureau of Economic Research*, Working Paper 3242.

DARRAT, A. F. (1988) 'On Fiscal Policy and the Stock Market', *Journal of Money, Credit, and Banking*, 20, 353–63.

DOOLEY, M. P. and MATHIESON, D. J. (1987) 'Financial Liberalization in Developing Countries', *Finance & Development* (Sept.), 31–4.

ELY, D. P. and ROBINSON, K. J. (1989) 'The Stock Market and Inflation: A Synthesis of Theory and Evidence', *Economic Review* (Federal Reserve Bank of Dallas) (Mar.), 17–29.

ERRUNZA, V. and LOSQ, E. (1989) 'Capital Flow Controls, International

Asset Pricing, and Investor's Welfare: A Multi-Country Framework', *Journal of Finance*, 44, 1025–37.

ERRUNZA, V. and LOSQ, E. (1985a) 'International Asset Pricing under Mild Segmentation', *Journal of Finance*, 40, 105–124.

ERRUNZA, V. and LOSQ, E. (1987) 'How Risky are Emerging Markets?', *Journal of Portfolio Management* (Fall) 62–7.

ERRUNZA, V. and LOSQ, E. (1985b) 'The Behavior of Stock Prices on LDC Markets', *Journal of Banking and Finance*, 9, 561–75.

FAMA, E. F. and FRENCH, K. R. (1988) 'Dividend Yields and Expected Stock Returns', *Journal of Financial Economics*, 22, pp. 3–25.

FISCHER, K. P., ORTIZ, E. and PALASVIRTA, A. P. (1991) 'The Industrial Group and Risk Management in Imperfect Capital Markets', in D. Dimon and R. Sarathy (eds), *Management and Economic Growth Prospects in Latin America and the Caribbean* (San Diego: University of San Diego) 55–77.

FRIEDMAN, B. (1980) 'Survey Evidence on the "Rationality" of Interest Rates Expectations', *Journal of Monetary Economics*, 6, 753–66.

GULTEKIN, N. B. (1983) 'Stock Market Returns and Inflation Forecasts', *Journal of Finance*, 38, 663–73.

HARVEY, C. R. (1991) 'The World Price of Covariance Risk', *Journal of Finance*, 46, 111–58.

JUDGE, G. S., GRIFFITHS, W. E., CARTER HILL, R., LÜTKEPOHL, H. and LEE, T.-C. (1985) *The Theory and Practice of Econometrics*, 2nd edn (New York: John Wiley & Sons).

KAUL, G. (1987) 'Stock Returns and Inflation', *Journal of Financial Economics*, 18, 253–76.

KENNEDY, C. R. and BAGLIONI, A. J. (1988) *A Model of Political Regime Change and Expropriation Risk*. Monograph. Academy of International Business, San Diego (July).

KOBRIN, S. J. (1979) 'Political Risk: A Review and Reconsideration', *Journal of International Business Studies* (Spring/Summer), 67–80.

KOBRIN, S. J. (1978) 'When Does Political Instability Result in Increased Investment Risk?', *Columbia Journal of World Business*, (Fall) 113–22.

KOBRIN, S. J. (1976) 'The Environmental Determinants of Foreign Direct Manufacturing Investment: An Ex Post Empirical Analysis', *Journal of International Business*, 7, 29–42.

LANGOHR, H. and VIALLET, C. (1984) 'The Reaction of the Paris Bourse to a Sequence of Major Events: The Case of the French Nationalization Program (1981–1982)', in G. A. Hawawini and P. A. Michael (eds), *European Equity Markets* (New York: Garland Publishing) 271–90.

LEVIS, M. (1979) 'Does Political Instability in Developing Countries Affect Foreign Investment Flows? An Empirical Examination', *Management International Review*, 19, 59–68.

MAHAJAN, A. (1990) 'Pricing Expropriation Risk', *Financial Management*, 19 (Winter) 77–86.

MCMILLIN, W. D. and LAUMAS, G. S. (1988) 'The Impact of Anticipated and Unanticipated Policy Actions on the Stock Market', *Applied Economics*, 20 377–84.

MISHKIN, F. S. (1983) *A Rational Expectations Approach to Macroeconometrics* (Chicago: University of Chicago Press).

NIGH, D. (1985) 'The Effect of Political Events on United States Direct Foreign Investment: A Pooled Times Series Cross-Sectional Analysis', *Journal of International Business*, 16 (Spring) 1–17.

OXELHEIM, L. and WIHLBORG, C. G. (1987) *Macroeconomic Uncertainty: International Risks and Opportunities for the Corporation* (New York: John Wiley & Sons).

PHILLIPS-PATRICK, F. J. (1989) 'The Effect of Asset and Ownership Structure on Political Risk', *Journal of Banking and Finance*, 13, 651–71.

ROBOCK, S. H. (1971) 'Political Risk: Identification and Assessment', *Columbia Journal of World Business* (July/Aug.), 1–20.

SELLIN, P. (1991) *Political Risk in the Capital Asset Pricing Model*, Proceedings of the French Financial Association (July).

SHAPIRO, A. C. (1978) 'Capital Budgeting for the Multinational Corporation', *Financial Management* (Spring) 7–16.

SOLNIK, B. (1991) *International Investments*, 2nd edn (New York: Addison-Wesley).

STULZ, R. (1981) 'On the Effect of Barriers on International Investment', *Journal of Finance*, 36, 923–34.

URICH, T. and WACHTEL, P. (1981) 'Market Response to the Weekly Money Supply Announcements in the 1970s', *Journal of Finance*, 36, 1063–73.

Part VI
Capital Markets

Part VI takes an analytical look at capital markets and makes important extensions of modern investments, portfolio theory as well as agency theory to take into account increased international competition and globalization of financial markets. Patterns of changes in the international capital markets are examined to determine their efficiency; conventional paradigms and research techniques are extended to test global efficiency and formulate new theories and tests for the case of emerging capital markets. The issues have attracted the attention of practitioners and researchers, but disagreements remain on the nature of global exchange markets. One point of concern refers to the degree of integration among international stock exchanges and their ability to process information. Shahriar Khaksari and Neil Seitz conduct new tests to answer this question. In Chapter 14, 'Real Test of International Market Efficiency', the authors aim at determining whether the mean-variance frontier available to an internationally diversified investor is affected by the choice of the country in which ultimate consumption is to occur. Limitations of previous studies are overcome by including dividends as well as price changes in computing equity returns, by including long and short-term debt securities as well as equity, and by adjusting returns for inflation so that both real and nominal return efficient frontiers could be examined. Empirical findings show that the location of the mean-variance efficient frontier is affected by the country in which ultimate consumption takes place. The chapter provides therefore evidence that international capital markets are not fully integrated. Chapter 15 analyzes risk management and corporate governance in imperfect capital markets as they exist in LDCs (specifically in Latin America). Chapter 16 takes the reader into the Korean financial market, and in Chapter 17 the authors examine equity markets of quotation systems in France.

14 A Real Return Test of International Capital Market Efficiency

Shahriar Khaksari and Neil Seitz

14.1 INTRODUCTION

The nature of the mean-variance efficient frontiers available to investors in various countries (when internationally diversified portfolios are constructed) is of interest for practical and theoretical reasons. First, there is the practical question of the benefits investors in various countries gain from international diversification. Secondly, to theoreticians (and policy makers as well) there is the question of whether international capital markets are fully integrated. If the markets are integrated, an extension of standard efficiency definitions leads to the prediction that investors in all countries will have identical efficient frontiers.

While the advantages of international portfolio diversification have been recognized for many years (see, for example, Grubel (1968), Lessard (1974), and Levy and Sarnat (1975), most studies in this area have been based on the perspective of investors in only one country. However, there are several papers which have compared mean-variance efficient portfolios constructed from the investors' point of view in more than one country. In the first study of this type, Levy and Sarnat (1975) looks at nominal return-efficient frontiers from the standpoint of American and Israeli investors in more than one country. They find the two frontiers to be substantially different. This evidence would indicate that the two markets are segmented and therefore not efficient.

Nahum Biger (1979) computes nominal return-efficient portfolios from the stock market indices of eleven industrialized countries from 1966 to 1976, considering the perspectives of investors in each of the eleven countries. These efficient sets are reported to be very similar, despite large variations in exchange rates. Thus, this research exhibits evidence of the efficiency of international capital markets since risky

189

assets are being priced similarly. Biger's conclusion therefore conflicts with the results reported by Levy and Sarnat.

The works of Biger (1979), and Levy and Sarnat (1975), however, share several limitations. First, both studies have used only common stock, ignoring all other types of investments. Secondly, both studies have relied solely on holding-period return measured by price change alone by ignoring the dividend component of return. Thirdly, both results hinge on nominal returns measured in purchasing power terms.

The importance of considering a broader range of assets has been stressed by Roll (1977). Neither Biger nor the Levy and Sarnat results give any justification for ignoring all securities except common stock. Presumably, they choose this truncated security structure simply as a matter of practical convenience of reducing the data collection effort to manageable proportions. However, it appears to us that ignoring all other securities in the experimental studies may have distorted the domestic and international efficient frontiers available to investors. The primary reason for ignoring dividends appears apparently also a design for tractability of data. However, the importance of dividends in measuring returns over a period of time is well documented (Lessard, 1974, p. 4).

The importance of inflation in computing returns has been recognized ever since the classic work of Irving Fisher (1930) came into being, and almost every economist has accepted that ever since (see, for example, Lintner (1975), Solnik (1978), Biger (1975), and Branch (1974)). In general, rational investors are expected to consider real rather than nominal returns. One possible justification for ignoring inflation is the assumption that the inflation rate is known. In this vein, Biger (1979) observes, 'in essence, the efficient set of portfolios for these investors is identical to the efficient set obtained by nominal considerations except that mean return for each security's nominal return and the price level changes'. That means then that there is no simple relationship between nominal and real efficient frontiers.

Having a due appreciation then that inflation has an impact upon both risk and return of securities, it is clear that a test of the efficiency of markets should be based on real returns.

14.2 OBJECTIVES OF THE STUDY AND HYPOTHESIS

In this chapter, we attempt to overcome some of the limitations of the earlier papers, and thus try to derive meaningful conclusions on the efficiency of the international capital markets. Specifically, we extend the work of Biger (1979) by including dividends in measuring common stock returns, by including debt securities as well as common stock in the opportunity set, and by using real returns to recognize the impact of inflation. In an effort to do that we test the following hypotheses:

(1) When a set of securities, denominated in more than one currency, is considered, the mean-variance efficient frontier (constructed in real terms) will be the same regardless of the country in which the eventual expenditure of portfolio returns is expected to occur.

(2) When a set of securities, denominated in more than one currency, is considered, the mean-variance efficient frontier (constructed in nominal returns) will be the same regardless of the country in which the eventual expenditure of portfolio returns is expected to occur.

14.3   RESEARCH DESIGN

In this chapter, we construct mean-variance efficient frontiers using common stock, bonds and money market instruments from each of five countries. Furthermore, we take into consideration returns in both real and nominal terms from the perspective of investors desiring to consume goods in each of the five countries. The primary test concerns whether or not the location of the efficient frontier varies with a change in the country in which consumption occurs.

14.3.1   The set of investments

Since our interest is to ascertain if financial markets in the various countries are integrated, it is not necessary to look at the individual securities in each country. An index of returns for each type of security for each country is adequate for this purpose. If indexes representing all securities of a particular type in each country display a lack of market integration, one can conclude without examining individual securities that the markets are not integrated.

Here we use three kinds of investments from each of five countries: the United States, Great Britain, France, Germany and Japan. These countries have been selected because: (i) data and information regarding different kinds of securities for the time period of the study are available for these countries; (ii) these countries represent a very large portion of international trade, direct and indirect investment; (iii) there is more trade and flow of capital among these countries than any other group or the rest of the world altogether. If the capital market of these countries are not collectively efficient or integrated, the rest of the world capital markets is not likely to be efficient or integrated either. For the set of investments, we use stock market indices, government bonds, and short-term money market instruments. In the case of stock market indices, dividend returns as well as price appreciation returns are used.

The period chosen for the study is 1965 to 1979, which in turn provides 56 holding periods that allow an adequate scope for statistical testing. This time period also has the advantage of spanning wide variations in market conditions. It gives approximately seven years of data before and after the collapse of the *Bretton Woods* system. It also spans periods of relatively low and relatively high inflation.[1] Thus, our findings are not limited to some narrowly described set of market conditions.

We use quarterly data on two grounds. First, it gives a reasonable number of intervals for the period of observation. Secondly, this becomes the shortest holding period for which data can be obtained for all the international assets during the quarterly period and does not sell them in the markets during the quarter.

Stock price indices for all five countries have been collected from *International Financial Statistics*, published by the International Monetary Fund. Dividend yields for all the countries in the sample are obtained from *Economic Statistic Monthly*, published by the Bank of Japan. The Bank of Japan's US dividend yield data are based on the *Standard and Poor's 500 Stock Index*. The yield is the monthly average of yields obtained each week by dividing the aggregate cash dividend by the total market value. The United Kingdom's average yield is on the basis of 750 common stocks. Germany's yield is the quotient of the aggregate of the dividend (including any stock dividend) and the aggregate market value at the end of each month for all quoted shares. France's average dividend yield is on the basis of end-of-the-month yield of 280 stocks listed on the Paris Stock Exchange.

The bond indices that have been used include government bonds with a maturity of 10 years in the case of US, United Kingdom and Japan. Because of the lack of data on bonds with the comparable maturity, bond indices from Germany and France are excluded from the portfolio. Three-month treasury bills have been used to represent short-term money market instruments for the US and United Kingdom. For Japan, Germany and France, call money rates are used. The International Monetary Fund recognizes these assets as short-term money market instruments. Comparable data are more readily available for these instruments than for other representatives of short-term rates. While these short-term assets are of similar risk, there is nothing in the design for our experiment that requires that their risk characteristics be identical.

14.3.2 Exchange rates

Exchange rates at the beginning and end of each quarter have been taken from *International Financial Statistics*. As Westerfield (1977) shows, the distribution of exchange rates is not exactly normal and therefore two parameter models (mean and variance) cannot define the distribution. However, Westerfield demonstrates that for many countries, the standard deviation results in the same variability as other measures. Therefore, the use of the mean-variance approach is justified.

14.3.3 Inflation index

There exist differing opinions as to what should be construed as proper inflation index. The consumer price index, wholesale price index, GNP deflator, and specific price indices have all been suggested (Cornell, 1977). The two most well-known indices, of course, are the wholesale price index and the consumer price index. The wholesale price index (WPI) includes only goods prices, while service prices are included in the consumer price index (CPI). Assuming that both wages and worker productivity in manufacturing are growing at the same rate, changes in price level do not affect per unit labour costs or final good prices and obviously the WPI will not be affected. If, on the other hand, the labour market is competitive, wages in the service industry grow as much as the manufacturing sector of the economy. Since service prices enter the CPI, these rising wages will push the index up. Thus it can be postulated that the inflation rate as measured by CPI exceeds the WPI in the countries that are experiencing a positive productivity growth.

In order to select one of the two indices as the inflation rate, the ultimate usage of the returns from the financial assets should be specified. If the returns are supposed to be reinvested, then WPI is the more relevant one. But if the investors contemplate ultimately consuming the returns from their investment, the CPI is more appropriate. In this study, it was assumed that investors measure the returns from their investment on the basis of satisfaction received from consumption. Thus we choose the CPI data for representing inflation.

14.3.4   Holding period returns

The returns on all three different assets are computed on a quarterly basis. For government bonds, quarterly holding period returns are calculated by assuming the purchase of a par value bond at the beginning of each quarter and the sale of the bond at the end of that quarter. Since the bond's market values usually are not available and even when they exist, they are not comparable, the following computational procedure have been used. The value of the bond at the beginning of the quarter is simply assumed to be $1000. Interest during the period is based on the yield at the beginning of the period. The value at the end of the period is then determined by discounting the stream of payments still due from such a bond using the yield to maturity on such bonds at the end of the period as the discount rate. Thus, it is possible to compute a holding period return rather than just using the reported yield to maturity for the period. The holding period returns for stocks are found by the standard procedure of using beginning price dividends during the period, and end of period prices. Returns on money market instruments are straightforward. Percentage holding period returns for this class of assets are directly obtained from *International Financial Statistics*. The International Monetary Fund classifies a number of assets from different countries as short-term money market instruments, as mentioned before. These assets are three-month treasury bills from the United States and Great Britain, and call money rates for Japan, Germany and France.

The next step is to convert returns denominated in different currencies to nominal returns in the currency of the country in which the investor resides ($R_{n,t}$):

$$R_{n,t} = \frac{(P_{t+1} + I)\, X_{t+1} - P_t\, X_t}{P_t\, X_t},$$

where X_t is the units of the currency of the investor's country required to purchase a unit of the foreign currency at the beginning of period t; I_t is the interest or dividend paid during period t; and P_t is the price of the security at the beginning of period t.

In order to convert these nominal returns to real returns, the Consumer Price Index of the investor's home country is used as follows:

$$R_{r,t} = (1 + R_{n,t}) [CPI_t/CPI_{t-1}]^{-1}$$

where CPI_t is the Consumer Price Index at the beginning of period t; $R_{r,t}$ is the real return for period t, and $R_{n,t}$ is the nominal return for period t.

14.3.5 Efficient frontiers

Real and nominal holding period returns are computed for each of the securities from the perspective of a United States investor who is willing to diversify internationally. Then individual holding period returns are used to compute the mean return for each security, variance for each security, and a covariance matrix of returns for the thirteen securities. This information is then used to construct real and nominal return efficient frontiers by the calculus of the minimization method. The process is repeated from the perspective of an investor in each of the other countries.

14.4 EMPIRICAL RESULTS

As the objective of this analysis is to compare locations of efficient frontiers, the composition of the efficient portfolios is not reported in detail here. However, it is worth noting that the efficient portfolios regularly contain debt instruments as well as common stock. Thus, the importance of including these instruments in the analysis is confirmed. This result holds for both real and nominal returns.

Systematic differences have existed between mean-variance efficient frontiers for investors in all countries during this period both in nominal and real terms, although the differences are greatest in real terms. While the absolute size of the differences are not very large, the differences are large enough not to be attributed to random

Table 14.1   Real return efficient frontiers

Per cent returns	Variance				
	Germany	France	UK	Japan	US
1	0.000 104 8	0.000 164 2	0.000 358 2	0.000 243 5	0.000 183 2
2	0.000 432 6	0.000 629 0	0.000 800 4	0.000 691 8	0.000 676 8
3	0.001 195 2	0.001 429 8	0.001 562 9	0.001 472 6	0.001 497 6
4	0.002 242 7	0.002 566 4	0.002 645 5	0.002 585 7	0.002 645 6
5	0.003 624 9	0.004 039 0	0.004 048 4	0.004 031 2	0.004 120 9
6	0.005 341 9	0.005 847 5	0.005 771 5	0.005 809 2	0.005 923 4
7	0.007 393 8	0.007 991 9	0.007 814 9	0.007 919 5	0.008 053 1
8	0.009 780 4	0.010 472 2	0.010 178 5	0.010 362 3	0.010 510 0
9	0.012 501 8	0.013 288 5	0.012 862 3	0.013 137 4	0.013 294 2
10	0.015 558 0	0.016 440 6	0.015 866 3	0.016 245 0	0.016 405 5
11	0.018 949 1	0.019 928 7	0.019 190 6	0.019 684 9	0.019 844 1
12	0.022 674 9	0.023 752 7	0.022 835 1	0.023 457 3	0.023 610 0
13	0.026 735 5	0.027 912 5	0.026 799 8	0.027 562 0	0.027 703 0
14	0.031 130 9	0.032 408 4	0.031 084 8	0.031 999 2	0.032 123 3
15	0.035 861 1	0.037 240 1	0.035 690 0	0.036 768 8	0.036 870 8
16	0.040 926 1	0.042 407 7	0.040 615 4	0.041 870 7	0.041 945 5
17	0.046 325 9	0.047 911 3	0.045 861 0	0.047 305 1	0.047 347 5
18	0.052 060 5	0.053 750 8	0.051 426 9	0.053 071 9	0.053 076 7
19	0.058 129 9	0.059 926 1	0.057 313 0	0.059 133 1	0.059 133 1
20	0.064 534 1	0.066 437 4	0.063 519 4	0.065 602 7	0.065 516 7

variation. The real and nominal return results are discussed separately below.

14.4.1   Real return efficient frontiers

The mean-variance efficient frontiers are constructed for the 1965–79 period in real terms from the view points of investors in Germany, France, the United Kingdom, Japan, and the United States. The efficient sets over the range of 1 per cent to 50 per cent annual rate of return are computed and used for statistical testing. Results for 1 per cent to 20 per cent are tabulated, and are exhibited in Table 14.1. Rankings do not change between 20 per cent and 50 per cent.

During this period, the real return mean-variance efficient portfolios yield the highest return per unit of risk for investors in France and the lowest return per unit of risk for investors in Japan, after adjusting for exchange rate gains and losses. This conclusion is based on examination and ranking of the portfolios by risk for each level of return. It should be mentioned that these rankings are not dependent on the rate of return on one country's securities. In other words, the capital markets of different countries are not being ranked, but rather the investment opportunities of investors in different countries. This is done on the assumption that investors in any of the five countries have the opportunity to invest in a portfolio composed of any desired combination of thirteen international securities.

Statistical significance

The Friedman two-way analysis of variance is used to test the significance of differences in risk for comparable levels of return. The Friedman test statistic is 187, which is significant at the 0.001 level, assuming a Chi-square distribution with 4 degrees of freedom. As a consequence, hypothesis I is rejected; when a set of securities denominated in more than one currency is considered, the mean-variance optimum frontier (constructed in real returns) is dependent on the currency of country in which eventual expenditure of portfolio return is expected to occur.

14.4.2 Nominal return efficient frontiers

The mean-variance efficient frontiers constructed in nominal terms are relatively more similar than those constructed in real terms, possibly indicating that inflation is not fully integrated into the investment decision. On the basis of the sum of the ranks, United Kingdom investors have the opportunity to earn the highest level of returns, followed by those of Japan, the United States, Germany, and France. The nominal return-efficient frontiers from 1 per cent to 20 per cent are shown in Table 14.2.

Statistical significance

The Friedman Test statistic for nominal returns is 192, which is significant at the 0.001 level, assuming Chi-square distribution with 4 degrees of freedom. Therefore, hypothesis II is rejected; when a set of securities, denominated in more than one currency, is considered, the mean-variance efficient frontiers (constructed in nominal terms) are dependent on the country in which eventual expenditure of portfolio return is expected to occur.

Table 14.3 compares the rankings of mean-variance efficient frontiers in real and nominal terms. It is interesting to note that the

Table 14.2   Nominal return efficient frontiers

Per cent return	Variance				
	Germany	France	UK	Japan	US
1	0.000 039 7	0.000 144 9	0.000 162 1	0.000 117 3	0.000 040 0
2	0.000 098 0	0.000 035 4	0.000 021 1	0.000 028 9	0.000 059 6
3	0.000 491 5	0.000 261 7	0.000 201 5	0.000 272 2	0.000 407 2
4	0.001 220 2	0.000 823 8	0.000 702 9	0.000 847 3	0.001 082 7
5	0.002 284 0	0.001 721 7	0.001 525 6	0.001 754 2	0.002 086 0
6	0.003 683 0	0.002 955 3	0.002 669 4	0.002 992 9	0.003 417 3
7	0.005 417 1	0.004 524 7	0.004 134 5	0.004 563 3	0.005 076 4
8	0.007 486 4	0.006 429 9	0.005 920 8	0.006 465 5	0.007 063 5
9	0.009 890 8	0.008 670 8	0.008 028 2	0.008 694 4	0.009 378 4
10	0.012 630 4	0.011 247 6	0.010 456 9	0.011 265 1	0.012 021 2
11	0.015 705 2	0.014 160 1	0.013 206 8	0.014 162 6	0.014 922 0
12	0.019 115 1	0.017 408 3	0.016 277 8	0.017 391 8	0.018 290 6
13	0.022 860 1	0.020 992 4	0.019 670 1	0.020 952 8	0.021 917 1
14	0.026 940 3	0.024 912 2	0.023 383 6	0.024 845 6	0.025 871 5
15	0.031 355 7	0.029 167 8	0.027 418 2	0.029 070 2	0.030 153 8
16	0.036 106 2	0.033 759 2	0.021 774 1	0.033 626 5	0.034 764 1
17	0.041 191 9	0.038 686 4	0.036 451 2	0.038 514 5	0.039 702 2
18	0.046 612 7	0.043 949 3	0.041 449 4	0.043 734 4	0.044 968 2
19	0.052 368 7	0.049 548 1	0.046 768 9	0.049 286 0	0.050 562 1
20	0.058 459 8	0.055 482 5	0.052 409 6	0.055 169 4	0.056 483 9

Table 14.3   Ranking of real and nominal return mean-variance investment opportunities by country of investor

	Real	Nominal
Germany	3	4
France	1	5
United Kingdom	2	1
Japan	5	2
United States	4	3

rankings of some of the countries change drastically. For example, in the nominal return mean-variance efficient frontiers, the opportunity set available to French investors is dominated by the sets available to all other countries while in real terms the mean-variance efficient frontiers available to the French dominated all others.

CONCLUSION

Although portfolio composition is not reported in detail in this chapter, the mean-variance efficient portfolios regularly contain debt as well as equity instruments. Thus, this study has shown that a test of international capital market efficiency must contain securities other than common stock. This result holds for both real and nominal returns.

When real and nominal return efficient frontiers are compared, the rankings of mean-variance investment opportunities by country change sharply. Thus, it is here the importance of using real returns when performing studies of market efficiency, particularly in the international markets is also demonstrated.

These results lead to the conclusion that markets are segmented in both real and nominal terms; similar assets do not have the same return in all markets. This phenomenon could be related either to the existence of barriers to the flow of capital among the markets or inefficiency in the information market.

Note

1. The analysis is also performed for two sub-periods: 1965–72 and 1972–9. Those results are not reported as they do not differ from the results for the entire period. However, they do provide evidence that the conclusions are not sensitive to the time period chosen for analysis.

REFERENCES

BENNETT, P. and KELLEHER, J. (1988) 'The International Transmission of Stock Price Disruption in October 1987', *Quarterly Review*, Federal Reserve Bank of New York, Summer, pp. 17–33.
BIGER, N. (1975) 'The Assessment of Inflation and Portfolio Selection', *Journal of Finance* (May), pp. 24–32.
BIGER, N. (1979) 'Exchange Risk Implications of International Portfolio Diversification', *Journal of International Business Studies* (Fall).
BRANCH, B. (1974) 'Common Stock Performance and Inflation: An International Comparison', *Journal of Business* (Jan.), pp. 48–53.
BREALEY, R. A. (1969) *An Introduction to Risk and Return from Common Stock Prices* (Boston: M.I.T. Press).

CORNELL. B. W. (1977) 'Which Inflation Rate Affected Interest Rates?', *Business Economics* (May), pp. 22–5.

ERRUNZA, V. and LOSQ, E. (1985) 'International Asset Pricing under Mild Segmentation: Theory and Test', *Journal of Finance* (Mar.) pp. 105–124.

ESSAYYAD, M. and WU, H. (1988) 'The Performance of U.S. International Mutual Funds', *Quarterly Journal of Business and Economics* (Autumn) pp. 32–46.

FAMA, E. F. (1970) 'Efficient Capital Markets: A Review of Theory and Empirical Evidence', *Journal of Finance* (May) pp. 383–417.

FISHER, I. (1930) *The Theory of Interest* (New York: The Macmillan Company).

GRAUER, R. and HAKANSSON, N. (1987) 'Gains from International Diversification: 1968–85 Returns on Portfolios of Stocks and Bonds', *Journal of Finance* (July) pp. 721–41.

GRUBEL, H. G. (1968) 'Internationally Diversified Portfolios: Welfare Gains and Capital Flows', *American Economic Review*, pp. 1299–1315.

HAUGEN, R., ORTIZ, E. and ARJONA, E. (1985) 'Market Efficiency: Mexico Versus the U.S.', *Journal of Portfolio Management* (Fall) pp. 28–32.

JORION, P. (1985) 'International Portfolio Diversification with Estimation Risk', *Journal of Business* (July) pp. 259–78.

JORION, P. and SCHWARTZ, E. (1986) 'Integration vs. Segmentation in the Canadian Stock Market', *Journal of Finance* (July) pp. 602–616.

KAMAROTOU, H. and O'HANLON, J. (1989) 'Informational Efficiency in the U.K., U.S., Canadian, and Japanese Equity Markets: A Note', *Journal of Business, Finance, and Accounting* (Spring) pp. 183–92.

LESSARD, D. R. (1974) 'World, National and Industry Factors in Equity Returns', *Journal of Finance* (May), pp. 379–91.

LEVY, H. and SARNAT, M. (1975) 'Analysis of International Investments', in Elton and Gruber (eds) *International Capital Markets* (North-Holland/American Elsevier).

LINTNER, J. (1975) 'Inflation and Security Returns', *The Journal of Finance* (May), pp. 259–80.

ROLL, R. (1977) 'A Critique of Assets Pricing Theory's Tests'. '*Journal of Financial Economics*, pp. 129–76.

SOLNIK, B. (1978) 'Inflation and Optimal Portfolio Choices', *Journal of Financial and Quantitative Analysis* (December), pp. 903–27.

WESTERFIELD, J. M. (1977) 'An Examination of Foreign Exchange Risk Under Fixed and Floating Rated Regimes', *Journal of International Economics* (May), pp. 181–201.

15 Risk Management and Corporate Governance in Imperfect Capital Markets

Klaus P. Fischer, Edgar Ortiz and A. P. Palasvirta

15.1 INTRODUCTION

Successful business in the developing countries has often evolved into complex industrial 'groups' – a sort of conglomerates. Although their accomplishments are often impressive, these firms have rarely become fully publicly owned corporations. Little or no common stock is sold, and ownership and control remains tightly held in a circle of family members and friends. We contend that such behaviour is a rational response to risk bearing by investors in the absence of arms length financial markets. It is an efficient market solution to uncertainty and political risk when efficient markets do not exist.

We built this alternative theory about 'groups' and risk management in Less Developed Countries (LDCs) on modern financial thought, mainly efficient markets theory, portfolio theory and agency theory. We assume the LDC native entrepreneur to be a wealth maximizing and risk-minimizing individual. The differences in outcome, in relation to entrepreneurs from Industrialized Countries (ICs), result from differences in the market environment. We present a thorough analysis of the alternatives that owner-managers (O-M) in the developing countries use to diversify portfolio holdings and improve the risk-return relationship in the absence of arm's length financial markets. Within this framework the persistence of this form of corporate governance, i.e. the developing country family owned industrial group, is a logical result of the subsistence of imperfect capital markets. We also argue that certain forms of risk, namely political risk – government economic intervention – plays a particularly strong role in the decision-making process of private investors of LDCs.

This conceptual framework on industrial groups in LDCs leads us to identify four important alternatives that entrepreneurs from LDCs have to diversify risk and to make three important propositions concerning corporate control and risk management under imperfect financial markets.[1] Freer market conditions are now being promoted around the world. In this respect, our model underlines the importance and nature of the changes that must be promoted in the developing countries to assert their modernization processes and further their economic growth.

15.2   THE ORGANIZATION AND MANIFESTATION OF THE GROUP

Successful family enterprises grow into many products and markets. In Latin America these conglomerates are known as *grupo industrial*, or simply *grupo*, which is common usage among researchers in the field. Operationally, we define a group as a 'relatively strong group of firms linked by capital and a global strategy designed by the decision making power of common majority equity owners and managers'. Further, we identify its existence with LDCs. In these countries most of the private sector manufacturing, trading and retailing activities, specially where large capital investments are required, is under the control of Groups, where their owners also participate as managers, with a small proportion of stock traded in local markets. From the organizational point of view, Groups are conglomerates of companies in a variety of product markets. A Group may have a monopoly position in one product market, but competes with other Groups or foreign firms in some of the other markets. Although examples of vertical integration exist, Groups typically diversify horizontally into weakly related industries by creating frequently several independent enterprises in each sector. One common and very important industry in which Groups diversify horizontally is the financial services industry: finance companies, private development banks and commercial banks. These types of institutions contribute to the diversification of the Group's portfolio of activities. But more importantly, they provide a mechanism by which to channel social savings to finance the Group's activities. For example, commercial banks under Group control attract funds (deposits and savings) from individual investors, at regulated rates, which are then used to lever up Group firms at very favourable terms. Moreover, their credit needs receive priority treatment in relation to other firms, irrespective of higher expected returns in the investments from other clients. Group development banks can also divert for Group use State originated or guaranteed foreign funds. Finally, industrial groups also get preferred loans from public development banks, which mobilize domestic savings and foreign loans. As a result of these institutional arrangements, both the debt holder and the debtor are controlled by the same interest, the Group, and the effective cost of borrowing, even if the borrowing firms are charged market rates, is very low. In sum, group-owned financial intermediaries and private or public development banks, provide the bulk of the non-equity financing that supplements the Groups' internal savings.

15.3 RISK AND FINANCIAL MARKETS: TWO ALTERNATIVE PARADIGMS

15.3.1 The competitive markets paradigm

According to the efficient markets paradigm, an arm's length financial market is one in which participants create financial claims against real assets. They issue these claims in efficient primary markets and trade them in efficient secondary markets. By creating specialized financial commodities, financial markets bundle risk. These financial commodities are then sold separately, as different types of claims against the firm's assets, e.g., debt and equity. All the participants in the market are fully informed about the risk-return characteristics of the claims and markets are competitive, i.e. there are no price-setting participants. This is the paradigm or 'base case' of modern financial theory. Financial markets from the United States are fairly representative of this situation.[2]

In an economy characterized by efficient financial markets, firms grow in size and market concentration is a natural product of being able to take advantage of economies of scale or scope that, due to increased demand, arise from the production, marketing, or distribution of their goods. As a corollary to this, growth of the firm ultimately contributes to the separation of ownership and control. The entrepreneur in the US economy generally holds ownership and control of the new start-up firm in his own hands.[3] For the mature corporate entity, ownership and control held in the same hands is the exception not the rule.

In an evolutionary context, a firm begins as an entrepreneurial experiment. If the idea is good, competent management relying on the findings of solid R&D and careful cash and capital budgeting results naturally in growth of the firm. However, growth leads to two types of problems which ultimately lead to the separation of ownership and control. First, the need for funds to finance the growth opportunities of the firm may outpace the entrepreneurs' ability to self-finance. That is, to materialize the growth potential of the firm, the owner manager must relinquish control. In fact, the greater the potential for growth, the greater the potential for loss of control.[4]

Second, even if the entrepreneur is able to supply enough internal financing to maintain growth, he may no longer wish to do so. Absolute risk aversion on the part of the entrepreneur will lead him to not increase the absolute size of the bet (the stake in the firm) as wealth increases with the size of the firm. He has more to lose than in the good old days. Relative risk aversion on the part of the entrepreneur will persuade him to attempt to lower the size of the bet as a proportion of his total wealth. That is, there will be a natural economic motivation on the entrepreneur to diversify risk relative to the holdings in his asset portfolio. Thus, separation of ownership and control arises when the capital needs of the firm outpace either the ability or the desire of the entrepreneur to secure sufficient capital on his account to fund all the positive net present value projects available, or both.

Separation of ownership and control requires an environment of efficient financial markets. In such efficient markets, most firms find it easy to communicate information and, consequently, financial claims are then priced correctly relative to their risk characteristics. Provided that a 'critical mass' of well informed investors ('smart money') operate in the market, prices reflect reasonably accurately the true value of financial assets as a function of the expected value and risk characteristics of the underlying cash flows. These prices, in turn, become a signalling instrument to uniformed investors who are also active in the market ('noise traders'). For the mature firm that has a large set of information already in the market place, it is easy to attract additional capital at prices that are well known. For entrepreneurial firms with a relatively small set of information about their opportunities already available in the market place, it is more difficult to attract capital. The owner-manager must offer a higher expected return to compensate the venture capitalist for the risk involved in investment, e.g., penny stocks, and surrender some control over the firm.

In a well-developed, arm's length financial market, the entrepreneur seeking to give up control and diversify his portfolio, finds it relatively easy to accomplish this. A well developed market for corporate control and risk bearing financial commodities, where information asymmetries are minimal and pricing is efficient, allows the entrepreneur to sell some part of his stake in the firm at a fair market price. Simultaneously, he can acquire a preferred portfolio of risk-bearing securities, also efficiently priced and protected by a network of minority-investors protection laws. Risk bundling is done automatically in the market place. Intermediaries such as insurance firms, securities markets, commercial banks, and investment banks are the primary creators of instruments which bundle subsets of the total variation of the cash flows generated by the real assets of the firm. The price at which these instruments are eventually traded in the market is a function of the investors' evaluation of the risk return trade-off inherent in the subset of cash flows upon which each instrument holder has a claim. That is, the value of the firm is ultimately established in the market. As Thomadakis (1992) correctly pointed out,

> It is clear that this theory of optimal firm behavior is grounded much more on what goes on outside the firm than what goes on inside it. It is the capital market environment which determines the process of valuation, and which gives rise to the benchmark of optimal investment choice and competitive performance.

Conditions in financial markets of industrialized countries provide for opportunities for risk dispersion by giving up control in favour of diversification into many firms. The common stock of open corporations allows residual risk to be spread across many residual claimants. Each claimant, in turn, chooses the extent to which he is willing to bear risk by diversifying through equity positions in the open capital markets. Portfolio theory asserts that by spreading the risk across corporations the cost of bearing risk can be reduced down to the cost of bearing the risk inherent in the economy as a whole. Given markets with reasonable information symmetry, investors expect to earn a return adjusted to compensate for exposure to the (systematic) risk inherent in the securities held, since all information about the value of the risky assets is already embodied in the market price of the security.

15.3.2   The alternative paradigm: Proposition 1

Corporate growth under imperfect financial markets

The contrast between the 'base' case example, described above, and the environment facing the investor in a developing country is sharp. In these economies arm's length primary or secondary markets in financial claims are either absent or underdeveloped. There are many reasons for this, but certainly there are two fundamental reasons: first, the institutional mechanisms to produce information about the stochastic characteristics of individual firms' cash flows are poorly developed; second, there is an absence of a large pool of risk-taking investors who seek reducing their risk exposure through a well diversified portfolio of securities. Instead, equity is held by a small group of large investors who may even have the power to influence price formation. The first fact contributes to large information asymmetries in the market place. The second contributes to a relatively thin and perhaps manipulated market for financial claims. Therefore, market prices routinely do not reflect the true value of the asset to the entrepreneur and risk diversification alternatives are scant. This leads us to our first proposition.

> PROPOSITION 1. In the absence of arm's-length real and financial markets and the existence of limited growth opportunities, entrepreneurs have no incentive to relinquish control and diversify risk through financial markets.

Discussion. In the absence of well developed arm's length financial markets, diversification possibilities through the acquisition of a financial portfolio are limited or altogether non-existent. If they do exist, the minority position is often unprotected and information asymmetries are substantial. The relatively common availability of monopoly profits, strong information asymmetries and the absence of a large pool of risk-taking investors are factors that discourage the entrepreneur from unloading his stakes in the firm and diversify through financial markets. Also, in a developing economy limited growth possibilities associated with relatively small markets, limits the growth potential of any one firm and therefore limits the demand for funds to finance investment projects in that firm, as well as the supply of funds financial intermediaries are willing to pass on to those firms.

To put our arguments into context, we must explain the role that *political risk* plays in any economy. Political risk exists in any economy. The degree to which it affects the variability of the cash flows of a portfolio of assets in any one economy is obviously different. We submit that the primary risk encountered by the domestic investor in an LDC is political risk, namely excessive State intervention, and discontinuities and sharp changes in economic policy making; political risk also involves excessive regulation and bureaucratism. All these facts reflect in high, undiversifiable, systematic risk.

This is our paradigm, our alternative to the 'base case' conventionally used to derive most optimal decision rules in modern finance. Not surprisingly, we should also expect that the optimal decision rules derived under this alternative paradigm are also different, including strategies for risk management.

The nature of the market

Decisions by entrepreneurs in developing countries are 'bounded' by market imperfections. Dominant among those that influence entrepreneur behaviour are:

(1) *In the goods markets*
   (a) Monopoly profits exist, and are not transient in nature. Either an actual monopoly position exists, because markets for goods are small, government protects domestic industries and domestic business in general, or monopoly profits are maintained through either explicit or implicit collusion by the producers.
   (b) The firm depending on only domestic demand for goods, is not likely to experience sufficient demand to exploit any scale or scope economies. This thinness of markets changes the growth dynamics for the firm. Since growth opportunities are low, so is the demand for funds to finance it. This situation changes when the firm faces export opportunities which require rapid and large capacity expansions.[5]
(2) *In the labour markets*
   (a) Strong union organizations, often supported by the state. A strong clientelist relationship between unions and the State has led to the establishment of very protective and inflexible labour laws. In turn this leads to unstable labour activity, overvalued labour costs, redundant employment, superfluous labour rights, excess privileges to labour leaders, detrimental allocation of resources, and low labour productivity.[6]
   (b) Inadequate labour training and recurrent insufficiency of

skilled labour for the existing technology and its changes. This induces corporations to hold on innovation.

(3) *In the financial markets*
   (a) Large information asymmetries,[7] total absence of, or thin markets for equity and debt instruments, makes the entrepreneur's rational choice to diversify difficult to implement. The true value of the entrepreneur's assets cannot be reliably priced in the market.
   (b) In the absence of a large pool of risk-taking investors, potentially available equity capital is concentrated in the few hands of the major entrepreneurs in the economy. This has two implications: first, these major equity investors become 'price makers' with ability to manipulate securities prices; and second, these investors most probably are 'rival' entrepreneurs, thus giving up control of the firms means giving it up to a competitor.

The above are powerful disincentives contributing to the discouragement of corporate growth and promote the continuation of a structure where ownership and control remain in the same hands. Optimally, the firm should not grow much beyond medium size in the LDC. The entrepreneur of a large firm would be exposed to much more risk because it would limit his diversification possibilities. Alternatively, the entrepreneur would face loss of control due to dilution of his equity share. Moreover, in the developing countries, the minority position is often unprotected.

The nature and role of political risk: Proposition 2

Our model could be conceived in the presence of zero or negligible political risk. However, political risk has been a pervasive form of uncertainty in most modern economies without well-developed arms-length markets. Policy makers have relied on market controls, promotional instruments, trade restrictions and outright production to spur industrial development. Many of the market distortions facing entrepreneurs have been the result of government controls. Although modernization policies have been recently undertaken by most LDC, many distortions still persist and need to be eliminated. This leads us to make a second proposition:

PROPOSITION 2. Under the conditions found in most LDCs economies, the political risk premium charged by domestic investors on domestic projects is relatively high and commensurate to the level of intervention of the state in the economy, even if this intervention is intended to 'protect' the domestic industry.

Discussion. State intervention occurs in both real and financial markets. In the real markets some of the most frequent forms of intervention are: capacity and investment licensing; investment incentives; public procurement; import controls; barriers to exit; and rules of origin and national content. Concrete manifestations of incoherent and excessive state intervention in the financial markets in LDCs are: financial repression,[8] institutional rigidities, outdated laws, excessive and inefficient, often corrupt, government financial intermediation, and lagged and unstable policy making. These constraints take the form of regulated interest rates; regulated, often multiple, exchange rates; institution of 'priority sectors' for bank lending; excessive control of assets and liabilities of banking institutions; creation of excessive financial, many marginal, intermediation institutions; promotion of financial intermediation concentration and monopoly institutions; and creation of excessive development banking institutions, as a political response to particular pressure groups.[9] The high level of control of financial markets is frequently accompanied by a network of laws and regulations that guarantee the viability of financial institutions. In addition to deposit insurance, tight barriers to exit for financial institutions shift the business risk assumed by these institutions to the state, and ultimately to the tax-payers.

State intervention in real and financial markets is a source of rent-generating opportunities for business entrepreneurs and are barriers to competition from either foreign producers or domestic new entrants. More importantly, projects undertaken by the entrepreneur may be viable only under the protected market conditions created by the state. In the extreme case entrepreneurs undertake projects at the prodding of the authorities who explicitly commit to guarantee their profitability through manipulation of both the markets and inputs and outputs. Even ignoring these special cases, under competitive conditions many of these projects would have been rejected by the entrepreneur or would not have financing. Thus, the value of these projects to the Group is highly sensitive to small variations on economic policy. Slight changes in the market control mechanisms or the financing conditions facing entrepreneurs can be catastrophic for the profitability of the project. For the same reason that these opportunities exist in the first place as a function of current state intervention, their continued existence is dependent in the retention of the political status-quo. However, management of status-quo under the social and political conditions found in many LDCs is quite difficult. In order to obtain legitimacy and consensus the state responds to many pressure groups and it is frequently unable to sustain consistent economic policies.

The idea that a high level of protection to industries *implies a high level of political risk to the beneficiaries of the control, a priori*, might not be obvious. However, upon reflection it makes sense that the level of political risk exposure is a positive function of the involvement of the government in the economy. Unlike economic processes such as savings and investments, which are largely dependent in fundamental factors which change only slowly over the long run, political processes can be swift and dramatic. Also, the higher the level of confrontation in society the higher is the chance that changes in the political leadership of the country may result in turns in economic policy. When the level of intervention of the government in the economy is low, the ability of the state for affecting the economic environment in which business operate is limited. In contrast, when this level of intervention is high, small changes in economic policy can deeply affect market conditions and future cash flows to a firm, a group of firms, or the whole business sector of a country. Similarly, when cash flows are highly dependent upon politically generated market segmentation such as import restriction, capacity licensing, national sourcing and state purchases, etc. cash flows are extremely sensitive to a small fluctuation in economic policy. *Ceteris paribus* political risk is also a negative function of the size of the markets. Smaller markets are typically more susceptible to government action than large markets or economies.

Summarizing, the risk involved in the allocation and/or reallocation of rents resulting from the structure of government regulations and controls will have three important characteristics:

(1) the magnitude of political risk is positively related to the level of intervention of the state in the economy;
(2) in the absence of appropriate models to assess the exact nature of political risk, it is difficult to price; this added uncertainty will result in higher market premiums;
(3) political events which introduce discontinuities in the system tend to affect the economy as a whole; thus hedging opportunities through domestic portfolio diversification – through real or financial assets – are limited;

The third characteristic of political risk leads to the conclusion that the level of systematic risk – non-diversifiable by the means available to an investor in the economy – is high. Another important connotation is that the nature of this risk will necessarily influence the mechanisms of assessing projects. More specifically, it will reflect in the premium charged by entrepreneurs on the required rate of return of the investment opportunities. Furthermore, *the political risk premium charged by a domestic investor for any domestic project can be expected to be higher than that charged by foreign investors.* The reason is that for any particular country and any foreign investor (to that country), the political exposure to which the foreign investors is exposed as a result of investing in the project, is diversified by project/investments in other economies. Further, foreign investors are better informed, on a global basis, than local investors.[10]

15.4 A THEORY OF RATIONAL INVESTMENT IN THE ABSENCE OF ARM'S LENGTH FINANCIAL MARKETS: PROPOSITION 3

Assuming our alternative paradigm – including the nature of political risk – it is possible to determine the reasons for groups as a particular form of governance in LDCs, as well as to discern the strategies available to the investor/entrepreneur to rationally hedge his portfolio of assets. Under the market conditions and diversification possibilities described above, what are the options available for risk bundling to the LDC entrepreneur, from the point of view of strict economic rationality? This leads us to our third, and we believe, more interesting proposition.

> PROPOSITION 3. The rational investor, operating in an environment of absence of arm's length financial markets utilizes four interrelated mechanisms to modify the risk return attributes of his opportunity set, namely:
> (a) export capital (international diversification)
> (b) diversify in the real sector through atomized projects, leading to the formation of 'industrial Groups'.
> (c) leverage up through group-based financial intermediaries
> (d) generate rent through monopoly profits.

Discussion. To discuss this proposition we will present and justify the validity of each of our four mechanisms suggested for risk management in the absence of perfect capital markets.

15.4.1 Capital exports

The first form of risk management available to LDC entrepreneurs is capital exports, more specifically:

> PROPOSITION 3.1. Investors in developing countries export capital to achieve: (i) international portfolio diversification in the conventional sense, and (ii) diversification of the high level of (domestically) non-diversifiable political risk to which they are exposed in the domestic market. *Ceteris paribus*, the proportion of assets an LDC investor invests abroad can be expected to be higher than that of an IC investor.

Discussion. International diversification hardly needs any explanation given the ample literature explaining its benefits to investors. In the developed countries adjustments in portfolio holdings lead to relatively symmetrical capital movements among them, movements taking place according to international interest rates. However, in the context of the environment found in most LDCs the importance of international portfolio alternatives as an instrument of rational risk management is enhanced. Due to the (relative) low level of State intervention in well developed financial markets, investors from LDCs associate them with low levels of political exposure. Thus, diversification into markets with lower political risks than the domestic one is one of the key reasons for export of capital by owner-managers based in LDC economies. It is an exercise in political risk diversification, a matter rarely considered in international portfolio research.

If the entrepreneur has the ability to export capital to economies with accessible and liquid financial markets, he will do so. If the LDC entrepreneur were able to duplicate risk/return opportunities available in international markets, he would simply invest (at least higher proportions) in the more familiar environment with presumably lower exchange rate risk and easier access to funds. Thus, the more developed capital markets provide crucial diversification opportunities for the LDC entrepreneur. But more importantly, they also provide a risk/return continuum which serves as the base level against which all risk of investing in the domestic LDC economy are compared. Thus, the risk-return trade-off opportunities available in world financial markets, become the benchmark of evaluation of every domestic (and foreign) investment opportunities available to the entrepreneur.[11]

15.4.2 Diversification in the real sector or the theory of the group

Bundling risk in the real assets market[12]

As pointed out earlier, in the presence of arm's-length financial markets and growth opportunities, owner-managers have an incentive to forego control of the firm. This is done either, to realize the firm's growth potential or to diversify the entrepreneur's portfolio of assets through financial markets to the point where the only risk borne by him is the undiversifiable risk of the economy as a whole. However, these opportunities are not available to the LDC entrepreneur. Thus, we state the following proposition:

PROPOSITION 3.2. The Model of corporate organization and control described as the '*Grups*' is an efficient risk diversification strategy in the absence of arm's length real and financial markets.

Discussion. Entrepreneurs facing the limited growth opportunities and the real and financial markets typical of LDCs, lack the incentives to give up control of the firm and diversify risk through financial markets. Limited growth opportunities reduce the need to seek external financing. Market conditions lead to discrepancies between the market price of assets and the true value of the same to the entrepreneur. Consequently, the entrepreneur in the LDC economy must bundle risk on his own account, so that risk diversification is internalized. In other words, the entrepreneur facing these markets cannot efficiently diversify by holding a portfolio of financial assets, but he must diversify by holding diversified real assets, or, as previously explained, holding titles outside its own markets; he must also seek greater coverage for his local investments.

Investment specific risk is diversified by holding many firms in one's portfolio of assets. However, portfolios of real assets are not perfect substitutes of portfolios of financial assets. Foremost among the imperfections associated with real assets as portfolio constituents are: (i) higher political risk exposure; (ii) they are lumpy, (iii) relatively illiquid, and (iv) transaction costs associated with portfolio rebalancing are high. Real assets in the specific LDC environment are more difficult to shield against political risk than portfolios of financial

assets. Lumpiness implies that they lack the divisibility characteristic of financial assets. Hence, adjustments in portfolio composition
are coarse and fine-tuning along the risk/return frontier is nearly
impossible. Although risk is reduced, the process is inefficient and
residual systematic risk remains high. Illiquidity implies that shallow
or no secondary markets exist to dispose of unwanted assets, again,
making portfolio adjustments onerous or altogether impossible. The
transaction costs associated with disposing/acquiring real assets are
usually much higher than those of financial assets. In addition, adjustments of lumpy assets implies major restructuring of portfolio
weights and capital transfers which are costly.

Thomadakis (1992) provides convincing arguments explaining the
specific mode in which this diversification by O-M into the product
markets takes place. Limited liability creates for the entrepreneur a
bundle of default options against debt and non-debt claimholders.[13]
As a result of these default options and a set of claims resulting from
contracts of explicit or implicit nature, three main behavioural consequences can be drawn:

(1) given an available set of investment opportunities, entrepreneurs
    will choose the riskier projects and investment policies;[14]
(2) given any particular investment opportunity, entrepreneurs will
    choose the combination of factor inputs tending to maximize the
    value of the default options;
(3) most importantly in terms of implications for the organizational
    strategy of the Group, given a set of projects among which to
    allocate the entrepreneur's own capital, he will have an incentive
    to constitute his projects as limited liability entities, i.e. as sep-
    arate firms rather than as extensions (i.e. divisions) of an existing
    firm.

As firms grow larger implementing projects, risk and failure of one
project is increasingly coinsured by other projects within the firm.
Such coinsurance can affect the cash flows of the firm. Thus, to
compartmentalize risk in the LDC economy, the entrepreneur creates as many firms as there are projects. Because of this he is not able
to exploit economies of scale or scope either through vertical or
horizontal merger, but he does minimize the cost of coinsurance of
this projects (Thomadakis, 1992). As long as the costs saved are
greater than the lost value of economies unexploited, this is an
efficient market response to economic conditions within the LDC
economy.

An extension of this argument is that, given finite sources, the O-M is able to hold more firms in his portfolio, if those firms are small to medium size. The rational investor in a LDC will keep his firm size within those bounds so as to keep down the cost of coinsurance between firms since individual firms will be able to maximize the return to the investor from limited liability. Thus, *ceteris paribus*, the value of limited liability in a risky environment is maximized by minimizing the value of the individual firm.

In markets with arm's-length financial transactions, when firms grow in size, or when market concentration develops, as a result of investment, mergers and acquisitions are a natural product of economies of scale or scope.[15] As firms become large, we argue that in the presence of efficient financial markets, there are economic incentives for a rather smooth process of separation between ownership and control. *Conglomerates* are largely the result of agency conflicts between management and equity holders. In the presence of an efficient market for financial claims it is cheaper for the investor to diversify equity risk by holding a diversified portfolio of equity claims (shares) than by holding shares in a firm with a diversified portfolio of projects. Diversification at the firm level, while perhaps advantageous to the incumbent management, is more costly and less effective than diversification via financial markets. A financial portfolio is much more liquid with lower transactions costs for portfolio management and rebalancing.[16]

Thinness of capital markets in LDCs increases the importance of dividends and retained earnings as a source of investments. The entrepreneur must therefore generate high levels of profits to cover for reinvestment needs and high dividend payments, which are the main stem of valuation of the firm, as correctly pointed out by Errunza and Rosenberg (1982). Similarly, due to the absence of well developed financial markets, short-term loans are the largest share of corporate liabilities. They are used to finance even fixed assets. Since these loans are spread in a number of smaller firms, their cost is higher than those that could be charged to larger loans. Moreover, they are riskier due to the recurrent refinancing that is required, and due to the pressures on the liquidity of the firm (Ortiz, 1979; Ortiz and Bueno, 1992). Consequently, firms must hedge against risk seeking higher returns and self-financing alternatives, i.e. monopoly profits. This practice also hedges against political risk because banking and credit variables are the most commonly affected by financial repression and the shifting policies of LDC governments.

Organization of the 'group' and the solution of the owner-manager agency conflict

Industrial groups from LDCs have been compared to industrial conglomerates of industrial economies. Both structures consist of bundles of firms over several industries. The similarity is more apparent than real. A closer look reveals two important differences: first, the set of incentives that lead to the formation of conglomerates are different from those that lead to the formation of the Group; second, the structure of control and legal linkages between holding firms is also different.

One standard assumption in modern corporate finance is that managers make decisions which maximize the market value of the firm. Only recently, with the development of modern agency and contingent contract theory, has the theory of finance taken an 'inside look' to the structure of incentives which influence the decision of the various parties involved in the institutional structure of business activity. This inside look has revealed that many times, contracting parties, as principal or agents, can undertake wealth maximizing decisions which do not necessarily translate into 'market maximizing' actions. One of its manifestations is the formation of conglomerates. The presence of agency problems between managers and stockholders raises incentives for their formation. Specifically, the agency problems arises in the presence of *ex-ante* fixed compensation packages, where managers, agents in the decision process, have an incentive to reduce cash-flow risk and the probability of default (Jensen and Meckling, 1976; Jensen and Smith, 1986). Corporate diversification through conglomerates is one of the mechanisms most frequently used by managers to reduce this risk. Cash flows originated by firms in different industries co-insure each other. The resulting effect is that the conglomerate results in a safe environment for managers. However, from the point of view of the shareholder, the cost of coinsurance and conglomerate control reflects in loss of share value. At any rate, the organizational strategy is one in which the parent company is held by a large number of relatively small investors or equity holders. The diversification into different projects and economic sectors is implemented by the agents by creating subsidiaries of the parent company. This in turn may control other subsidiaries, typically within a sector. Figure 15.1 (a) shows the structure of a conglomerate as they are commonly found in the most industrialized countries.

Groups result from a different set of incentives. Group-member

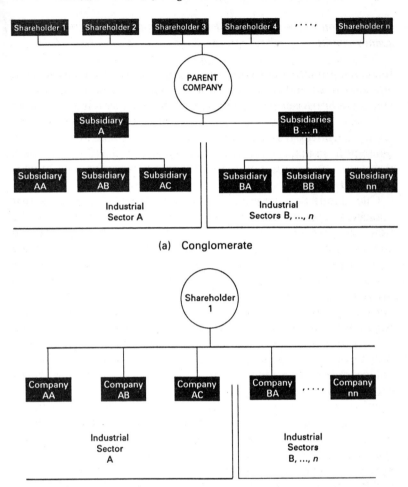

(a) Conglomerate

(b) Group

Figure 15.1

firms are frequently managed by the owners themselves or by rela-
tives and associates with very close social links. Hence conflicts
between managers and shareholders are either absent or checked
very closely by the controlling interest. Even when the management
is not tied to the owner by a strong implicit contract – a feature
common in the management of Group firms – managers are tightly
controlled by the owners who control a very high proportion – if not
the totality – of the stock outstanding. Thus, the controlling interest is

able to rapidly neutralize or reverse management (the agent) decisions that are in conflict with the interests of the owner (principal).

Yet, an entrepreneur, in the process of diversifying through projects in the real sector, as previously explained, creates a network of project firms over several industries. To avoid bearing the costs of cross-default insurance, the linkage between firms is designed to minimize cross-default liability. Typically, the only linkage between firms is the controlling position of the entrepreneur leading the group. The resulting structure is one in which the entrepreneur holds a bundle of project-firms over several industrial sectors. Figure 15.1(b) depicts the typical structure of the group.

The Group's entrepreneur, as an IC investor, holds a bundle of assets with minimal cross-default liabilities. The first holding a bundle of independent real projects, the second holding a bundle of limited liability financial assets in which cross-default liability is absent. Thus in the LDC economy a set of small firms maximizes O-M's wealth were one large firm cannot. This is a rational O-M's investment strategy in the face of the lack of opportunity to diversify through the holding of financial claims priced in the environment of efficient markets. Maintaining control of a well diversified group of project-firms provides the opportunity for risk dispersion otherwise not available in open capital markets.[17] This is, of course, the fundamental force driving the evolution of the so-called 'industrial Groups' in Latin America and elsewhere in the developing world.

15.4.3 Leverage up through group based financial intermediaries

The opportunity to lever up takes different characteristics in LDCs than it does in the presence of well developed arm's length securities markets. Often there is a large disparity between the need for funds arising from investment opportunities and the availability of internally generated funds. Given the precarious development of securities markets and the heavy reliance on intermediaries for financing, availability of bank-based debt becomes critical. However, LDC entrepreneurs also face a set of incentives which encourage high leverage and control by the Group of the financial intermediary. Hence our proposition that

> PROPOSITION 3.3 Given the model of diversification available to entrepreneurs and the level of political risk exposure, Groups have an incentive to lever up project/firms through Group controlled financial intermediaries.

Discussion. Incentives that encourage high leverage are: (i) the need to raise the rate of return of projects given the high systematic risk exposure of domestic products; (ii) the non-control nature of debt as opposed to equity; (iii) the incentive to dilute the relative size of equity commitment to individual projects and to spread it over a larger set of projects for portfolio management purposes; (iv) the unavailability of alternative sources of equity financing. Among the incentives that encourage the Group's control of financial institutions, we point to: (a) the availability of low interest rates through controls of borrowing and lending rates and priority financing for government specified industrial projects; (b) the opportunity to socialize project risk through government insurance of banks; and (c) virtual elimination of the agency conflicts between debt and equity holder and the associated monitoring costs. In countries with well developed arm's length financial markets many of these incentives simply do not exist or are priced away in the financial market's clearing process. However, this is not the case of most developing countries.

Access to securitized debt markets is either non-existent or, if available, subject to the same limitations as securitized equities markets. Moreover, while stocks retain their long-term investment characteristics, bonds in the developing countries are issued at most with short- and medium-term maturities. Since generally the firm cannot obtain funding by issuing bonds in the primary markets, an alternative source of funding is needed. However, in order to generate a higher required rate of return, it is helpful if the entrepreneur can lower his cost of borrowing such that it is lower than is commensurate with the risks of the cash flows involved. Also because of the atomization of firms by projects the average firm size is small. As a consequence, in order to leverage any one firm, the size of the loan needed is relatively small. The perfect institutional arrangement to carry out this type of strategy is a financial intermediary of some sort. It can borrow funds at low cost so that it can provide low cost loans to the Group members.[18] One would expect that some of the types of firms that the Group would covet as Group firms are therefore commercial banks, finance companies, and development banks.

Thomadakis (1992) also identifies incentives that encourage the O-M to control a bank. He affirms that this need stems from the potential disparity between the need for funds arising from investment opportunities and the availability of internally generated funds. The bank guarantees the availability of funds when needed without any claim on control over the project being financed. This is indeed a powerful argument and we fully agree with the motivation as well as the implications of this argumentation. However, we feel that there are some additional important incentives to attain control of a financial intermediary. These incentives arise from the mode of the diversification available to the O-M. The price of risk charged on individual projects/assets is a function of the systematic risk to which the investor is exposed. *Ceteris paribus* the lower the systematic risk the lower is the risk premium charged on the individual asset. Since the diversification mode available to the O-M in the absence of arm's length financial markets leads to a portfolio of lumpy real assets (firms), the residual systematic risk remains high. Thus, the premium charged on individual projects will be high. Leveraging projects through loans from a financial intermediary controlled by the O-M guarantees access to capital at the lowest possible cost (at the controlled deposit rate). Thus leveraging up projects with a loan from a Group-bank, not only reduces the equity stake (making the portfolio less lumpy) but also increases the rate of return on the investment. The implication is that many *investment opportunities could not be acceptable to the O-M should this mechanism of capturing low cost capital not be available*.

Other important reasons for groups for controlling financial intermediaries is capturing domestic and foreign savings[19] and socializing risk bearing. Low income among large sectors of the population in LDCs leads to a low propensity to save. The monetization of some sectors is also low. Their high liquidity needs are satisfied without the support of sight deposits in commercial banks. Thus, a large amount of deposits and savings in LDCs are institutional, mainly from the government. Those resources can be readily captured and channelled as credits and loans to firms from the group through a financial intermediary akin to them. This situation is also valid for the case of foreign loans, for which the government is its main mediator. However, as the group's financial intermediaries grow in size and importance, they will seek foreign resources in their own initiative.

Finally, socializing risk is another incentive to control a financial intermediary. In the absence of arm's length financial markets, the O-M finds limited demand for its securities. He himself finds restricted alternatives to hold a diversified portfolio. Thus he bears all the risk for his investments in real assets, unless he is able to find another alternative for risk bundling. Owning and controlling a bank offers him such alternative. First, he can obtain funds to hold more diversified portfolios in real assets. Second, risk is bundled among the clients of the bank from the private sector and with the government, who now have claims on the corporation. Furthermore, government banking insurance programmes and corporate incentives and rescue programmes establish an accepted and well known form of coinsurance among all participants.

15.4.4 Generate rents through monopoly profits

In the previous section we presented a string of actions entrepreneurs in LDCs take in financial markets to enhance their portfolio risk/trade-off function. In this section we will introduce actions by entrepreneurs in the real markets with the same purpose. Thus our proposition:

> PROPOSITION 3.4. In the absence of efficient markets and due to high political exposure, entrepreneurs will seek to introduce segmentation in the real markets which favour the entrepreneur or Group and offer the opportunity of permanent or transitory rent generation and enhance the return of projects.

Discussion. Industrial enterprises in every economy seek rent generating opportunities. Without them investors and firms would not have an incentive to invest. It is generally accepted that as a reward for innovation firms experience monopoly profits. However, these tend to be transient as a result of competitiveness among firms. Overall, this argument does not hold for LDCs. Groups obtain high and lasting returns because they hold a monopoly or oligopoly power both in innovation and in the market. Due to the small size of their enterprises research and development is unviable. Thus, they import foreign technology and can exploit it even beyond its useful life. Moreover, since imported capital goods are relatively labour intensive and since labour costs are low, really extraordinary monopoly profits can be obtained. A semiformal collusion with other groups generally exists because groups are suppliers among each other. In the absence of arm's length financial markets, the O-M seeks monopoly profits, colluding or seeking protectionism, in response to imperfections in the real market. However, this practice is also a rational response to financing needs and hedging for risk. Thinness of capital markets in LDCs, increases the importance of dividends and retained earnings as a source of investments. The O-M must therefore generate high levels of profits to cover for both reinvestment needs and pay high dividends payments.[20]

Incentives and protectionism from the state must also be mentioned. As we pointed out earlier, profitability of projects in LDCs is significantly dependent on controls introduced by the state. In fact, in many economies it is the predominant form of rent generation available to entrepreneurs in certain industries. Moreover, short of opportunities for rent generation, entrepreneurs have a strong incentive to make use of the political system to create these opportunities. Influencing government economic policy by any means available becomes an overriding objective. In this environment, often, the success of an entrepreneur depends less on his managerial skills to conduct successfully an efficient operation, than on his political skills to influence government economic policy to his benefit.

We must also refer to a quite common form of Group business activity: joint ventures with multinational corporations. These foreign ventures give local entrepreneurs access to fresh capital, unavailable at the local capital markets, and the opportunity to coinsure his business with proved lines of business and with continuous access to new technologies. This decision is also a rational response to risk bearing in the absence of arm's length financial markets, for it contributes to buffer business and political risks.[21] The local investor not only shares risks with another partner, but also improves his standing with the local government, for his joint venture has made possible new investments sought by local authorities. Thus, a joint venture is an association seeking mutual benefits in returns and risk bundling in the absence of well developed financial markets. However, it is worth noting that the local investor increases his risks in other ways, seldom considered in international finance studies. First, the local investor faces sharp criticisms from local opposition pressure groups for his 'irrational' and 'antinationalistic' decision. This could lead to further political risk. Second, he faces the risk of a take-over. A joint venture is basically a contractual relationship. Incompatibilities between multinationals and their local partners usually occur concerning strategic decisions, particularly in new start-ups. Thus, to avoid local interferences, multinationals resort to take-overs. This is not new, according to Vernon (1977) over a third of foreign subsidiaries in the developing countries were established through the acquisition of ongoing business. In the absence of developed financial markets and because the local investor holds an important number of shares, this take-over is made only through negotiation among the interested parties. Since the dispute is among two owner-managers the solution might be socially unsatisfactory.

Finally, we could not conclude this section without referring to corporate research and development. An important function of modern corporations is to develop new products and technologies to satisfy social needs, and then produce and market those goods or services to the final consumer. Groups have had a limited role in the innovative processes. Although their origin can be traced back to traditional industries, Groups have diversified into a great variety of products. However, their participation in product and technology development is limited. They concentrate in consumer goods and services. Technology and most intermediate and capital goods are imported.

To a great extent, this is the result of import substitution development models adopted by most developing countries after World War II, particularly in the case of the Latin American countries. Governments promoted import substitution, regardless of market size and emphasizing only local consumption. The government also undertook the development of some key industries, among them some in the capital goods sector (heavy metals) by creating state enterprises. Little promotion was made of technological development. Traditionally, investment in science and technology in these nations has been under 1 per cent of GNP per year *vis-à-vis* the 2–4 per cent prevailing among the developed countries (White, 1989). In the long run, this hindered the development of these nations, for in addition to the original ills that this strategy was meant to cure, other maladies appeared or the original ones manifested themselves in other forms. For instance, the original deficits in the balance of payments due to imports of consumer goods reappeared, but this time they were due to heavy imports of intermediate and capital goods. Similarly, local creativity was repressed. New products introduced in the local markets were follow ups of products derived abroad – a supply-led 'demonstration' effect. No serious marketing research and product development took place to satisfy local needs, and perhaps even exporting those goods to other countries. Similarly, new technologies were simply bought from foreign sources. Thus, a conservative, uncreative business environment has prevailed in LDCs.

However, this conservativeness and neglect should not be attributed entirely to cultural factors. It is also a strategy to manage risk in the absence of well developed capital markets. First, existing tax laws in most developing countries do not treat favourably corporate investments in science and technology. Thus, its costs and the uncertainty of future cash flows of such investments limit the feasibility of

product and technological development projects. The premia of discounted expected cash flows is insufficient to cover risks undertaken
by this type of innovative project. Moreover, uncertainty due to
unsteady and unpredictable government actions increases the required rate of return. Consequently, considering capital constraints,
the O-M selects to invest in products and technology already
tested and successful in other countries. Risk bearing for innovative
entrepreneurship is therefore 'deferred' until a more favourable business and political environment exists – until capital markets become
larger and efficient. Second, the lack of diversification alternatives in
the financial markets leads to the creation of project oriented firms
within the group, as already explained. Product and technology development are unviable owing to the lack of economies of scale and
scope, even though the group as a whole might be large. Finally,
thinness of capital markets limits the possibilities that O-Ms find
venture capitalists ready and capable of associating with them in
highly innovative enterprises. Indeed, that is a powerful reason why
domestic groups associate themselves in joint ventures with the government or with multinational corporations.

15.5 CONCLUSIONS

Our work presents a financial theory of corporate governance and
organization, and about risk management by owner-managers from
LDCs, in the absence of well developed arm's length financial markets. Two fundamental characteristics of these markets are poor
institutional mechanisms to produce and disseminate information
about the stochastic characteristics of individual firms' cash flows, and
there is an absence of a large pool of risk-taking investors who are
reducing their risk exposure through a well diversified portfolio of
securities. Furthermore, in these markets political risk – state intervention and unsteady policy making – constitutes a large proportion of the total systematic risk to which the entrepreneur is exposed.
These premises lead us to develop and examine three fundamental
propositions in terms of corporate structure and diversification
strategies undertaken by investors in these markets.

This analysis has important implications for capital markets development and economic development as well.[22] The primary implication is that underdeveloped capital markets restrain corporate
growth and limit social decision making concerning resource alloca-

tion for investments. To promote economic development governments from LDCs must promote the rise of publicly owned corporations through capital markets. This calls for creating significant incentives to entrepreneurs and investors, as well as implementing major reforms in the financial system. Markets should become an attractive alternative for rising funds for corporate growth and diversifying risk. New forms of securitization should be created and backed with innovative financial intermediation, so that entrepreneurs find relinquishing control attractive in pursuit of enhanced risk-returns in more efficient capital markets, and from increased operations from corporations that take advantage of domestic and international market opportunities and achieve economies of scale. Additionally, information mechanisms and information availability must be improved. Growth with equity should also be pursued, to ensure the existence of large pool of investors. Finally, financial repression must be reassessed. The scope of those programmes must be well determined and then the policies developed to carry new ones must be sustained, for the Latin American experience shows bitter results with financial liberalization, as well as failures in policy making due to shifts from the original plans. This also implies that strategic planning should be stressed.

Under current globalization trends all this means that LDCs should foster their capital markets to be able to sustain their growth plans and participation in international trade and finance. This is a challenge that must be completed during this decade, for otherwise LDCs will enter the twenty-first century with greater impediments to achieve their goals.

Notes

1. Our conceptual framework is based both on the rich empirical research on industrial groups in LDCs carried out by other authors, and in innumerable studies, including our own, on Latin American economics and finance. For ample references on these topics see: Fischer *et al.* (1991).
2. The diffusion of ownership and control and its social implications was first studied by Berle and Means (1933). More recent studies are those by Jensen and Meckling (1976), Fama and Jensen (1983), and Williamson (1988). They examine the separation between ownership and control as it operates under conditions of arm's length markets.
3. The entrepreneur can be a man or a woman. We acknowledge the

historic and ever-increasing role of women in business. The gender used throughout this chapter only seeks to simplify the style.

4. The proposition that growth opportunities are a factor in the diffusion of ownership is empirically corroborated by Demsetz and Lehn (1988). They find a significant negative relationship between firm size and insider ownership in the US. If we make the reasonable assumption that firm size is a proxy of realized growth opportunities, the implication is quite straightforward.

5. Market imperfections impact not only to the industrial sector, but all sectors of the economy. For instance, protectionism also promotes monopoly profits in distribution and retailing; similarly thinness of the market prevents such type of business to take advantage of economies of scale.

6. On the other hand, workers are also victims of market imperfections. Monopolies often undervalue their wages and attempt against their rightful historical gains.

7. In societies where monopoly and rent profits are highly dependent on political factors such as allocation of import quotas, preferential taxation and financing, allocation of development construction projects, etc., corporate secrecy and even intentional misinformation becomes a *need* for corporate survival. Secrecy is, of course, one of the idiosyncrasies attributed to LDC managers. Lack and unreliability of information has also been one of the factors which has hampered research on business finance in these markets.

8. Financial repression has been studied by Gurley and Shaw (1960), McKinnon (1973), Shaw (1973), and extended among others by Basant (1976; 1986), Mathieson (1979), Keller (1980), Courakis (1984) and Khan (1985); and Bruno (1979); Taylor (1983); van Wijnbergen (1983) and Buffie (1984). Kitchen (1986) also presents a full study of finance and development under financial repression.

9. The application of these types of policies have been extensively analysed for the Latin American case. See: Diaz-Alejandro (1985); Dornbusch and Reynoso (1989); Galbis (1979); Ibarra Puig (1989); Mathieson (1983); McKinnon (1986).

10. However, it must be stressed that multinational investors get higher returns than local investors because they invest in leading industrial sectors, where extraordinary (temporary) profits can be obtained. In addition multinational investors make better project evaluations, aided by sophisticated tools and a highly professional management.

11. In a world of increasingly integrated financial markets, assets are priced according to their contribution to systematic risk of the world market portfolio. Errunza and Losq (1985) provide the theoretical framework and ample empirical evidence that, from the perspective of the investor in a LDC with barriers to capital flows, financial markets are uni-directionally integrated. That is, although investors in the 'core' may be restricted in their ability to overcome barriers to capital flows, these barriers are ineffective from the perspective of investors in the 'periphery' seeking opportunities in the international markets.

12. This section benefits from some ideas presented by Thomadakis (1992).

Our extension, in affinity with Thomadakis, is at the hearth of the propositions. We have also benefited from our own earlier works and empirical evidence on Latin American Groups, cited in our previous work, Fischer *et al.* (1991).

13. Thomadakis (1992) makes the point that, although the conventional agency theory focuses its attention on debt claimholders, firms controlled by owner-entrepreneurs face a multiplicity of contingent claims based on explicit and implicit contracts with private and public agents.

14. This is a standard result of modern agency theory presented among others by Barnea, Haugen and Senbet (1985). See also Haugen and Senbet (1988) and Thakor (1989).

15. Mergers that make economic sense in this context are vertical and horizontal mergers. Conglomerate mergers in an efficient market environment are an aberration which point to the fact that US markets for corporate control are not as perfect as they should be, since they allow such an agency problem to exist. One would expect that as efficient capital markets evolve, only economic reasons would lead to large firms.

16. See Amihud and Lev (1981) for some empirical evidence.

17. As an example, Virmani (1985) notes how large private Korean corporations, with their diversified portfolio of product markets, 'provide a partial substitute' for equity markets found in developed countries.

18. This is particularly true in LDCs where financial repression is common and takes the form of a strict control of interest rates, both deposit and lending rates. Furthermore, regulation usually includes measures such as forcing banks to lend at subsidized rates a certain proportion of a bank's portfolio to primary and industrial sectors considered 'priorities'.

19. The works of Leff (1975; 1978) and Aubey (1979) stress the relationship between financial intermediation and business ownership and control in Latin America.

20. For the case agency issues and dividends in developed countries refer to Crutchley and Hansen (1989).

21. Joint ventures also take place between firms from developed countries. Managers might have similar motivations to those presented here. However, those ventures are carried out between managers of fully publicly owned corporations. We are stressing joint ventures as a portfolio alternative for O-Ms from LDCs to hedge political risk.

22. For important sets of capital markets development policies see: Fischer *et al.* (1991) and Ortiz (1992).

REFERENCES

AMIHUD, Y. and LEV, B. (1981) 'Risk Reduction as a Managerial Motive for Conglomerate Mergers', *Bell Journal of Economics*, vol. 12, no. 2 (Autumn), 605–17.

AUBEY, R. T. (1979) 'Capital Mobilization and the Patterns of Business Ownership and Control in Latin America: The Case of Mexico', in

S. Garfield *et al.* (eds), *Entrepreneurship in Cultural Context* (Albuquerque: University of New Mexico Press).

BARNEA, A., HAUGEN, R. and SENBET, L. (1985) *Agency Problems and Financial Contracting* (Englewood Cliffs, NJ: Prentice-Hall).

BASANT, K. K. (1976) 'Alternative Stabilization Policies for Less Developed Economies', *Journal of Political Economy*, vol. 84, no. 4 (Aug.) 777–95.

BASANT, K. K. (1986) *Studies in Inflationary Dynamics: Financial Repression and Financial Liberalization in Less Developed Countries* (Singapore: Singapore University Press).

BERLE, A. and MEANS, G. C. (1933) *The Modern Corporation and Private Property* (New York: Macmillan).

BRUNO, M. (1979) 'Stabilization and Stagflation in a Semi-Industrialized Economy', in R. Dornbusch and J. A. Frenkel (eds), *International Economic Policy*, (Baltimore: Johns Hopkins University).

BUFFIE, E. F. (1984) 'Financial Repression, the New Structuralist, and Stabilization Policy in Semi-Industrialized Economies', *Journal of Development Studies* (Netherlands), vol. x, no. 14 (Apr.) 305–322.

COURAKIS, A. S. (1984) 'Constraints on Bank Choices and Financial Repression in Less Developed Countries', *Oxford Bulletin of Economics and Statistics*, vol. 46, no. 4 (Nov.) 341–70.

CRUTCHLEY, C. E. and HANSEN, R. (1989) 'A Test of the Agency Theory of Managerial Ownership, Corporate Leverage and Corporate Dividends', *Financial Management* (Winter) 36–46.

DEMSETZ, H. and LEHN, K. (1988) 'The Structure of Corporate Ownership: Causes and Consequences', *Journal of Political Economy*, vol. 93, 1155–77.

DIAZ-ALEJANDRO, C. (1985) 'Good-Bye Financial Repression, Hello Financial Crash', *Journal of Development Studies*, vol. 19, no. 1/2 (Sept./Oct.) 1–24.

DORNBUSCH, R. and REYNOSO, A. (1989) 'Financial Factors in Economic Development', *American Economic Review*, vol. 79, no. 2 (May) 204–9.

ERRUNZA, V. R. and LOSQ, E. (1985) 'The Behavior of Stock Prices on LDC Markets', *Journal of Banking and Finance*, vol. 9, no. 4 (Dec.) 561–75.

ERRUNZA, V. R. and ROSENBERG, B. (1982) 'Investment in Developed and Less Developed Countries', *Journal of Financial and Quantitative Analysis*, vol. XVII, no. 5 (Dec.), 741–62.

FAMA, E. and JENSEN, M. C. (1983) 'Separation of Ownership and Control', *Journal of Law and Economics*, 26 (June), 19–37.

FISCHER, K. P., ORTIZ, E. and PALASVIRTA, A. P. (1991) 'The Industrial Group and Risk Management in Imperfect Capital Markets', in D. Dimon (ed.), *Proceedings, BALAS 1991* (San Diego: USD).

GALBIS, V. (1979) 'Inflation and Interest Rate Policies in Latin America. 1967–1976', *IMF Staff Papers*, vol. 26, no. 2 (Sept.) 334–66.

GURLEY, J. G. and SHAW, E. S. (1960) *Money in a Theory of Finance* (Washington, DC: Brookings Institution).

HAUGEN, R. A. and SENBET, L. W. (1988) 'Bankruptcy and Agency

Costs: Their Significance to the theory of Optimal Capital Structure', *Journal of Financial and Quantitative Analysis*, vol. 23, no. 1 (Mar.) 27–38.

IBARRA PUIG, V. I. (1989) 'Represion y Liberacion de las Actividades Financieras en los Paises en Desarrollo: El Caso de America Latina', *Comercio Exterior* (Mexico), vol. 39, no. 12 (Dec.), 1045–9.

JENSEN, M. C. and SMITH, C. W. (1985) 'Stockholder, Manager, and Creditor Interests: Applications of Agency Theory', in E. I. Altman and M. G. Subrahmanyam (eds), *Recent Advances in Corporate Finance*, (Homewood, Ill.: Richard D. Irwin) 93–131.

JENSEN, M. C. and MECKLING, W. H. (1976) 'Theory of the Firm: Managerial Behavior, Agency Cost and Ownership Structure', *The Journal of Financial Economics*, vol. 3, no. 4 (Oct.) 306–60.

KELLER, P. M. (1980) 'Implications of Credit Policies for Output and Balance of Payments', *International Monetary Fund Staff Papers*, vol. 27, no. 3 (Sept.) 471–78.

KHAN, M. S. (1985) 'Analytical Approach to Interest Rate Determination in Developing Countries', *Pakistan Development Review*, vol. 24 (Autumn/Winter), 494–5.

KITCHEN, R. L. (1986) *Finance for the Developing Countries*. (New York: John Wiley & Sons).

LEFF, N. H. (1975) 'Capital Markets in Less Developed Countries: The Group Principle', in R. I. McKinnon (ed.) *Economic Growth and Development* (New York: Marcel Dekker) 97–122.

LEFF, N. H. (1978) 'Industrial Organization and Entrepreneurship in the Developing Countries: The Economic Group', *Economic Development and Cultural Change*, vol. 26 (July) 661–75.

MATHIESON, D. J. (1979) 'Financial Reforms and Capital Flows in a Developing Economy', *International Monetary Fund Staff Papers*, vol. 26, no. 3 (Sept.) 450–59.

MATHIESON, D. J. (1983) 'Estimating Models of Financial Behavior During Periods of Extensive Structural Reform: The Experience of Chile', *IMF Staff Papers*, vol. 30, no. 2 (June), 350–93.

MCKINNON, R. I. (1973) *Money and Capital in Economic Development* (Washington: Brookings Institute).

MCKINNON, R. I. (1986) 'Financial Liberalization in Retrospect: Interest Rate Policies in LDCs', *Center for Economic Policy Research* (Stanford University), no. 74.

ORTIZ, E. (1979) 'Inflacion y Estructura Financiera de las Empresas Registradas en la Bolsa Mexicana de Valores', *Prospectivas de la Administracion en Mexico Hacia 1990* (Mexico: FCA/UNAM).

ORTIZ, E. (1992) 'Capital Market Reforms and Development in Latin America', in Khosrow Fatemi (ed.) *International Trade and Finance Association. 1992 Proceedings* (Laredo: LSU).

ORTIZ, E. and BUENO, G. (1992) 'Business Finance and Goal Programming in Imperfect Capital Markets', in K. P. Fischer and G. J. Pappaioannou (eds), *Business Finance in Less Developed Capital Markets* (Westport, CT: Greenwood Press).

SHAW, E. S. (1973) *Financial Deepening in Economic Development* (New York/London: Oxford University Press).

TAYLOR, L. (1983) *Structuralist Macroeconomics: Applicable Models for the Third World* (New York: Basic Books).

THAKOR, A. V. (1989) 'Strategic Issues in Financial Contracting: An Overview', *Financial Management* (Summer) 39–58.

THOMADAKIS, S. (1992) 'Enterprise Governance and Growth: Notes on the Theory of the Firm in Less-Developed Countries', in K. P. Fischer and G. J. Pappaioannou (eds), *Business Finance in Less Developed Capital Markets* (Westport, CT: Greenwood Press).

VAN AGTMAEL, A. W. and ERRUNZA, V. R. (1982) 'Foreign Portfolio Investment in Emerging Securities Markets', *Columbia Journal of World Business* (Summer) 58–63.

VAN WIJNBERGEN, S. (1983) 'Interest Rate Management in LDCs', *Journal of Monetary Economics*, vol. 12, no. 3 (Sept.), 433–52.

VERNON, R. (1977) *Storm Over Multinationals: The Real Issues* (Cambridge, Mass.: Harvard University Press).

VIRMANI, A. (1985) *Government Policy and the Development of Financial Markets: The Case of Korea.* World Bank Staff Working Papers, No. 747 (Washington: World Bank).

WHITE, E. (1989) 'Politicas e Instrumentos para el Desarrollo de las Nuevas Tecnologias en America Latina', *Comercio Exterior*, vol. 39, no. 11 (Nov.) 966–77.

WILLIAMSON, O. E. (1988) 'Corporate Finance and Corporate Governance', *The Journal of Finance*, vol. XLIII, no. 3 (July), 567–91.

16 Structural Changes in the Korean Financial Market

Joanna Poznanska

16.1 INTRODUCTION

One of the features of South Korea's impressive economic development is that it has been achieved without a developed financial
system. This sector has suffered from lack of autonomy, being closely
controlled by the government during the last thirty years. Governmental interventions have created not only phenomenal economic
success but also various structural problems and serious inefficiencies
in the national economy, among them a rather archaic financial
structure. This financial structure – banking and securities market –
has become a target of governmental reforms which have been inten-
sified lately.

There are a number of specific reasons for recent governmental
actions within the financial sector. One critical reason is that South
Korea currently suffers from a shortage of capital. The shortage is
reflected in very high prime lending rates, which were at 12.5 per cent
in 1991, with curb-market rates around 20 per cent. Moreover, there
are quantitative limits on the amount of official lending available.
Smaller companies have particular difficulty in obtaining loans (with
120 000 such companies having no access to bank credit at all). These
financial difficulties prevent small firms from setting up businesses in
the areas being abandoned by *chaebol* (e.g. in the textile industry).

Another reason for financial liberalization is that the commercial
banks have not yet learned how to be very profitable and highly
productive (e.g. Korea's productivity still represents only to 10 per
cent of the level of their Japanese counterparts (Clifford, 1991, p. 70)
even though they benefit from a generous gross interest margin of
more than 4 per cent (between lending and deposit); profit rates are
low. Banks suffer from a lack of qualified managers who are trained
to make credit decisions and market loans.

The need to liberalize the financial market becomes more apparent in the face of the latest effort by the government to sterilize the current account surplus of 1986–9. Currency appreciation and import liberalization helped to reduce the impact of trade surplus on domestic money stock and keep inflation in check. The government realized in the process that another sterilization instrument, an open market operation by the Bank of Korea, can not be used in the absence of a well developed market for government securities.

The Korean government has been implementing a programme of fundamental changes in the financial system. These reforms involve: first, privatization of commercial banks; second, shifting from direct to indirect control and allowing for open market operations; third, deregulation of interest rate fixing; fourth, liberalization of exchange rates; fifth, increasing the role of the securities market; and sixth giving foreign investors access to the country's banking and securities system.

Currently, privatization is a less important form of economic liberalization than measures aimed at deregulation. This is not surprising, since the share of state assets in the national capital of Korea has always been relatively low. For example, in 1976 the state sector accounted for 9 per cent of the total product, while, for comparison, in Taiwan the state sector represented 27 per cent of the total output (Johnson, 1988, p. 149).

16.2 REFORMS IN THE BANKING SYSTEM

16.2.1 Privatization programme

Privatization has become a world-wide phenomenon. It started in the advanced capitalist countries and then developing countries adopted the strategy as well. The latest additions are the economies of Eastern Europe and the former Soviet Union, all abandoning their decades-old, state-run economies based on public ownership. China has not engaged in the divestment of public enterprises, but it has allowed a very dynamic growth in its non-state sector (including the municipal manufacturing industry, and family-based agriculture).

Among the most important reasons for reconsidering the role of state-owned organizations – in manufacturing, banking or transportation – is not only the relative inefficiency of such arrangements and the great expense to state budgets. In many cases, particularly in developing nations, the reason for privatization has also been the rise of local entrepreneurial classes which are able to assume financial risk in large-scale operations.

Before 1945, the climate in South Korea for entrepreneurship was unfavourable, but during the following years a large pool of talented businessmen has emerged. Particularly important for the expansion of an aggressive local entrepreneurial class has been the great opening of the economy. It has exposed domestic businessmen to international competition in a fluid market environment. Now, the strong internal business class is ready to take over state activities in crucial sectors of the economy, including banking.

In 1961, the government of South Korea nationalized the banks while the privatization of banking started with the government selling to the general public its majority share holdings in Hanil Bank in 1981. This sale set a trend for privatization of all major commercial banks. During the next two years such banks as Chohung Bank, Commercial Bank of Korea, Korea First Bank, and Bank of Seoul were privatized and now they are majority owned by large conglomerates.

The two other nationwide commercial banks, Shinhan Bank and KorAm Bank, have become joint-venture banks. KorAm is a joint-venture between the Bank of America, with 49 per cent equity, and a consortium of Korean companies; while Shinhan Bank is a joint venture involving private Korean companies and individual Korean residents in Japan. The KorAm Bank and Shinhan Bank enjoy more independence than other commercial banks in Korea (e.g. appointments of bank presidents are not controlled by the government).

The primary motive behind privatization has been to make the banking system more profitable without releasing governmental control over them. Although commercial banks have been privatized a long time ago, the impact of this reform has been very limited. Bank ownership is fragmented since no individual shareholder is permitted to own more that 8 per cent of the total stock. This dispersed ownership allows the Ministry of Finance to tightly control the banking sector.

Despite privatization, the commercial banks continue to act as bureaucratic organizations which dispense loans following governmental guidelines. Existing guidelines on credit allocation offer comfortable profit margins so that opposition to governmental interference is mitigated. They are still mostly implementing decisions made by the Ministry of Finance (e.g. rates on both loans and deposits are regulated by the ministry). The Ministry of Finance continues to be the most critical player, not even challenged by the central bank (this is clearly a replica of the Japanese model).

The Bank of Korea is tightly controlled by the Ministry of Finance, which decides on most of the important aspects of monetary policy. Given the circumstances, the Bank of Korea has been pressing for as fast a financial liberalization as possible. Such liberalization would allow the BOK to be more active in controlling money supply. The government maintains effective leverage over banks, in part because the banks suffer from large, non-performing loans which were provided under state guidelines to strategic industries during the last two decades. It is estimated that the value of non-performing loans amounted to 2.2 trillion won in 1991. Commercial banks have to convert a large portion of their profits to finance their loan-loss reserves. Several more years will be required for the banks to write off the bad debts.

16.2.2 Banking deregulation

The banking system in South Korea is under heavy state control, similar to the conditions present in Japan and Taiwan. In all these cases, the banking system has been used by the respective states as a major instrument for controlling the economies of those countries, i.e. activities of the private sectors. The credit system has been employed in particular to channel supplies of capital to priority projects, viewed by the governments as conducive to the overall economic strategy of the state (as was the case during the 1970s with shipbuilding and chemicals in South Korea).

Strict rationing of credit and fixing of interest rates charged on loans lasted till 1980–83, when the Korean government officially denationalized commercial banks. For comparison, in Taiwan the banks continue to be mostly state owned. In Japan, commercial banks are mostly private, with majority of them controlled by large holdings, i.e. *zaibatsu*. However, Japan's major financial institution – postal saving system – is totally controlled by the state (Johnson, 1988, p. 148).

The South Korean conglomerates – *chaebol* – differ from Japanese *zaibatsu* in one important way, namely groups typically do not include their own banks. *Chaebol* have to rely instead on credit institutions which are heavily controlled by the government. This financial link provides the state with a powerful instrument of economic intervention. Mason (Mason *et al.*, 1980, p. 267) states that: 'the most potent instru-

rt"),]())()

ments for implementing economic policy have undoubtedly been control of bank credit and access to foreign borrowers.'

Korean banks prefer to lend to *chaebol* rather than to small firms, and favour all firms over consumers. Still *chaebol* is interested in acquiring a stronger control over banking by obtaining shares in particular banks.

Despite announced restrictions on credit to *chaebol*, its share in total bank credit has not changed. Typically, the debt equity ratio for most *chaebol* is 350 per cent which makes commercial banks quite vulnerable. According to available evidence about one third of *chaebol* loans comes from non-banking institutions (e.g. insurance companies, trusts, etc.). About one half of non-banking financial institutions is owned or co-owned by *chaebol*.

The role of the government has been particularly important in setting interest rates and in differentiating them for particular customers in the industry. For instance, in 1971, the interest rate charged on general bank loans was 22 per cent, while borrowing for export-related projects carried only 6 per cent (World Bank, 1987, p. 113). Traditionally, the criteria for bank lending are determined by the government. It decides on what conditions potential borrowers have to meet in order to qualify for credit. Moreover, the government determines in all cases of so-called 'bad' loans whether financing should be continued or not.

The over-regulation of the capital market has resulted in the development of a substantial informal, underground financial sector. Capital raised in this way is applied mostly to the financing of current operations and to short-term credit for consumers. These funds are provided mostly by small groups of investors who typically offer money at rates exceeding the rates charged by commercial banks by two or three times. For example, in 1971, when general bank loans carried a 22 per cent rate, the 'curb' interest rate was close to 46.4 per cent (World Bank, 1987).

More than 30 per cent of the total loan volume in 1991 was financed by underground or non-bank institutions which do not follow government policy-guidelines (Leung, 1991, p. 22). These extensive activities outside of the governmental control have reduced the effectiveness of state actions during the last years. In fact, concern for the expansion of non-bank lending and the growth in 'curb' market operations has greatly contributed to the recent decision by the government to relax direct controls and start relying more on indirect interventions in the financial sector.

Table 16.1   Market share of banks, non-banks

	1985	1986	1987	1988	1989
Deposits					
Banks	45.2	42.3	39.3	36.5	33.1
Non-banks	54.8	57.7	60.7	63.9	66.3
Loans					
Banks	59.1	57.4	54.1	52.6	52.0
Non-banks	40.9	42.6	45.9	47.4	48.0

Source: Bank of Korea, 1990.

During the last few years, the government has tried to deregulate interest rates but with rather limited success. In 1988, bank lending rates were nominally decontrolled but the central bank reimposed restrictions through window guidance when rates began to increase. The slow pace of reform can be attributed to the fears of the Ministry of Finance that deregulation would have adverse effects, in particular that it could cause high interest rates and lead to a cost-push inflation. The Ministry was also afraid that the financial system could not instantly adjust to the new rules of the game.

In 1991, the government announced a new plan to free interest rates by 1996. It intends to proceed with liberalization of rates in a gradual fashion. Several principles will be adopted here, among them that long-term rates will be freed before short-term rates, and that lending rates will be liberalized before deposit rates are decontrolled. Such a gradual reform would require that the government has enough power to enforce its programme, while there are signs that in fact the state may quickly lose control over the timetable.

By mid-1992, the long-term deposit rates and certificates of deposit are to be decontrolled in order to reverse the shift of deposit money away from banks to non-bank institutions, e.g. insurance companies (banks' share in total deposits fell from 45.2 per cent in 1985 to 33.1 per cent in 1989, see Table 16.1). By the end of 1993, all bank loan rates and corporate bonds will be freed, and by 1996 all deposits other than bank debenture and demand deposits are to be liberalized.

The government expects serious resistance to the financial reforms from the commercial banks. For bank managers the reforms will be very unsettling since they remove the old practice of guaranteeing a fixed spread between lending and deposit rates. The spread has been the source of about one-third of banks' profits and the banks have not learned how to earn money from fee-based operations. Commercial banks are likely to oppose rate liberalization by forming cartel agreements and fixing both rates to enhance their profits.

16.2.3 Internationalization

South Korea allowed foreign banks to enter its market in 1967, with the objective of bringing foreign capital and import managerial skills. At that point, foreign banks were given certain privileges as an incentive to set up their businesses in Korea. Chase Manhattan Bank opened its branch first in the same year, and the number of foreign banks has increased rapidly since that time. There were 66 foreign bank branches, mostly placed in Seoul and Pusan, as of the end of 1989 (most of them from the United States and Japan).

During the mid-1980s, the special privileges for foreign banks were phased out. The right of foreign bank branches to use a swap system with the Bank of Korea to exchange foreign capital for local currency was gradually reduced. Their exclusion from a local requirement to provide certain policy loans for strategic industries was revoked as well. Foreign banks were forced to subscribe to money stabilization bonds, a tool used by the central bank of South Korea to manage money supply.

The government policy to apply the principle of national treatment to foreign banks also included the easing of some restrictions used only with respect to foreign banks, such as those on the purchase of real estate. Another step was that foreign banks were allowed access to the rediscount window of the central bank (though they have to pay an interest rate which is 2–5 per cent higher than that paid by the locals, a result of collusion by the latter, (Butler, 1991, p. 11). They were also permitted to enter trust business and issue certificates of deposit.

Foreign banks are innovative and, for example, they have entered retail banking, this without any limitations by the government (a case in point being the American CitiBank). Recently these banks have shifted their focus from corporate banking to a new type of consumer banking. Foreign banks have introduced a number of up-to-date banking instruments, such as an options market, currency swaps and other practices. Their high skills are reflected in above average profits (e.g. in 1990, the return on the total assets of foreign banks was estimated at 1.39 per cent compared with 0.68 per cent for their Korean counterparts, see Table 16.2).

Table 16.2   Foreign banks: share of Korean banking business

	1986	1987	1988	1989	1990	June 1991
Total assets	8.9	7.7	6.4	5.7	5.2	6.0
Total loans	10.9	10.2	8.5	6.8	6.0	6.6
Total deposits	1.7	1.5	1.1	0.9	1.0	0.9
Return on assets	1.19	1.42	1.8	1.83	1.39	—
Average return big 5 Korean banks	0.15	0.16	0.38	0.79	0.68	—
Net earnings (units Won 100 m)	801	1068	1366	1434	1326	—

Source: Ministry of Finance, Seoul, 1991.

Foreign banks are becoming actively involved in foreign exchange transactions, which are increasingly important as the government eases the currency controls. The daily market average of the foreign exchange system was introduced in 1990 to increase the role of market forces. In 1991, the Bank of Korea allowed exchange rates to fluctuate at a daily range of 0.6 per cent, rather than 0.4 per cent as in 1990 (before that year, rates were determined arbitrarily). This reform offers a great opportunity for foreign markets which have more experience in that kind of dealing.

Banks of foreign origin have been in an advantageous position since they have been allowed to offer loans at unregulated rates. In 1991, the Korean commercial banks were lending at the effective rate of 20 per cent, while foreign banks asked only 15 per cent for their credit money. If bank funds were allocated by the price – interest alone – all business would flow to the foreign banks. This, in part, explains why domestic banks tend to act as cartels to steer customers away from foreign banks.

Despite certain advantages, the foreign banks' share of the Korean banking industry has slightly declined during the last decade and a half. Their share of total bank assets declined from 8.9 per cent in 1986 to 6.0 per cent in 1991. Foreign banks' share of the total number of loans changed from 10.9 per cent in 1986 to 6.6 per cent in 1991, while their share in the total deposits went from 1.7 per cent in 1986 to 0.9 per cent in 1991. Clearly, the foreign banking sector has assumed the role of a peripheral element in the whole banking structure of Korea.

16.3 CHANGES IN SECURITIES MARKETS

16.3.1 Securities market

There are two ways of financing capital expansion by a company: first, through self-financing based on revenues raised by a particular producer (i.e. from current profits); and second, through the so-called capital market, where investors take advantage of external sources (i.e. national pool of savings). The weight of each source may differ in particular economies, though in any modern economy both of these forms of financing tend to coexist.

Business literature distinguishes two basic forms of a capital market: first, one market form is based on bank credit, either independent of the state or subordinate to a state (as in post-war Japan); and second, a market based on securities, i.e. stocks and bonds. Historically, the credit-based financial system precedes the security market, which represents a more flexible form (as it allows for change in repayment deadlines through operations in the secondary market).

The South Korean financial system can be characterized as one with a domination of external financing of capital expansion. This is reflected in a very high ratio of financial exposure, i.e. debt/equity coefficient of firms. This ratio in South Korea was about 300–400 per cent in 1980, which was very close to the level reported in Japan, but higher than in Taiwan where the respective ratio was about 160–200 per cent. For example, in 1991 Samsung had four times more debt than equity, while another *chaebol*, Goldstar, had 28 times more in debt (Darlin, 1992, p. 18). The South Korean ratio was several times higher than in the United States and Great Britain.

Another feature of the South Korean capital market is that securities markets are very weak, while the bulk of the external financing comes to companies from the banking system. In 1980, about 80 per cent of capital assets in South Korea were formed through loans extended by commercial banks, with the balance coming from internal sources (i.e. equity). For comparison, 50 per cent of capital assets were financed internally in the United States in 1980 (Lim, 1981, p. 26).

The stock market was officially opened up in South Korea in 1956 and allowed to operate with very little governmental regulation until 1977, when typical instruments of state intervention were introduced. At this moment, the stock market was still relatively small, but such a late development of a market for securities is not unusual for countries at the

Table 16.3   Composition of the financial market, South Korea
(in per cent)

Year	1965–9	1970–74	1975–9	1980–84	1985–9
Credit system	46.1	55.1	48.0	46.6	40.7
Banks	38.2	44.0	31.9	23.7	17.2
Non-banks	7.8	12.2	16.1	22.7	23.5
Securities Market	9.1	14.3	21.4	19.9	24.5
Shares	8.3	11.1	11.8	11.6	14.4
Bonds	0.8	3.2	9.7	8.3	10.1
Government funds	0.9	0.3	0.0	1.9	2.3
Commercial Paper	0.0	0.8	1.7	3.3	6.5
Foreign capital	27.9	21.3	15.9	6.0	3.0
Other sources	16.9	7.2	13.0	22.4	23.0
Total	100.0	100.0	100.0	100.0	100.0

Source: Bank of Korea, Financial System in Korea (various years).

level of economic growth as that of South Korea. The securities market accounted for 8.3 per cent of the financial system during 1965–8, and it increased its share to 14.4 per cent during 1985–9 (see Table 16.3).

16.3.2   Foreign operations

During most of the post-war period foreigners were limited to investing in the South Korean stock market through a few mutual funds and trusts. In 1991 the Korean stock market was valued at 114 billion dollars. This was not only one of the most substantial markets within the medium developed world but also one with great prospect for further expansion. Various restrictions made foreigners unable to benefit from these rapidly expanding securities operations, causing a lot of friction.

One important reason for the recent decision by the Korean government to open the stock market to foreigners has been the growing pressure from the United States and Western Europe. Both have been pressing Korea for many years to liberalize its foreign trade, and more recently the focus of these demands has shifted to the Korean service sector. The United States, with its considerable comparative advantage in banking services has been particularly interested in opening Korean securities (the recent GATT negotiations in Uruguay have provided convenient outlet for pursuing this policy).

In 1992, in its efforts to reform securities, the government opened the Seoul stock market to direct foreign investment. Foreigners will be allowed to buy up to 10 per cent of the outstanding companies listed on the stock market. For companies involved in so-called 'strategic' industries, ranging from mining to banking services, the limit will be 8 per cent. There will be some exclusions such as Kepco, the giant electricity company, where foreign ownership will not be allowed at all.

The government determined that any individual foreign investor would be allowed a maximum 3 per cent equity stake in a single Korean company, while collectively foreigners would be permitted to own up to 10 per cent. With respect to 45 Korean companies where foreign ownership has already exceeded the 10 per cent limit, through direct investment and bond conversions, the government established a 25 per cent limit.

Simultaneous with the opening of the stock market to foreigners, foreign brokers were issued branch licences allowing them to conduct business in South Korea. Opening a branch in Seoul is rather costly and requires a minimum expense of $13.5 million. By 1992, only European and American security companies were issued branch licences. The primary source of revenue for the brokerage companies will be involvement in booking Korean equity.

In mid-1991 the stock market surged in response to the earlier announcement by the Ministry of Finance that foreigners will be allowed to access the stock market. The volume of transactions reached a record level of 1.1 billion dollars during one of the daily sessions during that time – with a large portion of the new money that joined the stock market coming from the underground economy. Among contributing factors was not only the confidence that foreign participation will invigorate the market but also the poor performance of real estate and good showing of the national economy.

Internationalization of the Korean capital market also involves increased ceilings for Korean companies to enter foreign securities markets. According to the recently enacted law, South Korean companies will be permitted to issue up to a total of $1.5 billion in overseas markets, up from last year's limit of $0.7 billion. The ceiling for individual companies will be increased from $150 million to $200 million. Companies will also be allowed to issue securities, not once a year, but several times a year.

The above measures were designed to boost the competitiveness of manufacturing companies by expanding their access to foreign funds at cheaper rates. Priority was given to high-technology sectors. The amount of securities issued abroad by Korean companies expanded from $60 million in 1989 to $290 million in 1990, and to $1 billion in 1990. A good example of such utilization of foreign capital markets is Samsung Electronics in Hungary. It is about to issue shares on the Budapest stock exchange, in order to avoid high local bank interest rates and the risk involved in borrowing hard currency (Denton, 1992, p. 21).

16.4 CONCLUSION

The South Korean economy is under increasing pressure to modernize its financial sector, i.e. diversify and liberalize it. Such reforms are needed to mobilize financial resources required by the ongoing restructuralization of the economy: particularly the shift from labour-intensive to technology based production. Financial reforms are also needed to create the proper conditions for an effective monetary policy. The pace of the actual reforms have been slow, mostly due to the decisions made by the key actor, the Ministry of Finance.

One possible event which could accelerate the liberalization process is the unification of both Koreas. Such a unification may result in an enormous demand for capital and the government's effort to gradually reform the financial system will not work. Korea, whether united or not will most likely follow Japan's financial model rather than the Anglo-American model, centred around an independent central bank.

REFERENCES

BUTLER, S. (1991) 'Battering Rams Poised', *Financial Times*, 29 October 1991, p. 11.
CLIFFORD, M. (1991) 'On a Short Leash', *Far Eastern Economic Review*, 17 October 1991, p. 70.
DARLIN, D. (1992) 'Foreign Buying of Korean Stocks Likely to Be Cautious, Analysts Say', *The Asian Wall Street Journal Weekly*, 6 January 1992, p. 18.
DENTON, N. (1992) 'Budapest Flotation for Samsung Hungarian Unit', *Financial Times*, 11 February 1992, p. 21.
JOHNSON, C. (1988) *Political Institutions and Economic Performance: The*

Government-Business Deletions in Japan, South Korea and Taiwan (Stanford, CA: Stanford University Press) pp. 148–9.

LEUNG, J. (1991) 'First Step of Seoul to Liberalize Interest Rates Draws Mixed Reactions', *The Asian Wall Street Journal Weekly*, 22 November 1991.

LIM, Y. (1981) *Government Policy and Private Enterprise: Korean Experience in Industrialization* (Berkeley, University of California) p. 26.

LINDER, D. J. (1992) 'Foreign Exchange Rate Policy, Monetary Policy and Capital Market Liberalization in Korea', presented at AEA meeting, January 1992.

MASON, E. and KIM, *et al.* (1980) *The Economic and Social Modernization of the Republic of Korea* (Seoul, Korea: Korea Development Institute) p. 267.

PARK, SOON POONG (1989) 'Financial Repression and Liberalization in Korea', *Monthly Review of Foreign Exchange Bank* (October) pp. 3–23.

RHO, CHOONG-HWAN (1989) 'Money Market Development in Korea', *Monthly Review of Korea Exchange Bank* (December) pp. 3–15.

WORLD BANK (1987) *Korea: Managing the Industrial Transition*, vol. 1 (Washington DC: The World Bank) p. 113.

17 An Analysis of Equity Markets of Quotation Systems[1]

Gilles Duteil and
Abraham Mulugetta

17.1 INTRODUCTION

Technological and organizational revolutions of recent years have profoundly affected the operation of the financial markets. However, these have also raised increasing concerns regarding the safety and the soundness of the financial system, especially since the 1987 market crash.

The main role of financial markets are:

(1) Intermediation between the buyers and sellers of financial assets.
(2) Financing capital needs.
(3) Processing and dissemination of all relevant information to the market participants.

The quality of a financial market may be assessed in terms of its ability to perform these three roles which, in turn, are closely associated with the organizational structure of the market itself.

Rather than discussing 'the quality' of the market, it should be emphasized that the market has various 'qualities' and not just 'the quality'. The following are some of the related qualities: liquidity, visibility, depth, operational efficiency, reliability, safety, immediacy, equal accessibility and equal treatment (see the Appendix for explanation).

In terms of importance in the determination of market quality, liquidity appears to be one of the major criteria.

The financial theory focused mainly on measuring market efficiency through the analysis of the role of information integration in the process that rules price behaviour. Fama (1970) defined an efficient market as a market yield of a financial asset (based on available information) which is equal to the theoretical probability distribution of that same asset. It assumes that the price of a security fully reflects all available information at that point in time.

$$E(P_{j,t+1} \mid \Phi_t) = [1 + E(r_{j,t+1} \mid \Phi_t) P_{j,t} \tag{1}$$

where E is the expected value operator, $P_{j,t}$ is the price of security j at time t, $P_{j,t+1}$ is the price of security j at time $t + 1$, $r_{j,t+1}$ is the one period per cent rate of return for security j during period $t, t + 1$ and Φ_t is the set of information that is assumed to be 'fully reflected' in the security price at time t.

Examination of the financial market has been the subject of numerous studies. Critical evaluation of these duties can highlight an important issues which have been previously assumed away. That is, most financial markets do not seem to be as efficient as Fama (1970) stated. Therefore the assumption of market efficiency has been challenged by Shiller (1981), who shows that the observed yield volatility on financial markets is much larger than the one that should prevail under an assumption of efficiency. Thus, the concept of efficiency seems to be somewhat counterproductive to use in particular to evaluate market quality.

The missing link in the concept of efficiency appears not to lie at the level of information integration, but at the level of the price formation process. Therefore, a more detailed analysis requires a deep knowledge of the market microstructure.

Market operational efficiency can be assessed in terms of the liquidity of securities it deals with. Liquidity is a first class indicator for traders, especially for institutional investors, since it allows measurement of the impact of a large trading volume on the market volatility and market organizational structure on the stock price behaviour (the institutional investor is often at risk of selling large blocks of illiquid equities, therefore, incurring significant losses).

Is there a better measure of market efficiency than the ability to process all the information, which is the basis of the Efficient Market Hypothesis? Market efficiency in terms of information processing may not be the ideal measure of market quality. Therefore, a better measure of market quality may be one that combines efficiency and safety. These two factors may be captured by liquidity of equity markets.

In order to do that, a detailed analysis of the market microstructure and the price formation process must be performed. This chapter attempts to do just that.

Organizationally, following the definition of liquidity, the impact of market organization on liquidity will be analysed. Then some measures for estimating liquidity in the equity market in France by using data quoted on Cotation Assistée en Continu (CAC) for the period April 1988 to December 1989 will be proposed.

The data analysis shows that there are shortcomings with the proposed quotation system that the exchange authorities, Société des Bourses Françaises (Bourse), are now contemplating implementing the CAC system (It should be noted that the proposed quotation system is not to create a *de facto* rating system which may prematurely set the liquidity pattern of various corporate equities.)

17.2 TWO DIMENSIONS OF LIQUIDITY

17.2.1 The economic definition

Hicks (1962) first proposed the notion of liquidity. He argued that liquidity is the fact that a monetary asset can be easily transformed into another financial asset. Liquidity is therefore closely linked to the 'manoeuvring capacity' of an investor holding a financial asset (see Duteil, 1991).

17.2.2 The financial market definition

Cooper, Groth and Avera (1985) defined liquidity as the relationship between the volume of trading and changes in market prices. The purpose of their study is to analyse how price and volume variables behave with relation to each other in order to measure the liquidity risk which is defined as the risk of having a loss when selling a large number of stocks.

According to Marsh and Rock (1986), liquidity represents the degree to which a financial asset can be exchanged at a relatively stable price over a relatively short period of time. A liquid stock is an asset in which large transaction volumes can be carried out with minimal pressure on prices. This implies, of course, that market orders must be executed at minimal cost. However, as will be shown later, liquidity does not imply price stability or the lack of volatility.

This definition of liquidity is also accepted by Hui and Huebel (1986) who state that the more liquid a stock is, the less dramatic is its price response to changes in volume traded. In other words, large asset transactions must translate into small price variations and, therefore, into less risk, in order for the financial asset to be considered liquid.

Among the US researchers who have applied operational liquidity measurements are Cooper, Groth and Avera (1985) and Hui and Huebel who view liquidity as a market's ability to absorb orders without experiencing sizeable price fluctuations.

The measures are respectively:

$$LIQ = \frac{VP}{\sum |\% \ \Delta P|} \tag{2}$$

where *VP* is the dollar volume of trade for a stock over a 4-week period, and $\sum |\% \ \Delta P|$ is the sum of the daily absolute percentage price changes in the 4-week period.

$$LQ = \frac{(P_{max} - P_{min})}{P_{min}} \times \left[\frac{(V)}{(SP)}\right] \tag{3}$$

where *(SP)* is the dollar value of shares outstanding (on average closing price for a 5-day period), P_{max} is the average daily high price for a 5-day period, P_{min} is the average daily low price for a 5-day period, and *V* is the volume of shares traded.

Both studies used measurement intervals that are too long to capture the liquidity or illiquidity effects being sought. That is the reason why intra-day data are used in this study.

Throughout the literature, no measure fully explains the concept of liquidity.[2] The main problem is that price changes do not have the same origin or meaning. Random price changes generated by 'noises' prompt price variations in response to new information that is essential in markets where prices are the key signals to fundamental values and expectations. A liquid market keeps random price changes to a minimum level irrespective of the size and number of transactions. An efficient market lets prices move fast when investors change their perceptions of a company. This means that simple measures of liquidity may only represent a sort of weighted average of the frequency with which new information affects one stock compared with another, and the paradox is that liquidity by itself is likely to lead to less, rather than more, efficiency (see Bernstein, 1987). As a consequence, more efficient markets may not attract many active investors, because price variations will tend to be discontinuous, so that knowledgeable investors would not be able to take advantage of pricing errors. Yet, liquid and efficient markets both need a great number of active investors.

Despite the difficulties encountered in measuring liquidity, this characteristic has become a desirable feature for investor strategy. This interest in liquidity is motivated by difficulties some investors have faced trying to sell large blocks of an illiquid stock in the past and by the desire of security exchanges to gain some insight to improve their operational efficiencies.

Traders, investors, and financial analysts are concerned about liquidity, but so far, no one in France has come up with a satisfactory quantitative measure of it. Considering the growing interest of institutional investors and security exchanges in the notions of liquidity, as an interim measure, the ratios used in the United States are tested on French stocks.

17.3   FRENCH MARKETS MICROSTRUCTURE

Since 1986, the Paris Bourse has gradually replaced its traditional oral Walrasian batch auction (*cotation à la criée*) with an automated continuous quotation system which was inspired from the Toronto Stock Exchange CATS System.

Like the centralized markets of the United States, the opening price is processed by a batch auction, where all market orders and limit orders that correspond to the opening price (and entered into the system before market opening) are executed. After this opening auction, the market operates on a book order basis without the assistance of a market specialist and the trades are executed when matching orders are placed. Only market and limit orders are accepted. Stop orders were discontinued in 1989.

In fact, the Paris market is essentially a centralized market where orders are entered by Sociétés de Bourse, which act mainly as brokers and since 1989 a few of them also act as dealers. Over-the-counter trades are not frequent and are not always reported to the public, thus depriving the investors of some valuable information.[3]

The main publicly available information is provided by the Société de Diffusion de l'Information Boursière (SDIB) which is a 100 per cent sister company of the French Stock Exchange Authorities, La Société des Bourses Françaises. This market information is released through a satellite system which gives price and volume data on each trade as well as the five best bid-ask limits of the order book. In the

Paris Bourse, most equities are not actively traded and, therefore, lack depth. As a result, this continuous transaction automated system faces the following types of risk:

(1) *Execution risk.* When an investor places a limit order in the market, he does not know if and when it will be executed.
(2) *Market impact effect.* If an investor introduces a limit order with a high volume, he does not know, a priori, at what price his order will be executed.

For example, suppose an investor enters a market and places a buy order of 1000 shares of 'ABC'. At this moment, if the book-order shows the following:

Q	P_{ask}	P_{bid}	Q		
500	502				
500	501				
300	500			market	
				spread	
				is	498/500
		498	250		
		497	500		
		496	800		

where Q is the quantity of shares, P_{ask} is the ask price and P_{bid} is the bid price.

The order will be executed in the following manner:

300 shares at 500 FRF
500 shares at 501 FRF
200 shares at 502 FRF

resulting in an average price of 500.90 FRF per share. And if no new orders reach the market, the new market spread will be 498/502.

Given that a large number of equities quoted in the Paris Bourse are traded in very thin markets, the market impact effect might be more drastic for orders whose volume is larger than the average traded volume for a given stock. Because of this, investors tend to split their orders, thus lessening immediacy in their trading and/or facing losses in bloc trading.

(3) Delay in price discovery (that is, adjustments in prices as new information becomes available) could be longer due to lack of

information concerning all trades, including over-the-counter transactions. This can lead, in a thin market, to higher volatility when new information hits the market.

17.4   THE TAXONOMY OF STOCKS IN THE FRENCH MARKET

French equity markets are segmented into three divisions:

(1) *La Cote Officielle* which is divided into two categories. *Le règlement mensuel* where the most active stocks whose settlement is done once a month are traded. *Le marché comptant* is where less active stocks are traded on immediate settlement basis. Stocks are designated to be traded in one of the above categories by the Paris Bourse authorities.

(2) *Le second marché*. This division was created in 1983 and was inspired by the London Unlisted Securities Market. The requirements for being listed on 'second market' are less stringent than those needed for the *Cote officielle*, allowing medium-sized companies access to the financial market. But as only 10 per cent of the company's capital has to be put into public hands, the average number of shares outstanding is rather low.

(3) *Le marché hors-cote* is a non-regulated market where no special requirement is needed for trading. Some stocks are actively traded and others do not even have one trade per term. This market is not considered an official market but rather an over-the-counter market. This market *Hors cote* is not well thought of by the public because it lacks an adequate supervisory body and minimum requirements which allows it to become a theatre of financial scandals, discouraging small individual investors.

These divisions arose because of listing requirements and volume traded. The Société des Bourses Françaises is in the process of improving French market qualities, especially with regards to liquidity. It announced, in late 1990, a plan for the creation of trading categories regardless of the divisional origin of the stock, but took into account the degree of liquidity of stocks. The announced quotation categories are the following:

• First category: stocks bearing a 'natural liquidity' (which was not further defined) and traded in a continuous market.

- Second category: stocks having 'sufficient liquidity', but needing the assistance of a 'specialist' (the role of the specialist was not clearly defined), and traded on a continuous market.
- Third category: stocks with moderate liquidity and traded on a discontinuous market system (*cotation à clapets*) where quotations are set only when counterparts exist.
- Fourth category: stocks with low trading activity, whose quotation is to be established only upon demand from a *société de bourse*.

This foresees the creation of a unique market whose quotation process would change according to the degree of liquidity of stocks. Besides, it introduces for the first time, the services of 'specialists' in France. This new approach will bring a desirable depth in stock trading because of the intervention of specialists, trading for their own accounts on designated stocks, in a competitive environment. But at the time the above project was announced, the criteria for each category were not defined. Later, the Stock Exchange authorities realized that these categories may imply a *de facto* rating by investors with consequent influence on stocks' behaviour.

The trading categories were implemented on the CAC system on 2 December 1991.[4] Unfortunately, definitions of the categories were also changed making it difficult to understand the extent of liquidity in the French equity market.

The newly defined categories are as follows:

(1) Equities which are traded in the first category must meet *one* of the following requirements:
  (a) > 250 000 FRF volume traded per working day;
  (b) > 20 trades per working day;
  (c) average market spread < 1 per cent.
  - Trading hours: 10 am–5 pm.
  - Trading circuit breakers: trades are put on hold for 15 minutes when price change is larger than 10 per cent compared with the last closing price,[5] then normal transactions are resumed until price changes by another 5 per cent when trading is again halted. For the day, one more 5 per cent change is allowed, that is, a maximum variation of 20 about per cent.[6]

(2) Equities which are traded in the second category need to meet *one* of the following criteria:
  (a) > 50 000 FRF volume traded per working day;
  (b) > 5 trades per working day;

    (c) average market spread > 2 per cent.
- Trading hours: 10 am–5 pm.
- Trading circuit breakers: trades are put on hold for 30 minutes when price change is larger than 5 per cent compared to the last closing price, then two more 2.5 per cent prices changes are allowed for the day.

(3) Equities which do not meet one of the above requirements are traded on the third category.
- Trading in this category does not take place on a continuous book order market but in batch auctions which are held twice a day at 11:30 am and a call back at 4:00 pm. Stocks are quoted only if the price change does not exceed 5 per cent on the ups or downs from previous quotation.

(4) Stocks with low trading activity are introduced into the CAC system (in the third category) upon request, but are removed from the quotation system, at the end of one month, if they do not show sufficient activity.

The categories are scheduled to be up-dated by the Stock Exchange authorities every semester.

These trading categories do not accurately represent the level of liquidity of stocks, in which they are traded, because of the insignificance of eligibility requirements differentiating various categories. That is the reason for this study, to develop a better liquidity factor.

17.5   METHODOLOGY AND RESULTS

Very few financial data banks are available in France. A data base called AFFI-SBF was used in this study. It contains price and volume date on 208 French stocks of the *Cote officielle* quoted on the CAC system. The period of analysis is from 5 April 1988 to 29 December 1989 and the data set consists of every transaction (intraday) by these 208 firms over the entire period.

All prices were adjusted for capital modifications.[7] Daily prices were calculated on the basis of weighted average of all transactions of the day.

$$PMP_{ij} = \frac{\sum_{k=1}^{n} (VT_{j,k} COCOR_{j,k})}{\sum_{k=1}^{n} VT_{j,k}} \tag{4}$$

where PMP_{ij} is the average price weighted by volumes for stock (j), calculated for day (i), $COCOR_{j,k}$ is the adjusted price of a stock (j) for a transaction (k), $VT_{j,k}$ is the volume of transactions (k) for stock (j), and n is the number of transactions for stock (j) on day (i).

This PMP (weighted average price) represents the average price an investor would have paid to the market since each transaction has a weight proportional to its volume. Berkowitz, Logue and Noser (1988) consider this indicator as being the price a 'naive' trader can expect to obtain. Any intraday price can be compared to the PMP which acts as a benchmark.

Price changes were calculated on PMP basis:

$$RENT_{ij} = \text{Log} \left((PMP_{ij} + DIVCOR_{ij})/(PMP_{i-1j}) \right) \qquad (5)$$

where: $RENTPMP_{ij}$ is the logarithm price change for stock (j) on day (i), i is day (i), j is stock (j), and $DIVCOR_{ij}$ is the adjusted dividend, if any occurred on day (i).

Two daily liquidity ratios were calculated, the first one in the manner of Cooper, Groth and Avera (1985):

$$LIQ_{ij} = \frac{\sum_{k=1}^{n} COCOR_{j,k} VT_{j,k}}{\sum_{k=1}^{n} | \delta COCOR_{j,k} |} \qquad (6)$$

where $\delta COCOR_{j,k} = \text{Log} (COCOR_{j,k}/COCOR_{j,k-1})$.

The second one in the manner of Hui and Huebel:

$$LQ_{ij} = \frac{(VT_{ij}/TIT_j)PMP_{ij}}{(Ph_{ij} - Pb_{ij})/Pb_{ij}} \qquad (7)$$

where VT_{ij} is the volume of shares traded on stock (j) during the day (i), TIT_j is the number of shares outstanding for stock (j), Ph_{ij} is the highest price of stock (j) for day (i), and Pb_{ij} is the lowest price of stock (j) for day (i).

These two liquidity ratios obtained from equation (6) and (7), were then regressed against the following variables:

VT, daily volume of shares traded
VTM, average daily volume traded
PMP, daily average weighted price
ABSRENT, absolute value of RENT.

The average results obtained, in terms of multiple correlation (R) are the following:

$LIQ; R < 0.4$

$LQ; R < 0.6$

As those results were not adequate enough in explaining liquidity, this study attempted to intuitively adapt a modified version of Hui and Huebel model to the characteristics of French market.

Considering that the French equity market is rather thin and that the average volume of transactions is low, it was assumed that the global level of activity of the market might have a strong influence on liquidity measurement. In order to account for this factor, the ratio was transformed as:

$$LIQD_{ij} = \frac{(VT_{ij}/VTMAR_i)PMP_{ij}}{1 - [(Ph_{ij} - Pb_{ij})/Pb_{ij}]} \tag{8}$$

where $LIQD_{ij}$ is the liquidity indicator and $VTMAR_i$ is the total number of shares traded during the day on the market, for all stocks.

$$LIQD_{ij} = \alpha + \beta_1 (VT) + \beta_2 (VTM) + \beta_3 (PMP)$$
$$+ \beta_4 (ABSRENT) + \varepsilon \tag{9}$$

After regressing this new liquidity indicator against the same variables as above, an average multiple correlation coefficient, $R > 0.8$, was obtained. This is a significant increase in terms of explanation from earlier models used. It essentially confirms the intuitive expectation that the level of market activity must also be incorporated in the measurement of liquidity.

For over 90 per cent of the cases, the main explanatory variable was VT. First, an attempt was made to differentiate the stocks in terms of explanatory behaviour of their liquidity ratio. For each stock the contribution of the independent variables in the overall variance explained (R^2) was calculated. Then a non-hierarchical cluster analysis was performed (FASTCLUS procedure of the SAS system) based on the value of the contribution of the independent variables, *XVT*, *XVTM*, *XPMP*, and *XABSRENT* (these are the contribution of R^2 from VT, VTM, PMP and ABSRENT respectively). Once the clusters were obtained, a discriminant analysis was performed in order to confirm or reject the previous clusters.

From the results obtained, three clusters are formed. Cluster 1 shows the preponderance of *XVT* with a mean of 0.861784 indicating that the volume of shares traded has the largest influence on liquidity and *XABSRENT* has the smallest mean value among the three groups. This could indicate that the average return between two transactions does not greatly affect the level of liquidity of stocks in this cluster.

Cluster 2 is characterized by the lowest mean value of *XVT* (0.474206) but the highest mean value of *XABSRENT* (0.026981). It may indicate that liquidity behaviour of stocks classified in this cluster is closely linked to the relationship between price changes and volumes. But the average R^2 is only 0.59 indicating that other unknown factors affect the liquidity ratio. Stocks in this group have the highest average share volume per trading day of 66,480 and average market capitalization of 2.30^{10} FRF.

In the last cluster, the mean of *XVT* (0.712983) shows the dominance of the volume traded in the formation of liquidity, but still is significantly lower than that in cluster 1. However, the mean of *XABSRENT* is higher. This may indicate that, in this group, returns are given more weight than in the first cluster.

Additionally, a regression analysis was performed to test whether the values of *LIQGDM* (the arithmetic mean of $LIQD_{ij}$ calculated for each stock) are adequately explained by the independent variables. The regression equation is:

$$LIQGDM = \alpha + \beta_1 \, (XVT) + \beta_2 \, (XVTM) + \beta_3 \, (XPMP)$$
$$+ \beta_4 \, (XABSRENT) + \varepsilon \qquad (10)$$

where: α and β_1 are regression coefficients, ε is the residual term, *XVT* is the contribution of VT in R^2 in equation (9), *XVTM* is the contribution of VTM in R^2 in equation (9), *XPMP* is the contribution of PMP in R^2 in equation (9) and *XABSRENT* is the contribution of ABSRENT in R^2 in equation (9).

The variations between the observed variables and the ones predicted by the model is 0.0463. Assuming that there is no relationship between *LIQGDM* and the model, the results show that there is at least a 5.9649 per cent probability that the predicted variability is as much as 0.0463. This constitutes weak statistical evidence that the model adequately fits the observed values of *LIQGDM*. However, the Box–Cox power transformation analysis suggests that the logarithm of *LIQGDM* may give a better fit. So after excluding the extreme cases, the following model was regressed:

$$\text{Log}_{10}(LIQGDM) = \alpha + \beta_1 (XVT) + \beta_2 (XVTM)$$
$$+ \beta_3 (XPMP) + \beta_4 (XABSRENT)$$
$$+ \varepsilon \tag{11}$$

In this case, the variation between the observed variables and the ones predicted by the model is 0.1459. Assuming that there is no relation between $\text{Log}_{10}(LIQGDM)$ and the model, there is now a 0.0005 per cent chance that the variability is as large as estimated. This represents strong statistical evidence that the model adequately fits the observed values of $\text{Log}_{10}(LIQGDM)$.

The analysis of the variance (ANOVA) shows the following results:

Response: $\text{Log}_{10}(LIQGDM)$

Source	DF	SS	MS	F	Pr > F
XABSRENT	1	3.307	3.307	14.53	0.0002
XVT	1	1.531	1.531	6.728	0.0102
XPMP	1	0.736	0.736	3.233	0.0737
XVTM	1	0.366	0.366	1.606	0.2066

XABSRENT and *XVT* have an effect on the expected value of $\text{Log}_{10}(LIQGDM)$ significantly greater than the mean level of disturbance. This is consistent with previous research. The resulting model is:

Term	DF	Estimate	Std	T	Pr > |T|
INTERCEPT	1	0.863	0.255	3.338	0.0009
XABSRENT	1	7.479	1.962	3.812	0.0002
XPMP	1	–8.338	4.637	–1.798	0.0737
XVT	1	–0.819	0.316	–2.594	0.0102
XVTM	1	–0.770	0.608	–1.267	0.2066

$$\text{Log}_{10}(LIQGDM) = 0.863 + (7.479 * XABSRENT)$$
$$- (8.338 * \text{XPMP}) - (8.819 * XVT)$$
$$- (0.770 * XVTM) \qquad (12)$$

On the basis of these data, a cluster analysis was performed which, this time, used the variable $\text{Log}_{10}(LIQGDM)$ instead of $LIQD_{ij}$ as a measure of liquidity. Based on the results of the cluster analysis, a discriminant analysis was done to confirm the validity of the previous clusters.

The cluster analysis differentiates between 19 distinct classes of stocks. This was also confirmed by the discriminant analysis. The division between stocks comes from more subtle interactions between liquidity ratio, *XVT* and *XABSRENT*. The most active French stocks appear to be in classes 2, 4, 5, 6 and 17.

These results need to be analysed further in terms of the original (buy or sell) trades, market capitalization, and others to give more sense to the differentiation of stocks.

17.6 CONCLUSION

Investors clearly recognize liquidity as a desirable feature for portfolio investment strategy. But at this point of the study, the measures used do not fully explain liquidity as defined earlier. In France, empirical research regarding market 'qualities' has been considerably limited because of lack of available data. Recent changes in French market microstructure have not yet provided the proof of any amelioration in terms of depth in equity trading. An analysis of the empirical results of this study suggests several observations. First, the average liquidity ratio has a high positive correlation with the market value. Second, the liquidity ratio cannot simply be compared from one stock to another using market value because it is also significantly influenced by this price change. But it can be used as a measure of dynamic liquidity behaviour for a given stock, after this change has been computed for a standard number of shares. This, then can be used as a benchmark. Third, the quotation categories introduced by the Société des Bourses Françaises are not likely to improve market depth, except for the third category, where batch auction trading seems to be more adequate in terms of depth and price discovery for moderate active stocks. The actual market organization does not seem to be suitable for block trading (except OTC) and for future growth and expansion in the current context of harmonization of financial services in Europe. The active competition of London Seaq International market, in which most of French 'blue chips' are traded by market-makers, is likely to increase, as it provides firm prices and immediacy to block traders. The latter does not have to face execution risk and market impact effect and enjoys low commission cost and no tax.

Finally, we conclude that further research on liquidity, depth, and market microstructure would be useful to investors for decision making and portfolio management, as well as for market authorities, who are willing to adapt the organization of French equity markets.

APPENDIX

Liquidity. The possibility to get in or out of the market at any moment without facing heavy losses (i.e. with a reasonable price change).

Visibility. The possibility to work in satisfactory conditions across the board with all the relevant information available to all participants.

Depth. The capacity of the market to supply or absorb large quantities of stocks without abnormally increasing its volatility.

Operational efficiency. The fact that the market assures, with a minimum delay, the settlement of trades, and reflects exactly the status of any transaction.

Reliability. The fact that no investor can manipulate prices, that no intervention alters the truth of transaction and that all participants have equal access and equal treatment.

Immediacy. The minimum delay in allowing an investor to make 'buy-sell' transactions.

Notes

1. Because of shortage of space, appendixes II and III are not included in this version. Interested readers may contact the authors for a copy. The authors would like to thank the Société des Bourses Françaises (Paris) and the SAS Institute (European Division) for their financial support and

encouragement for this research project. Comments are welcome. For any query, contact G. Duteil, CETFI, 18, rue de l'Opéra, 13100 Aix-en-Provence, France.
2. See in particular, Amihud, Mendelson and Wood (1990); Bernstein (1987); Biais (1990); Branch and Echevarria (1991); Garman (1976); Glosten (1987); Hasbrouck and Schwartz (1986; 1988); Karpoff (1987); Mann and Seijas (1991); Marsh and Rock (1986); Sanger and McConnel (1986); Reinganum (1990); Roll (1984); and Stoll (1989).
3. Except for block trades, transacted on the Bourse upon mutual agreement between institutional investors, and which are known as 'applications'.
4. Bours'Info, *Bulletin d'information de la Société des Bourses Françaises*, September 1991.
5. The base price that is going to be used as a reference price to compute the allowable price change can be the last traded price or the best ask price if the stock was 'reserved' on the high or the best bid if it was given. On the low given, they are not beyond the first circuit breaker prices.
6. Exactly 18.78 per cent on a downward swing and 21.28 per cent on an upward swing.
7. Such as stock split or reverse split.

REFERENCES

AMIHUD, Y., MENDELSON, H. and WOOD, R. A. (1990) 'Liquidity and the 1987 Stock Market Crash', *Journal of Portfolio Management* (Spring) p. 65–9.
BERKOWITZ, S. A., FINNEY, L. D. and LOGUE, D. E. (1988) 'Quality of Markets Provided on Toronto Stock Exchange', *Revue Banque*, no. 482, April 1988.
BERKOWITZ, S. A., LOGUE, D. E. and NOSER, E. A. Jr (1986) 'The Total Cost of Transactions on the NYSE', *Journal of Finance*, vol. 63, no. 1 (Mar.) pp. 97–112.
BERNSTEIN, P. L. (1987) 'Liquidity, Stock Markets, and Market Makers', *Financial Management*, Summer, pp. 54–62.
BIAIS, B. (1990) 'Price Formation and the Supply of Liquidity in Fragmented and Centralized Markets', Paper presented at the 6th World Congress of the Econometric Society, 1990.
BRANCH, B. and ECHEVARRIA, D. (1991) 'The Impact of Bid-Ask Prices on Market Anomalies', *Financial Review*, vol. 26 (May) pp. 249–68.
COOPER, K. S., GROTH, J. C. and AVERA, W. E. (1985) 'Liquidity, Exchange Listing and Common Stock Performance', *Journal of Economics and Business* (Feb.) pp. 21–33.
DUTEIL, G. (1991) 'French Equity Market: Does Liquidity Exist?', Paper presented at the International Trade and Finance Association 1991 Conference, Marseille, France, 30 May–3 June 1991.
FAMA, E. (1970) 'Efficient Capital Markets: A Review of Theory and Empirical Work', *Journal of Finance*, vol. 25, no. 2 (June) pp. 383–417.

GARMAN, M. B. (1976) 'Market Microstructure', *Journal of Financial Economics*, no. 3, pp. 257–75.

GLOSTEN, L. R. (1987) 'Components of the Bid-Ask Spread and the Statistical Properties of Transaction Prices', *Journal of Finance*, vol. 62, no. 5 (Dec.) pp. 1293–1307.

HASBROUCK, J. and SCHWARTZ, R. A. (1986) 'The Liquidity of Alternative Market Centers: A Comparison of the New York Stock Exchange, and the NASDAQ National Market System', American Stock Exchange Transactions Data Research Project Report 1, January 1986.

HASBROUCK, J. and SCHWARTZ, R. A. (1988) 'Liquidity and Execution Costs in Equity Markets: How to Define, Measure, and Compare Them', *Journal of Portfolio Management* (Spring) pp. 10–16.

HICKS, J. R. (1962) 'Economic Theory and the Evaluation of Consumers' Wants', *Journal of Business*, vol. 35, no. 3, pp. 256–63.

HUI, B. and HUEBEL, B. (1984) *Comparative Liquidity Advantages Among Major U.S. Stock Markets* (Lexington, MA: Data Resources).

KARPOFF, J. M. (1987) 'The Relation Between Price Changes and Trading Volume: A Survey', *Journal of Financial and Quantitative Analysis*, vol. 22, no. 1 (Mar.) pp. 1098–126.

LIPPMAN, A. S. and McCALL, J. J. (1986) 'An Operational Measure of Liquidity', *American Economic Review* (Mar.) pp. 43–55.

MANN, S. V. and SEIJAS, R. W. (1991) 'Bid-Ask Spread, NYSE Specialists, and NASD Dealers', *Journal of Portfolio Management* (Fall) pp. 54–58.

MARSH, T. and ROCK, K. (1986) 'Exchange Listing and Liquidity: A Comparison of the American Stock Exchange with the NASDAQ National Market System', American Stock Exchange Transactions Data Research Project Report No. 2, January 1986.

REINGANUM, M. R. (1990) 'Market Microstructure and Asset Pricing', *Journal of Financial Economics*, no. 28, pp. 127–47.

ROLL, R. (1984) 'A Simple Implicit Measure of the Effective Bid-Ask Spread in an Efficient Market', *Journal of Finance*, vol. 39 (Sept.) pp. 1127–39.

SANGER, G. C. and McCONNEL, J. J. (1986) 'Stock Exchange Listing, Firm Value, and Security Market Efficiency: The Impact of NASDAQ', *Journal of Financial and Quantitative Analysis*, vol. 21, no. 1 (Mar.) pp. 1–25.

SHILLER, R. J. (1981) 'The Use of Volatility Measures in Assessing Market Efficiency', *Journal of Finance*, vol. 36, no. 2 (June) pp. 291–304.

STOLL, H. R. (1989) 'Inferring the Components of the Bid-Ask Spread: Theory and Empirical Tests', *Journal of Finance*, vol. 64, no. 1 (Mar.) pp. 115–134.

Part VII

Taxes, Distortions and International Banking

Part VII of the book brings out tax issues and models of tax structure under closed and open economies, and examines various facets of this type of price distortion, discusses the implications of existing municipal taxation systems in Mexico on the North American Free Trade Agreement. In this part, focus is also put on international banking globalization. Historical patterns of globalization of the French banking system and the details of off-shore banking trends are examined. Alejandra Cabello's 'Economic Integration and Mexican Municipal Finances' (Chapter 18) attempts to study the implications of existing municipal taxation systems in Mexico on the North American Free Trade Agreement (NAFTA). She puts forth an important point: potential benefits to Mexico from its integration with Canada and the United States might be limited due to existing asymmetries among the three nations. Uneven regional development is a factor that could create severe bottlenecks in the North American integration processes, hindering Mexico's trade and investment opportunities that could be gained from the NAFTA. This conclusion is reached after a careful analysis of Mexican municipal finances. To this effect, she first reflects on the interrelationships between economic integration and municipal development and finances. Taking another approach in closed and open economy frameworks, Dilip K. Ghosh and Shyamasri Ghosh present optimum structure of distortions in different postulated set-ups, and discuss the issues on possible tax structure. Then, the authors attempt to ascertain when uniform rather than differentiated and when differentiated rather than uniform tax structure would be optimal for the taxing country. In this context, the authors provide conditions for successful trade liberalization and thus creation of trading blocs and customs unions. In Chapter 20, 'Socio-history of French Banks and Banking: Role Model for Global Banking', Irene Finel–Honigman turns to historical evidence to asses patterns of internationalization and draws lessons to the present banking internationalization. The author finds that fear of speculation and risk since the financial fiascos of the eighteenth century coupled with a sense of historical presence and cultural identity have led France to adopt long-term, well hedged protective policies while developing and maintaining vast intercountry and international banking networks. French banking has always depended on effective government intervention from Napoleon III 'Saint Simonien' capitalism (1860–71) to de Gaulle's nationalization of major banks (1946) to Mitterand's complex manoeuvres from nationalization to privatization (1981–88). Aggressive and innovative banking management has led to a higher degree of competition in international banking. To enhance their competitiveness, US banks have established offshore banking centres to strengthen their international operations. Offshore centres allow them to lower costs and overcome limitations due to tax laws or regulatory policies meant to ensure sound banking management and confidence on the financial system. As a result, US banks carry out a significant amount of foreign lending activities through offshore banking centres. In the last chapter of this book, 'Offshore Banking Centres: Prospects and Issues' (Chapter 21), Emmanuel Roussakis, Krishnan Dandapani and Arun Prakash focus on the main issues surrounding this international banking practice. They present the environment of offshore banking and explicate the problems thoroughly, and then shed some light on its prospects. They conclude with their significant empirical analysis that barriers all over the world are crumbling and the world is becoming a global market place. In this changing environment of international financial markets the offshore banking centres which can provide excellent quality of service and can maintain high regulatory and supervisory standards can be expected to survive in decades to come, and this requirement will in turn strengthen the banking system worldwide.

18 Economic Integration and Mexican Municipal Finances

Alejandra Cabello

18.1 INTRODUCTION

Economic and financial globalization is leading to profound changes in national policy making, as well as in international economic relationships. Leaving behind economic development models instrumented at the end of World War II, influenced by neo-Keynesian thought and also by structuralist paradigms in the case of the Latin American nations, countries are now looking to market forces to promote economic growth. Full liberalized global economic activity is, however, far from being complete. GATT has failed to create an adequate institutional framework for freer international trade, due to the dissimilar interests of its members, particularly among the developed countries. As a result, countries are strengthening their ties with neighbouring countries and forming economic blocs.

The bloc conformed by the North American countries, Canada, United States and Mexico is a step in this direction. Mutual benefits are expected for the three nations. For Mexico, however, benefits might be limited due to existing asymmetries in economic development with its trading partners. Its ability to take advantage of investment opportunities derived from North American integration could be hindered by bottlenecks arisen from sharp differences in infrastructure, technological innovation, labour training, institutional development, income distribution and national regional development.

Although the Mexican–US border region offers many opportunities for corporate investments, the area is also plagued by many economic problems. In addition, concentration of economic activity in the area could reaffirm distorted regional and social development which has characterized contemporary Mexico. In this respect, to take full advantage of integration with United States and Canada, investments should be promoted along the entire country, favouring

263

less developed areas. Thus, one of the most important challenges that Mexican authorities face is to promote greater regional development. Local economic development reflects differences in endowments. To a great extent, their utilization depends on local public finances. They provide local governments with the financial resources necessary to build up the infrastructure, education, institutions and markets needed to attract investments to the area. Similarly, full knowledge of local needs and finances provide national governments with the information necessary to implement regional development plans. This work is a contribution in this direction. It makes a thorough analysis of Mexican public revenues and public expenses at the municipal level. Its intention is to pinpoint differences and determine the root for existing dissimilarities, so that policies can be instrumented to provide municipal governments with additional resources and the ability to promote their own development.

18.2 ECONOMIC INTEGRATION AND MUNICIPAL DEVELOPMENT AND FINANCES

Technological advances taking place during the last two decades have led to profound transformations in production, and innovative patterns in world trade and finance. As a result, institutions have also had to change, spurred by the market as the underlying force of economic activity. Within this framework, two tendencies characterize the end of the millennium: globalization and the conformation of economic blocs. Although these phenomena are apparently contradictory, they are rather complementary. Due to limited advances in GATT negotiations, countries are grouping themselves to face competitively the challenges and opportunities of globalization. Integration is not only seen as a means to increase local markets and increase welfare thanks to economies of scale and scope of integrated countries. It is also seen as a means to exploit their complementarities to increase their productivity and economic exchanges with other nations or regional groups.

The North American Free Trade Agreement (NAFTA) falls within these schemes. Canada, Mexico, and United States, breaking ancient taboos which characterized their relationships, particularly those existing between Mexico and United States, have decided to cooperate to conform a unique economic bloc: one which associates two developed countries with a less developed one. They intend to promote greater welfare for their populations by restructuring and optimizing their productive and financial processes, lowering corporate costs and enhancing their competitivity in relation to European and Japanese corporations.

The association is however asymmetrical.[1] Table 18.1 pinpoints the differences in socioeconomic development among the three North American countries. Some basic indicators must be emphasized. Mexico's Gross Domestic product is only 5 per cent of US aggregate output. Canadian GDP doubles Mexican output which is therefore 10 per cent of US GDP. Thus, 85 per cent of the 'largest world economic bloc' consists of the US economy. Trade between Mexico and Canada remains low, but for both nations their exchanges with US is very important. Mexico imports from US 65.21 per cent of its total imports; Mexican exports to US amount to 69.73 per cent of its total exports. Canada presents similar trends. Its exports to US are 70.3 per cent and its imports from US are 74.58 per cent of its totals. Canada and Mexico are the first and third trading partners for US, respectively. Nevertheless, US exports to Mexico only amount to 5.9 per cent of US total exports. US imports from Mexico are 3.86 per cent of its total imports.

Mexico has a competitive advantage in costs. Minimum hourly wages in US dollars are 0.54 cents in Mexico, 5.05 in Canada and 4.75 in United States. As a result some labour groups in US and Canada fear job losses due to massive plant relocations in Mexico. They affirm that capital moves to places with lower production costs, lower taxes, and limited regulation, specially on environmental matters. They emphasize that integration with Mexico will lead to a convergence to a lower common denominator, instead of pulling the entire region to higher welfare standards. They also point out that Mexico will undergo some undesirable changes as a result of inappropriate exploitation of its resources by multinational corporations.[2] Their view is, however, limited. First, integration should lead to gains in all countries. Second, corporations exploit market imperfections such as differential wages, but to be able to take advantage of them they must also count in their prospective location places with adequate infrastructure, labour training, local sourcing, political stability, etc. Otherwise, investments would be booming in countries like Haiti where labour costs are the lowest in the Western hemisphere. In this respect, since labour productivity is higher in United States and Canada and technological innovation is fairly developed in both nations, Mexico has more to fear from plant relocations, particularly

Table 18.1 Economic and social indicators of Mexico, Canada and United States

Economic indicators, 1991

	Mexico		Canada		United States	
GDP*	282.50		592.80		5 672.60	
%US	5.00		10.40			
GDP per capita	3 217.00		21 596.00		22 412.00	
%US	14.30		96.30			
Exchange rate (annual)	3 018.40		1.15		1.00	
Cons. price index (%)	22.70		5.60		4.20%	
Interest rates – Treasury Bills	19.28		8.73		5.41%	
Exports*	27.12		127.82		418.51	
to Mexico			0.78	0.61%	24.90	5.90%
to Canada	0.58	2.13%	–		89.55	21.50%
to US	18.91	69.73%	89.72	70.30%	–	
Imports*	38.18		120.08		490.11	
from Mexico	–		0.58	0.48%	18.91	3.86%
from Canada	0.78	2.05%	–		89.72	18.30%
from US	24.90	65.21%	89.55	74.58%	–	
Trade balance*	–11.06		+7.54		–73.60	
Current account*	–13.26		–24.16		–8.66	
Capital account						
Direct for investment*	4.7615		0.907		–7.30	
Foreign portfolio investment*	7.5400		17.003		–5.36	

Social indicators, 1990

Extension square km.	1 958 200	9 996 140	9 372 610
Population millions (91)	87.70	27.30	253.10
Active econ pop. (%)	35.40%	50.40%	48.90%
Min wages ($US)	0.54	5.05	4.75
Income 10% highest	37.99%(77)	24.20%(87)	25.0%(85)
Income 20% lowest	1.08%(77)	5.70%(87)	4.7%(85)
Infant mortality/1000	39.20	6.60	9.50
Population < 14 years (%)	37.30%	20.90%	21.60%
Urban population (%)	72.60%	77.10%	75.00%
Life expectancy	69.70	77.40	76.00
Calories/day	3 052.00	3 482.00	3 871.00
Population/care	15.10	2.10	1.70
Prof/elementary school students	30.50	15.70	17.00

* Billion dollars.

Sources: Banco de Mexico, *Indicadores Economicos*, various issues, 1992; Banco Nacional de Comercio Exterior, *Comercio Exterior* vol. 41, no. 7 (Mexico, July 1991); International Monetary Fund, *International Financial Statistics Yearbook, 1992*, and July 1992; World Bank, *Social Indicators of Development*, 1991–1992, 1992.

considering that its development is so uneven as shown by economic indicators in Table 18.1. Moreover, social indicators shown in the same table confirm the asymmetries existing among the North American countries. Infrastructure and social differences are so sharp that they could lead Mexico to serious economic setbacks if policy makers do not consciously take steps to prevent friction that could arise due to differences on levels of economic development with its trading partners.[3] Integration can only be successful to the extent to which the North American countries can harmonize their development policies, and their laws and institutions.

Macroeconomic and sectoral analysis have been carried out to diagnose the situation. Consequently, some provisions have been taken in the North American Free Trade Agreement, NAFTA. Liberalization will proceed at a slower pace in Mexico than in Canada and United States in some key sectors, mainly the agricultural and financial sectors. However, further analyses are necessary to promote in Mexico the changes needed to take advantage of economic integration and globalization.

An important aspect that needs to be examined is regional economic development. Regional development plans must be implemented to ensure smooth economic integration and to promote a steady, balanced growth of the entire economy. In a closed economy, the potential growth of a local economy is a function of the resources available in the area, the size of its market and nature and magnitude of economic interactions with other domestic units. Exchange with other nations also influence local development, but their impact is bounded by limitations on mobility on the factors of production. Economic integration changes this situation because a higher mobility of factors of production is promoted. Indeed, in the North American context, NAFTA is also an agreement to promote investments and financial integration in the area. Capital should therefore flow more freely in the area. Labour movements should also increase, due to increased economic activity, geographic closeness and agreements reached in this respect. In sum, regional growth will be also conditioned by external determinants.

However, the spatial points of a large developing economy such as Mexico show great contrasts. As a result, overall economic development can be restrained by bottlenecks derived from uneven regional development. Similarly, in an economic integration context, investment opportunities might be less due to inadequate regional development. Finally, development might favour some areas and remain

Table 18.2   Mexican regional economic indicators, 1989*
(Percent participation)

	National GDP	Savings	Savings[†] Per Capita	GDP[†] Per Capita
Most developed Federal entities				
Distrito Federal	27.47	44.93	9.30	16.50
Mexico	10.68	1.05	0.18	5.40
Jalisco	6.94	10.55	3.41	6.50
Nuevo Leon	5.93	10.66	5.89	9.50
Veracruz	5.14	2.64	0.72	4.10
Total	56.16	69.83		
Least developed Federal entities				
Baja California Sur	0.39	0.23	1.24	6.10
Campeche	0.45	0.20	0.66	4.20
Quintana Roo	0.46	0.23	0.80	4.60
Colima	0.51	0.29	1.17	5.90
Tlaxcala	0.66	0.18	0.40	4.30
Total	2.47	1.13		

* Estimated by Instituto Nacional de Estadistica, Geografia e Informatica (INEGI).
† Millions pesos.

Source: Banco Nacional de Mexico (Banamex), *Examen de la Situacion Economica de Mexico*, vol. LXVI, no. 779 (Oct. 1990) p. 485.

confined to an assembling process (*maquila*) at border areas, which has been the case under the 'silent' integration that has taken place between the United States and Mexico during the last two decades. The magnitude of regional uneven development is depicted in Table 18.2. Mexico is a federal state composed of 31 states and a Federal District (Mexico City). Nevertheless, according to recent census figures the Federal District and five other states account for 56.16 per cent of total national output. These entities also account for 69.83 per cent of total national savings. Moreover, Mexico City concentrates 27.47 per cent of total Gross Domestic Product and 44.93 per cent of national savings. In sharp contrast, the five least developed states account for only 2.47 per cent of total national output and 1.13 per cent of domestic savings.

Thus, potential development poles must be identified to promote regional development of wider areas through forward and backward linkages. An important part of those schemes must be devoted to municipal development for it allows closer attention to local problems and local citizens participation. Since municipal underdevelopment in countries like Mexico is highly related to a lack of resources, inadequate allocation of funds, and limited investment opportunities, closer attention should be paid to local finances. Local governments should increase their resources and allocate them more efficiently. This would allow Mexico to offer better conditions for investment and trade to firms from the North American countries and to take full advantage of the benefits derived from economic integration with its more developed Northern neighbours. Greater regional development would also contribute to strengthen and integrate domestic markets. Financial markets would also flourish at the national level, and link the country to the international financial markets. These changes, pushed by municipal development, would allow Mexico to accelerate its economic growth and promote greater equity, which ultimately should lead it to become a part of the developed world.

18.3   FINANCIAL ANALYSIS OF MEXICAN MUNICIPALITIES

Municipal finances have seldom been analysed for the case of the developing countries. Public finances of these countries are commonly analysed on an aggregate basis, focusing on the central government. Taking as point of departure the conceptual framework previously presented, this section makes a comprehensive analysis of municipal revenues and expenditures for the Mexican case, for the 1970–86 period. Tendencies, structure and growth of local government finances are examined in real terms to make a diagnosis about the origin and allocation of resources of Mexican municipalities. Data utilized comes from the Instituto Nacional de Estadistica, Geografica e Informatica and it is the most recently available desegregated municipal financial information.[4]

18.3.1   Growth and structure of municipal revenues

In real terms, revenues tend to decrease towards 1986. It is worth noting that revenue shares (distributed by the federal government to the local governments) show an increase from 1970–84, but decrease in 1985 (− 1.35 per cent) and 1986 (− 10.53 per cent) (see Figure

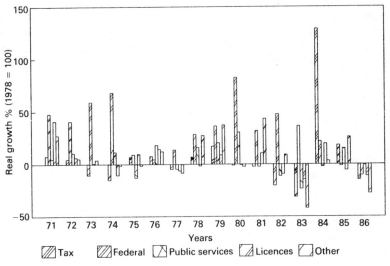

Figure 18.1 Municipal gross revenues

18.1). In absolute terms negative growth was even more dramatic for the last two years of the period under study, the federal share decreased from $15 312.30 million pesos in 1984 to $15 105.02 and $13 514.00 million pesos in 1985 and 1986, respectively (see Table 18.3).

More disturbingly, the structure of municipal revenues also tended to deteriorate. From 1970 to 1986 municipal effective ordinary revenues (taxes, public services, licences and fees, and other municipal taxes) tend to decrease while the share of federal revenue shares tend to increase, as a result of changes in the coordination of revenue collecting, which have led to a highly centralized tax system in Mexico. Local governments collect for the federal government; in turn the federal government shares revenues with the municipalities. That is, local control of taxes is limited in Mexico.

Figure 18.2 shows the relative increase in federal revenue shares throughout 1970–86. By 1970 federal tax shares amounted to 4.2 per cent of total local effective revenues; local taxes were 37.2 per cent fees and licences 20.1 per cent, other revenues 21.4 per cent; and public services 17.1 per cent. Throughout the years the importance of federal income shares increased, as shown in Figure 18.2. By 1973, federal income shares increased to 11.01 per cent; by 1979 they increased to 25.11 per cent; in 1983 this item corresponded to 67.6 per cent of total municipal revenues; finally in 1986 federal tax shares

Table 18.3 Municipal revenues and expenses
Million pesos, 1978 = 100

	Gross revenues	Taxes	Federal tax share	Public services revenues	Licencing permit revenues	Other	Public debt	Revenue collections non-municipal	Beginning disposable balance	Non-cash expenditures
1970	6 554.18	1 990.71	222.91	916.41	1 074.30	1 142.41	349.85	585.14	266.25	6.19
1971	7 352.94	2 141.18	326.47	947.06	1 191.18	1 461.76	258.82	697.06	282.35	47.06
1972	8 016.81	2 226.89	459.38	1 044.82	1 257.70	1 535.01	246.50	845.94	341.74	58.82
1973	8 920.00	1 987.50	727.50	1 052.50	1 297.50	1 540.00	422.50	1 545.00	297.50	50.00
1974	9 791.92	1 684.85	1 208.08	1 157.58	1 167.68	1 507.07	503.03	2 165.66	387.88	10.10
1975	10 361.40	1 796.49	1 305.26	994.74	1 273.68	1 484.21	357.89	2 710.53	333.33	105.26
1976	11 389.39	1 922.73	1 368.18	1 165.15	1 456.06	1 668.18	542.42	2 772.73	327.27	166.67
1977	11 446.53	1 830.79	1 552.29	1 103.41	1 376.03	1 537.02	383.08	3 273.80	306.70	83.43
1978	12 716.00	1 970.00	1 968.00	1 283.00	1 348.00	1 942.00	656.00	3 160.00	325.00	64.00
1979	15 334.19	2 293.57	2 665.82	1 541.46	1 471.24	2 643.82	664.13	3 472.93	456.85	124.37
1980	18 440.72	2 257.20	4 852.65	2 002.68	1 465.51	2 574.68	442.73	3 917.62	623.58	304.09
1981	21 668.76	2 195.71	6 354.79	1 942.44	1 616.95	3 680.27	663.00	3 967.56	1 024.07	223.97
1982	20 432.48	1 734.85	9 351.78	1 696.64	1 441.37	3 962.12	627.47	958.50	597.83	61.92
1983	19 695.06	1 198.07	12 677.51	1 317.51	1 229.40	2 324.03	566.00	70.16	228.42	83.54
1984	25 895.08	2 751.41	15 312.30	1 298.89	1 469.48	2 391.87	1 097.52	201.46	459.22	912.93
1985	26 462.77	3 208.23	15 105.02	1 492.03	1 390.76	2 991.12	1 189.91	388.07	685.69	11.94
1986	22 741.68	2 600.43	13 514.00	1 471.91	1 224.99	2 167.63	1 204.52	274.40	283.53	0.27

Real growth

1971	12.19	7.56	46.46	3.34	10.88	27.95	-26.02	19.13	6.05	660.00
1972	9.03	4.00	40.71	10.32	5.58	5.01	-4.76	21.36	21.03	25.00
1973	11.27	-10.75	58.36	0.74	3.16	0.32	71.40	82.64	-12.94	-15.00
1974	9.77	-15.23	66.06	9.98	-10.01	-2.14	19.06	40.17	30.38	-79.80
1975	5.82	6.63	8.04	-14.07	9.08	-1.52	-28.85	25.16	-14.06	942.11
1976	9.92	7.03	4.82	17.13	14.32	12.40	51.56	2.29	-1.82	58.33
1977	0.50	-4.78	13.46	-5.30	-5.50	-7.86	-29.38	18.07	-6.29	-49.94
1978	11.09	7.60	26.78	16.28	-2.04	26.35	71.24	-3.48	5.97	-23.29
1979	20.59	16.42	35.46	20.14	9.14	36.14	1.24	9.90	40.57	94.32
1980	20.26	-1.59	82.03	29.92	-0.39	-2.62	-33.34	12.80	36.49	144.51
1981	17.50	-2.72	30.96	-3.01	10.33	42.94	49.75	1.27	64.23	-26.35
1982	-5.71	-20.99	47.16	-12.65	-10.86	7.66	-5.36	-75.64	-41.62	-72.35
1983	-3.61	-30.94	35.57	-22.35	-14.71	-41.34	-9.80	-92.68	-61.79	34.90
1984	31.48	129.65	20.78	-1.41	19.53	2.92	93.91	187.15	101.04	992.84
1985	2.19	16.60	-1.35	14.87	-5.36	25.05	8.42	92.63	49.31	-98.69
1986	-14.06	-18.94	-10.53	-1.35	-11.92	-27.53	1.23	-29.29	-58.65	-97.75

Source: Developed by the author from information in INEGI, *Finanzas Públicas Estatales y Municipales, 1970–1982*, and *1976–1986* (Mexico, 1984 and 1990).

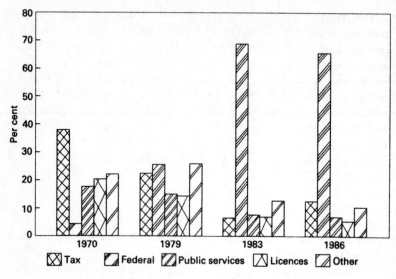

Figure 18.2   Effective municipal spending

increased to 64.42 per cent of total municipal revenues. Thus, local revenues decreased continuously to the point that by 1986 local taxes were 12.40 per cent; public services 7.02 per cent; fees and licences 5.84 per cent; and other revenues 10.83 per cent of total municipal revenues. Moreover, it is worth noting that during 1983 federal income shares correspond to 67.63 per cent of total municipal revenues.

18.3.2   Growth and structure of municipal expenditures

Table 18.4 shows the trends in real terms in municipal expenditures in Mexico for the period under analysis. Public works and development projects showed important increases from 1970–81, except for 1977. Growth was remarkable in some years; particularly in 1981; then growth in public works and development projects increased by 44.6 per cent. After 1982 growth was rather irregular, showing sometimes sharp increases (45.9 per cent in 1984) and decreases (−25.7 per cent in 1986). Administrative expenditures show healthy growth rates from 1970 to 1981 but they became irregular for the 1982–86 period. Moreover, in 1982 administrative expenditure changed by −26.0. Finally, transfers showed irregular growth throughout the entire 1970–86 period.

The structure of municipal expenditures also shows unfavourable patterns of change. Administrative expenditures were the most important item of total municipal expenditures. On the average they amounted to 65.8 per cent for the entire 1970–86 period. Public works and development projects averaged 28.32 per cent of total municipal expenditure for the 1970–86 period. It is worth noting that administrative expenditures were relatively more important from 1970 to 1980 in relation to public services and transfers. From 1981 to 1986 administrative expenditure decreased in relative terms.

One important thing to note is the relationship between federal revenue shares and local administrative expenditure. In real terms, from 1970 to 1981 local administrative expenditure was much higher than federal revenue shares. For instance in 1970 local administrative expenditures amounted to $4170.28 million pesos, while federal revenue shares were $222.9 million pesos. By 1981 local administrative expenditures were $12 330.72 million pesos and revenue shares were $6354.8 million pesos. From 1982 to 1985 this relationship changes. Federal revenue shares exceeded local administrative expenditures ($15 105.2 versus $14 440.23 million pesos, respectively, in 1985). However, in 1986 local expenditures ($13 615.0 million pesos) exceeded again federal revenue shares (£13 514.0). Thus, local administrative expenditures were 'covered' with federal revenue shares and some additional local resources, leaving limited resources for public works and development.

18.3.3 Fiscal balance

Table 18.4 shows the fiscal balance for the Mexican municipalities. Differences between ordinary effective revenues and ordinary effective expenditures (no virtual items included) shows that on the aggregate Mexican municipalities show deficits in 14 years of the 17 years under analysis. Surplus balances were present during 1982–84, but municipalities were unable to maintain them. For this reason, municipalities had to contract debt to finance their expenditures.

Debt was mainly contracted with national development banks, and to a lesser extent with private commercial banks. Development banks channel funds for especial projects from funds obtained from federal sources, international development agencies, and international financial markets.

Table 18.4 Effective municipal spending† (million pesos, 1970–86)

	Current			Real*			Real growth		
	Administrative	Public works and development	Transfers	Administrative	Public works and development	Transfers	Administrative	Public works and development	Transfers
1970	1 347	451	94	4 170	1 396	291			
1971	1 478	514	153	4 347	1 512	450	4.2	8.3	54.6
1972	1 773	601	149	4 966	1 683	417	14.3	11.4	-7.3
1973	2 105	770	225	5 263	1 925	563	6.0	14.4	34.8
1974	2 984	1 090	192	6 028	2 202	388	14.6	14.4	-31.0
1975	3 507	1 492	244	6 153	2 618	428	2.1	18.9	10.4
1976	4 586	1 813	242	6 948	2 747	367	12.9	4.9	-14.3
1977	6 118	2 196	525	7 189	2 580	382	3.5	-6.1	4.2
1978	7 747	2 783	516	7 747	2 783	516	7.8	7.9	35.1
1979	10 777	4 080	1 254	9 118	3 452	1 061	17.7	24.0	105.6
1980	16 123	6 398	1 003	10 799	4 285	672	18.4	24.2	-36.7
1981	23 564	11 844	1 451	12 331	6 198	759	14.2	44.6	13.0
1982	27 710	17 288	2 212	9 127	5 694	729	-26.0	-8.1	-4.0
1983	69 384	36 589	3 591	11 321	5 970	586	24.0	4.8	-19.6
1984	133 550	88 337	8 799	13 199	8 711	868	16.6	45.9	48.1
1985	231 002	139 376	19 404	14 440	8 713	1 213	9.4	0.0	39.8
1986	405 613	192 744	29 831	13 615	6 470	1 001	-5.7	-25.7	-17.5

	Percent			Real*		
	ADM/EMS	PUB SERV/EMS	TRANSF/EMS	Effective revenues	Effective spending	Differences
1970	71.19	23.84	4.97	5 347	5 858	-511
1971	68.9	23.96	7.13	6 068	6 309	-241
1972	70.27	23.82	5.91	6 524	7 067	-543
1973	67.9	24.84	7.26	6 605	7 750	-1145
1974	69.95	25.55	4.5	6 725	8 618	-1893
1975	66.89	28.46	4.65	6 854	9 198	-2344
1976	69.06	27.3	3.64	7 580	10 062	-2482
1977	70.82	25.42	3.76	7 400	10 152	-2752
1978	70.13	25.19	4.67	8 511	11 046	-2535
1979	66.89	25.32	7.78	10 616	13 630	-3014
1980	68.54	27.2	4.26	13 153	15 756	-2603
1981	63.93	32.13	3.94	15 790	19 288	-3498
1982	48.49	30.25	3.87	18 187	15 550	-2637
1983	63.33	33.4	3.28	18 747	17 876	871
1984	57.95	38.24	3.81	23 224	22 777	447
1985	59.269	35.76	4.98	24 187	24 366	-179
1986	64.57	30.68	4.75	20 979	21 086	-107
AVG	65.77	28.32	4.89			
STD	5.74	4.28	1.31			

* 1978 = 100
† EMS = Effective Municipal Spending

Source: Same as table 18.3.

18.4   PROPOSAL FOR MUNICIPAL ANALYSIS AND CONTROL

An analysis of revenues and expenditures reveals the nature and trends of municipal finances in Mexico. A limitation that the preceding analysis makes clear is that municipalities in Mexico have few sources of their own. The federal government gets most revenues, even though they might originate in and be collected by the municipalities. To promote regional development, an alternative that Mexican authorities should consider, is to give local governments more control on their own taxation systems.

Previously, this has been considered non-viable, mainly owing to a lack of adequate training at the local level. Indeed, local accounts show many deficiencies. Indicators about some important local decision processes such as local wealth, investments, liquidity, indebtedness, operating results are either weak or absent.

In this respect, one important step to foster sound municipal financing is to develop an accounting system which allows better control and decision making.[5] Taking these needs into consideration an option for local government accounting can be an adaptation of conventional accounting statements to public financing.[6]

The benefits of this proposal can be seen in Table 18.5. There the coefficients for local investments structure, indebtedness, revenues turnover, and operating results are shown. These coefficients have been derived from 'normalized' financial statements for the Mexican municipalities. Normalized refers to the adaptation of the statistical information published by the municipalities to the conventional balance sheet and income statements used by public and private corporations. Due to the nature of the information, the statements so derived are mainly flow accounts, but cumulative results could lead to stock accounts which, for instance, would allow to identify investments made, as well as to know equity owned by each municipality – something currently totally unknown by municipalities in Mexico.[7]

Analysing the coefficients shown in Table 18.5, it is seen that holdings in cash and banks averaged 6.33 per cent of total municipal investments (assets). This seems a reasonable figure. Moreover, the averages can be used as a benchmark to analyse the performance of individual municipalities.

Similarly 50 per cent of total (average) municipal assets were devoted to public works and development. A figure that remained

Table 18.5 Normalized coefficients, 1970–86

	Structure of investment		Debt		Revenues turnover	Margin	
	A (%)	B (%)	C (%)	D (times)	E (times)	MOO (%)	MNO (%)
1970	10.25	53.75	13.47	11.91	2.06	22.05	24.07
1971	8.71	46.64	7.99	9.09	1.87	28.36	28.11
1972	9.85	48.55	7.11	10.78	1.88	23.84	25.86
1973	7.78	50.33	11.05	8.69	1.73	20.36	30.68
1974	9.19	52.18	11.92	10.06	1.59	10.36	31.72
1975	6.38	50.10	6.85	10.65	1.31	10.24	38.39
1976	6.53	54.79	10.82	11.22	1.51	8.35	32.75
1977	6.08	51.13	7.59	10.32	1.47	2.84	34.37
1978	6.27	53.73	12.66	8.34	1.64	8.98	32.05
1979	6.62	50.04	9.63	9.81	1.54	14.11	34.41
1980	6.76	46.48	4.80	10.91	1.43	17.89	36.14
1981	8.20	49.63	5.31	14.81	1.26	21.91	37.56
1982	4.04	38.46	4.24	28.79	1.23	49.81	50.27
1983	1.87	48.80	4.63	22.99	1.53	39.61	35.21
1984	2.79	52.88	6.66	22.94	1.41	43.17	36.17
1985	4.02	51.12	6.98	21.12	1.42	40.3	36.53
1986	2.32	52.98	9.86	25.15	1.72	35.1	31.76
Avg	6.33	50.09	8.33	14.56	1.56	23.37	33.89
Std	2.51	3.73	2.84	6.53	0.22	13.57	5.64

A = $ + Bank holdings/total assets; B = Public works/total assets; C = Total Liabilities/Total Assets; D = Operating margin/public debt amortization; E = Revenues/total assets; MOO = Operating Margin; MNO = Net margin.

Source: Developed by the author from information in Table 18.3.

fairly constant throughout the 1970–86 period. Important comparisons could be developed for the case of different municipalities.

In relation to debt, the normalized accounts reveal that on the average amortization had a coverage of 14.56 times. This coverage would be lower considering interest payments. No desegregated data was available to develop a times interest earned ratio.

Revenue turnover measures the efficiency, and on the average it was 1.56 times, which appears to be reasonable. Since this ratio stresses investments and does not consider administrative expenses (which makes local finances deficit spending units), further refinements are necessary, for instance, examining further revenues and total expenditures.

Other ratios can be developed by adopting to local finances 'financial statements formats'. However, as pointed out earlier improved and more detailed accounting figures are necessary; otherwise some coefficients would be incomplete and not too useful for decision making. This is the case in the 'margin' ratios shown in Table 18.5

18.5 DECENTRALIZATION OF PUBLIC FINANCES AND MUNICIPAL DEVELOPMENT

Improving the systematization and accounting of local finances sets forth an adequate framework to manage them more efficiently and promote municipal development. It also sets forth the right framework to promote greater decentralization. As shown by the empirical findings, the Mexican economy is characterized by excessive centralism, even though this is a federation. This has been the result of historical conditions and social pacts which, seeking political stability and a democratic development, led the rise of 'presidentialism' and a strong central, paternalistic government. This situation was somewhat compatible with an economy emerging from centuries of traditionalism. However, it is not compatible with an economy that has been finally taking very decisive steps towards its modernization along the lines of the most recent world trends.

Parallel to its economic reforms, which are indeed impressive, Mexico must implement political reforms to strengthen its democracy and federalism. Congruent with liberalization and deregulation schemes, the market at the local levels must be strengthened and federal economic intervention on the states and local governments must be eased. In this respect, the Solidarity Programme established by the federal government is an innovative instrument to respond to local needs with local participation and local matching of funds.[8] The establishment of a new Ministry in charge of social development and environmental protection is also an important step to promote regional development. However, stronger federalism and long-range regional development still need to be consolidated and made consistent with each other. In sum, federal – state – and local relations must be redefined to reflect both the constitution and maturity in economic growth. State and local finances must be strengthened to promote regional and local markets development. Socioeconomic responsibilities must be clearly determined for each level of government so that fair and innovative tax systems can be implemented to support economic growth and stronger trade and investment relations with other nations, particularly with the US and Canada.

Federalism and state and local public finances from Canada and the United States can provide some important lessons to Mexico. The Canadian tax system should be carefully studied, for it is by far the most truly harmonized than those from other federations, including some highly centralized; however, it is not free from problems and errors (Bird, 1985; 1986; Ip, 1991; Ip and Mintz, 1992). Some important lessons that can be applied from the experiences from those nations are:

- Decentralization of education, health, housing, welfare, recreation and local investing and operating needs, which should be supported by local taxation and local public expenditure financing.
- Planned redistribution schemes based on a rigorous identification of state and local wealth differences, indexing state and local output, savings, taxes and other socioeconomic indicators.[9]
- States and municipalities should partially raise their revenues from personal and corporate income taxes. Harmonization schemes with federal tax programmes should be implemented to prevent friction. However, state and local tax rates should be set freely by those levels of government to formulate their own fiscal incentives for investments. Other tax revenues could be derived from sales taxes, real estate and property taxes, personal wealth taxation, royalties on the exploitation of local resources, and various forms of licensing.
- Independent search for debt financing at local and international capital markets. State and municipalities should be able to issue their own debt securities.

These policies should be accompanied with long-range economic development plans. Important aspects that they should include are: (a) Development of transportation and overhead needed to increase trade among national regions and with its neighbouring countries, and other trade partners from other latitudes; (b) Identification of state and municipal comparative advantages to promote investments in products and services that can lead to the establishment of a competitive edge in specific municipalities; and (c) plan and instrument tax changes consistent with laws in their trading partners, for greater linkages with them will create pressures for tax harmonization (Gordon, 1990).

18.6   CONCLUSIONS

The conformation of economic blocs is a response to meet the challenges of increased economic and financial globalization. NAFTA is a step in this direction. It should accrue mutual benefits to Canada, Mexico and the United States. However, this might be limited by existing asymmetries among them. Uneven domestic regional development is a factor that could create bottlenecks in the North American integration processes, hindering particularly Mexico's trade and investment opportunities that could be derived from NAFTA.

The Mexican–US border offers attractive conditions for investments. However, the area has some limitations which could lead to distorted and limited development. To take full advantage of NAFTA trade and investment opportunities, Mexico should promote local development. An important aspect of this strategy should be closer attention to local public finances.

An empirical analysis on the main patterns of change and structure in Mexican municipal finances, shows serious limitations and distortions. Generally, the growth of revenues and expenditures tended to diminish towards 1986. Federal revenue shares became the most important source of local revenues. In relation to expenditures, administrative expenditures take the biggest share of local finances. One problem that can be found in municipal finances is inadequate accounting systems. They need to be improved. Improvement in municipal accounting could also be used to improve control and decision making of local governments. Moreover, improved accounting could be used to develop adaptations of the financial statements model to find out key relationships in municipal financing.

However, the most important step that Mexican authorities should implement to further local economic growth is to strengthen its federalism by decentralizing economic responsibilities and decision making. Particularly, states and local governments should be allowed greater control in taxation and expenditures, applications could be derived from its neighbouring countries, which are also federations. Particularly, close attention should be given to the Canadian case. It can offer Mexico important lessons because its taxation system is well developed and relations between the federation and provinces and local governments are well harmonized. Drawing from the experiences from its Northern neighbours, Mexico should decentralize some activities such as education, health, housing, welfare and recreation. Similarly, state and local governments should be allowed to raise revenues from personal and corporate taxes, sales taxes, real estate and property and wealth taxation, royalties and licences. Tax rates should be set independently by each State or municipal community, but harmonizing their interest with the federation, to be able to promote trade and investments using fiscal policies. States and local communities should also be allowed to issue their own debt securities and issuing them at local and international financial markets. Finally, equalization systems should be developed to promote development of less developed states and communities. All these strategies should be integrated with long-range regional and local development plans. Steady and balanced regional development would allow Mexico to strengthen its real and financial markets to take full advantage of NAFTA and make important contributions of its own and to increased welfare for the North American countries.

Notes

1. It is worth noting that asymmetric socioeconomic conditions have been one the strongest arguments put forth against NAFTA in Mexico. See, for instance the work edited by Benito Rey Romay (1992).
2. Many Canadian analysts have been particularly sensitive to these issues and therefore oppose NAFTA. See Faux and Rothstein (1991), (1991; 1992), and Stanford (1991). Kreklewich and Patroni; Their views are shared by labour unions, environmental oriented groups and analysts from many countries. For a report on along these lines see the work by Kreklewich and Patroni (1992).
3. Some labour groups and economists feel that free trade could favour a relocation of plants from Canada and Mexico to the United States to take

advantage of economies of scale in production and management. Inadequate regional development could further induce these changes (Martin, 1991).

4. *Finanzas Públicas Estatales y Municipales, 1970–1982, and 1976–1986* (Mexico: INEGI, 1984) 1990.

5. Technical notes have been developed by some institutions: Centro de Estudios de Administración Municipal (CEAM) del Instituto Nacional de Administración Pública (INAP); Centro Nacional de Estudios Municipales de la Secretaría de Gobernación; and the Instituto Nacional para el Desarrollo de las Haciendas Municipales (INDETEC). See, for instance, 'Elaboración y Ejercicio del Presupuesto de Egresos', *Guía Técnica No. 4* (Mexico: INAP/CEAM, 1985); 'La Contabilidad y la Cuenta Pública Municipal,' *Guía Técnica No. 5* (Mexico: INAP/CEAM, 1985); and *Guías Técnicas de Gobierno y Administración Municipal* (Mexico, D.F.: CNEM), various issues. However, they have not been applied fully and have not included a full accounting system like the one proposed here.

6. For a full development and presentation of this model see: Alejandra Cabello (1992).

7. Further developments of the model here presented and further empirical studies now in process, will attempt to fill information gaps related to transfer payments and interest payments to make feasible full ratio analysis for Mexican municipalities.

8. Mexico's Solidarity Programme, *Programa Nacional de Solidaridad* (Pronasol) was established by President Salinas, 6 December 1988. Its objectives include improving socioeconomic conditions for peasants, indigenous people, and dwellers from popular complexes and *barrios*; promote a balanced regional development and creating conditions for productive improvements in social welfare; and promoting and strengthening the participation in development projects of local nongovernmental organizations and local authorities. See Consejo Consultivo del Pronasol, 'El Combate a la Pobreza', *El Nacional* 1990.

9. 'Wealth indexes', based on tax revenues are for instance used by the Provincial government of Quebec to assess regional development needs. Similarly, at the federal level, Canada applies a considerable amount of redistribution across provinces which is an equalizing component of the system (Broadway and Flatters, 1989). A related more contemporary issue is that of stabilization policies at the provincial level. For an assessment of provincial–federal coordination for stabilization programmes see the work by Scarth (1991).

REFERENCES

BIRD, R. M. (1985) 'Federal Finance in Comparative Perspective', in T. J. Courchene, D. W. Coklin, and G. C. Cook (eds), *Ottawa and the Distribution of Money and Power*, vol. I (Toronto: Ontario Economic Council).
BIRD, R. M. (1986) *Federal Finance in Comparative Perspective*. (Toronto: Canadian Tax Foundation).

BROADWAY, R. and FLATTERS, F. (1989) 'Federal – Provincial Fiscal Relations Revisited: Some Consequences of Recent Constitutional Policy and Policy Developments', in M. McMillan (ed.) *Provincial Public Finances: Plaudits, Problems and Prospects*, vol. 2 (Toronto: Canadian Tax Foundation).

CABELLO, A. (1992) 'Análisis Financiero Municipal, 1970–1986', mimeo (Centro de Investigacion y Docencia Economicas, Mexico, D. F.).

FAUX, J. and ROTHSTEIN, R. (1991) 'Fast Track, Fast Shuffle. The Economic Consequences of the Administrations's Proposed Trade Agreement with Mexico' (Canadian Centre for Policy Alternatives).

GORDON, R. H. (1991) 'Canada–U.S. Free Trade and Pressures for Tax Harmonization', Working Paper (National Bureau of Economic Research).

GRINSPUN, R. (1991) 'North American Free Trade Area: A Critical Economic Perspective.' (Canadian Centre for Policy Alternatives, Ottawa).

GRINSPUN, R. (1992) 'A Note on Economic Integration and the Transformation of Civil Society', Paper presented at the International Conference on Economic Integration, Migration Policies and Human Rights in North America, Mexico City, 28–29 February 1992.

IP, I. K. (1991) *Big Spenders. A Survey of Provincial Government Finances in Canada* (Toronto: C. D. Howe Institute).

IP, I. K. and MINTZ, J. M. (1992) *Dividing the Spoils. The Federal–Provincial Allocation of Taxing Powers* (Toronto: C. D. Howe Institute).

KREKLEWICH, R. J. and PATRONI, V. (1992) 'Critical Perspectives on North American Integration: A Rapporteur's Report', CERLAC Discussion Papers Series, No. 2 (York University).

MARTIN, F. (1991) 'Measuring the Impact of Free Trade: Local Analysis versus Regional and National Models', *International Regional Sciences Review*, vol. 14. no. 1, pp. 1–14.

REY ROMAY, B. (1992) *La Integration Comercial de Mexico a Estados Unidos y Canada. ¿Alternativa o Destino?* (Mexico, D. F.: Siglo XXI).

SCARTH, W. M. (1991) 'Provincial Stabilization Policy: Coordination Issues', in H. G. Grubel, D. D. Purvis, and W. M. Scarth, *Limits to Government. Controlling Deficits and Debt in Canada* (Toronto: C. D. Howe Institute).

STANFORD, J. (1991) 'Going South. Cheap Labour as an Unfair Subsidy in North American Free Trade' (Canadian Centre for Policy Alternatives).

INSTITUTIONAL REFERENCES

Banamex (1990) 'Ahorro Financiero y Distribucion del Ingreso', *Examen de la Situacion Economica de Mexico*, vol. LXVI, no. 729 (Oct., pp. 484–9).

Banco de Mexico (1992) *Indicadores Economicos*, various issues, 1992.

Banco Nacional de Comercio Exterior (1991) *Comercio Exterior*, vol. 41, no. 7, Mexico, July.

Centro Nacional de Estudios Municipales. *Guias Tecnicas de Gobierno y*

Administracion Municipal (Mexico, D. F.: CNEM) various issues.

Consejo Consultivo del Pronasol (1990) 'El Combate a la Pobreza', *El Nacional*.

Instituto Nacional de Administración Pública (1985) 'Elaboracion y Ejercicio del Presupuesto de Egresos', *Guia Tecnica 4*. Centro de Estudios de Administración Municipal (Mexico, D. F.: INAP).

Instituto Nacional de Administración Pública (1985). 'La Contabilidad y la Cuenta Publica Municipal', *Guia Tecnica 5*. Centro de Estudios de Administracion Municipal (Mexico, D. F.: INAP).

Instituto Nacional de Estadistica, Geografía e Informatica. *Finanzas Publicas Estatales y Municipales*, 1970–1982, and 1976–1986 (Mexico, D. F.: INEGI, 1984, and 1990).

International Monetary Fund. *International Financial Statistics*, Yearbook 1992: and July 1992.

World Bank (1992) *Social Indicators of Development 1991–1992*.

19 Optimum Distortions in Closed and Open Economies: Some Aspects of the Theory of Second Best

Dilip K. Ghosh and Shyamasri Ghosh

19.1 INTRODUCTION

Substantial advance has been made in the exploration of optimum policies in a given economic environment. The Theory of Second Best has been quite a challenging field of research particularly since the publication of the excellent paper by Lipsey and Lancaster (1956), and it has been extended over to the open economies by the powerful pencrafts of Corden (1957), Bhagwati and Ramaswami (1985), Johnson (1965), Ghosh (1979), and many others. In the framework of the closed economies very many crops have been available at intervals. But what have been found so far are various piecemeal researches and findings for the economic society striving for better economic conditions in the imperfect market setting through different possible measures of policy manipulation, and, therefore, what is lacking is a coherent structure of optimum distortions. In this chapter we build the structure of optimum distortions in different postulated set-ups. First, we discuss possible tax structure in closed and open economic frameworks, and then try to ascertain when uniform rather than differentiated and when differentiated rather than uniform tax structure would be optimal for the taxing country. This issue of uniform versus non-uniform tax system has been important in consideration of economic efficiency, equity and administrative simplicity for quite a long time, and, therefore, we would like to look into it in some detail. Here we consider only one factor of production, labour measured in units of man-hour.

19.2   THE CLOSED ECONOMY FRAMEWORK

In this section we take the closed economic framework, a framework where there is no international trade taking place; domestic production rate is the domestic consumption rate. We postulate constant returns to scale in the production technology, and hence output price of each good can be taken as given. Here there are n goods to consider (for consumption as well as for production): $C_1, C_2, \ldots, C_n$. The first good is construed as leisure in our model. The utility function (which is the index of social welfare) is described by

$$U = U(C_1, C_2, \ldots, C_n) \tag{1}$$

where

$$U_i \equiv \partial U/\partial C_i > 0, \ U_{ii} \equiv \partial^2 U/\partial C_1^2 < 0,$$

and

$$U_{ij} \equiv U_{ji}, \ i = 1, 2, n,$$

and

$$\begin{bmatrix} U_{11} & U_{12} & \cdots & U_{1n} \\ U_{21} & U_{22} & \cdots & U_{2n} \\ U_{n1} & U_{n2} & \cdots & U_{nn} \end{bmatrix}$$

is negative definite matrix, i.e., the minors of this Hessian utility matrix alternate in sign, starting from negative. The production transformation locus in this model would be a hyperplane since there is one factor of production and $n(> 1)$ commodities. This transformation locus would be

$$X_0 = \sum_{i=1}^{n} A_i C_i \tag{2}$$

where X_0 is the total man-hour available in a given static state of the economy (and, therefore $X_0 - A_1 C_1 \equiv$ labour supply where $A_1 \equiv 1$). In such a theoretical paradigm we know that the social optimum will obtain when the production transformation hyperplane becomes the supporting plane for the utility surface.[1] The dual to (2) would be

$$P_i^* = A_i w \qquad \text{for all } i \tag{3}$$

where $w \equiv$ wage rate and P_i^* is the producer price of the ith good.

In situations characterized by no kind of distortion the maximization of (1) subject to (2) defines the optimum C_i's. But suppose now that the scope for the imposition of taxation for each good of consumption exists. That is, the wedge between the producer and the consumer prices may be made as follows:

$$P_i = P_i^*(1 + t_i) \tag{4}$$

where P_i is the consumer price of the ith good and t_i is the *ad valorem* tax or subsidy rate on the consumer. If $t_i > 0$, it is the tax on the ith good and if $t_i < 0$, it is the subsidy on the ith good. Equation (3) can now obviously be rewritten in the following form:[2]

$$P_i = A_i w(1 + t_i).$$

Now the problem the consumer faces is as follows:[3]

Max $U = U(C_1, C_2, \ldots, C_n)$

sub to $X_0 = (1/(1 + t_i)) \sum_{i=1}^{n} A_i(1 + t_i) C_i.$

This maximization operation will yield the following solution:

$$C_i = C_i(t_1, t_2, \ldots, t_n) \qquad i = 1, 2, \ldots, n.$$

So, we would find that the utility function can be expressed as the function of the tax rates, $(t_1, t_2, \ldots, t_n)$, and hence we can immediately recognize that these tax rates could be effectively used in such a framework as the control variables in the optimization of the welfare function. The t_i's which would maximize U would render

$$\partial U/\partial t_i = 0,$$

and hence correspondingly the compensatory income change would be necessitated if the original utility level is to be maintained. We know from the basic theory of consumer's behaviour that

$$\sum_{j=1}^{n} P_j \cdot \partial C_j/\partial P_i \,\big|_{dU=0} = 0 \tag{5}$$

and hence we have the following:

$$w \sum_{j=1}^{n} A_j (1 + t_j) \frac{\partial C_j}{\partial P_i} \bigg|_{dU=0} = 0 \tag{5'}$$

From relation (2) we obtain:

$$\sum_{j=1}^{n} A_j \frac{\partial C_j}{\partial P_i} \bigg|_{dU=0} = 0 \tag{2'}$$

and, therefore, the substitution of (2') into (5') yields:

$$\sum_{j=1}^{n} A_j A_j \frac{\partial C_j}{\partial P_i} \bigg|_{dU=0} = 0 \tag{6}$$

Therefore, the expansion of equation (6) for all i would give us the following:

$$\begin{bmatrix} \dfrac{\partial C_1}{\partial P_1}\bigg|_{dU=0} & \dfrac{\partial C_2}{\partial P_1}\bigg|_{dU=0} & \dfrac{\partial C_n}{\partial P_1}\bigg|_{dU=0} \\[2em] \dfrac{\partial C_1}{\partial P_2}\bigg|_{dU=0} & \dfrac{\partial C_2}{\partial P_2}\bigg|_{dU=0} & \dfrac{\partial C_n}{\partial P_2}\bigg|_{dU=0} \\[2em] \dfrac{\partial C_1}{\partial P_n}\bigg|_{dU=0} & \dfrac{\partial C_2}{\partial P_n}\bigg|_{dU=0} & \dfrac{\partial C_n}{\partial P_n}\bigg|_{dU=0} \end{bmatrix} \begin{bmatrix} A_1 t_1 \\[2em] A_2 t_2 \\ \vdots \\ A_n t_n \end{bmatrix} = \begin{bmatrix} 0 \\[2em] 0 \\ \vdots \\ 0 \end{bmatrix} \tag{6'}$$

It is now the standard exercise to show that the assumption of negative definiteness on the $[U_{ij}]$ matrix gives us that

$$\begin{bmatrix} \dfrac{\partial C_1}{\partial P_1}\bigg|_{dU=0} & \dfrac{\partial C_2}{\partial P_1}\bigg|_{dU=0} & \dfrac{\partial C_n}{\partial P_1}\bigg|_{dU=0} \\[2em] \dfrac{\partial C_1}{\partial P_2}\bigg|_{dU=0} & \dfrac{\partial C_2}{\partial P_2}\bigg|_{dU=0} & \dfrac{\partial C_n}{\partial P_2}\bigg|_{dU=0} \\[1em] \vdots \\[1em] \dfrac{\partial C_1}{\partial P_n}\bigg|_{dU=0} & \dfrac{\partial C_2}{\partial P_n}\bigg|_{dU=0} & \dfrac{\partial C_n}{\partial P_n}\bigg|_{dU=0} \end{bmatrix}$$

is also a negative definite matrix. Hence it appears that the system of equations given through (6′) yields the trivial solution that all t_i's are zero.[4] But a more close inspection would suggest that non-trivial solution for t_i's exists. If we carefully look at relation (2′) and plug it in (6) we get quite easily the following structure:

$$
\begin{bmatrix}
\dfrac{\partial C_2}{\partial P_1}\Big|_{dU=0} & \dfrac{\partial C_3}{\partial P_1}\Big|_{dU=0} & \dfrac{\partial C_n}{\partial P_1}\Big|_{dU=0} \\[2ex]
\dfrac{\partial C_2}{\partial P_2}\Big|_{dU=0} & \dfrac{\partial C_3}{\partial P_2}\Big|_{dU=0} & \dfrac{\partial C_n}{\partial P_2}\Big|_{dU=0} \\[2ex]
\vdots & & \\[1ex]
\dfrac{\partial C_2}{\partial P_n}\Big|_{dU=0} & \dfrac{\partial C_3}{\partial P_n}\Big|_{dU=0} & \dfrac{\partial C_n}{\partial P_n}\Big|_{dU=0}
\end{bmatrix}
\begin{bmatrix}
A_2(t_2 - t_1) \\[2ex]
A_2(t_3 - t_1) \\[2ex]
\vdots \\[1ex]
A_n(t_n - t_n)
\end{bmatrix}
=
\begin{bmatrix}
0 \\[2ex]
0 \\[2ex]
\\[1ex]
0
\end{bmatrix}
$$

This $(\partial C_j/\partial P_j\,|_{dU=0}$ matrix is $n \times (n-1)$ ordered. We can neglect the first row of this above matrix and consequently our system reduces to:

$$
\begin{bmatrix}
\dfrac{\partial C_2}{\partial P_2}\Big|_{dU=0} & \dfrac{\partial C_3}{\partial P_2}\Big|_{dU=0} & \dfrac{\partial C_n}{\partial P_2}\Big|_{dU=0} \\[2ex]
\dfrac{\partial C_2}{\partial P_3}\Big|_{dU=0} & \dfrac{\partial C_3}{\partial P_3}\Big|_{dU=0} & \dfrac{\partial C_n}{\partial P_3}\Big|_{dU=0} \\[2ex]
\vdots & & \\[1ex]
\dfrac{\partial C_2}{\partial P_n}\Big|_{dU=0} & \dfrac{\partial C_3}{\partial P_n}\Big|_{dU=0} & \dfrac{\partial C_n}{\partial P_n}\Big|_{dU=0}
\end{bmatrix}
\begin{bmatrix}
A_2(t_2 - t_1) \\[2ex]
A_2(t_3 - t_1) \\[2ex]
\vdots \\[1ex]
A_n(t_n - t_n)
\end{bmatrix}
=
\begin{bmatrix}
0 \\[2ex]
0 \\[2ex]
\\[1ex]
0
\end{bmatrix}
\quad (6'')
$$

This $(\partial C_r/\partial P_s\,|_{dU=0})$ matrix (where $s, r, = 2, 3, \ldots, n$) is not null and hence we must have:

$$t_2 = t_3 = \cdots = t_n = t_1$$

(since the labour coefficients A_i's would be non-zero). Therefore, we obtain the following proposition:

> if labour is taxed at a certain percentage, the consumption of all other commodities should be subsidized at the same percentage (and vice versa).

Let us visualize this fact with the aid of the following diagram (Figure 19.1)

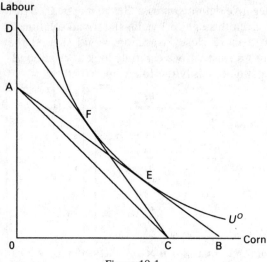

Figure 19.1

Suppose U^o was the original utility level attained with the transformation surface (in this two-dimensional space) at point E. The horizontal axis measures corn and the vertical axis measures labour. If labour is taxed at the rate CB/OB, then the transformation locus shrinks down to AC which will reduce the welfare level definitely, and to maintain the utility at its original level we need the AC line to blow up like CD to be tangential with U^o at F. In this diagram, what we see very easily is the fact that the maintenance of the constant utility level after the imposition of taxation on labour requires the imposition of subsidy on corn price. One does not need diagrammatics or mathematics for this result; one's immediate common sense is good enough to arrive at that fact. But what we can see through mathematics is the fact that the rate of subsidy has to be the same for all goods, which fact perhaps we do not see immediately through our common-sense logic.[5] But whatever way one may like to justify the algebraic operations as above, we can say that we have arrived at no startling or surprising result at all. So, let us step forward.

Next, let us suppose that because of certain political or administrative reasons or otherwise, some subset of commodities cannot be subjected to any kind of distortion. Suppose $t_1, t_2, \ldots, t_m$ rates of taxes are already imposed on the subscripted commodities respectively, and those taxes cannot be further manipulated. So, the only instruments available would be $t_{m+1}, t_{m+2}, \ldots, t_n$. When the situation is as such, the equation set-up given by (6′) reduces to the following:

$$
\begin{bmatrix}
\left.\dfrac{\partial C_{m+1}}{\partial P_{m+1}}\right|_{dU=0} & \left.\dfrac{\partial C_{m+2}}{\partial P_{m+1}}\right|_{dU=0} & \left.\dfrac{\partial C_n}{\partial P_{m+1}}\right|_{dU=0} \\[2ex]
\left.\dfrac{\partial C_{m+1}}{\partial P_{m+2}}\right|_{dU=0} & \left.\dfrac{\partial C_{m+2}}{\partial P_{m+2}}\right|_{dU=0} & \left.\dfrac{\partial C_n}{\partial P_{m+2}}\right|_{dU=0} \\[2ex]
\vdots & & \\[1ex]
\left.\dfrac{\partial C_{m+1}}{\partial P_n}\right|_{dU=0} & \left.\dfrac{\partial C_{m+2}}{\partial P_n}\right|_{dU=0} & \left.\dfrac{\partial C_n}{\partial P_n}\right|_{dU=0}
\end{bmatrix}
\begin{bmatrix}
A_{m+1}t_{m+1} \\[2ex]
A_{m+2}t_{m+2} \\[1ex]
\vdots \\[1ex]
A_{n}t_{n}
\end{bmatrix}
=
\begin{bmatrix}
-\sum\limits_{j=1}^{m} A_j t_j \left.\dfrac{\partial C_j}{\partial P_{m+1}}\right|_{dU=0} \\[2ex]
-\sum\limits_{j=1}^{m} A_j t_j \left.\dfrac{\partial C_j}{\partial P_{m+2}}\right|_{dU=0} \\[1ex]
\vdots \\[1ex]
-\sum A_j t_j \left.\dfrac{\partial C_j}{\partial P_n}\right|_{dU=0}
\end{bmatrix}
$$

$$(6''')$$

From $(6''')$ we then get the following solution:

$$
t_h = -\frac{1}{A_h} \cdot \frac{\displaystyle\sum_{i=m+1}^{n} \sum_{j=1}^{m} B_{ih} A_j t_j \left.\dfrac{\partial C_j}{\partial P_i}\right|_{dU=0}}{|B|}
\tag{7}
$$

where

$$
|B| \equiv \det \left(\left.\frac{\partial C_j}{\partial P_i}\right|_{dU=0} \right)_{i,\, j = m+1,\,\ldots,\, n}
$$

and B_{ih} is the cofactor of $(i-j)$ element of (B) matrix.
We have already known that

$$
\sum_{j=1}^{n} A_j \frac{\partial C_j}{\partial P_i}\bigg|_{dU=0} = 0
$$

and hence

$$
\sum_{j=1}^{m} A_j \frac{\partial C_j}{\partial P_i}\bigg|_{dU=0} = -\sum_{s=m+1}^{n} A_s \frac{\partial C_s}{\partial P_i}\bigg|_{dU=0}
$$

Therefore, plugging it in (7) we obtain:

$$
t_h = \frac{1}{A_h} \frac{\displaystyle\sum_{i=m+1}^{n} \sum_{s=m+1}^{n} B_{ih} \frac{\partial C_s}{\partial P_i}\bigg|_{dU=0} \cdot A_j t_j}{|B|} \cdot
$$

It comes out then that for $h = s$ the sum total of the coefficients of $A_j t_j$ would be equal to $A_j t_j$ would be equal to $1/A_h$ since

$$\sum_{i=m+1}^{n} \sum_{s=m+1}^{n} B_{is} \frac{\partial X_s}{\partial P_i}\bigg|_{dU=0} = |B|.$$

So, we can rewrite (7) as follows:

$$t_h = \frac{1}{A_h} \sum_{j=1}^{m} \alpha_j A_j t_j \qquad \text{where } \sum_{j=1}^{m} \alpha_j = 1.$$

Let us at this point postulate that $\partial C_j / \partial P_i\big|_{dU=0}$ for all i and j, i.e., all goods are substitutes in Slutsky sense. With this assumption in hand, we see that t_h is a linear combination of the given tax rates, and $t_h > 0$. The complementarity between goods may make $t_h < 0$. If we want to normalize further that all A_i's are equal to unity we see that $t_h(h = m + 1, \ldots, n)$ is the convex combination of the given t_j's. That is,[6]

$$t_h \, \varepsilon \, (\underline{t}, \, \bar{t})$$

where $\underline{t} \equiv \min (t_2, t_2, \ldots, t_m)$ and $\bar{t} \equiv \max (t_2, t_2, \ldots, t_m)$.

Next, let us pose the problem in a little different way.[7] Here we have a target of tax revenue[8]

$$T = \sum_{j=1}^{n} t_j C_j,$$

as the additional constraint in our maximization. So, the problem before us is to

$$\max U = U(C_1, C_2, \ldots, C_n)$$

$$\text{sub to } \sum_{i=1}^{n} P_i C_i = X_o$$

$$\text{and } X_o - \sum P^*_i C_i - T = 0.$$

Then, the Lagrangean to be maximized is given by the following:

$$L = U(C_1, C_2, \ldots, C_n) + \lambda \sum_{i=1}^{n} (P_i C_i - X_o) + \mu(X_o - \sum_{i=1}^{n} P^*_i C_i - T)$$

which can be rewritten as follows:

$$L = U(C_1, C_2, \ldots, C_n) + \frac{\lambda}{\gamma}\Sigma(U_iC_i - X_o)$$
$$+ \mu(X_o - \Sigma P_i^*C_i - T). \tag{8}$$

The maximization of this Lagrangean with respect to C_j's give the following:

$$\frac{\partial L}{\partial C_j} = U_j + \frac{\lambda}{\gamma}\Sigma(U_{ij}C_i + U_j) - \mu P_j^* = 0$$

$$\therefore U_j\left(1 + \frac{\lambda}{\gamma}\right) + \frac{\lambda}{\gamma}\Sigma U_{ij}C_i = \mu P_j^*$$

$$\therefore \gamma P_j\left(1 + \frac{\lambda}{\gamma} + \lambda P_j \Sigma \frac{U_{ij}}{U_j} C_i = \mu P_j^*\right.$$

or

$$P_j\left[\gamma + \lambda - \lambda\Sigma\left(-\frac{U_{ij}}{U_j} C_i\right)\right] = \mu P_j^*.$$

Let us define $\Sigma(-(U_{ij}/U_j)C_i) \equiv U^j$, which is the marginal utility of C_i good.

We have now

$$P_j[\gamma + \lambda(1 - U^j)] = \mu P_j^*$$

or,

$$t_j = P_j^*\left(\frac{\mu U^j - \gamma}{\gamma + \mu(1 - U^j)}\right) = \frac{\mu U^j - \gamma}{\gamma + \mu(1 - U^j)} \qquad \text{therefore } P_j^* = 1.$$

The optimal t_j's are thus determined, and we find that the optimum structure of taxation will be uniform if $\Sigma_{i=1}^n U_{ij}C_i = 0$, i.e., if the utility surface is homogeneous of the first degree. So, homotheticity on the utility space is a sufficient but not a necessary condition to ensure optimal tax structure in the framework we have used in our model.

So far we have discussed essentially in terms of a closed economic framework, and, therefore, let us now look at the open economy model.

19.3   THE OPEN ECONOMY FRAMEWORK

In this model we assume that the foreign terms of trade $(\beta_1, \beta_2, \ldots, \beta_n)$ are given, and the taxing country (let us call it the home country) is incapable of changing the international terms of trade. That is, we take the usual 'small country' assumption to frame our model. Without any loss of generality, we can assume here $\beta_1 = \beta_2 = \ldots = \beta_n = 1$. The home country is postulated to put up the following wedge on the ith good.

$$P_i = \beta_i (1 + \tau_i)$$

or

$$P_i - \beta_i = \tau_i.$$

The domestic consumer and the producer prices are assumed identical (but not unity, as was assumed in the previous section). Since we are now discussing the open economy our consumption level is different from the domestic production level for the ith good. We use $(C_1, C_2, \ldots, C_n)$ to describe the consumption level of the subscripted good, and $(X_1, X_2, \ldots, X_n)$ stand for the respective domestic production levels. That is,

$$C_i - X_i = E_i \qquad i = 1, 2, \ldots, n$$

where E_i stands for the import volume (if $E_i > 0$) or export volume (if $E_i < 0$). In this framework the consumer will try to maximize the given utility function

$$U = U(C_1, C_2, \ldots, C_n) \tag{9}$$

subject to

$$\sum_{i=1}^{n} \beta_i C_i = \sum_{i=1}^{n} \beta_i X_i. \tag{10}$$

The change in utility level can be computed as follows:

$$dU = \sum_{i=1}^{n} U_i \, dC_i. \tag{11}$$

But

$$U_i = \gamma P_i. \tag{12}$$

Now, plugging in $U_i = \gamma P_i$ in (11) would yield:

$$\frac{dU}{\gamma} = \sum_{i=1}^{n} P_i \, dC_i. \tag{13}$$

Total differential of (10) gives the following:

$$\sum_{i=1}^{n} \beta_i \, dC_i = \sum_{i=1}^{n} \beta_i \, dX_i. \tag{14}$$

Adding and subtracting both $\sum_{i=1}^{n} P_i \, dC_i$ and $\sum_{i=1}^{n} P_i \, dX_i$ on both the sides of (14) we obtain:

$$\sum_{i=1}^{n} (\beta_i - P_i) \, dC_i + \sum_{i=1}^{n} P_i \, dC_i = \sum_{i=1}^{n} (\beta_i - P_i) \, dX_i + \sum_{i=1}^{n} P_i \, dX_i. \tag{15}$$

Therefore, in view of (13), we can write (15) as follows:[9]

$$\frac{dU}{\gamma} = \sum_{i=1}^{n} (\beta_i - P_i) \, dX_i - \sum_{i=1}^{n} (\beta_i - P_i) \, dC_i$$

or

$$\frac{dU}{\gamma} = \sum_{i=1}^{n} \tau_i \, (dC_i - dX_i) \tag{16}$$

therefore

$$\frac{1}{\gamma} \frac{dU}{d\tau_j} = \sum_{i=1}^{n} \tau_i \left[\frac{dC_i}{d\tau_j} - \frac{dX_i}{d\tau_j} \right] = \sum_{i=1}^{n} \tau_i \left[\frac{dC_i}{dP_j} - \frac{dX_i}{dP_j} \right]. \tag{16'}$$

The maximality of U requires the left-hand side of (16') to be zero, and hence we obtain:

$$\sum_{i=1}^{n} \tau_i \left[\frac{dC_i}{dP_j} - \frac{dX_i}{dP_j} \right] = 0$$

and from this we get:

$$\tau_j^{\text{optimal}} = \frac{-\sum_{i \neq j}^{n} \tau_i \left[\dfrac{dC_i}{dP_j} - \dfrac{dX_i}{dP_j}\right]}{\left[\dfrac{dC_j}{dP_j} - \dfrac{dX_j}{dP_j}\right]} = \frac{\sum_{i \neq j}^{n} \tau_i \left[\dfrac{dC_i}{dP_j} - \dfrac{dX_i}{dP_j}\right]}{\sum_{i \neq j}^{n} \left[\dfrac{dC_i}{dP_j} - \dfrac{dX_i}{dP_j}\right]}.$$

Hence if $dC_i/dP_j > 0$ and $dX_i/dP_j \leq 0$ for $i \neq j$ – that is, if the ith good and jth good are substitutes in the consumption side and substitutes or independent in the production side, then we have here, through these derivations, that optimal τ_j lies between the lowest and highest values of the given τ_i's. The demand and the technology characteristics determine the optimal value and characterization of the optimum τ_j's, given other predetermined τ_i's. If some τ_i's are positive and other τ_i's negative, we might have some sector completely tariff-free. If we assume that $(\partial C_i/\partial P_j)$ matrix is negative definite and $(\partial X_i/\partial P_j)$ matrix is positive definite, then it turns out quite easily in the same way (as we have shown earlier) that

$$\tau_i = \tau^* \qquad \text{for all } i$$

if we can use all τ_i's to optimize the welfare index. So, we find that optimal tariff structure is necessarily uniform in such a derivative system.[10] A careful reflection would prompt one quite immediately that the existence of the non-traded goods in this model would not affect the structural aspects of optimum tariff rates, although it would obviously affect the magnitudes thereof.[11]

Now, we shall take a more close look at relation (16). Before that let us look at the equation (14):

$$\sum_{i=1}^{n} (dC_i - dX_i) = 0 \qquad \text{therefore } \beta_i = 1$$

or

$$\sum_{i=1}^{n} \left(\frac{dC_i}{d\tau_n} - \frac{dX_i}{d\tau_n}\right) = 0 \qquad (14')$$

therefore

$$\left(\frac{dC_n}{d\tau_n} - \frac{dX_n}{d\tau_n}\right) = -\sum_{j=1}^{n-1}\left(\frac{dC_j}{d\tau_n} - \frac{dX_j}{d\tau_n}\right). \tag{14''}$$

From (16′) we have:

$$\frac{1}{\gamma}\frac{dU}{d\tau_n} = \tau_n\left(\frac{dC_n}{d\tau_n} - \frac{dX_n}{d\tau_n}\right) + \sum_{j=1}^{n-1}\tau_j\left(\frac{dC_j}{d\tau_n} - \frac{dX_j}{d\tau_n}\right). \tag{16''}$$

Now, from the substitution of (14″) in (16″) we obtain:

$$\frac{1}{\gamma}\frac{dU}{d\tau_n} = \sum_{j=1}^{n-1}(\tau_j - \tau_n)\left[\frac{dC_j}{d\tau_n} - \frac{dX_j}{d\tau_n}\right]. \tag{16'''}$$

Here also we find that when $dC_j/d\tau_n > 0$ and $dX_j/d\tau_n \leq 0$, the welfare level increases with the decrease in τ_n if $\tau_j < \tau_n$. Therefore, what we obtain is a very clear proposition that reduction of the extreme tariff rate is welfare-augmenting (when the goods are, of course, gross substitutes). This result has its immediate suggestion for trade liberalization, and has the definite policy relevance in the case of custom union. Vanek (1964) has suggested the same policy prescription, though Meade (1955) and Ozga (1955) obtained somewhat the opposite policy recommendation. This seemingly contradictory Meade–Ozga result is easily resolved if one notes that in the Meade–Ozga analyses $(dC_j/d\tau_n - dX_j/d\tau_n) < 0$ (i.e., the goods are complementary in both the consumption and the production or complementarity dominates on the overall measure). However, it should be noted that this complementarity destroys the stability of the structure, and in that case comparative static exercises of any kind breaks down. Hence, as it transpires, the extreme distortions should be reduced until these are within the open or closed set of the given unalterable tariff rates – a result we have obtained earlier. Given the fact that the existing unalterable tariff rates given through the national pressure group or the international agreement or something like that are uniform it then comes out as a natural corollary to our previous proposition that all tariff rates should be uniform in the optimum situation.

A few more observations are in order now also. If τ_n is not an extreme rate, but lies in between other tariff rates then it is possible that manipulation of τ_n is of no consequence in so far as the welfare change is concerned as $\Sigma(\tau_j - \tau_n)\,\partial C_j/\partial\tau_n - \partial X_j/\partial\tau_n$ may be equal to zero.[12] But, if in balance $\Sigma(\tau_j - \tau_n) > 0$ (or < 0), then increase (or decrease) in τ_n has the effect of increasing welfare.

This result is quite consistent with the result established by Foster and Sonnenschein (1970), and Bhagwati (1971), and like Lloyd (1974) we can smack of (through this result) the conclusion reached by Bhagwati (1968) and Kemp (1968) that the restricted trade is better than no trade, if, of course, non-inferiority in consumption of all goods exists, and other distortions due to consumption or production taxes remain. The result has its further appeal in the context of the formation of customs union, since we can check if the creation of the customs union is a step toward ensuring higher welfare level or not.

For that purpose let us suppose that all goods are gross substitutes in our sense (i.e., $dC_j/dP_i - dX_j/dP_i > 0$) and $\tau_n > \tau_i$ for all $i \neq n$. If now because of the formation of customs union the tariff rates (τ_1, $\tau_2, \ldots, \tau_k$) all reduce to zero, what would be the effect of variation in the extreme tariff rate? The answer is same as before; the reduction of the extreme tariff rate for the non-member of the customs union would be welfare increasing. But if $\tau_n < \tau_i$ for all $i \neq n$ τ_1, $\tau_2, \ldots, \tau_k$ are all set to zero (because of customs union agreement), the manipulation of τ_n may be of any effect – welfare-increasing, not affecting welfare at all, or welfare-reducing. The case where increase in the extreme tariff rate would be welfare-augmenting is the one where the customs union goods (good 1 through good k) are complementary, the non-customs union goods (good $k + 1$ through good n) are substitutes and $\tau_n > \tau_i$ for all $i \neq n$.

Many more specific cases can be handled and different queries may be answered. We have only looked at the problem of tariff manipulations, and hence a more general approach to consider all types of distortion – consumption tax (subsidy), production tax (subsidy), and the tariff (subsidy) rates – would be another framework for theoretical analysis. We have looked more closely at the issue like trade liberalization in terms of the reduction of extreme tariff rate. But the issue of trade liberalization goes far beyond, and hence one may discuss more in terms of tariff changes and world welfare. Baldwin (1973), Kenen (1974) have made some limited progress in the exploration of the issues raised, but a more general treatment is lacking still in the literature.

Notes

We are indebted to Professor Winston Chang and Kazuo Saso who have been extremely helpful in clarifying some of the points.

1. We assume that the interior solution exists.
2. If we normalize by assuming $A_i = 1$ all i and $w = 1$, then t_i can be conceived as the unit tax also.
3. $t_1 < 0$ implies tax rate and $t_1 > 0$ implies subsidy.
4. This solution is really the first-best solution – the solution that would retain if the economy remains free of any pre-existing distortion.
5. The result is rather strikingly different from the result of Corden (1957), Corlett and Hague (1953–4) and Kenen (1974). The intuitive logic perhaps in this case suggest that the tax rate on labour should be compensated by the weighted average rate of subsidy on other commodities. The result derived is a special case of the intuitive derivation.
6. This is the result derived by Foster and Sonnenschein (1970), Komiya (1967) and Little (1950).
7. This is the way the problem has been treated in Komiya (1967).
8. If we consider the *ad valorem* tax rates, then the constraints of tax revenue would look like $T = \Sigma_{j=1} P_j^* t_j X_j$. Here, without loss of generality, we assume all $P_j^* = 1$, w as unity, and hence $T = \Sigma t_j X_j$.
9. Along the transformation surface, $\Sigma P_i dX_i = 0$, and hence we obtain equation (16).
10. If the pre-existing tariff rates are uniform, then the whole tariff structure is uniform in the optimal welfare situation. The setting of the tariff rate at the hand of the policy maker different from the uniform pre-existing tariff rates would define suboptimality.
11. The magnitudes of the tariff rates would depend upon the consumption, production elasticity and the marginal propensity to consume each good. Komiya (1967) has shown how the existence of the non-traded goods affect the import elasticity.
12. A similar situation will be obtained if one subset of the commodities are substitutes and the other subset complementary. Then the reduction of extreme distortion may not be of any help in changing (raising) the welfare level.

REFERENCES

ATKINSON, A. B. and STIGLITZ, J. E. (1972) 'The Structure of Indirect Taxation and Economic Efficiency', *Journal of Public Economies*, 1.
BALDWIN, R. E. (1973) 'Customs Unions, Preferential Systems and World Welfare', in M. Connally and A. Swoboda (eds), *International Trade and Money* (London: George Allen & Unwin).
BHAGWATI, J. N. (1971) 'The Generalized Theory of Distortions and

Welfare', in J. Bhagwati *et al.* (eds), *Trade, Balance of Payments, and Growth: Papers in International Economics in Honor of Charles P. Kindleberger* (Amsterdam: North-Holland).

BHAGWATI, J. D. (1968) 'Gains From Trade Once Again', *Oxford Economic Papers*, 20 (July).

BHAGWATI, J. D. and RAMASWAMI, V. K. (1985) 'Domestic Distortions, Tariffs and the Theory of Optimum Subsidy', *Journal of Political Economy*, 71 (Feb.).

BOND, E. W. (1990) 'The Optimal Tariff Structure in Higher Dimensions', *International Economic Review*, vol. 31, no. 1, (Feb.).

CORDEN, W. M. (1957) 'Tariffs, Subsidies and the Terms of Trade', *Economica*, 24 (Aug.).

CORLETT, W. J. and HAGUE, D. C. (1953–4) 'Complementarity and the Excess Burden of Taxation', *Review of Economic Studies*, vol. XXI, no. 54.

DAVIS, O. and WHINSTON, A. (1965) 'Welfare Economics and the Theory of Second Best', *Review of Economic Studies*, 32.

ELDOR, R. and LEVIN, D. (1990) 'Trade Liberalization and Domestic Monopoly: A Welfare Analysis', *International Economic Review*, vol. 31, no. 4, (Nov.) pp. 773–82.

FOSTER, E. and SONNENSCHEIN, H. (1970) 'Price Distortion and Economic Welfare', *Econometrica*, 38.

GHOSH, D. K. (1979) 'Optimum Tariffs in a Multi-Commodity World', *Southern Economic Journal* (Oct.).

GHOSH, D. K. (1984) *Trade, Distortions and Growth* (New Delhi: Concept Press).

GHOSH, D. K. (1993) 'NAFTA in a Bloc of Non-Unified Exchange Rates: An Examination', presented at the International Symposium, 'Beyond NAFTA: Financial Integration and Development', Mexico City, Mexico, January 1993.

GREEN, H. A. J. (1961) 'The Social Optimum in the Presence of Monopoly and Taxation', *Review of Economic Studies*, 29.

HATTA, T. (1986) 'Tax Reform and Strong Subsidies', *International Economic Review*, vol. 27 (June) pp. 303–15.

JOHNSON, H. G. (1965) 'Optimal Trade Intervention in the Presence of Domestic Distortions', in R. E. Caves, H. G. Johnson and P. B. Kenen (eds), *Trade, Growth and Balance of Payments*, (North-Holland: Amsterdam).

KEMP, M. C. (1968) 'Some Issues in the Analysis of Trade Gains', *Oxford Economic Papers*, 20 (July).

KENEN, P. B. (1974) 'A Note on Tariff Changes and World Welfare', *The Quarterly Journal of Economics*.

KOMIYA R. (1967) 'Non-Traded Goods and the Pure Theory of International Trade', *International Economic Review*, 8 (June).

KRISHNA, K. (1989) 'Trade Restrictions as Facilitating Practices', *Journal of International Economics*, vol. 26 (May) pp. 251–70.

LIPSEY, R. G. and LANCASTER, K. (1956) 'The General Theory of Second Best', *The Review of Economic Studies*, 24.

LITTLE, I. M. D. (1950) 'Direct Versus Indirect Taxes', *The Economic*

Journal, 1951, and also his *A Critique of Welfare Economics* (Oxford: The Clarendon Press).

LLOYD, P. J. (1974) 'A More General Theory of Price Distortions in Open Economies', *Journal of International Economies*, 4.

MEADE, J. E. (1955) *Trade and Welfare* (London: Oxford University Press).

OZGA, S. A. (1955) 'An Essay in the Theory of Tariffs', *Journal of Political Economy* (Dec.).

VANEK, J. (1964) 'Unilateral Trade Liberalization and Global Welfare', *Quarterly Journal of Economics*, Feb.

20 Socio-History of French Banks and Banking: Role Model for Global Banking

Irene Finel-Honigman

20.1 INTRODUCTION

'It is part of the folklore here that land and catholicism have left the French unfit for capitalism.'[1]

The French attitude toward the banking profession has oscillated between catholic condemnation and pragmatic necessity, between Rousseau's morally and economically self-enclosed nation state and Voltaire's quest for economic liberalism and ideological tolerance.

From the time Philippe the Fair resolved his conflict with his bankers the Knights of Malta, by outlawing the order and beheading the Grand Master for sorcery in 1314, the relationship between government and banking has remained fraught with tension and ambivalence. Although banking as an institution has been deemed a necessary evil, and after 1848 respected as a symbol of the State, bankers were branded as little better than usurers and money dealers. At worst accused of being part of an international conspiracy, at best praised for their skills in global expansion and foreign markets, French bankers respect for the French heritage and identity, *patrimoine* has been viewed with suspicion.

At the start of the Renaissance, France benefited from a centralized monarchy and a modern geopolitical identity, yet it remained a backwater for economic, commercial and financial regulatory activity. Ideally situated to become a key financial market, French merchants tended to distrust divesting themselves of tangible property (land and gold) and conservatively saved rather than invested their assets.

It was only in the 1570s, that France despite the wars of Religion, underwent an economic modernization by increasing exports in goods and labour, suppressing baronial mints and consolidating circulation of monies and minting privileges. At the convocation of the Etats Generaux in 1576 a monetary commission of economic scholars was created to standardize the livre tournois, to establish the gold ecu as account 'super money', increase trade, control the money supply and curb rampant inflation in grain prices. Small private banks like the Banque Courtois (1592) began to appear until the 1680s when again repressive isolationism, heavy defence expenditures and limited trade created a growing tension between the merchant class and the corrupt, passive aristocracy.

Molière's witty satires stigmatized merchants and financiers as avaricious, *L'Avare*, uneducated, *Le Bourgeois gentilhomme*, and grovelling before the aristocracy, *Don Juan*, yet this social class unlike the nobility was free of debt, possessed tangible assets and the skills and dynamism to exploit resources. But, unlike England's powerful merchant bankers turned landed gentry, French financiers remained socially marginal and politically repressed. From 1661 Louis XIV's minister Colbert called for reforms in the monetary system and increases in trade but without a state bank and state credit, it was impossible to channel and control financial policies.

20.2 THEOLOGY AND IDEOLOGY VERSUS ECONOMIC PROGRESS

A perfect illustration of Weber's theories of capitalism's dependence on Protestantism's exoneration of success and profit, France's movements between economic repression and initiative coincided with the liberalization of religious policies from the Edit de Nantes to Napoléon's decrees on religious freedom. The Revocation of the Edit de Nantes in 1685 banning Protestant banking and merchant families from exercising their functions limited economic progress. By 1703 Paris only had 21 bankers (51 in 1721 and 66 in 1776). Between 1704 and 1709, inflation, bad harvests, war losses and *agiotage*, speculation between the devalued louis d'or and paper money led to corruption and financial chaos. By 1715 the public debt exceeded 3.5 million, underwritten in part by loans from Geneva's bankers.

The French economic press, theatre and literature traces the

French fear of financial speculation and risk to the fiasco of the Mississippi Bubble in 1718–1720.

The name John Law reappeared as a dire warning following the crash of 1866, the bank failures of 1892 and the end of Chirac's overactive stock market in 1987. However, John Law's basic premise to use paper money as a form of monetary stability was sound advice. When he arrived in 1718 in France, he persuaded the regent Philip d'Orléans to create the first Royal Bank, by issuance of 3 billion worth of paper shares on future speculation in Louisiana land and tobacco development. Besieged by buyers, Law's scheme becomes the first stock speculation boom, which broke down social barriers as valets, aristocrats and merchants competed to buy shares. By 1720 with only 500 million in specie, payments had to be suspended, the bank dismantled but the impact of the 'Mississippi Bubble' revolutionized French financial philosophy. It forced the government to establish financial institutions (the Stock Market opened in 1726), to stabilize the louis d'or and silver ecu against the livre tournois, to call for regulation and state control to offset 'Madame Deficit'. Reflected in the plays and essays of Beaumarchais, Sedaine and Voltaire, aristocratic disdain for banking, investment, and foreign trade changed to respect and gratitude toward a mobile merchant class which associated its interests with saving rather than exploiting the State.

On 13 February 1800, with 30 million francs, Napoléon opened the Banque de France. The French government, more than a century after the Bank of England (1694), finally understood the need to consolidate monetary policies and State control in one Central Bank.

The Restoration and beginning of the Louis Philippe regime brought about a serious Catholic right-wing backlash. Nostalgic for an idealized protectionist monarchy, Balzac in literature like Daumier in art caricaturized bankers as foreign usurpers.

> On a value of 1000 francs it earns each day twenty-eight francs by the grace of God and the laws of the bank, powerful royalty invented by the Jews in the twelfth century and which today dominates thrones and nations.[2]

Balzac's diatribe was a reaction to Prime Minister Guizot's motto in 1830 'Enrichissez-vous'. Guizot did not advocate greed, but economic liberalism, and open credit policy to promote a more capitalist, commercial and investment prone environment, similar to England.

20.3 CORPORATE PATERNALISM TO GLOBALIZATION

Under Saint Simon and Auguste Comte's philosophy a ruling oligarchy discharged its democratic obligations to all classes by increasing the wealth and economic welfare of the State. Napoléon III's advent to power in 1852 brought in new energy to revitalize and expand France's role in domestic and international markets and legitimized policies of corporate paternalism. The discount rate was lowered, and the Stock Market vastly expanded from 118 shares quoted in 1850 to 407 shares quoted in 1869. By 1866, at his death, the Regent of the Bank of France left his only son a diversified portfolio of over one million francs in bank shares, National Life and Fire Insurance shares, Russian, Austrian and Egyptian securities, and a stock portfolio of railroad shares.

While literature denigrated the financier (Vallès's *L'Argent*, Flaubert's *L'Education sentimentale*) the government encouraged the banker as symbol of a strong and prosperous nation.

By 1863 after ten years of steady economic growth, banking needed new credit and investment facilities and regional centres.

In May 1863 the government passed legislature which allowed companies with a minimum of 20 million francs to become SARL (limited responsibility incorporate statute) shareholder corporations. Henri Germain, Lyonnais industrial and financier, incorporated the first SARL in Lyons with 40 000 shares of 500 francs and on 1 July 1863 the Crédit Lyonnais opened as the first major independent deposit bank in France: Its goals were 'to create a large client base in all classes of the population, as well among the craftsmen and small capitalists as among business merchants and rich industrialists. We want loyalty in our relationships, quick and efficient execution of transactions and fair conditions'.[3]

In 1865 the Banque de France controllers report commented 'The Crédit Lyonnais is involved in all imaginable financial operations from the most prudent to the most risky. It is a zealous company in all meanings of this strong term. The present leadership has a lot less experience and wisdom than ambition.' (Bouvier, p. 167).

In 1867 there were over 2500 client accounts, including 38 in Africa, 18 in Asia and 12 in America. It also dealt in municipal bonds, French tobacco securities, Italian and Turkish railroad bonds. A policy of prudence and carefully calculated risk combined to steadily increase the bank's profits between 1865 and 1871. At the time of the market crash and credit restrictions in 1866, Germain had already realized the need to expand abroad. The first Crédit Lyonnais branch opened in 1872 in London, followed by branches in Madrid, Cairo, Alexandria, and Constantinople in 1875. By 1901 there were over 20 branches abroad including Moscow, St Petersburg, Jerusalem, and Lisbon. The Crédit Lyonnais was closed out of only two major markets, India due to the hegemony of British interests and the United States due to protectionist tariffs against foreign banks and companies.

After the defeat of the Franco-Prussian war, French banks' sound reserves, and regional and foreign assets allowed the Banque de France to pay back 5 billion gold francs in war damages to Bismarck in under two years. The war and the subsequent popular revolt, the Paris Commune, taught the Crédit Lyonnais two valuable lessons: it reinforced the need to seek secure investments and set up branches abroad and it consolidated the psychological strength of the banking establishment. F. Jourde, in charge of the Commune's finances, former employee of the Banque de France accepted the Regent Rouland de Ploeuc's small subsidies but never sought to appropriate or nationalize the bank's 2.4 billion gold francs in reserve: 'While the Commune received just enough to barely survive, Versailles presented a bill of acceptance drawn on the Bank of France for 257.6 million to fight the insurgents in Paris'.[4]

By the 1880s, at the height of prosperity and colonial power French bankers again became the target of religious and political attacks. Involved in the excessive speculation in Ottoman Empire investment schemes, the main Catholic bank, l'Union Générale went bankrupt in 1892. In *L'Argent*, Zola, the press and politicians accused bankers of pandering to international conspiracies. Maurice Barrès in 1898 wrote 'Capital speculates, destroys, becomes more and more international and aspires no longer to be in solidarity with the destiny of France'.[5]

Following the Dreyfus affair bankers were judged as enemy of the anticapitalist, isolationist, Right and Marxist symbol of exploitation and personal greed. Malraux's *La Condition humaine* (1933), presents a scathing condemnation of old line reactionary bankers who refuse short-term risk and demand long-term guarantees. The character Ferral 'who wants that a bank be a gambling house',[6] a colonial financier who created a consortium of financial interests in precommunist China seeks to defend his risk-laden philosophy of investment, increased credit and expansion. While Ferral loses out to the government and corporate bankers who were detrimental to France's progress in world markets from the 1920s to the 1960s, he represents the very attitude that France finally espoused in the 1970s.

After 1945 the slow rebuilding of France's economy under the Marshall Plan began with de Gaulle's decision to nationalize the Société Générale, the Crédit Lyonnais in 1946 and the merged Banque Nationale de Paris in 1952. France in the 1950s and 1960s underwent a period of introspection, and denial of history. De Gaulle's vision of France's international mission and renewed sense of national pride was a first step toward re-entry into the global market. De Gaulle detested money and finance, yet with the guidance of economic advisers, Raymond Aron, Jean Monnet, Robert Schumann, he advocated a strong stable franc, corporate paternalism and State support for the small and middle market corporations.

20.4 'PRAGMATISM AND COOPERATION HAVE TO PREVAIL OVER IDEOLOGY'[7]

In order to fully integrate banking as a respected profession in harmony with the best interests of the State, a more profound change in attitude towards money, profit and globalization had to take place.

Favouring conservative steady growth, French banking remains a sophisticated exercise in casuistic analysis justifying its actions in the name of a higher goal, prosperity and enhancement of the State.

American 'cowboy' banking philosophy of high risk, heavy lending, fast-moving decisions, is no longer valid at a time of disarray in the banking industry, and inability to shake loose the remnants of Glass Steagal, weakened by a lack of cohesive monetary policies, and leaning toward right-wing isolationism. When the only American bank (Citicorp) is in 18th place among the top twenty, French banking in comparison appears no longer coyly protective of its assets, interventionist and restrictive but sound, well placed in world markets and able to take on calculated risks, offer new financial operations with solid guarantees and a record of no failures or closings.

Between 1966 and 1980 France became one of the top ten banking powers. The Crédit Agricole, Crédit Lyonnais, BNP and Société Générale have remained in the top category despite government changes, the market crashes of 1987 and 1989 and the incursion of Japanese banks since 1980. In November 1991, the Crédit Agricole ranked in 8th place, the Crédit Lyonnais in 10th, BNP in 9th and the privatized Société Générale in 22nd.[8]

French banks have modernized their technology, image and product through new marketing strategies and research and development. Addressing themselves to the small and medium corporations (PME/PMI) and to individual investors the banks want to be seen as a partner in corporate decisions. From 1976 to 1986 the number of checking accounts grew from 33 to 71 million. Between 1980 and 1985, French banks became the most computerized in the world (*monétique*), adapting to high technology, revitalizing their personnel and training policies.

The initial period of nationalization in 1981–3 of all private and semi-private banks with assets of over 1 billion francs encouraged modernization and technology but restricted the spirit of expansion. By 1983, the end of the period of austerity and nationalization was justified as a necessary pragmatic move towards American type capitalism, growth in the Stock Market, opening of the Second Market, creating new financial instruments (MATIF, Futures in 1983), the first ECU issues and a new aggressive push for investment abroad. By 1984 French banks' motto was 'profitability, security and liquidity'[9] with a renewed sense of prosperity and a push towards Europe.

In March 1987 Jacques Maisonrouge (former Minister of Industry under Chirac and former head of IBM) could declare to an American audience: 'The French now like business and understand what it takes to be successful in world markets'.[10] French bankers and businessmen became instrumental in re-educating their colleagues and in creating new programme and a new orientation for French business schools with emphasis on marketing, investment and international studies. Privatization between 1985 and 1988 was more a rhetorical device to explain partial denationalization as in practice the largest numbers of shareholders in privatized companies (Société Générale, in 1987) remained State banks and major State companies.

The complex legal distinction between state owned, private, privatized became less important than a government policy of a high profile financial presence in Europe and in the United States, a major role in large bank syndications and a key player in all world markets.

After the 9 December 1991 Maastricht Summit, the path towards European monetary unification, and the creation of a hyperstructure European system of Central Banks (EuroFed) appeared inevitable.

Whether located in London, Frankfurt or Strasbourg, the model will have to be a strong institution with long-term international experience and success in regulating global markets. The issues of national sovereignty, symbolized in the Central banks will have to be integrated and subsumed to the greater issue of European Community Sovereignty.

It seems historically unrealistic to assume that the fledgling economies of Eastern Europe with limited banking experience will adopt American banking philosophy. Russian finance is in a position similar to early nineteenth-century France. A network of interdependent regional banks with a strong central regulatory bank could quickly lead to the creation of independent deposit and credit banks which would promote industrial and commercial endeavours. The philosophy which fostered the Crédit Lyonnais and Société Générale, Paribas, in the 1870s and Mitterand's unique blend of socialist control and capitalist expansionism offers a far more compatible model. In competition with German banks, the French still have a discreet advantage.

The value of historical affinities and quiet diplomacy cannot be underestimated. The largest bank in St Petersburg in 1917, the Crédit Lyonnais lost vast assets, yet immediately after World War II, began to re-establish contacts and in 1972 became the only Western bank to open a representative office in Moscow. Actively involved in leasing and joint ventures, it helped establish the International Moscow Bank in October 1989, as shareholder with three Soviet and four other foreign banks.[11]

The Crédit Lyonnais's appeal as representative of the State and leader in global banking is both financial and psychological. It offers Russian finance a means of transition between stringent State regulation and capitalist initiative. These initiatives, the cultural appeal of France in Eastern Europe, choosing Jacques Attali, socialist, intellectual and historian to head the Bank for Development and Reconstruction in Eastern Europe, illustrate French finances' ability to finally reconcile the paradoxical and achieve a Cartesian synthesis.

Notes

1. Jane Kramer, 'Letter from Europe', *The New Yorker*, 6 August 1984, p. 74.
2. Balzac, *Illusions Perdues* (1837) (Paris: Garnier, 1961) p. 592.
3. Jean Bouvier, *Le Crédit Lyonnais de 1863 à 1882* (SEVPEN, 1961) p. 157.
4. Hippolyte Lissagaray, *Histoire de la Commune de 1871* (Bruxelles, 1876) p. 227.
5. Maurice Barrès, *Les Deracinés* (Paris: Plon, 1967) p. 249.

6. André Malraux, *La Condition Humaine* (Gallimard, 1946) p. 328.
7. Serge Bellanger, 'French Business', in J. Frommer and J. McCormick (eds), *Transformations in French Business. Political, Economic and Cultural Changes from 1981 to 1987* (Quorum Books, 1989) p. 36.
8. 'Une Année Douloureuse', *Le Nouvel Economiste*, *Special 5000*, November 1991.
9. Pierre Beaudeux, 'Les Banquiers à la Rose', *Expansion*, 24 May 1984.
10. Jacques Maisonrouge, 'Introduction', in J. Frommer and J. McCormick (eds), *Transformations in French Business*, p. VIII.
11. 'Crédit Lyonnais, an Innovative Bank in the USSR', *Business in the USSR* (Paris: Groupe Expansion, June 1990).

21 Offshore Banking Centres: Prospects and Issues

Emmanuel N. Roussakis, Krishnan Dandapani and Arun J. Prakash

21.1 INTRODUCTION

The total cross-border banking assets had risen from $2.7 trillion in 1982 to over $6.0 trillion in 1992. Expansion of existing international banking and financial centres in recent decades has been accompanied by the emergence of a number of new financial centres and regions around the globe and the trend is expected to continue. Concomitant with the expansion of international financial markets, the international banking system has experienced a robust growth. The international financial flows at the close of the past decade were estimated to be in excess of $200 trillion per year, about fifty times as much as the total world trade volume of $4 trillion. Cross-border financial flows are expected to grow further in the current decade as a result of the economic integration of Europe, the shift of the communist bloc countries into market economies, the gradual revitalization of Latin America, opening of new markets in Asia, and the globalization of trade and removal of trade barriers in North America. The implications of this growth for banking centres are enormous. Hence, in this chapter, we evaluate the prospects and issues with regard to the growth of offshore banking centres in the coming decade.

21.2 DEFINITION AND DEVELOPMENT

Historically, banking was primarily a domestic enterprise until the early part of the twentieth century. But since World War II, an international financial community has started emerging, and the international effort undertaken to reconstruct Europe and other war-ravaged countries led to the development of global financial institutions. Also over the last decade the pace of integration of global financial management practices has been accelerating. In the early stages, the international financial centres were extensions of domestic centres and primarily were developed to assist their clientele in trade and investment. Based on their differing operations, these centres were variously identified as International Financial Centre, World Financial Centre, Offshore banking Centre, International Banking Facilities and Regional Financial Centre. The comprehensive definition of Offshore Banking Centres (OBCs) could be attributed to McCarthy,[1] who identified them as:

> Cities, areas or counties which have made a conscious effort to attract offshore banking business, i.e. nonresident foreign currency-denominated business, by allowing relatively free entry and adopting a flexible attitude where taxes, levies and regulations are concerned.

Another conceptual and operational definition of an offshore banking centre is based on the type of banking transaction. We can identify four possible banking transactions: between domestic borrowers and domestic lenders, between domestic borrowers and foreign lenders, between domestic lenders and foreign borrowers, and between borrowers and foreign lenders. While the first is a purely domestic situation, the three remaining cases are examples of international banking transactions. By definition, entrepôt financial centres permit all three kinds of international transactions. Offshore banking term is used usually only for the last category in which transactions are conducted between two or more parties. Most governments discourage the mixing of foreign banking with domestic banking, and hence entrepôt centres are subject to far greater regulation than offshore centres.

Up until the 1970s, the development of the banking and financial centres was concentrated in the important centres of international finance, mainly London and New York. The existence of support facilities, technical expertise and communication capabilities greatly aided in their development. However, over time, other centres rose in prominence mainly due to favourable government and tax policies. The necessary prerequisite conditions for the existence and operations of an OBC are depicted in Table 21.1. These conditions enable the successful operation of an OBC. The other major and minor factors which promote the growth and successful operation of the

Table 21.1

Category A
Prerequisite factors. Important requirements, those without which offshore financial activities would be considered impossible:

(1) low- or non-existent domestic taxes,
(2) political stability,
(3) confidentiality of records,
(4) flexible banking laws and regulations,
(5) no currency conversion limitations.

Category B
Major factors. Conditions that aid significantly in the development and maintenance of offshore financial services, such as:

(1) possession of adequate infrastructure, such as telex, telephone, etc., and availability of qualified personnel,
(2) advantageous geographical location.

Category 3
Minor factors. Conditions which are generally considered of minor importance, but which can greatly enhance the attraction of a specific Offshore Financial Centre. Examples of these are:

(1) low costs of operation,
(2) governmental policies,
(3) mentality of the general population towards the offshore business,
(4) reasonable fees and levies, languages and others.

---

offshore banking centre are also identified and are widely shared by all successful OBCs.

While the overall OBCs' assets have been growing, the share of the well known global financial centres have started declining over the last decade; by the end of 1982 London, a leading international banking centre had a 20 per cent market share of the offshore banking. This was closely followed by US with about 10 per cent of the market share and Bahamas, France and Switzerland with approximately 5 per cent each. Since 1982, while international lending and deposit taking have been growing at roughly 15 per cent annually, a considerable portion of international banking activity occurs in offshore banking markets. A variety of factors has provided an impetus to the growth of banking activities overseas, mainly to aid in trade activities and attract the investment clientele. The development of the Middle Eastern economies and Asian markets led to the development and establishment of more offshore banking centres competing with existing financial centres. OBCs have also been facilitating complex financing transactions, often in foreign currencies through the conduit of a domestic bank. Borrowing costs, hence, are also substantially lower for corporations because minimal tax and banking regulations enable corporations to raise capital at a lower cost. However, one major factor in favour of the existing financial centres is that the growth of a financial centre is synchronized with the growth of the capital markets. Table 21.2 identifies some of the major existing OBCs, world-wide and a cursory examination reveals that most of the successful conditions for the existence of an OBC exists in these regions.

21.3 GROWTH AND ANALYSIS OF OFFSHORE BANKING CENTRES

The importance of the OBCs in the 1980s and their share of the Eurocurrency market[2] may be seen in Table 21.3 which presents an analysis of the external currency market, by major country grouping. As seen in this table, at year-end 1991 OBCs gross Eurocurrency liabilities amounted to $1285.7 billion, which represented an approximate fourfold increase over the 1982 level. OBCs share of the Eurocurrency market in 1991 accounted for 21.0 per cent and reflected a compounded annual growth rate of 17.4 per cent, compared with a 16.4 per cent rate for the entire market. This growth contributed to the decentralization of the Eurocurrency market, which until 1970 existed almost exclusively in London and in a few other Western European centres.

Although OBCs represent a substantial slice of the multibillion dollar global banking, there is some product differentiation between centres on the basis of services offered, cost, and, in some cases, geographic location. Depositor preferences of OBCs are often determined by personal, cultural and even emotional factors, such as local language or political status. In addition, many depositors prefer to diversify their investment to more than one centre to assure safety. As a result, some banks have established offices in more than one centre.

Table 21.4 identifies some of the major OBCs and the size of their Eurocurrency business for the years 1982–91. As seen in this table, the competition for offshore banking is very intense and crowded in

Table 21.2   Major existing offshore and financial centres

The European Region

Campione	Luxembourg
Channel Islands	Malta
Gibraltar	Monaco
Greece	Netherlands
Ireland	Sark Lark
Isle of Man	Switzerland
Liechtenstein	United Kingdom

Caribbean Offshore Financial Centres

Anguilla	Costa Rica
Antigua	Jamaica
Aruba	Montserrat
Bahamas	Netherlands Antilles
Barbados	Panama
Bermuda	Puerto Rico
British Virgin Islands	St Vincent
Cayman Islands	

The Far East and Oceania

Cook Islands	Nauru
Hong Kong	Philippines
Macau	Singapore
Micronesia	Vanuatu

The Middle Eastern and African Offshore Financial Centres

Bahrain	Seychelles
Israel	United Arab Emirates
Liberia	

Eastern Europe

Hungary
Soviet Union
Austria

the Carribean and is represented by four major centres (Bahamas, Cayman Islands, Netherlands Antilles and Panama). On the basis of size, however, the largest single OBC, at year-end 1991, was Belgium/Luxembourg which has recorded a notable 20.0 per cent annualized growth rate. Likewise, Singapore and Hong Kong have also exhibited remarkable annual growth rates, 34.3 per cent and 22.3 per cent, respectively. Singapore is the fourth largest foreign

Table 21.3 Gross Eurocurrency liabilities, 1982–91* (billions of dollars, at year end)

Countries/centres	1982	1983	1984	1985	1986	1987	1988	1989†	1990	1991‡	Annual growth rate (per cent)
Non-oil developing countries	$101.0	$110.9	$170.5	$177.3	$195.3	$229.8	$236.9	$242.3	$321.1	$351.1	15.84
Oil exporting countries	147.6	131.2	140.5	159.9	143.8	169.6	178.5	179.6	215.2	223.0	5.22
Offshore banking centres	318.1	349.5	439.4	510.8	691.5	907.5	999.5	1069.5	1307.4	1285.7	17.35
Industrial countries	950.8	996.3	1242.4	1482.0	1936.1	2581.5	2848.6	3044.7	3805.7	3634.4	16.72
Other	102.9	114.3	123.7	146.4	212.8	313.0	357.1	388.1	479.8	620.2	22.86
Total	$1620.4	$1702.2	$2116.5	$2476.4	$3179.5	$4201.4	$4620.6	$4924.2	$6129.2	$6114.4	16.41
OBCs as a % of Total	19.63	20.53	20.76	20.63	21.75	21.60	21.63	21.72	21.33	21.03	

*These are considered 'gross' liabilities because interbank claims have not been netted out.
† At end of September 1989.
‡ At end of March 1992.

Source: Bank of England, Quarterly Bulletin, various issues.

319

Table 21.4 Gross Eurocurrency liabilities of major offshore banking centres, 1982–91 (billions of dollars at year end)

OBCs	1982	1983	1984	1985	1986	1987	1988	1989*	1990	1991‡	Annual growth rate (per cent)
Bahamas	$81.6	$90.1	$98.1	$99.4	$112.6	$121.1	$127.8	$120.7	$135.7	$140.7	6.39
Bahrain	16.9†	15.1†	19.1	18.2	18.9	24.0	24.9	22.4	19.5	18.3	1.84
Cayman Islands	60.2	72.3	77.9	85.4	119.1	135.9	154.6	180.9	195.2	222.1	15.94
Hong Kong	27.6	34.1	63.7	82.1	130.6	224.1	262.7	277.3	345.4	317.2	34.34
Belgium/Luxembourg	75.9	76.3	87.8	111.9	154.2	210.5	218.8	233.4	355.3	356.1	20.05
Netherlands Antilles	10.6	12.2	15.8	19.5	25.4	30.8	30.2	28.4	42.4	44.6	18.46
Panama	16.0	18.3	22.1	24.2	28.5	30.8	25.3	26.4	25.3	40.9	12.72
Singapore	29.3	31.1	54.9	70.1	102.2	130.3	155.3	180.0	188.5	145.9	22.32
Total	$318.1	$349.5	$439.4	$510.8	$691.5	$907.5	$999.6	$1,069.5	$1,307.3	$1,285.8	17.35

* At end of September 1989.

† Estimated.

‡ At end of March 1992.

Source: Bank of England, *Quarterly Bulletin*, various issues.

exchange trading centre in the world and a financial catalyst in the economic development of the Asian-Pacific region. A substantial amount of the funds flowing in the Singapore market is supplied by the offshore market in London. Singapore has become the funding centre for the Asian-Pacific region, a position achieved, in part, by its initiative in the late 1960s to establish the Asian Currency Market, and assisted by the absence of withholding tax on non-resident interest at a time when Hong Kong levied such a tax.[3]

Singapore's offshore sector operates primarily as a banking centre for institutions engaging in large fund-raising exercises, or large volume trading. Singapore is attractive as an offshore centre because (1) profits generated in the offshore centres are significantly less taxed than domestically generated profits, (2) most banking regulations governing domestic institutions do not apply to the offshore banks, and (3) its infrastructure is one of the best in Asia. As a result, the number of offshore banks in Singapore has grown significantly over the past several years (from 14 in 1974 to 200 in 1991).[4]

Hong Kong is the only offshore haven that compares with Singapore in terms of the depth and expertise of its offshore financial activities. In spite of all of its advantages, Hong Kong's future as a base for offshore holding companies is suspect after the communist Chinese takeover in 1997. The up-coming expiration of the 99-year-lease with England is raising important concerns about the future growth of this centre. Another issue, of a more immediate nature, is the rising cost of maintaining holding companies in Hong Kong. As a result of these two issues, several offshore holding companies are reassessing about continuance in the island and have elected to register themselves elsewhere (i.e. British Virgin Islands or the Cayman Islands). However, many companies are still maintaining an administrative and management presence for the time being. In this regard, Hong Kong's growth in recent years has been more as a service and administrative centre rather than as a pure offshore centre.[5]

An important development in the Asian dollar market, which was expected to impact the growth and status of both Singapore and Hong Kong, was the establishment of the Japanese offshore market (JOM), in December 1986. JOM is Tokyo's only real presence as an offshore financing median, with its primary function being the facilitation of currency transactions between non-resident financial institution and foreign banks operating locally.[6] Although Tokyo is one of the world's leading financial centres in terms of institutions and infrastructure, offshore dealings have been virtually limited to inter-bank flows enabling Japanese banks to engage in the continuous short-term funding of their long-term assets. The limited scope of this market is likely to persevere as long as the current bureaucratic practices and regulatory standards remain intact. This type of en-vironment makes it impossible for Tokyo to emulate the openness and internationalism exhibited by both Hong Kong and Singapore. This coupled with rising costs, has adversely affected offshore deal-ings in Tokyo.

The Asian/South Pacific region has also become home to many other lesser known offshore centres. Vanuatu and the Cook Islands are the two major financial centres of this region, as both have experienced notable growth in recent years.[7] Other island nations in the area that play a limited financial role include Nauru and Western Samoa. Though neither of these two centres has really 'taken off', the potential is still there given the region's benefits. Locale is probably the single strongest advantage for the South Pacific centres as they chase after the much desired Asian Dollar. Specifically, Asian inves-tors can conduct business during their own business hours, which proves to be a major convenience factor. Other significant benefits are (1) freedom from taxation or foreign exchange controls, (2) exemption of offshore entities from domestic laws, and (3) strict secrecy provisions with any breaches thereof punishable by imprison-ment.

The Caribbean sector contains some major offshore financial cen-tres in its own right. Virtually all of the major centres in this region offer the advantages of political stability, freedom from taxation, and low registration and maintenance costs. However, all of these centres have information exchange agreements with the US Government, in an effort to eliminate criminal elements from the region and simul-taneously add some much needed credibility.

Both the Bahamas and Cayman Islands achieved respectable growth rates during the 1982–91 period, amounting to 6.4 per cent and 15.9 per cent, respectively. As seen in Table 21.4, Bahamas was the largest OBC in 1982, accounting for 25.7 per cent of the group's total foreign liabilities. By 1991 however, the Bahamas had sunk to fifth place. Some of the reasons frequently cited for this decline include the Bahamas' complacency by its past success; negative pub-licity about drug trafficking and corruption; rising fees, bureaucratic delays and inefficiency; and reports of drug-related crime and viol-ence in Nassau. The Bahamas' slow down proved very beneficial for the neighbouring Cayman Islands. Although the Cayman Islands have been in the offshore business since the mid 1960s, the first real boost came when the Bahamas won independence from Britain in 1973. A 'Bahamianization programme' that denied work permits to foreigners if local talent was available, induced some institutions to transfer their business to Cayman.[8] However, the Bahamas' more recent problems, coupled with the political crisis in Panama, have served to help transform the Cayman Islands into the leading OBC in the Caribbean region. The Cayman Islands have gone to great lengths to shore up their regulations and surveillance of offshore banks in an effort to dampen money laundering and, more recently, to enhance their image in the wake of the Bank of Credit and Commerce International scandal.

It is worth noting that both the Bahamas and Cayman Islands are tax havens and also permit foreign banks to operate through 'shell branches'. These facilities allow parent companies to conduct their business elsewhere but enter the transactions in the shell's books. Hence the reference to these centres as 'booking centers'. The shell often requires no more than a single employee and a post-office box. Consequently, it is not uncommon in the Bahamas to find a single attorney 'running' ten different banks. Recent pressure from central banks and foreign tax authorities has led to some change in that tendency.

Unlike the Bahamas and the Cayman Islands, Panama prohibits shell operations. That is, licensed banks must maintain actual premises and staff. Panama's entry into the world of international busidates from the 1960s when it designated a free zone for bonded warehousing and manufacturing within the city of Colon and enacted legislation favourable to the shipping industry. With a substantial shipping business intact and a significant experience in handling large-scale international transactions, Panama took steps in 1970 to establish itself as an OBC. Its growth as an international banking centre, however, came in the 1970s as a result of the massive recycling of petrodollars to Latin America. At the same time, capital flight from Latin America was well under way, and some Panamanian banks attracted large amounts of private offshore deposits. Total bank assets in Panama reached a peak of $49.3 billion in September 1982. From that date on, however, Panama began to decline as an international banking centre. The onset of the Latin America Debt Crisis, followed by debt rescheduling and the virtual halt of new bank lending to this region undermined the growth of this centre. More importantly, however, a political crisis which began in June 1987 and culminated in the US invasion in December 1989 shook up international confidence in Panama. As a result, Panama's offshore banking activity had dropped dramatically during this period, and new corporate business was driven elsewhere. However, as conditions began to normalize, Panama experienced a sizeable rise in its gross foreign liabilities. Specifically, liabilities increased from $25.3 billion at year end 1990 to $40.9 billion at year end 1991, an increase of 61.7 per cent. This increase may be signalling the recovery of Panama's stature as an international banking centre.

The Netherlands Antilles, formerly Dutch island colonies off the coast of Venezuela, constitute another important OBC. Curacao, the most important island in the Netherlands Antilles, came into its own as a financial centre during World War II by becoming a safe haven for Dutch companies during the Nazi occupation of Holland. After the war, the United States and the Netherlands signed a tax treaty which was extended to the Netherlands Antilles in 1955. Curacao's prominence as an OBC, however, came after the signing of a tax treaty with the United States, followed by similar agreements with Britain and the Netherlands. These treaties led to the establishment of local companies exempt from virtually all taxes in Curacao, except for a low income tax of 2.4 per cent to 3 per cent. To foreign investors in the United States, these companies offered exemption from withholding taxes on interest, dividends and royalties under the terms of the US tax treaty. It was not long before international investors grasped the opportunities offered by Curacao and moved to establish a corporate presence there. In the 1970s and 1980s major US banks and corporations followed suit and established a presence in Curacao. These latter moves helped launch Curacao in the world of international banking and made it an important Eurobond issuing centre.

Curacao's increasing role as a tax haven led the United States in mid-1987 to revoke its tax treaty (effective 1 January 1988) which eventually undermined the island's importance as a Eurobond issuing centre. Offshore banks have not been directly affected by the revocation of the US tax treaty, since their operations were not mainly treaty-related. On the other hand, with most of the offshore banking activity geared towards Latin America, Curacao has felt the effects of the Latin American debt crisis. Most of the current activity is conducted with Venezuela and Colombia, and offshore banks continue to lend to these countries on a selective basis. In catering to these interests, Curacao is competing with neighbouring Aruba which seceded in 1986 from the Netherlands Antilles and is now actively competing for its share of the offshore business.

In the years between 1982 and 1991 Belgium/Luxembourg grew by an annual rate of 20.0 per cent and at year end 1991 was the largest OBC. Although landlocked, Luxembourg is one of the oldest and most established OBCs. Catering primarily to European interest (e.g. Germany), Luxembourg began to establish itself as a financial centre in 1929, when it exempted holding companies from significant taxation. Another important measure that encouraged Luxembourg's growth was its approval of strict bank secrecy laws, an action that further enhanced its attractiveness to foreign institutions. Moreover, support personnel is frequently multilingual, and receives smaller salaries than its counterpart in London. That fact, coupled with Luxembourg's lower property values (compared with London's), have in many instances made the establishment and operation of a Luxembourg bank less costly than running a bank in London. Some banks, in fact, have found that they can buy commercial space in Luxembourg for about the equivalent cost of renting the same amount of space in London for a year.

Moreover, Luxembourg's regulatory policies have attracted banking business. In comparison with the strict banking policies in neighbouring Germany, Luxembourg places no reserve requirements on Eurocurrency deposits and no withholding tax on interest. This liberal regulatory climate, combined with some of the considerations stated above, are credited for making Luxembourg a major Eurocurrency and Eurobond centre in Europe.

The European Community (EC) will have an important effect into the nature and stature of offshore financial centres in Europe, particularly in light of the deregulation of the banking industry. In fact, the concept of offshore business runs contrary to the spirit of the EC which strives for uniformity of treatment. One unsettled issue is the indefinite continuation of Luxembourg's privileged status within the EC. Some banking clients already prefer to access Luxembourg indirectly – they use a bank in Switzerland as a conduit for their investments in Luxembourg. In addition to its role in Eurobond issuance, Luxembourg has become the leading centre for managed investment funds called UCITs (Undertaking Collective Investments in Transferable Securities.[9] UCITs are open-ended unit trusts, or mutual funds, whose tax efficient status was established by the EC. UCITs are regarded by many investment houses as the mutual funds of the future.

Another OBC identified in Table 21.4 is Bahrain, which both in terms of size and growth rate is trailing the other OBCs listed in this table. Relatively new to the international banking scene, Bahrain, in the Gulf, has emerged as the newest major OBC. Its stature has been enhanced by a special treaty with Great Britain that designates Bahrain as the centre of British administration in the discharge of its Gulf responsibilities. Among other things, this arrangement has resulted in the development of transport and telecommunications facilities, which in turn have benefited the local service offerings and have made Bahrain more attractive as an international finance centre. Another important factor has been its success in convincing other Gulf governments to use its market instead of depositing their reserves in London or New York. As a result of this development, Bahrain has emerged over the years as an important collection centre – that is, it engages primarily in outward financial intermediation. The low absorptive capacity of the region's economies has led to the channelling of the surplus savings accumulated in Bahrain to other centres. Thus Bahrain has emerged as a net supplier of funds to the Singapore Asian dollar market.

Bahrain has been very selective in granting permits, issuing them only to prestigious banks. Bahrain does not permit shell operations, any loan booked there must be administered locally. This has had a positive effect on the local financial community, though it diminishes some of the convenience to foreign banks. Finally, confidentiality of banking transactions is assured in Bahrain. Unauthorized disclosure of confidential information is covered by the Bahrain Penal Code, and offending bank officers are subject to fines and imprisonment.

Since 1989, Bahrain has steadily conceded in terms of size. The region was particularly hit hard following the Gulf War which served to 'taint' the region, labelling it unstable. During the Gulf crisis, vast amounts of money left the region and evidently, have not yet returned.

21.4 FUTURE PROSPECTS OF EXISTING AND EVOLVING OFFSHORE BANKING CENTRES

In analysing the prospects of OBC in future, we shall analyse them regionwise.

Asian Region

In the Asian region, the growth of the OBCs are largely fuelled by the Asian giants. A comprehensive survey by M. A. Goldberg reveals that Tokyo, Hong Kong, and Singapore are the places where international banking occurs and are the ideal locations for banks in Asia. The secondary locales like Vanatu, Taipei, and Manila have minor roles to play in the international financial arena in the Asia Pacific region.[10]

The Japanese government is encouraging Tokyo to become an international financial centre. Tokyo, as the capital of Japan has great potential, being the international financial centre with a total of 21 000 corporate businesses headquartered there. A vast information network interlining with a network of satellites has helped Tokyo enter an entirely new dimension of growth and dynamism.[11] However, foreign banks and brokerage houses are seriously re-evaluating their continued presence there because of their inability to penetrate the local market. For example, while 20 per cent of the Tokyo Stock Exchange membership is foreign, they account for only 4.5 per cent of the exchange's turnover.[12] Japan's OBC was established to permit domestic banks to conduct business with non-residents, without being encumbered by deposit insurance and reserve requirements, and to encourage the use of the yen as an international currency. Japanese banking centre had assets exceeding those of the older New York and Singapore operations. However, it is difficult to assess the success of Japan's OBCs. The rapid growth is mainly because of the fact that the Japan offshore market has become a surrogate domestic yet inter-bank market. Japan's OBCs currently limit seepage to the domestic account to 5 per cent of a bank's previous month's average balance of transactions with non-residents. Large international banks have withdrawn funds from the Japan offshore market accounts through their overseas branches and then brought the funds back on shore through an interoffice yen swap.[13]

Hong Kong's securities business is the main driving force behind Hong Kong's status as an international financial centre, and the attraction for an increasing number of foreign brokerage houses and investment banks. The Japanese houses are willing to buy investor goodwill at a price, thus posing a formidable challenge to the local and global players. Hong Kong, however does not have a central bank and a central monetary authority. The functions of the central bank are carried out by the Monetary affairs branch of the Government Secretariat. The type of financial institutions in Hong Kong include, licensed banks, restricted licence banks and representative offices of foreign banks and deposit taking companies. As of 1990 the number of licensed banks was a record and there were several new entrants in the market.[14] While the telecommunication network of Hong Kong is superior even to that of London, its base for offshore investment is under threat because of communist Chinese jurisdiction. Hong Kong accounts for 65 per cent of the direct foreign investment in the neighbouring Guongdong province. However, improving relations between Taiwan and China endanger and erode Hong Kong's attractiveness as an OBC.[15] The resumption of Chinese sovereignty over Hong Kong in 1997, the stock market volatility, and the political uncertainty have made many question Hong Kong's future as an international financial centre. Over the last decades, Hong Kong had a convenient location, a fair and open regulatory system, a generous tax regime, well-educated, English speaking labour force, including professional, clerical, and administrative staff. However, the possible disruption in Guongdong, and the political instability, have diminished the attractiveness of Hong Kong and it is already losing trained professionals due to emigration, mainly at middle levels.[16] These developments will lead to a diminished role for Hong Kong as a future OBC.

Increasingly Singapore is acting as a magnet for trade within the Asia-Pacific region and hope to benefit from Hong Kong's losses. The offshore banking units mostly are in trade-related business and in foreign exchange. Singapore's OBCs have heavily invested in computerized trade finance networks and other infrastructure. One of the major constraining factors in the growth of Singapore is that its currency cannot be internationalized. Hence with the saturation of Singapore's market, the non-convertibility of the currency will hinder further growth. Singapore has to move boldly with a package of reforms that will include internationalization of currency and other privatization to be successful in the intensely competitive market.[17] In spite of serious barriers to newcomers, Singapore is seen as the third vital link in the Asian region, after Tokyo and Hong Kong. In the 1970s, numerous Japanese banks established offices in Singapore. In the current decade, Japanese stockbroking companies, and OBCs and financial institutions find the Singapore government's package very attractive for migration and are expanding.

While the Republic of Korea has an excellent infrastructure and manufacturing base to support OBCs, the Korean market retains a cautious approach to capital market reforms. One major hurdle in Korea becoming an OBC is that its interest rates are strictly fixed and monitored by Korean authorities. More liberalization is needed for Korea to become a major international financial and offshore banking centre.

Taiwan, like the Republic of Korea has very high levels of savings and investment, but the financial markets are still in the process of liberalization. In addition the $75 billion capital reserves held Taiwan, its central location, the broad manufacturing base to support the financial industry and absence of conflict of interest law portend well for Taiwan.[18] Taiwan adopted a $300 billion, six year, National Development Plan in the summer of 1991. An important part of the plan is to permit banks to engage in universal banking activities. A three-stage action plan to make Taiwan the financial centre of Western Pacific Region has been adopted and the short-term plans include developments of new financial products and trading of foreign exchange; a medium term plan is to broaden the scope of offshore banking units and the long-term goal entails the internationalization of the New Taiwan dollar.[19] However, the inappropriate timing of privatization move by the Taiwanese government have set back its ability to achieve full potential.

A major attraction of Thailand, for foreign OBCs are its average growth rates and developing economy. In Macau, the government has an objective of transforming Macau into an international financial centre along the lines of Hong Kong or Singapore and is planning to introduce a number of banking and insurance restructuring measures. However, the absence of a stock market and the low capital base of its existing banks will prove to be a big hurdle in its development.[20] Another growing OBC is Labuan, Malaysia's offshore tax haven. Three commercial banks, 8 trust companies, 20 offshore companies, and one insurer have been granted approval to operate on Labuan. Labuan can become a major OBC in Asia because of the government's commitment to the expected growth in the region. The preliminary experience has been successful. However, continued migration of banks are needed to maintain long-term viability and profitability. Labuan's major weakness continues to be its proximity to established low-tax regimes, such as Singapore and Hong Kong and the intense competition from established OBCs. The public bank of Malaysia is expected by 1992 to launch an OBC in Colombo. Cheap land and labour are attracting investors to Johore, Malaysia's southernmost state. Singapore's investments there have mushroomed and competition in the domestic market is forcing big Singapore's banks to look abroad for investment opportunities. The next focus may be Vietnam and Burma. An oligopoly structure of banking in the Philippines, and the resultant higher profit margins, is hindering the corporate cost of borrowing.[21] The central bank authorized the Offshore Banking Units to deal in export letters of credit up to $400 million in 1991 and also handle foreign remittances. However, two Philippine government initiatives will squeeze bank profitability: one is the restriction on holding foreign exchange assets and the other is the liberalization of the banking sector leading to increased competition. At present, the banks are expected to focus only in retail banking.[22]

The major problems of OBCs in Asia are that the existing banking structure and the lack of regulation. Banking is highly concentrated in the Philippines, Thailand, and Malaysia. For example in the Philippines 40 per cent of all banking assets are held by the top four banks. The regulatory lax problem is more serious in existing OBCs. For example, in Hong Kong the absence of regulation has allowed over 400 specialized leveraged companies. In Taiwan there has been an expansion of Margin Trading and some estimate the size of overnight sums outstanding to be in excess of $200 million. Fraudulent activities, unnecessary trades and falsification of records could tarnish the reputation of the centres and lead to a collapse.[23] Excellent regulatory control and supervision are required to maintain the continued integrity of future OBCs.

European Region

The European integration has changed the landscape of the offshore banking market in Europe. The European Community's comprehensive package for the establishment of a competitive European financial area include a full liberalization of capital movements, an amendment on the flow of capital between member states and third countries, and a facility to provide support for balance-of-payments difficulties and deal with surpluses.[24] This liberalization initiative could create a powerful, international financial centre. The rationale behind 1992 is that increased competition will bring economic benefits to the entire European Community (EC). Eliminating barriers will exert more pressure on profit margins as competition increases. Non-European institutions will play an increasing role in the financial market. As the financial sector becomes more open and efficient, EC firms should be in a better position to compete in third country markets.

UK banking markets will experience more changes than those in countries with more closed financial systems. Some business, driven offshore by restrictions, might return to London.[25] London's dominant position as an international financial centre has reflected the generally relaxed and informal regulatory environment, and over-regulation could threaten this position. US money centre banks remain committed to their London presence. Japanese banks remains deeply entrenched in the UK's economy, but their presence in London depends on the regulation. European banks make up over 40 per cent of the total foreign presence in London. The worldwide trend toward less regulation, combined with large savings surpluses in some European countries, has fostered this growth.[26] London has the potential to be a pre-eminent leader because of its strengths. It is the only European centre that has the network of markets and activities parallel to the domestic markets of other European community members. If after 1992, European business and financial markets structure gets more integrated, London will emerge as the major winner and will continue to grow as an OBC.

Amsterdam is making an effort to promote itself as an international financial centre and an intermediary between major European centres like London, Frankfurt, and Paris and smaller financial markets of Brussels, Milan, Dusseldorf, Zurich and other European cities. The Amsterdam Financial Centre Foundation was created in 1989 to reinforce Amsterdam's competitive situation and to provide intensive training to banking and finance professionals.[27] Amsterdam's attractions include its location for a number of multinationals and institutional investors, a strong currency, a stable and open economy, low interest rates, a well developed infrastructure, and a number of large, internationally oriented banks.[28] Cyprus has also been undergoing a change in the structure of its financial sector. In addition to the central bank it houses eight on-shore commercial banks, 19 offshore banking units. While the British legal system, cheap land, low income corporate tax rates are helpful in its OBC development, instability in Middle East, recession induced by low oil prices, and the high cost of telecommunications and the local bureaucracy hinder its growth.

France has the largest and most important securities market in Europe after the UK with Paris having the fourth largest stock exchange in the world. The growth of the futures and options market and the restructuring of the securities market could increase the attractiveness of France. Gibraltar also has emerged as a prosperous centre for offshore banking. With the decline of British military presence Gibraltar needs to rely on its status as an offshore financial centre to promote economic growth.

Italy's strengths in the intermediate technology and its developing trade relations in Asia have helped the regional Italian banks in Asia to grow. The framework for the development of OBCs has already been established by Italian banks of correspondent relationships with overseas banks and Italy has a major presence in most major international financial centres.[29] Madeira in Portugal has been promoted as an offshore centre to strengthen and diversify the island's economy. Recent legislation enacted to provide a free trade zone and OBCs will enable it to grow in the future.

Malta has a good potential to grow as an important OBC. The government has actively been pursuing policies to prohibit illicit activity and has established an independent supervisory authority. A watch-dog group in the form of a nominee company has also been established to ensure the integrity of Malta as an international financial centre and could attract insurance and banking firms. A membership in the European community, and a market oriented economy could help it succeed. Malta's geographic location historically has shaped its politics and economy. Malta's orientation towards service industries and international investment recently got an added boost when the Maltese government introduced new incentives for the industrial investor. The legislation establishes the framework upon which a complete international financial centre can be established, including provisions for upgrading the island's infrastructures. It features a low tax rate on offshore companies; offshore trading companies, banks, and insurance companies. The legislation further establishes a new independent authority for assisting and monitoring offshore business. The emergence of Malta as a financial centre should provide an opportunity to utilize the insurance market's technical resources.[30]

In securities trading, money management and trade finance Swiss banks have dominated the world for long as the best in the business. However, Switzerland may be forced to look outside its borders for growth. Foreign exchange depreciation has affected confidence in Switzerland overseas banking. Continued global pressures has forced Switzerland to end the long-time pledge of absolute secrecy of investor accounts. Liechtenstein, the world's smallest sovereign state is rapidly overtaking Switzerland as Europe's number one tax haven. It has benefited from a series of Swiss banking scandals, which has forced the banks to pierce the veil of secrecy.

Turkey's ability to become the Middle East's OBC and to draw
large-scale foreign investment depends on its ability to turn its economy around in the near future, control its chronic inflation, and
increase exports. Turkey expects to be a major recipient of foreign
investment and loans from the West and from moderate, pro-
Western Arab and Islamic countries should it join as the 13th member of the European Community by the end of this decade. Istanbul
has been designated as Turkey's first OBC, and the government is
planning to establish several new free trade zones by 1992, which
would be tax-free and duty-free and would be considered outside
Turkey's custom boundaries. One major requirement is that the
nation must also maintain its high growth rates and further build up
its foreign exchange reserves to be a viable OBC.[31] Turkish banks
have become more efficient because of increased competition from a
profusion of foreign and domestic institutions. The invasion of
Kuwait had little direct impact on the banks. Construction and rebuilding in the region will provide an industrial base. The Gulf crisis,
and the aggressive moves by the government in the aftermath of
Iraq's invasion of Kuwait, creating an OBC in Istanbul and enabling
free conversion of Turkish lira, and removal of restrictions on the
dealing in foreign exchange will help in the development of OBCs. A
vastly improved communication system and the development of new
products and markets will help it to grow in the future.[32]

Middle East Region

Unlike the early 1980s, when Arab banking was a worldwide force,
only a few banks now command international respect: the rest are
focused almost exclusively on domestic markets. Declining oil prices
and operating pressures are decreasing their worldwide presence.
Saudi Banks are playing a growing role in funding public-sector
development. Despite being damaged by the collapse of Bank of
Credit and Commerce International (BCCI), earnings in the United
Arab Emirates (UAE) have remained reasonably healthy. However,
the BCCI affair will likely delay plans to start an OBC in the UAE. In
Bahrain, many of the offshore banks are facing serious problems. In
Kuwait, the banks' recovery from the Gulf War has been slow and
most are focusing on internal rebuilding; only the national bank of
Kuwait has maintained a credible international presence.[33]
The Gulf crisis has resulted in a fundamental restructuring of

Kuwait's banks and a major reappraisal of Bahrain's offshore banking. The major international banks have been reduced to Arab Banking Corporation, Gulf International Bank in Bahrain and Arab Banking Corporation in Jordan. Most of the banks are now concentrating in large-scale lending to shore up state industries. Some Islamic banks are also exploring opportunities in the former USSR regions and Algeria.[34]

Bahrain for long has held the pre-eminent position in the Middle East as an international and regional banking centre, mainly based on its offshore activities attracting both Arab and international financial institutions. The telephone, fax and telex rates are among the cheapest in the world and the cost of labour is relatively inexpensive. The growth of the Bahrain's stock market and the liberal investment and ownership law and the complete absence of personal, corporate and withholding tax and 100 per cent foreign ownership are other impetus for the continued growth of Bahrain as an OBC.[35] Despite firmer oil prices, Bahrain, with reserves of about 130 million barrels and production levels of 40 000 barrels a day, cannot rely on oil revenues for much longer, with falling oil prices. Diversification is more critical for it than any other Gulf nation. The government is keen to industrialize, hoping for 30 per cent industrial contribution by the end of the 1990s. Current plans call for the Aluminum Bahrain project, airport expansion, and improvements for the telecommunications network and water system. The main concern of banks now are the expected higher capital requirements of the Bahrain Monetary Agency and its impact on profitability.[36] However, both local and offshore banks have now largely completed recapitalization and restructuring programmes and profitability and long-run stability are expected. Three major problems for the continued success of Bahrain as an OBC are the lack of indigenous business, its banks Third World debt charges, and the lack of liquidity in the banking sector. These have to be addressed for Bahrain to become a successful OBC.

Qeshm, the largest island in the Gulf, has sprung to prominence as the pragmatists in Tehran seek to capitalize on the strategically placed island's potential as a tourist resort, industrial zone, and offshore banking centre. The area has some one billion barrels of oil reserves and over 2.2 trillion cubic metres of proven natural gas reserves. Qeshm is seen as a means of increasing Iran's role in international trade as well as boosting industrial growth and technology transfer. Qeshm is fast developing its infrastructure, but plans for offshore banking are still at an early stage. Allowing foreign banks to enter Qeshm would be a major step for Iran, but it would be easier in Qeshm's free zone than on the mainland. It also has a separate legal and social code.[37]

Australian Region

Mauritius and Sydney are the two possible centres for the development of an OBC in the region. Mauritius is now launching a major worldwide campaign to attract foreign investors to participate in the island's second phase of economic development. The economy, based on sugar, textiles, manufacturing and an expanding OBC, has grown to an average rate of 8 per cent and help in the development of an OBC.[38] The government has plans of promoting Sydney as an OBC. However, it is still in the infant stage and has to wait for the development of other infrastructure.

Caribbean Region

The Caribbean region OBCs have been undergoing a systematic change. Bermuda has been making a sustained effort to become a premier OBC. The country is able to tap a talent of finance professionals. The absence of income, capital gain and corporate tax, and the abolition of stamp duty on international business transactions in 1990 make it one of the most favoured locations. Other features like a 100 per cent foreign ownership of an exempt corporation, ease of any nationality to create a trust and the absence of cumbersome filing requirements portend well for its future growth.[39] Bahamas has over 40 years of steady growth and experience in the offshore banking industry. Confidentiality, lack of corporate, personal income tax, capital gains tax and inheritance tax provide great advantage. In 1990, the government launched the Investment Protection Programme to encourage and accelerate the flow of capital and transfer of technology from around the world. Added to the fact of excellent location, technological and communication facilities, skilled educated work-force and low fees these factors would make Bahamas more successful in future.[40] Offshore banking was introduced in Barbados in 1979 with the Offshore Banking Act. The Central Bank of Barbados is responsible for the administration of the Act. Barbados is part of the growing tax treaty network, and, accordingly, while secrecy and confidentiality are respected and enshrined in statute, equal respect is given to exchange of information provisions contained in tax treaties and agreements.[41] Barbados main attraction has been its double tax treaties with the US, Canada and the UK. Treaty negotiations are underway with Germany. These have to be continued for Barbados to be a successful OBC.

The cumulative effect of political turmoil, capital flight, US sanctions and bank disclosures have been devastating in the Panamanian economy. The government is in default on $3.9 billion of foreign debt and two thirds of it is owed to commercial banks. Between 1986 to 1988 the banking system's assets fell by 63 per cent to $15 billion, and offshore deposits fell by 72 per cent and offshore loans fell by 69 per cent. One possible beneficiary of Panama's decline is Puerto Rico, which has 16 commercial banks with total assets of $19 billion. While Puerto Rico is a more favoured tax haven than any of the Caribbean centres, for an offshore bank to be successful there, a wide range of banking activities have to be developed and bank confidentiality and secrecy have to be maintained.[42]

British Virgin Island has been wooing international business companies and enacted an ordinance permitting companies to carry on any lawful activities except insurance, and these corporations were also exempt from local income tax. This measure enabled the increase in offshore companies from 7000 in 1988 to over 13 000 in 1990. The importance of offshore banking may also be growing.

North America

The North American Free Trade Agreement has changed the landscape of banking in the continent. In Mexico, the fall in interest rates, the possible growth of a manufacturing base and major international financial centre and the possibility of starting and securing a business with relative ease are attracting many investors to Mexico. The low cost of operation will also aid in the development of OBCs. The International Financial Centres and OBCs can provide Canadian companies with useful services and help improve the Canadian competitive position in terms of international financial expertise. These two countries are good potential sources for the development of future OBCs.

CONCLUSIONS

The barriers all over the world are crumbling and the world is becoming a global market place. With increased integration of the global community due to the advancements in telecommunications and technology, we can expect that international banking activity will gravitate to the financial centres wherein the banking operators and banking practices are highly regulated and supervised. In the last two decades there were several significant developments in the legal and political arena with regard to bank secrecy, which limit bank secrecy worldwide. This will become more and more necessary due to varied problems induced by fraud, political corruption and money laundering. Hence only those OBCs which can provide excellent quality of service and maintain high regulatory and supervisory standards can be expected to survive in the decades to come. A high level of competitiveness and internationalization of banking will require that the OBCs be efficient and profitable and this in turn will strengthen the banking system worldwide.

Notes

An earlier version of this paper was presented in the International Trade and Finance Association Meeting in Laredo, Texas, April 1992.

1. I. McCarthy (1983), 'Offshore in the Asian Pacific Area', in R. Moxon *et al.* (eds), *Asia Pacific Dynamics* (Greenwich CT: JAI Press).
2. Eurocurrency is any currency deposited in a bank outside the country where that currency is the unit of account.
3. Singapore removed its 40 per cent withholding tax in August 1968, but it was not until 1982 that Hong Kong did likewise. See E. Sarver, *The Eurocurrency Market Handbook* (New York: Institute of Finance, 1987) pp. 122.
4. See N. Balakrishnan, 'Banking by Concession', *Far Eastern Economic Review*, (5 March 1992) pp. 34.
5. See M. Taylor, 'A City of Secrets', *Far Eastern Economic Review* (5 March 1992) pp. 32.
6. See A. Rowley, 'Off the Map', *Far Eastern Economic Review* (5 March 1992) pp. 44.
7. See A. Deans, 'Treasure Islands', *Far Eastern Economic Review* (March 1992) pp. 38.
8. E. N. Roussakis (ed.), *International Banking: Principles and Practices*, (New York: Praeger, 1983) pp. 88.
9. J. Bartholomew, 'Continental Shelf', *Far Eastern Economic Review*, (5 March 1992) pp. 40.

10. M. A. Goldberg, 'Asia Pacific International Financial Centres', *International Journal of Bank Marketing*, vol. 9 (1991) pp. 4–10.
11. F. Tsuchiya, 'Natural Forces in the Building of a City', *Business Japan*, vol. 34, issue 7 (July 1989) pp. 37–43.
12. See N. Holloway, 'Markets: Tokyo's Heavy Toll; Secret of Success', *Far Eastern Economic Review*, vol. 143, issue 9 (2 Mar. 1989) pp. 80–82.
13. 'Japanese Banking Booms Offshore', *Economist*, vol. 309, issue 7578 (26 November 1988) pp. 87.
14. See, 'International Banking: Hong Kong', *International Financial Law Review* (September 1991) pp. 98–104.
15. M. Taylor, 'Hong Kong', *Far Eastern Economic Review*, vol. 155 (5 Mar. 1992) pp. 32–4.
16. J. Bonello, 'Center of Attraction', *ReActions*, issue: 2 (Feb. 1989) pp. 39–41.
17. N. Balakrishnan, 'Singapore: Changing the Old Order', *Far Eastern Economic Review*, (9 July 1992) pp. 39–42.
18. M. Montagu-Pollock, 'Taiwan: New Star in the Making', *Asian Business* (Hong Kong), vol. 26 (March 1990) pp. 28–34.
19. L. S. Liu, 'A Road Map for Taiwan's Financial Reform in the 1990s?', *International Financial Law Review*, vol. 10 (Aug. 1991) pp. 26–8.
20. G. Field, 'The Challenge of Transforming Macau's Financial System', *Euromoney* (May 1992) pp. SS5–SS6.
21. R. Tiglao, 'Money in High Places: Pressure Builds to Break Up Philippine Oligopoly', *Far Eastern Economic Review* (Hong Kong), vol. 151 (28 March 1991) pp. 62–3.
22. E. Guyot, 'Philippine Banks Face Tougher Times', *Asian Finance* (Hong Kong), vol. 17, issue 5 (15 May 1991) pp. 15.
23. M. Montagu-Pollock, 'Forex: Reining in the Cowboys', *Asian Business* (Hong Kong), vol. 27 (Feb. 1991) pp. 58–61.
24. David C. Donald, 'Toward a Single European Capital Market: The European Economic Community's Directive to Liberalize Capital Flows', *Law and Policy in International Business*, vol. 20, issue 1 (1988) pp. 139–62.
25. M. Blanden, R. McDougall and C. Jones, 'The Thoughts from the European Commission', *Banking World*, vol. 7, issue 10 (Oct. 1989) pp. 28–9.
26. M. Blanden, R. McDougall and C. Jones, 'Financial Center: London – Preserving the Liberal Climate', *Banker*, vol. 139, issue 765 (November 1989) pp. 35–42 and 53–87.
27. R. Janssen, 'Amsterdam: Building an International Financial Center', *Europe* (Sept. 1992) pp. 20–21.
28. S. Geschwindt, 'Recapturing the Market', *ReActions*, issue 6 (June 1989) pp. 40–43.
29. B. Roy, 'Northeast Italy and Asia: An Emerging Partnership', *Asian Finance*, vol. 14, issue 11 (15 November 1988) pp. 55–82.
30. John Bonello, 'Center of Attraction', *ReActions*, issue 2 (Feb. 1989) pp. 39–41.
31. M. Demirsar, 'In the Postwar Middle East, Turkey Takes Center Stage', *Global Finance*, vol. 5, issue 4 (April 1991) pp. 24–8.

32. A. Dugan, 'Turkey: The Golden Scenario', *Euromoney* (Nov. 1990) pp. 88–92.
33. M. Blanden and S. Timewell, 'Top 1,000: Local Heroes', *Banker*, vol. 142, issue 797 (July 1992) pp. 81–82.
34. S. Timewell, 'Top 100 Arabs: There's No Place Like Home', *Banker* (Nov. 1991) pp. 44–56.
35. 'Bahrain', *Euromoney, Offshore Financial Centers Supplement* (May 1992) pp. 15–19.
36. A. Dugan, 'Bahrain: When the Wells Run Dry', *Euromoney* (Mar. 1990) pp. 13–14.
37. S. Timewell, 'Iran: Singapore of the Gulf?'. *Banker*, vol. 141, issue 780 (Feb. 1991) pp. 46–7.
38. P. Graig, 'Mauritius, a Success Story of the 1980s, is Looking for Investors to Participate in the Next Development Phase', *Business America*, vol. 113, issue 6, (23 March 1992) pp. 28–9.
39. Offshore Financial Centers Supplement, *Euromoney* (May 1992) pp. 20–24.
40. 'The Bahamas', *Euromoney: Offshore Financial Centers Supplement* (May 1992) pp. 5–14.
41. T. A. Carmichael, 'International Banking: Barbados', *International Financial Law Review* (International Banking Supplement), Sept. 1991, pp. 27–30.
42. N. Peagam, 'Panama Puts Out More Flags; Puerto Rico Tries Again', *Euromoney* (Treasure Islands Supplement), May 1989, pp. 77–88.

Index

339